RAMPAGE JACKSON
STREET SOLDIER

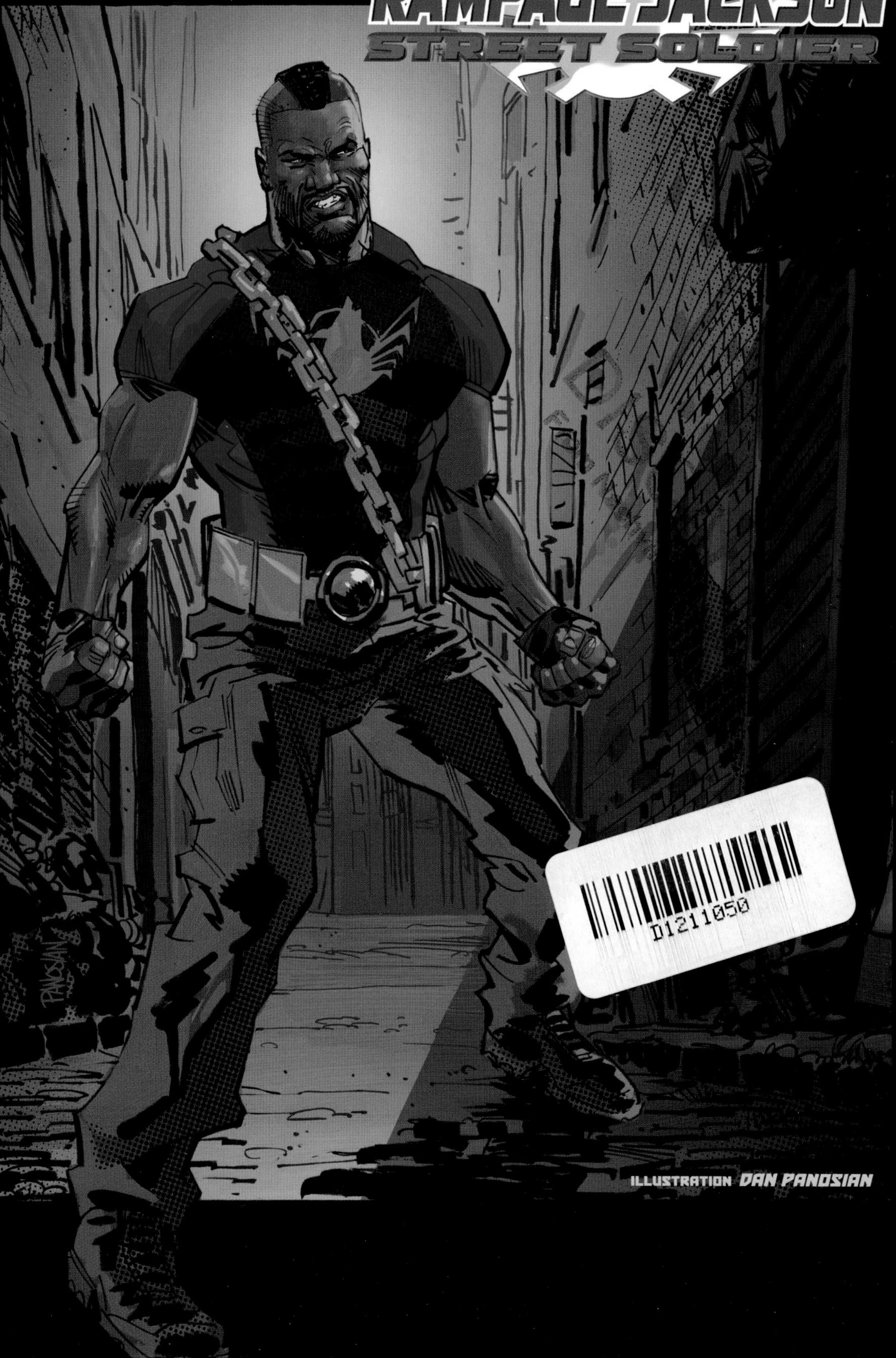
PANOSIAN

ILLUSTRATION *DAN PANOSIAN*

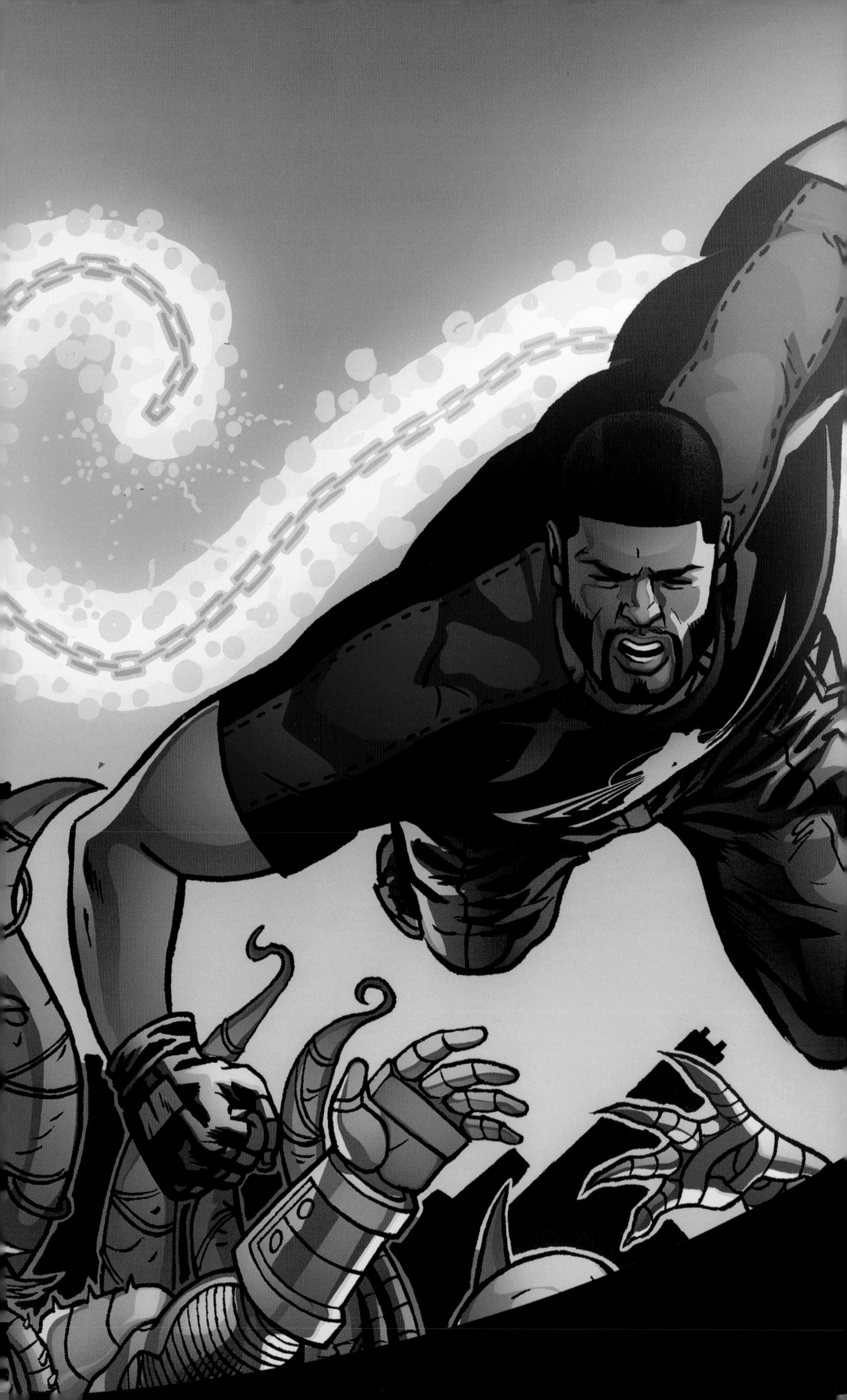

www.LIONFORGE.com

LION FORGE COMICS

f Facebook.com/LionForge
t Twitter @LionForge
YouTube.com/LionForge

ISBN: 978-1-63140-379-8

18   17   16   15   1   2   3   4

IDW®
www.IDWPUBLISHING.com
IDW founded by Ted Adams, Alex Garner, Kris Oprisko, and Robbie Robbins

Ted Adams, CEO & Publisher
Greg Goldstein, President & COO
Robbie Robbins, EVP/Sr. Graphic Artist
Chris Ryall, Chief Creative Officer/Editor-in-Chief
Matthew Ruzicka, CPA, Chief Financial Officer
Alan Payne, VP of Sales
Dirk Wood, VP of Marketing
Lorelei Bunjes, VP of Digital Services
Jeff Webber, VP of Digital Publishing & Business Development

Facebook: facebook.com/idwpublishing
Twitter: @idwpublishing
YouTube: youtube.com/idwpublishing
Tumblr: tumblr.idwpublishing.com
Instagram: instagram.com/idwpublishing

BORN TO FIGHT

WRITER FABIAN NICIEZA ILLUSTRATOR LEONARDO ROMERO

GIANT MONSTER ISLAND

WRITER MIKE BARON ILLUSTRATOR LEONARDO ROMERO

MICKEY SINN

WRITER BARBARA RANDALL KESEL ILLUSTRATOR LEONARDO ROMERO

INSIDE OUT

WRITER MARTIN PASKO ILLUSTRATOR LUCAS WERNECK

ACROSS TIME

WRITER TOM PEYER ILLUSTRATOR LUCAS WERNECK

BUKI

WRITER ADAM BEECHEN ILLUSTRATOR LUCAS WERNECK

UNDERMINED

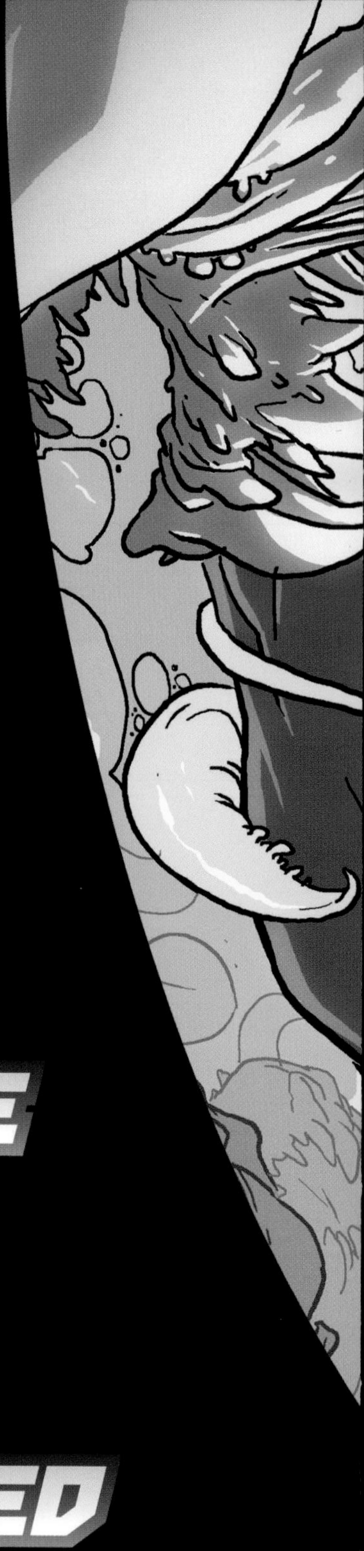

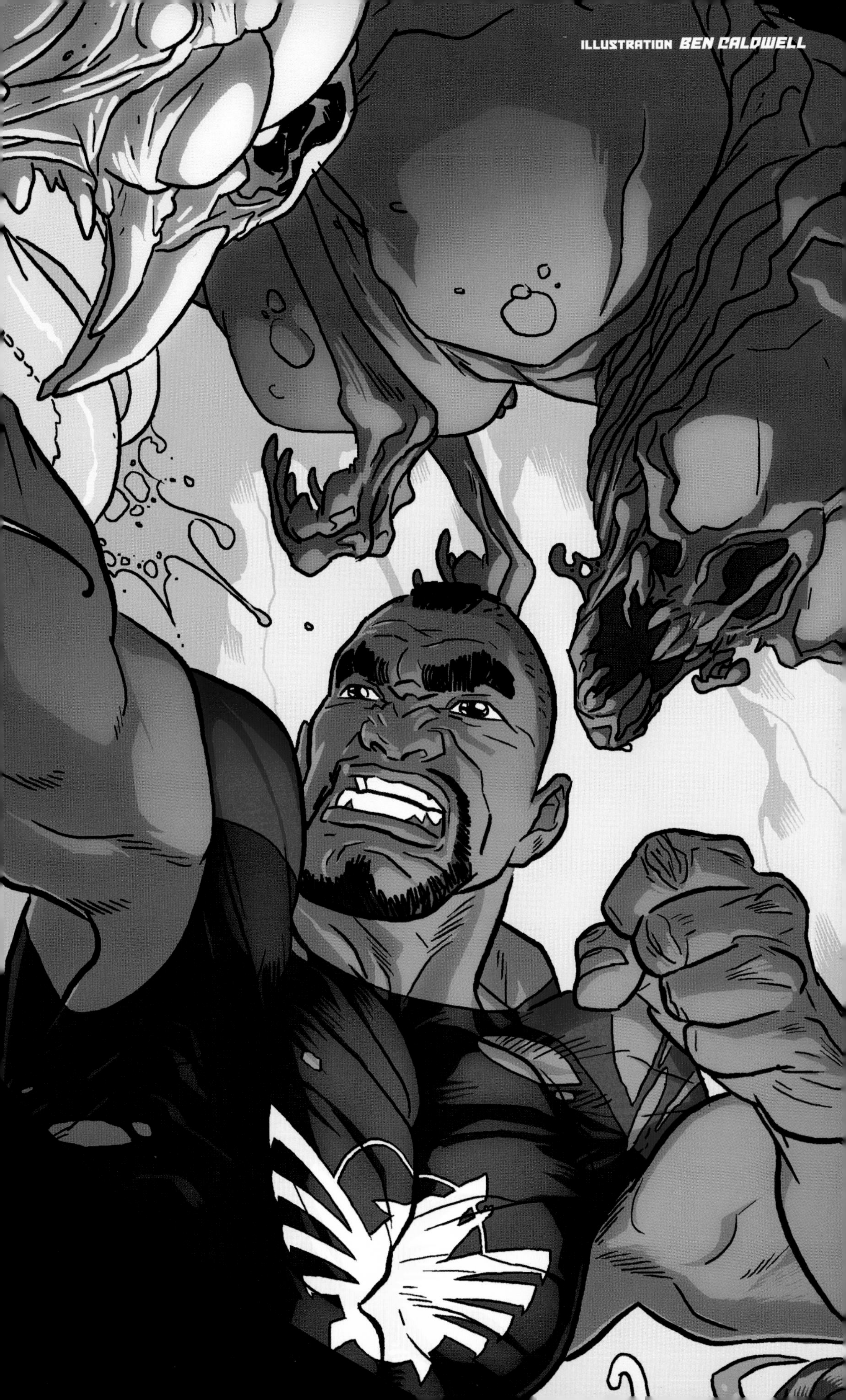
ILLUSTRATION BEN CALDWELL

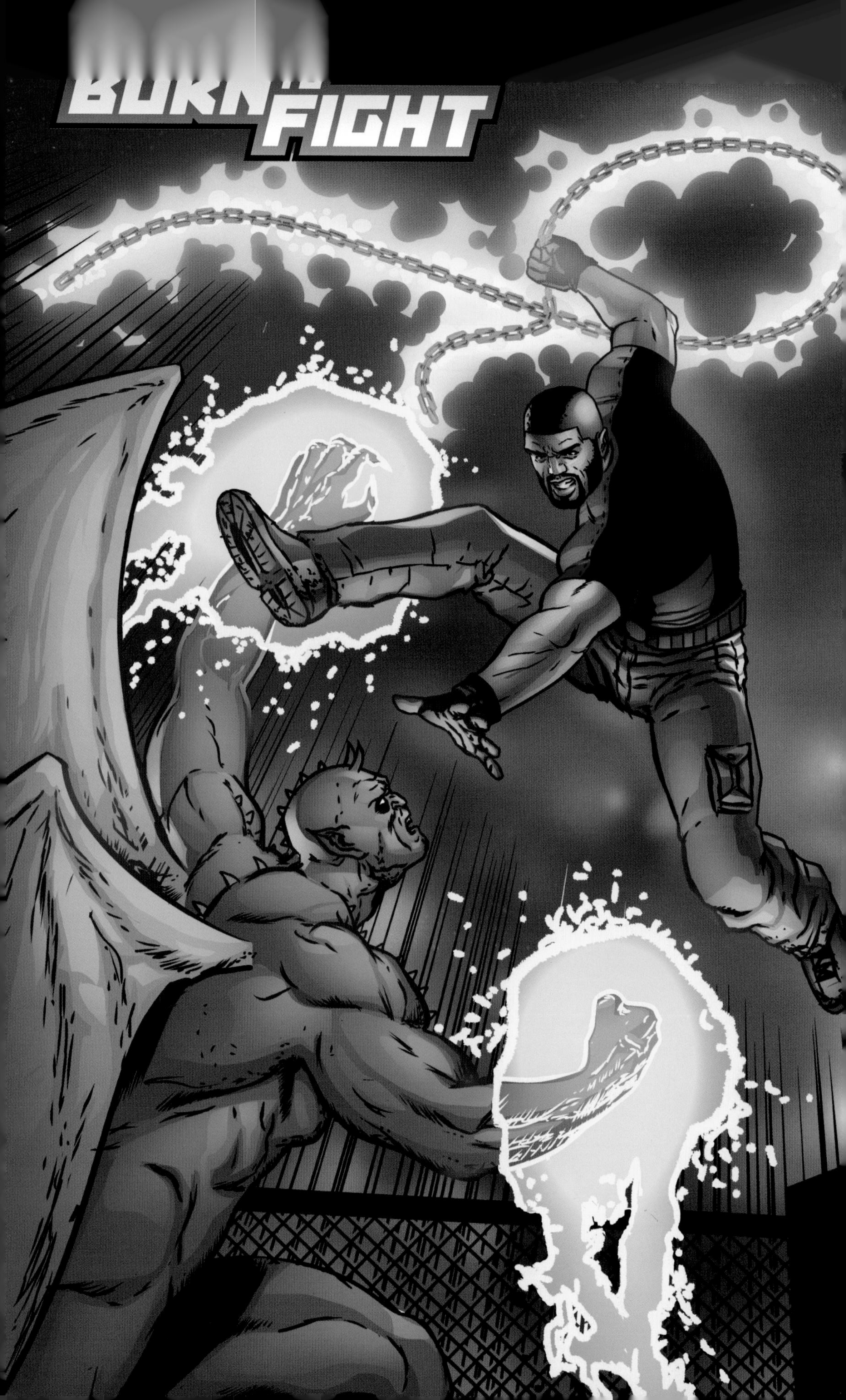

FIGHT

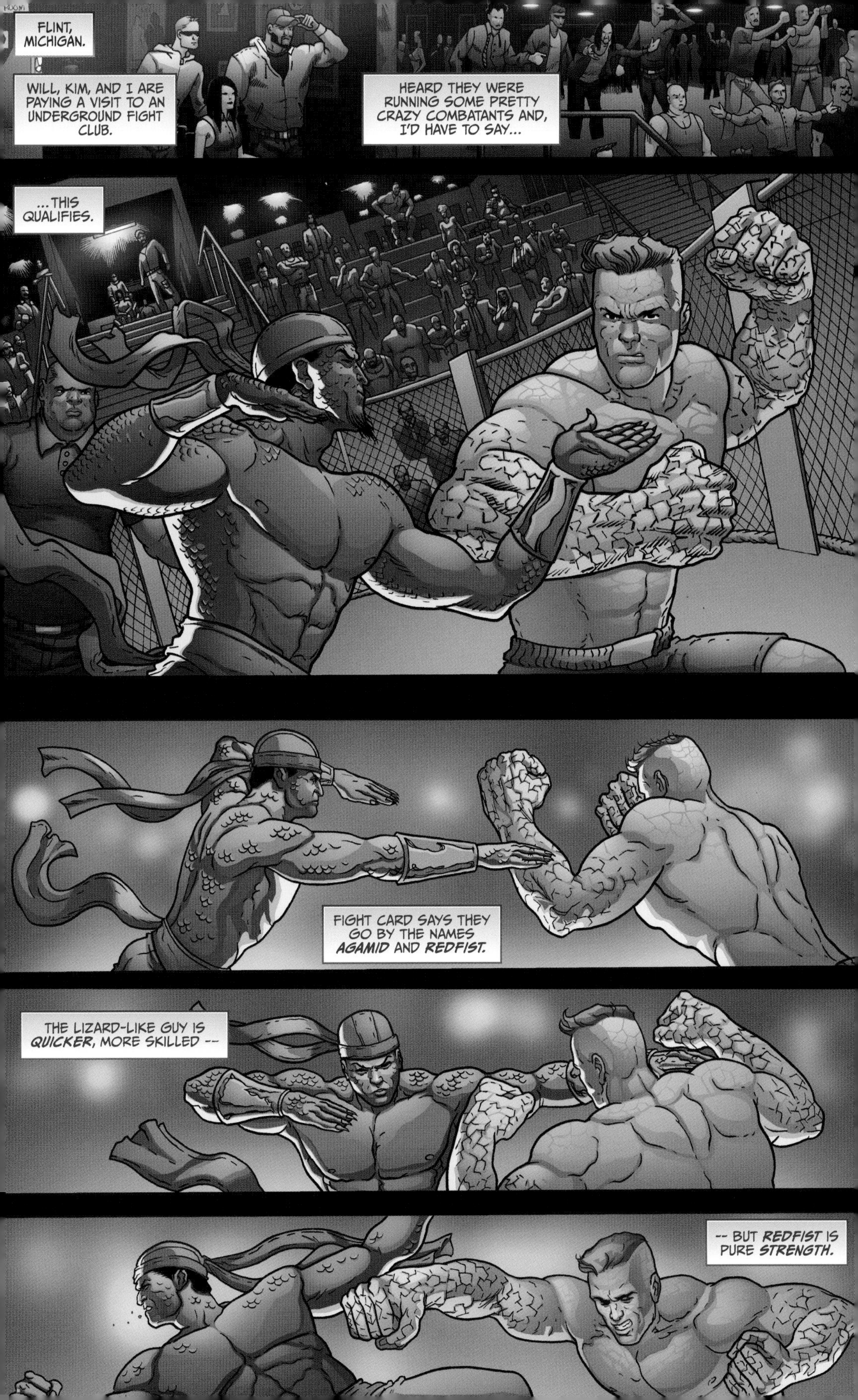
FLINT, MICHIGAN.
WILL, KIM, AND I ARE PAYING A VISIT TO AN UNDERGROUND FIGHT CLUB.
HEARD THEY WERE RUNNING SOME PRETTY CRAZY COMBATANTS AND, I'D HAVE TO SAY...
...THIS QUALIFIES.
FIGHT CARD SAYS THEY GO BY THE NAMES *AGAMID* AND *REDFIST.*
THE LIZARD-LIKE GUY IS *QUICKER*, MORE SKILLED --
-- BUT *REDFIST* IS PURE *STRENGTH.*

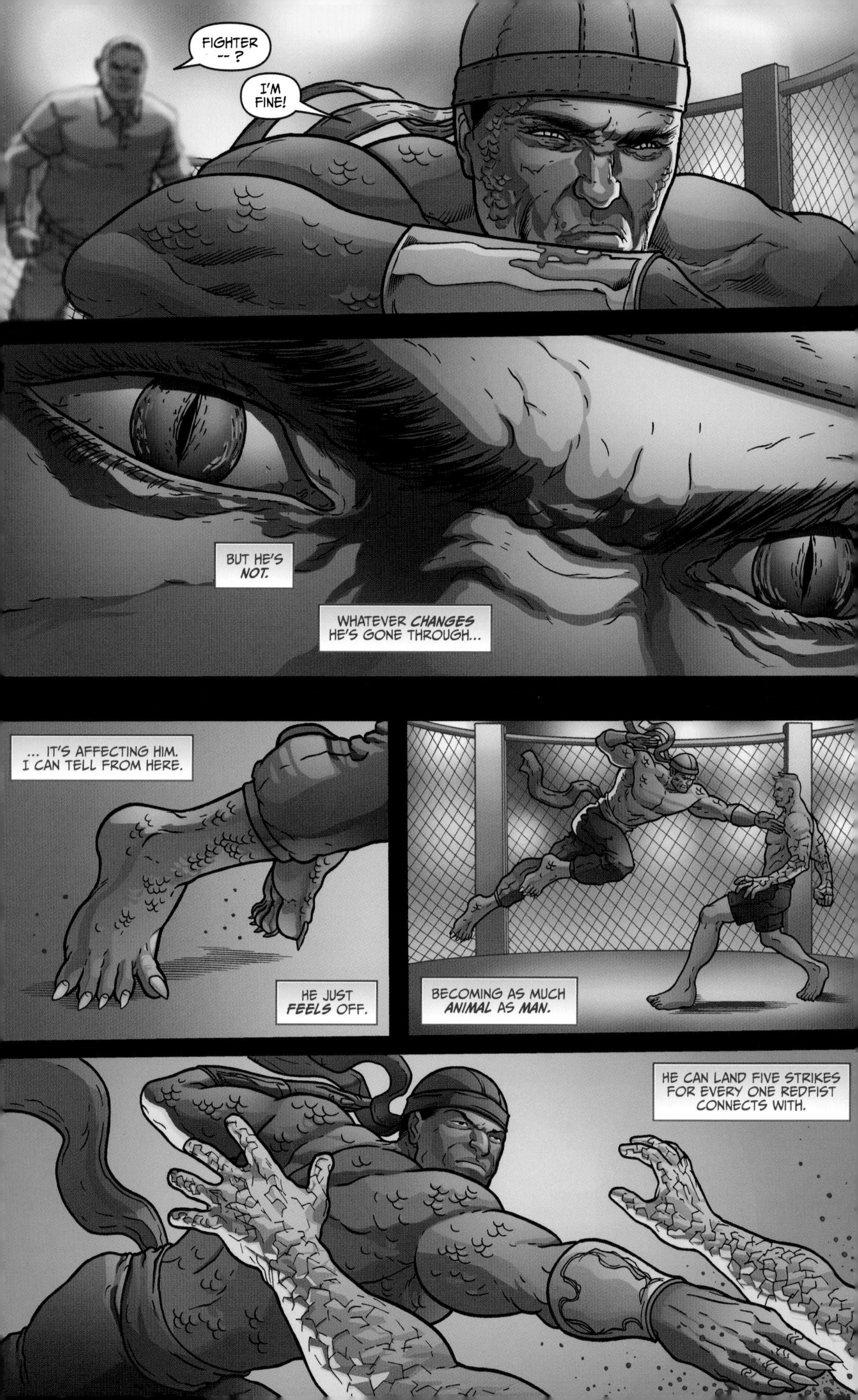
FIGHTER -- ?
I'M FINE!
BUT HE'S NOT.
WHATEVER CHANGES HE'S GONE THROUGH...
... IT'S AFFECTING HIM. I CAN TELL FROM HERE.
HE JUST FEELS OFF.
BECOMING AS MUCH ANIMAL AS MAN.
HE CAN LAND FIVE STRIKES FOR EVERY ONE REDFIST CONNECTS WITH.

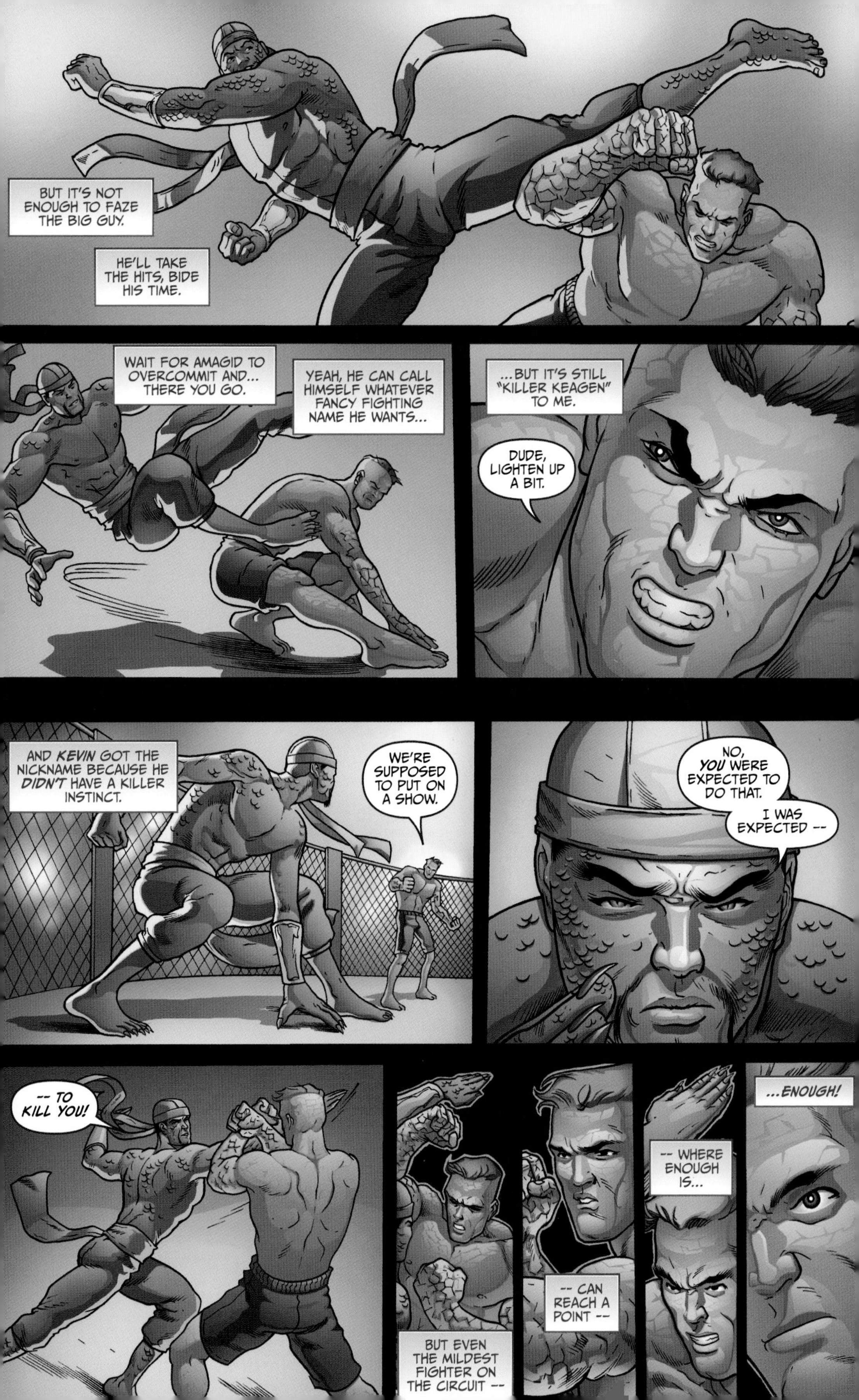
BUT IT'S NOT ENOUGH TO FAZE THE BIG GUY.
HE'LL TAKE THE HITS, BIDE HIS TIME.
WAIT FOR AMAGID TO OVERCOMMIT AND... THERE YOU GO.
YEAH, HE CAN CALL HIMSELF WHATEVER FANCY FIGHTING NAME HE WANTS...
...BUT IT'S STILL "KILLER KEAGEN" TO ME.
DUDE, LIGHTEN UP A BIT.
AND KEVIN GOT THE NICKNAME BECAUSE HE DIDN'T HAVE A KILLER INSTINCT.
WE'RE SUPPOSED TO PUT ON A SHOW.
NO, YOU WERE EXPECTED TO DO THAT.
I WAS EXPECTED --
-- TO KILL YOU!
BUT EVEN THE MILDEST FIGHTER ON THE CIRCUIT --
-- CAN REACH A POINT --
-- WHERE ENOUGH IS...
...ENOUGH!

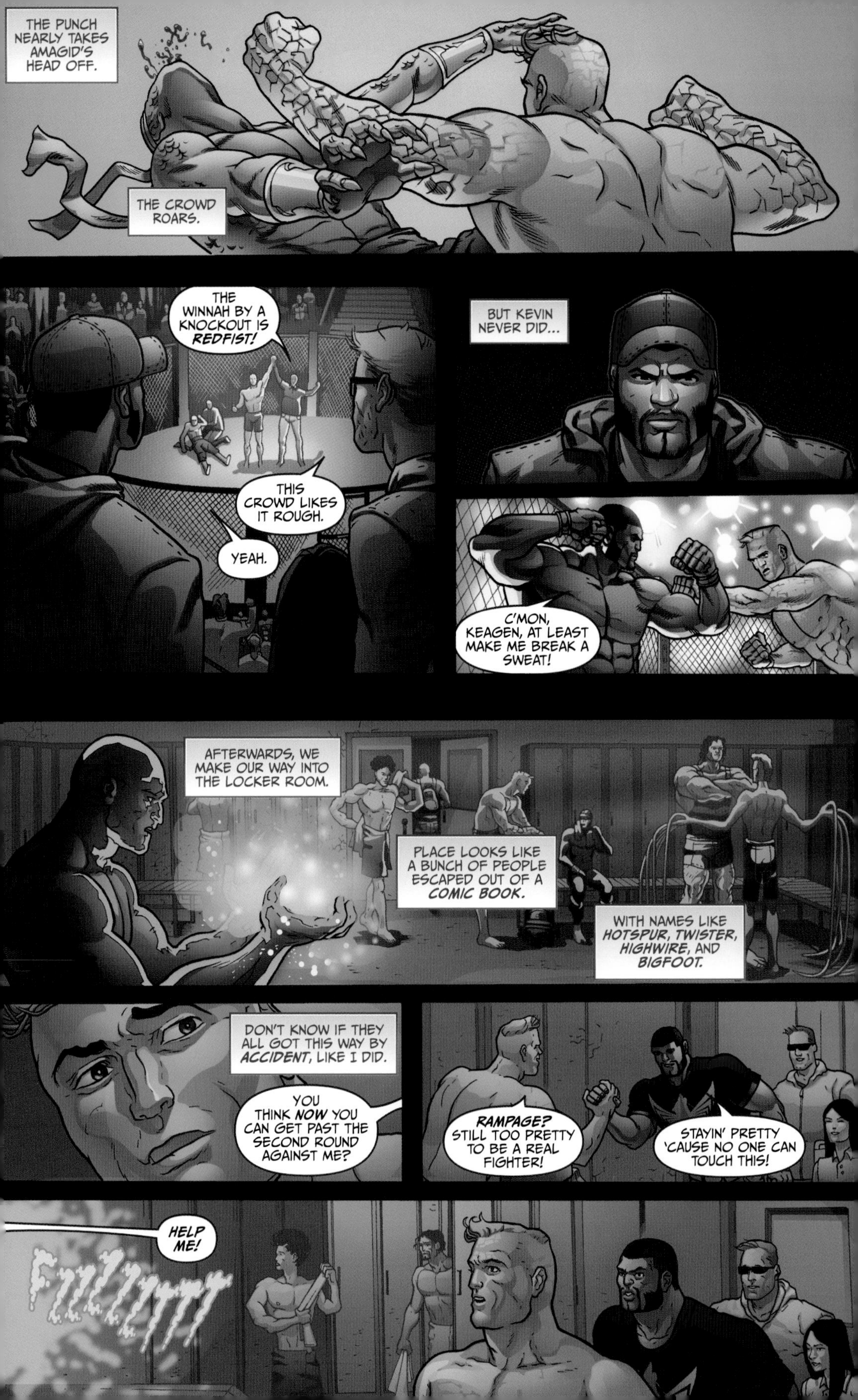
THE PUNCH NEARLY TAKES AMAGID'S HEAD OFF.
THE CROWD ROARS.
THE WINNAH BY A KNOCKOUT IS *REDFIST!*
THIS CROWD LIKES IT ROUGH.
YEAH.
BUT KEVIN NEVER DID...
C'MON, KEAGEN, AT LEAST MAKE ME BREAK A SWEAT!
AFTERWARDS, WE MAKE OUR WAY INTO THE LOCKER ROOM.
PLACE LOOKS LIKE A BUNCH OF PEOPLE ESCAPED OUT OF A *COMIC BOOK.*
WITH NAMES LIKE *HOTSPUR, TWISTER, HIGHWIRE,* AND *BIGFOOT.*
DON'T KNOW IF THEY ALL GOT THIS WAY BY *ACCIDENT*, LIKE I DID.
YOU THINK *NOW* YOU CAN GET PAST THE SECOND ROUND AGAINST ME?
RAMPAGE? STILL TOO PRETTY TO BE A REAL FIGHTER!
STAYIN' PRETTY 'CAUSE NO ONE CAN TOUCH THIS!
HELP ME!
FZZZZTTT

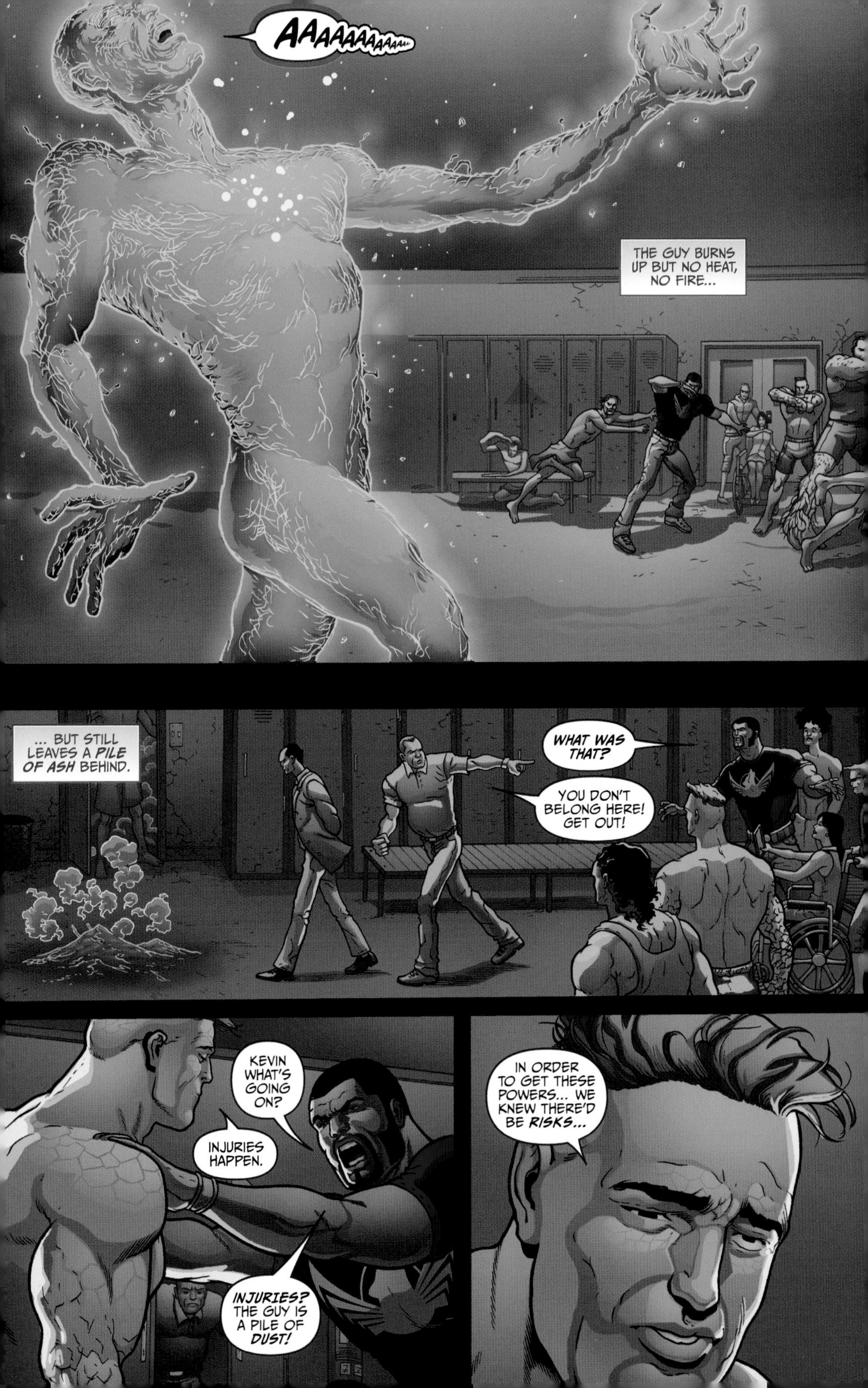
AAAAAAAAAAAA...
THE GUY BURNS UP BUT NO HEAT, NO FIRE...
... BUT STILL LEAVES A PILE OF ASH BEHIND.
WHAT WAS THAT?
YOU DON'T BELONG HERE! GET OUT!
KEVIN WHAT'S GOING ON?
INJURIES HAPPEN.
INJURIES? THE GUY IS A PILE OF DUST!
IN ORDER TO GET THESE POWERS... WE KNEW THERE'D BE RISKS...

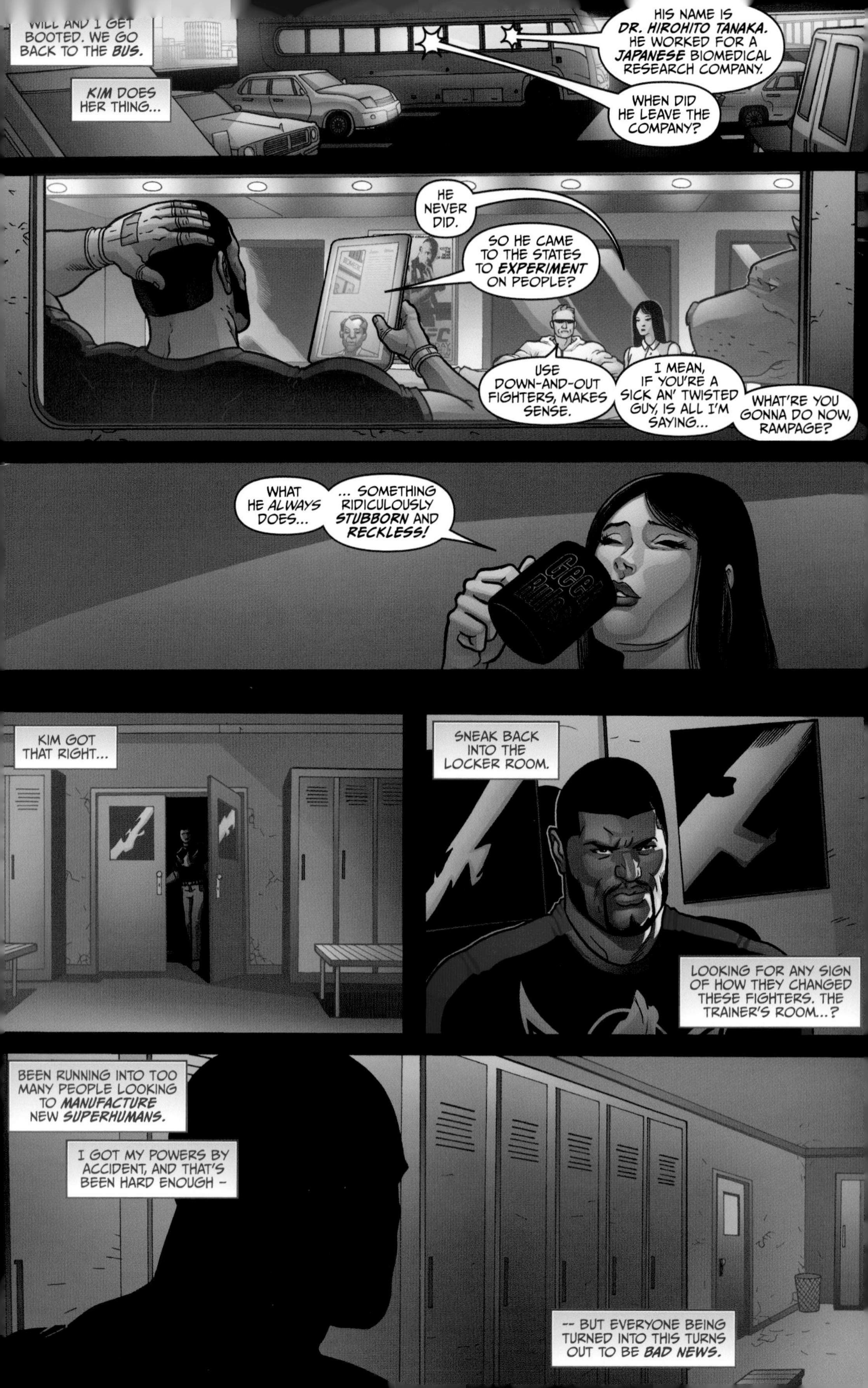
WILL AND I GET BOOTED. WE GO BACK TO THE BUS.
KIM DOES HER THING...
HIS NAME IS DR. HIROHITO TANAKA. HE WORKED FOR A JAPANESE BIOMEDICAL RESEARCH COMPANY.
WHEN DID HE LEAVE THE COMPANY?
HE NEVER DID.
SO HE CAME TO THE STATES TO EXPERIMENT ON PEOPLE?
USE DOWN-AND-OUT FIGHTERS, MAKES SENSE.
I MEAN, IF YOU'RE A SICK AN' TWISTED GUY, IS ALL I'M SAYING...
WHAT'RE YOU GONNA DO NOW, RAMPAGE?
WHAT HE ALWAYS DOES...
... SOMETHING RIDICULOUSLY STUBBORN AND RECKLESS!
KIM GOT THAT RIGHT...
SNEAK BACK INTO THE LOCKER ROOM.
LOOKING FOR ANY SIGN OF HOW THEY CHANGED THESE FIGHTERS. THE TRAINER'S ROOM...?
BEEN RUNNING INTO TOO MANY PEOPLE LOOKING TO MANUFACTURE NEW SUPERHUMANS.
I GOT MY POWERS BY ACCIDENT, AND THAT'S BEEN HARD ENOUGH –
-- BUT EVERYONE BEING TURNED INTO THIS TURNS OUT TO BE BAD NEWS.

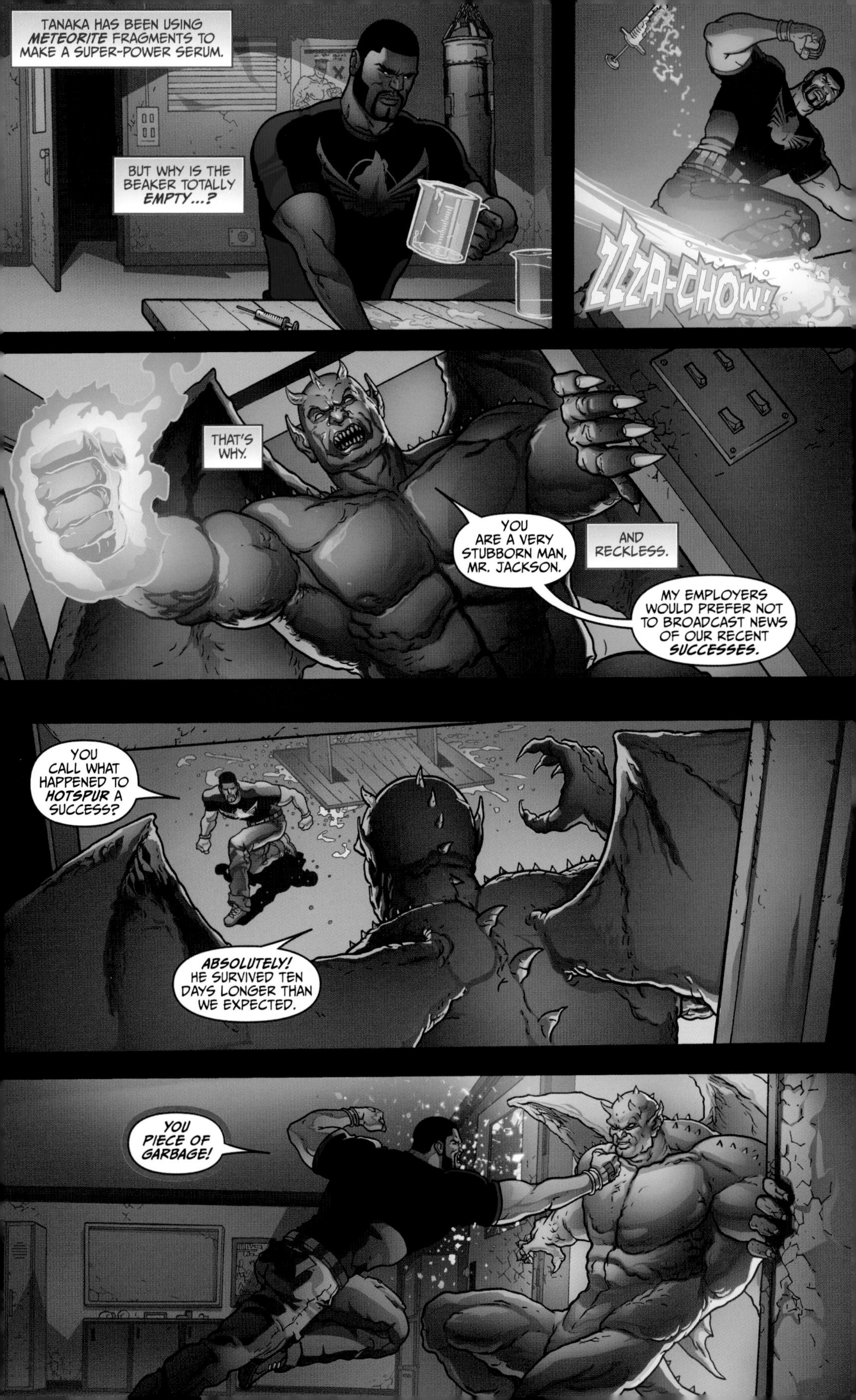
TANAKA HAS BEEN USING *METEORITE* FRAGMENTS TO MAKE A SUPER-POWER SERUM.
BUT WHY IS THE BEAKER TOTALLY *EMPTY...?*
ZZZA-CHOW!
THAT'S WHY.
YOU ARE A VERY STUBBORN MAN, MR. JACKSON.
AND RECKLESS.
MY EMPLOYERS WOULD PREFER NOT TO BROADCAST NEWS OF OUR RECENT *SUCCESSES.*
YOU CALL WHAT HAPPENED TO *HOTSPUR* A SUCCESS?
ABSOLUTELY! HE SURVIVED TEN DAYS LONGER THAN WE EXPECTED.
YOU PIECE OF GARBAGE!

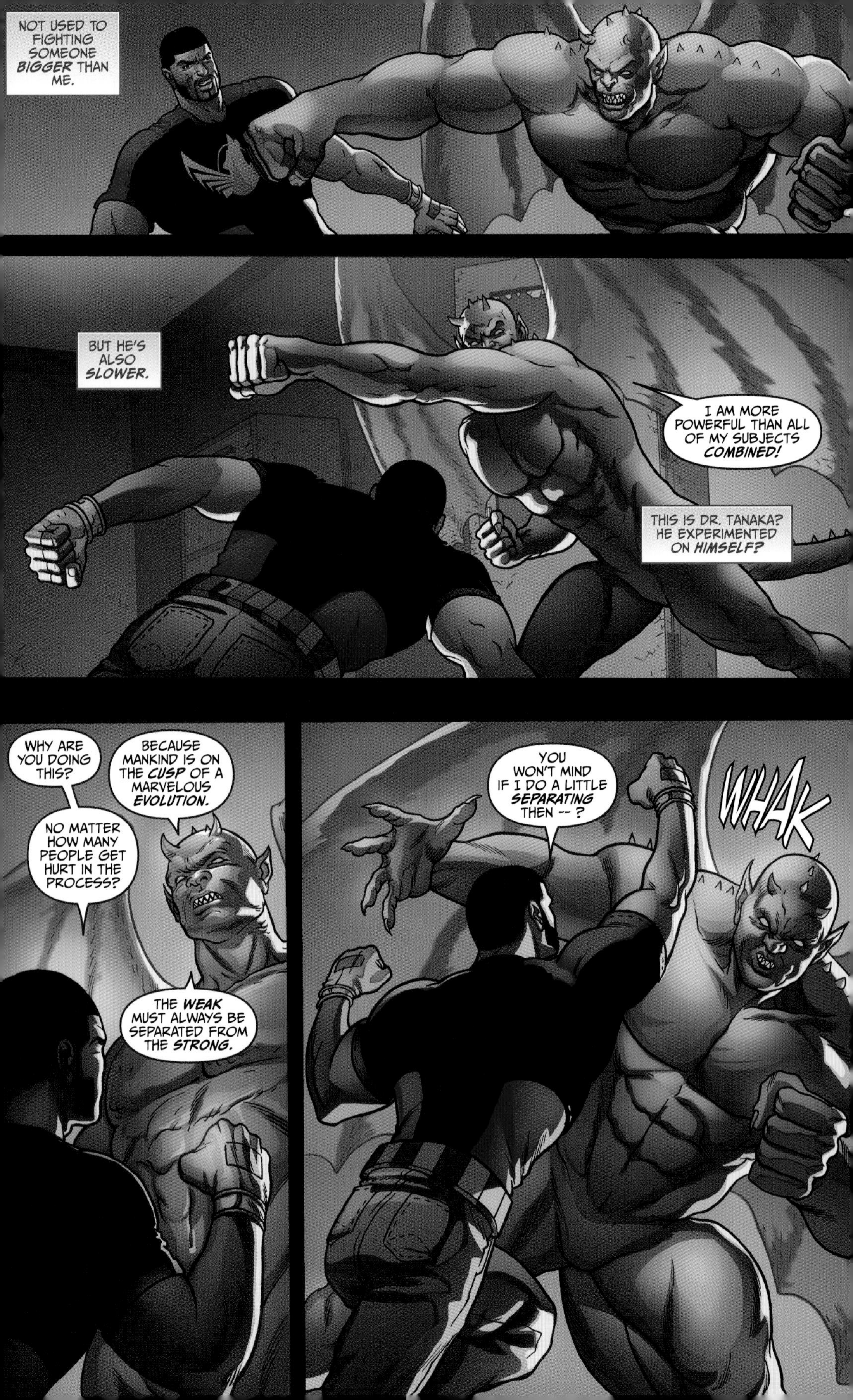
NOT USED TO FIGHTING SOMEONE BIGGER THAN ME.
BUT HE'S ALSO SLOWER.
I AM MORE POWERFUL THAN ALL OF MY SUBJECTS COMBINED!
THIS IS DR. TANAKA? HE EXPERIMENTED ON HIMSELF?
WHY ARE YOU DOING THIS?
BECAUSE MANKIND IS ON THE CUSP OF A MARVELOUS EVOLUTION.
NO MATTER HOW MANY PEOPLE GET HURT IN THE PROCESS?
THE WEAK MUST ALWAYS BE SEPARATED FROM THE STRONG.
YOU WON'T MIND IF I DO A LITTLE SEPARATING THEN -- ?
WHAK

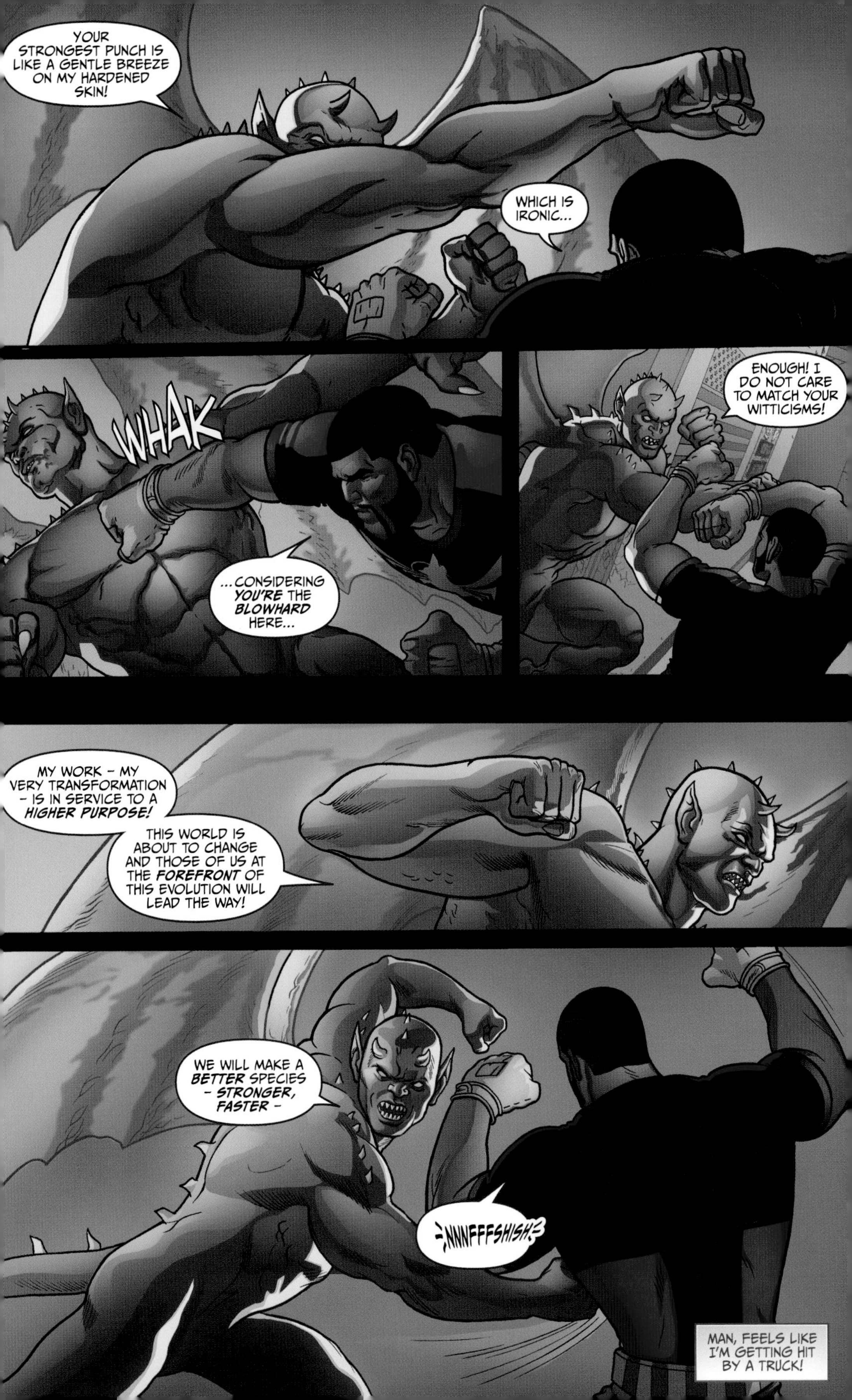
YOUR STRONGEST PUNCH IS LIKE A GENTLE BREEZE ON MY HARDENED SKIN!
WHICH IS IRONIC...
WHAK
...CONSIDERING *YOU'RE* THE *BLOWHARD* HERE...
ENOUGH! I DO NOT CARE TO MATCH YOUR WITTICISMS!
MY WORK - MY VERY TRANSFORMATION - IS IN SERVICE TO A *HIGHER PURPOSE!*
THIS WORLD IS ABOUT TO CHANGE AND THOSE OF US AT THE *FOREFRONT* OF THIS EVOLUTION WILL LEAD THE WAY!
WE WILL MAKE A *BETTER* SPECIES - *STRONGER, FASTER* -
NNNFFFSHISH
MAN, FEELS LIKE I'M GETTING HIT BY A TRUCK!

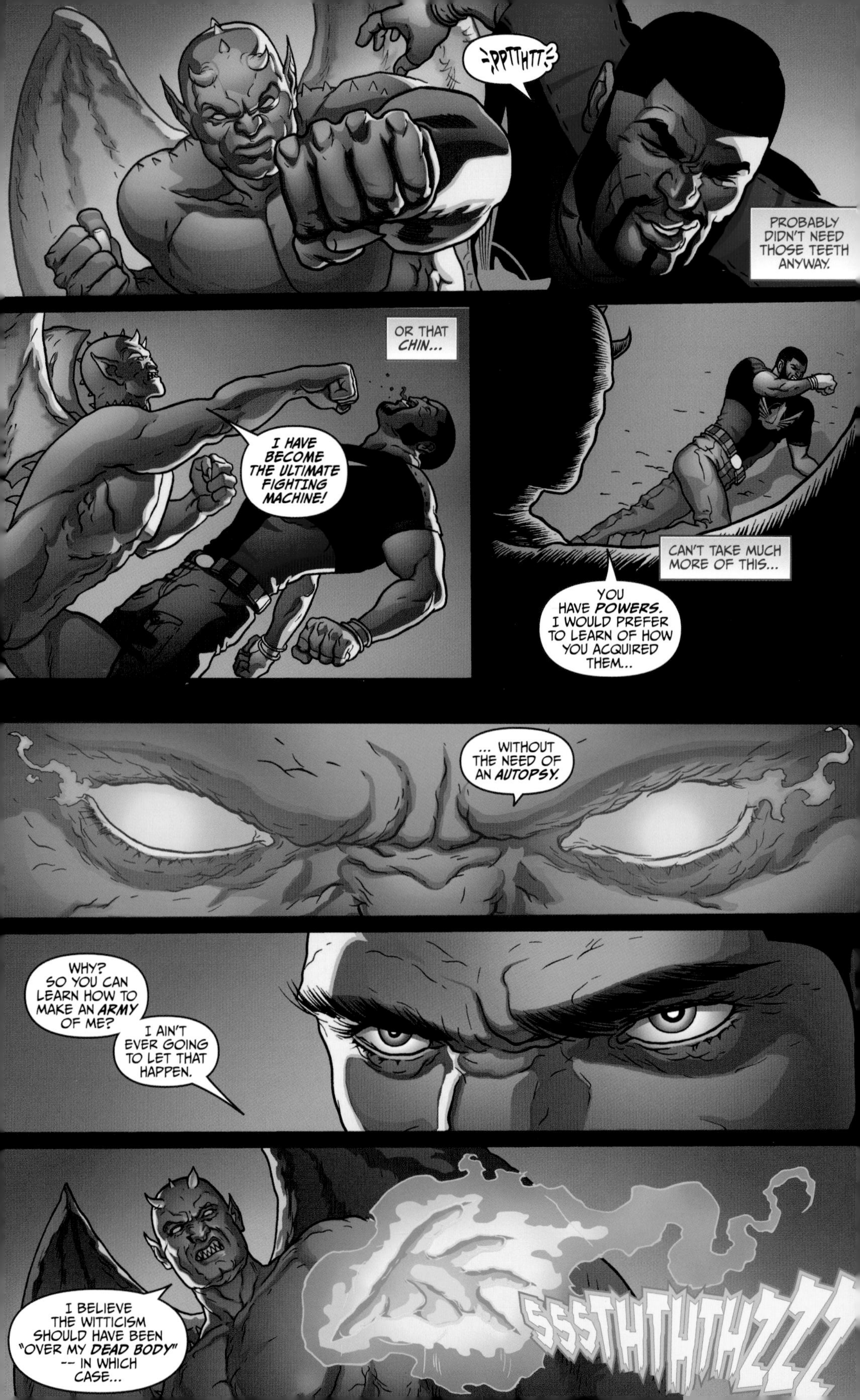
-PPTTHTT-
PROBABLY DIDN'T NEED THOSE TEETH ANYWAY.
OR THAT CHIN...
I HAVE BECOME THE ULTIMATE FIGHTING MACHINE!
CAN'T TAKE MUCH MORE OF THIS...
YOU HAVE POWERS. I WOULD PREFER TO LEARN OF HOW YOU ACQUIRED THEM...
... WITHOUT THE NEED OF AN AUTOPSY.
WHY? SO YOU CAN LEARN HOW TO MAKE AN ARMY OF ME?
I AIN'T EVER GOING TO LET THAT HAPPEN.
I BELIEVE THE WITTICISM SHOULD HAVE BEEN "OVER MY DEAD BODY" -- IN WHICH CASE...
SSSTHTHTHZZZ

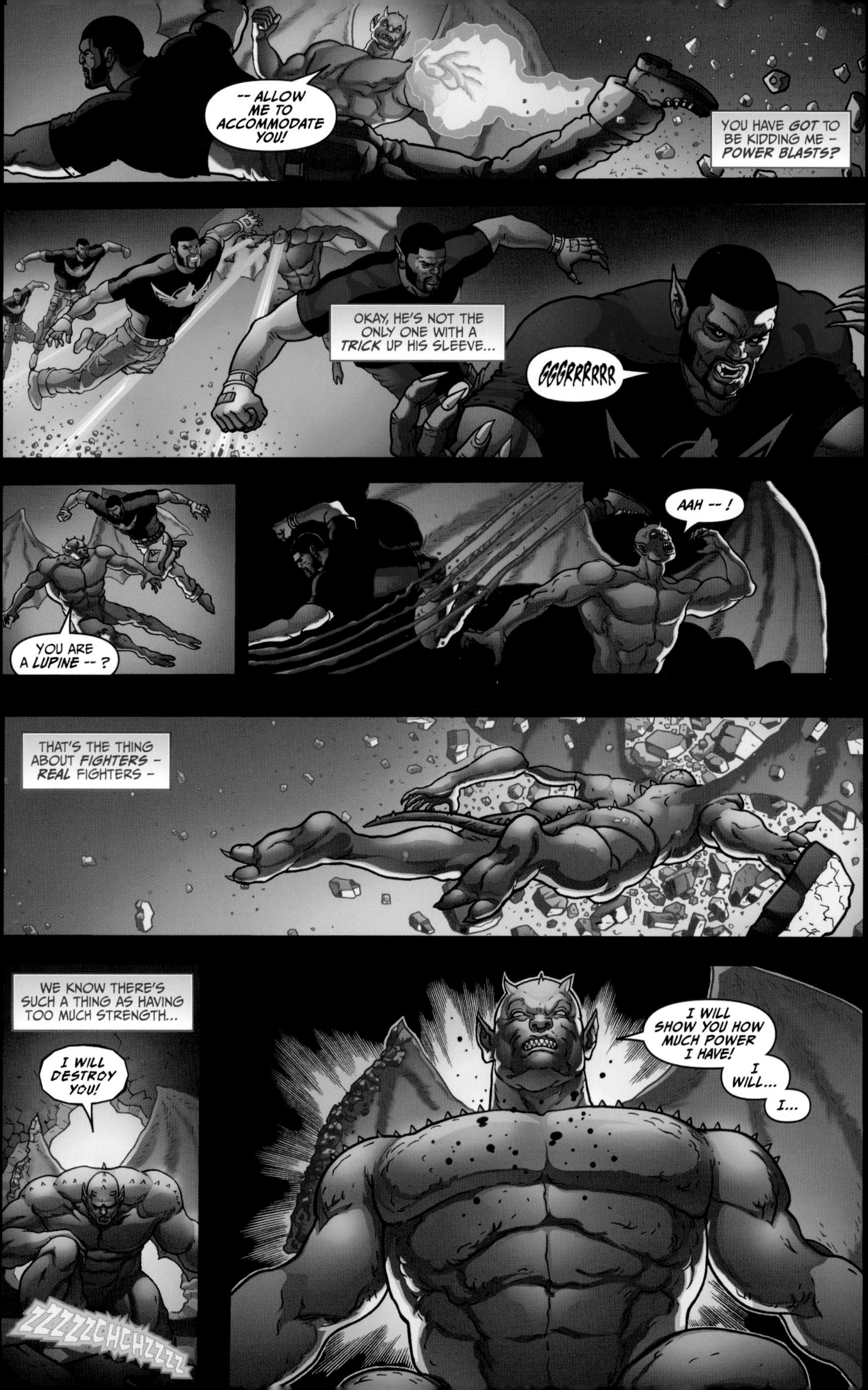
-- ALLOW ME TO ACCOMMODATE YOU!
YOU HAVE GOT TO BE KIDDING ME – POWER BLASTS?
OKAY, HE'S NOT THE ONLY ONE WITH A TRICK UP HIS SLEEVE...
GGGRRRRRR
YOU ARE A LUPINE -- ?
AAH -- !
THAT'S THE THING ABOUT FIGHTERS – REAL FIGHTERS –
WE KNOW THERE'S SUCH A THING AS HAVING TOO MUCH STRENGTH...
I WILL DESTROY YOU!
ZZZZZCHCHZZZZZ
I WILL SHOW YOU HOW MUCH POWER I HAVE!
I WILL...
I...

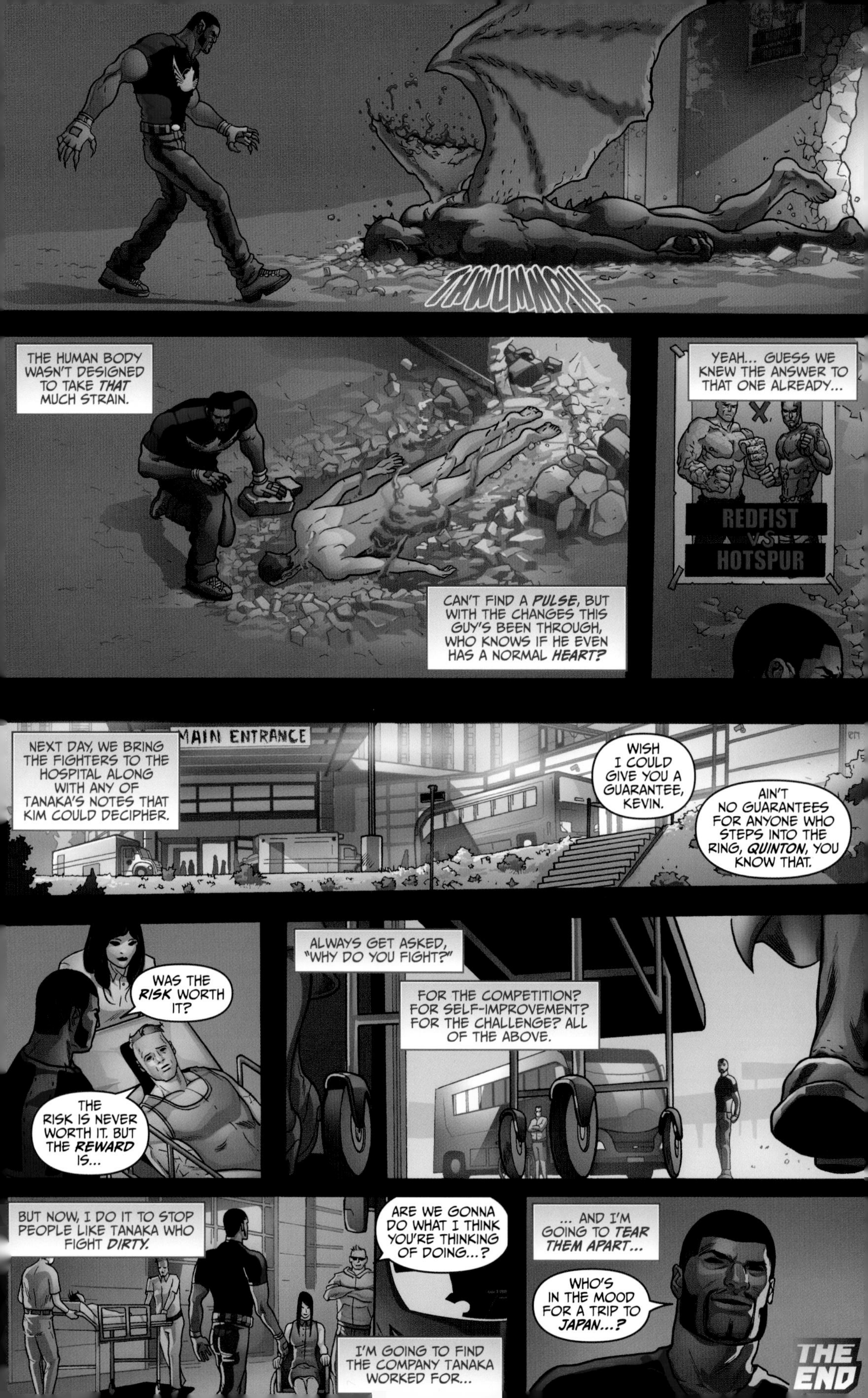
THWUMMPH!
THE HUMAN BODY WASN'T DESIGNED TO TAKE THAT MUCH STRAIN.
CAN'T FIND A PULSE, BUT WITH THE CHANGES THIS GUY'S BEEN THROUGH, WHO KNOWS IF HE EVEN HAS A NORMAL HEART?
YEAH... GUESS WE KNEW THE ANSWER TO THAT ONE ALREADY...
REDFIST
VS
HOTSPUR
MAIN ENTRANCE
NEXT DAY, WE BRING THE FIGHTERS TO THE HOSPITAL ALONG WITH ANY OF TANAKA'S NOTES THAT KIM COULD DECIPHER.
WISH I COULD GIVE YOU A GUARANTEE, KEVIN.
AIN'T NO GUARANTEES FOR ANYONE WHO STEPS INTO THE RING, QUINTON, YOU KNOW THAT.
WAS THE RISK WORTH IT?
THE RISK IS NEVER WORTH IT. BUT THE REWARD IS...
ALWAYS GET ASKED, "WHY DO YOU FIGHT?"
FOR THE COMPETITION? FOR SELF-IMPROVEMENT? FOR THE CHALLENGE? ALL OF THE ABOVE.
BUT NOW, I DO IT TO STOP PEOPLE LIKE TANAKA WHO FIGHT DIRTY.
ARE WE GONNA DO WHAT I THINK YOU'RE THINKING OF DOING...?
I'M GOING TO FIND THE COMPANY TANAKA WORKED FOR...
... AND I'M GOING TO TEAR THEM APART...
WHO'S IN THE MOOD FOR A TRIP TO JAPAN...?
THE END

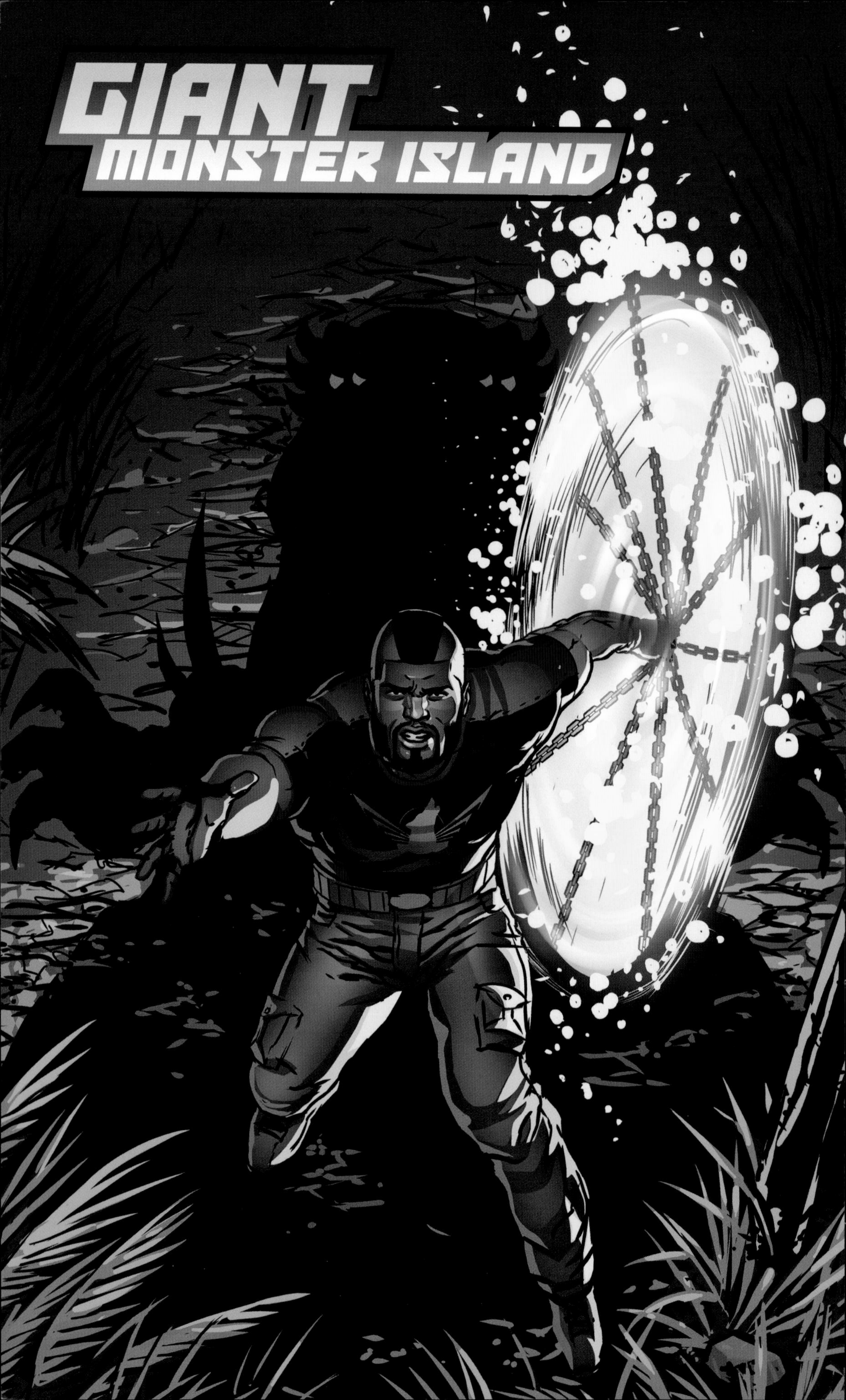
GIANT
MONSTER ISLAND

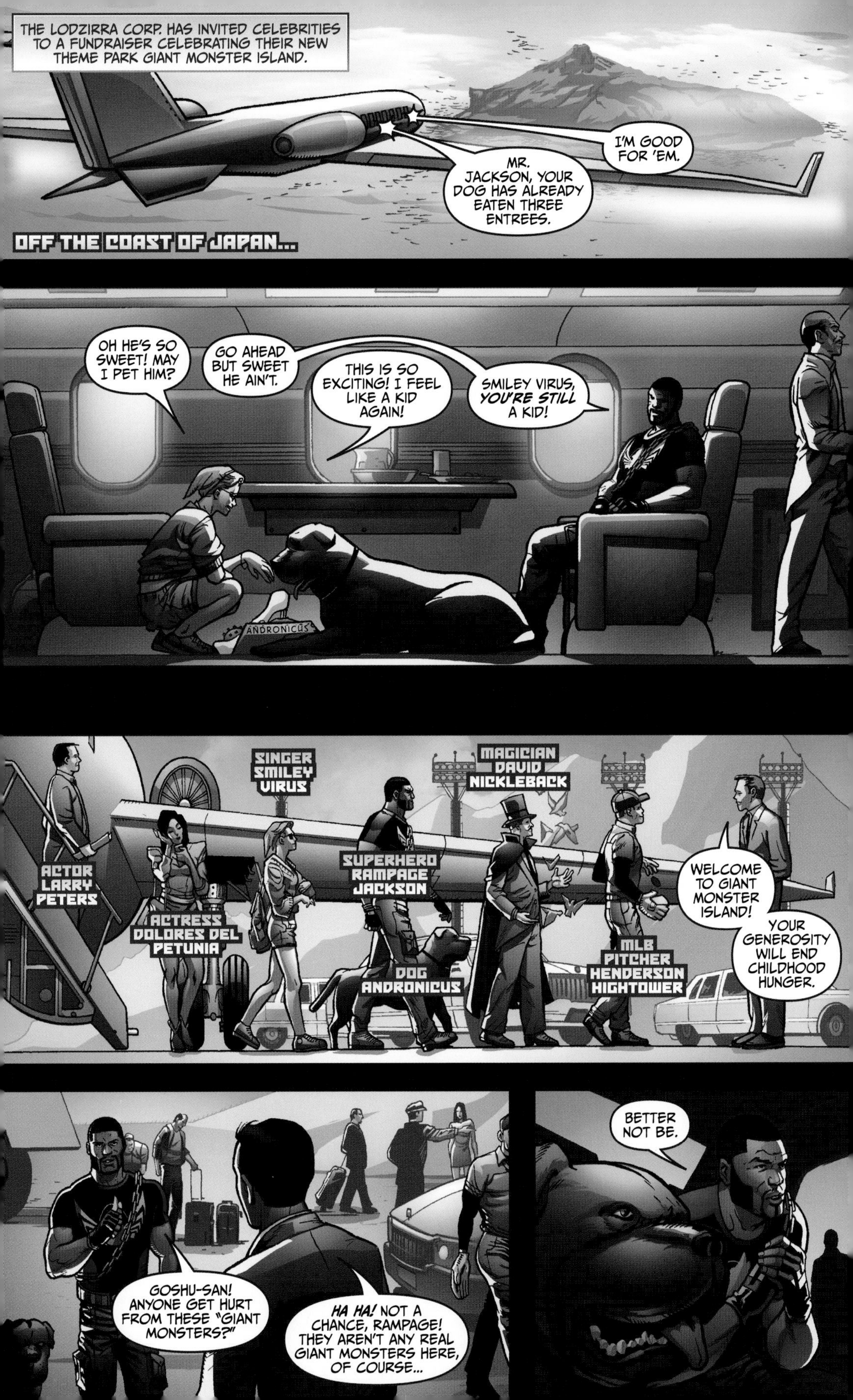
THE LODZIRRA CORP. HAS INVITED CELEBRITIES TO A FUNDRAISER CELEBRATING THEIR NEW THEME PARK GIANT MONSTER ISLAND.
MR. JACKSON, YOUR DOG HAS ALREADY EATEN THREE ENTREES.
I'M GOOD FOR 'EM.
OFF THE COAST OF JAPAN...
OH HE'S SO SWEET! MAY I PET HIM?
GO AHEAD BUT SWEET HE AIN'T.
THIS IS SO EXCITING! I FEEL LIKE A KID AGAIN!
SMILEY VIRUS, YOU'RE STILL A KID!
ANDRONICUS
ACTOR LARRY PETERS
ACTRESS DOLORES DEL PETUNIA
SINGER SMILEY VIRUS
SUPERHERO RAMPAGE JACKSON
DOG ANDRONICUS
MAGICIAN DAVID NICKLEBACK
MLB PITCHER HENDERSON HIGHTOWER
WELCOME TO GIANT MONSTER ISLAND!
YOUR GENEROSITY WILL END CHILDHOOD HUNGER.
GOSHU-SAN! ANYONE GET HURT FROM THESE "GIANT MONSTERS?"
HA HA! NOT A CHANCE, RAMPAGE! THEY AREN'T ANY REAL GIANT MONSTERS HERE, OF COURSE...
BETTER NOT BE.

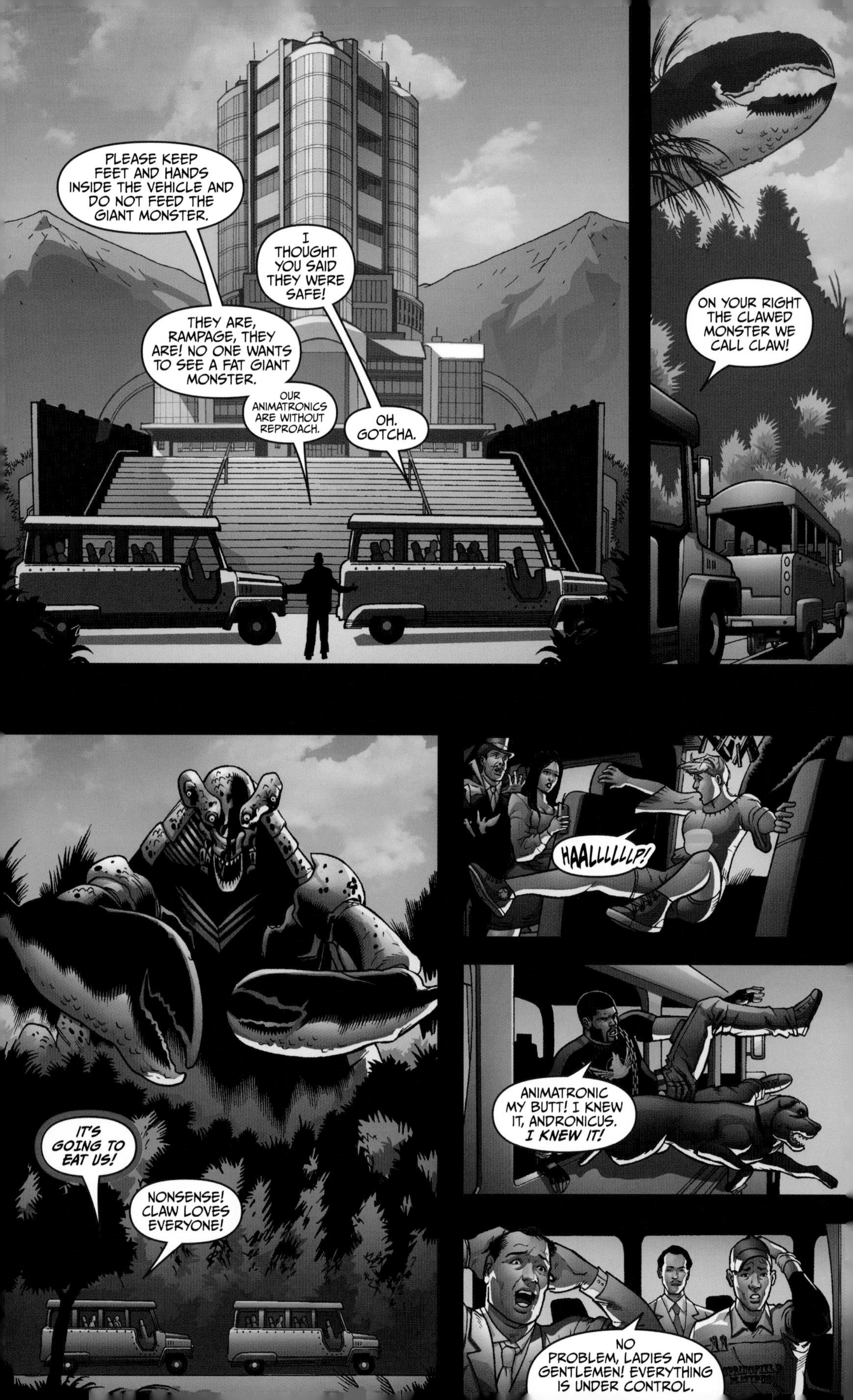
PLEASE KEEP FEET AND HANDS INSIDE THE VEHICLE AND DO NOT FEED THE GIANT MONSTER.
I THOUGHT YOU SAID THEY WERE SAFE!
THEY ARE, RAMPAGE, THEY ARE! NO ONE WANTS TO SEE A FAT GIANT MONSTER.
OUR ANIMATRONICS ARE WITHOUT REPROACH.
OH. GOTCHA.
ON YOUR RIGHT THE CLAWED MONSTER WE CALL CLAW!
IT'S GOING TO EAT US!
NONSENSE! CLAW LOVES EVERYONE!
HAALLLLLLP!
ANIMATRONIC MY BUTT! I KNEW IT, ANDRONICUS. *I KNEW IT!*
NO PROBLEM, LADIES AND GENTLEMEN! EVERYTHING IS UNDER CONTROL.

WE WON'T CATCH IT RUNNIN'.

GET ON THE TREE! UP, BOY, UP!

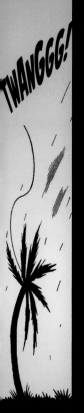

TWANGGG!

THWACK!

EEYOW! LIKE HITTING ONE OF KIM'S BISCUITS!

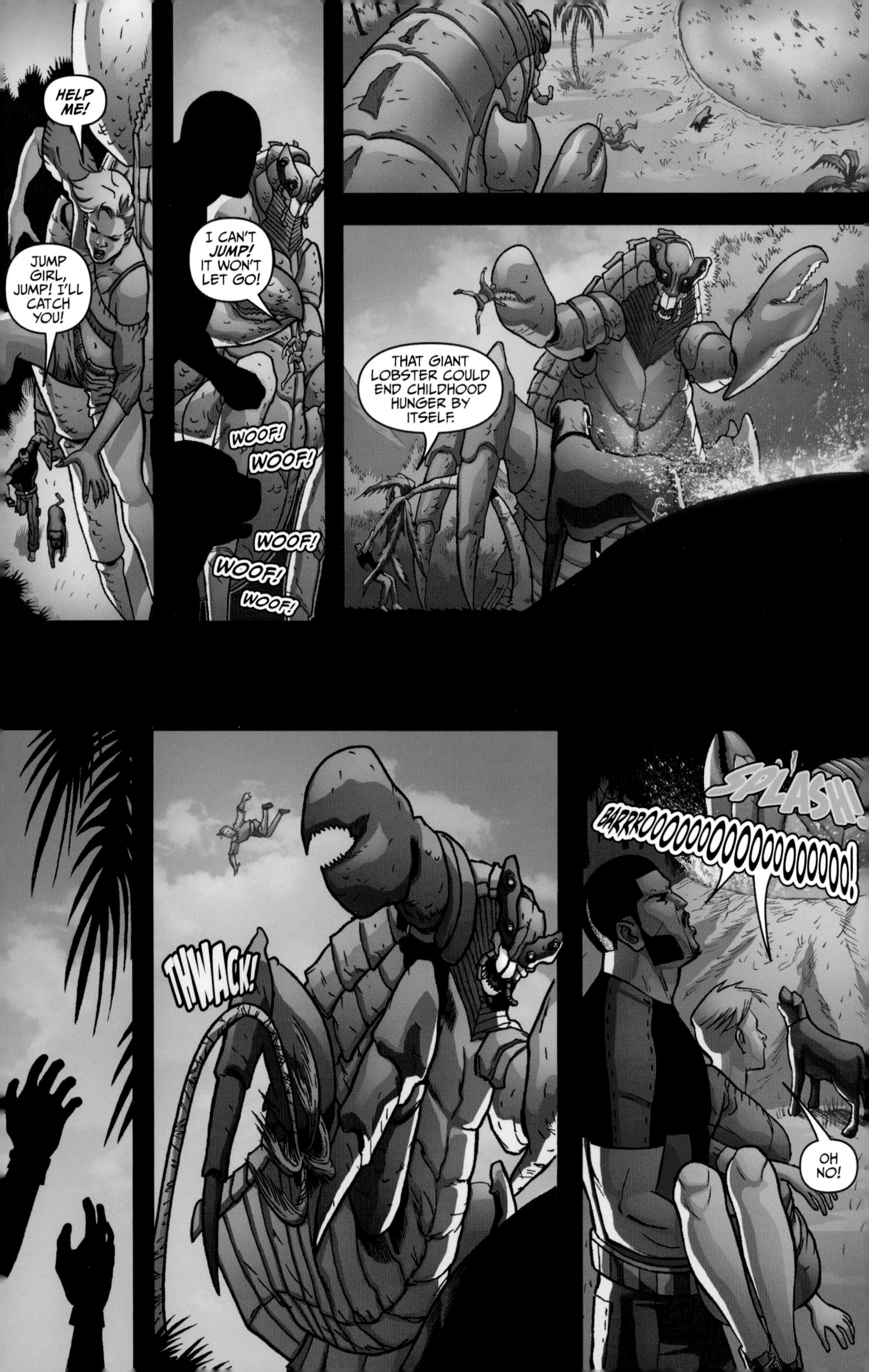

HELP ME!
JUMP GIRL, JUMP! I'LL CATCH YOU!
I CAN'T JUMP! IT WON'T LET GO!
WOOF!
WOOF!
WOOF!
WOOF!
WOOF!
THAT GIANT LOBSTER COULD END CHILDHOOD HUNGER BY ITSELF.
THWACK!
SPLASH!
BARRROOOOOOOOOOOOOOOOOOOO!
OH NO!

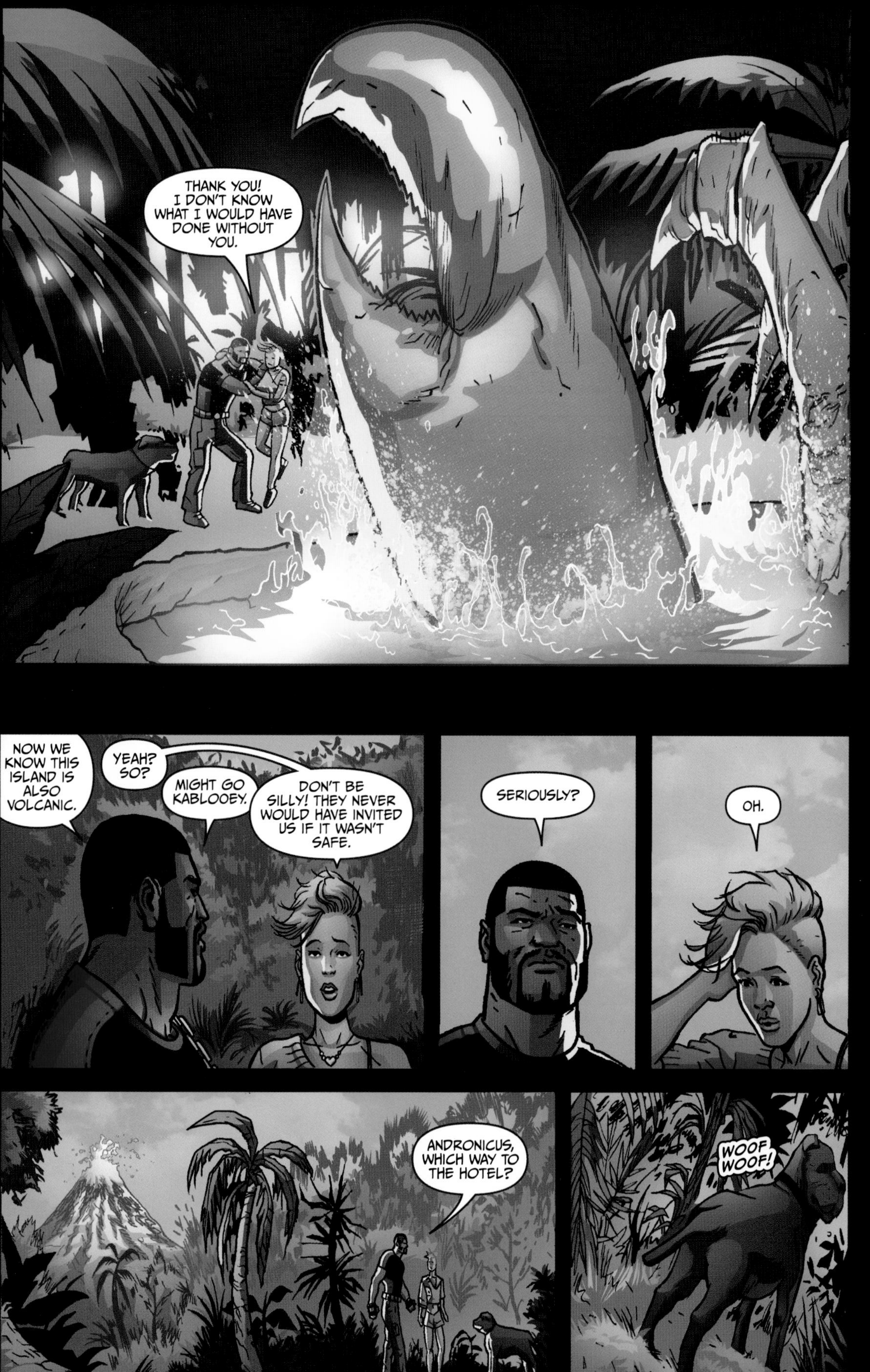
THANK YOU! I DON'T KNOW WHAT I WOULD HAVE DONE WITHOUT YOU.
NOW WE KNOW THIS ISLAND IS ALSO VOLCANIC.
YEAH? SO?
MIGHT GO KABLOOEY.
DON'T BE SILLY! THEY NEVER WOULD HAVE INVITED US IF IT WASN'T SAFE.
SERIOUSLY?
OH.
ANDRONICUS, WHICH WAY TO THE HOTEL?
WOOF WOOF!

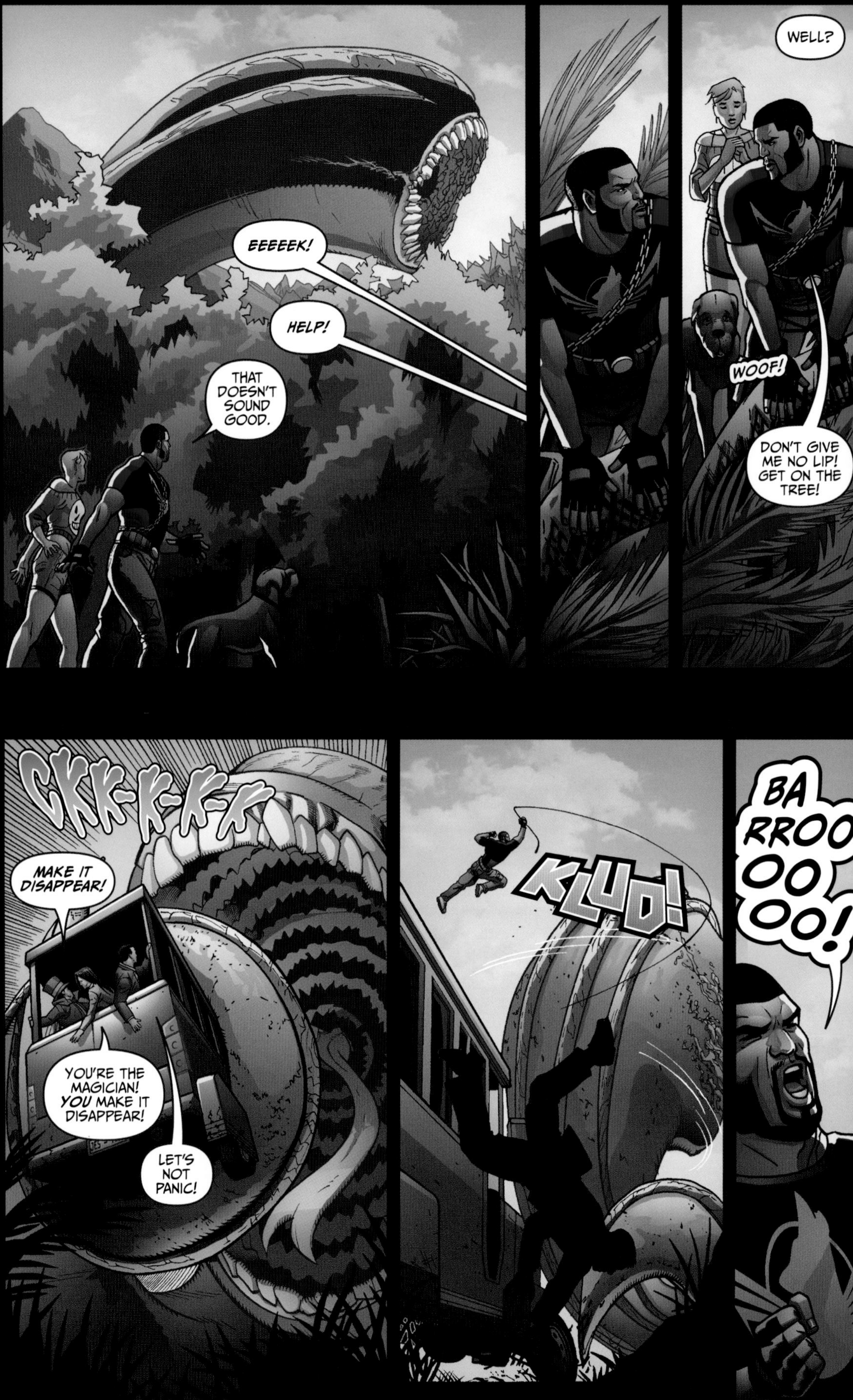

EEEEEK!
HELP!
THAT DOESN'T SOUND GOOD.
WELL?
WOOF!
DON'T GIVE ME NO LIP! GET ON THE TREE!
CKK-K-K-K
MAKE IT DISAPPEAR!
YOU'RE THE MAGICIAN! *YOU* MAKE IT DISAPPEAR!
LET'S NOT PANIC!
KLUD!
BA RROO OO OO!

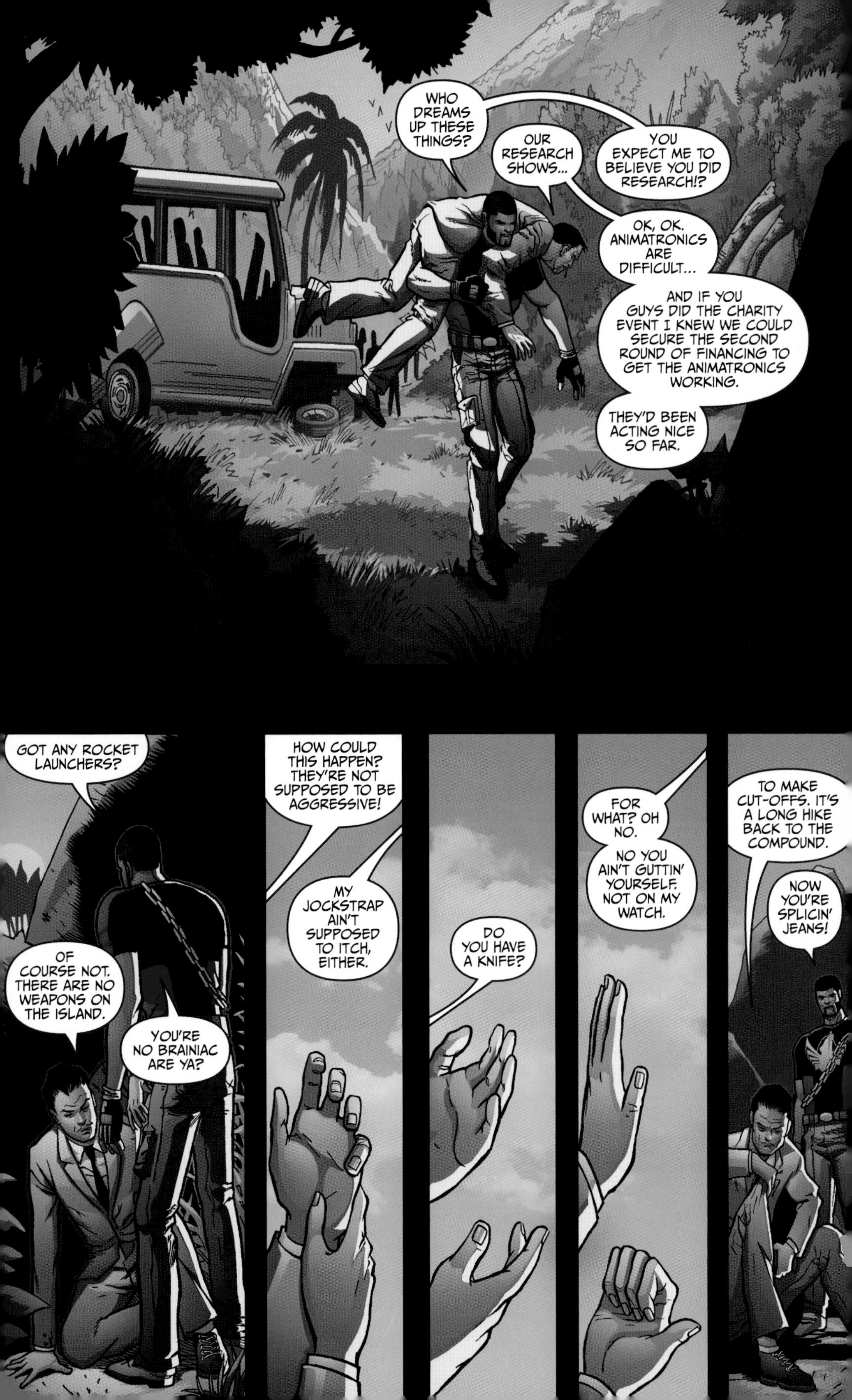
WHO DREAMS UP THESE THINGS?
OUR RESEARCH SHOWS...
YOU EXPECT ME TO BELIEVE YOU DID RESEARCH!?
OK, OK. ANIMATRONICS ARE DIFFICULT...
AND IF YOU GUYS DID THE CHARITY EVENT I KNEW WE COULD SECURE THE SECOND ROUND OF FINANCING TO GET THE ANIMATRONICS WORKING.
THEY'D BEEN ACTING NICE SO FAR.
GOT ANY ROCKET LAUNCHERS?
OF COURSE NOT. THERE ARE NO WEAPONS ON THE ISLAND.
YOU'RE NO BRAINIAC ARE YA?
HOW COULD THIS HAPPEN? THEY'RE NOT SUPPOSED TO BE AGGRESSIVE!
MY JOCKSTRAP AIN'T SUPPOSED TO ITCH, EITHER.
DO YOU HAVE A KNIFE?
FOR WHAT? OH NO.
NO YOU AIN'T GUTTIN' YOURSELF. NOT ON MY WATCH.
TO MAKE CUT-OFFS. IT'S A LONG HIKE BACK TO THE COMPOUND.
NOW YOU'RE SPLICIN' JEANS!

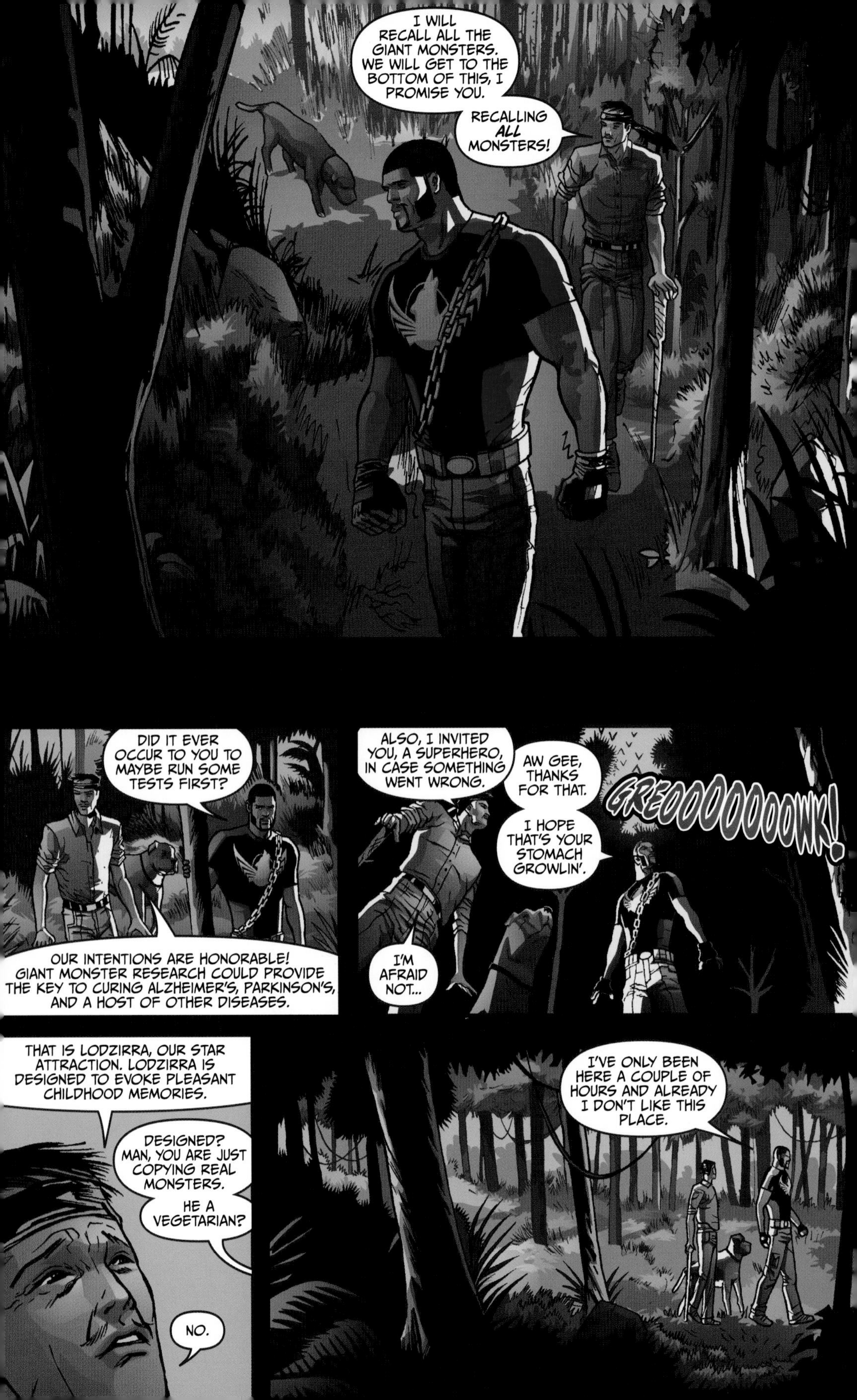
I WILL RECALL ALL THE GIANT MONSTERS. WE WILL GET TO THE BOTTOM OF THIS, I PROMISE YOU.
RECALLING *ALL* MONSTERS!
DID IT EVER OCCUR TO YOU TO MAYBE RUN SOME TESTS FIRST?
OUR INTENTIONS ARE HONORABLE! GIANT MONSTER RESEARCH COULD PROVIDE THE KEY TO CURING ALZHEIMER'S, PARKINSON'S, AND A HOST OF OTHER DISEASES.
ALSO, I INVITED YOU, A SUPERHERO, IN CASE SOMETHING WENT WRONG.
AW GEE, THANKS FOR THAT.
GREOOOOOOOOWK!
I HOPE THAT'S YOUR STOMACH GROWLIN'.
I'M AFRAID NOT...
THAT IS LODZIRRA, OUR STAR ATTRACTION. LODZIRRA IS DESIGNED TO EVOKE PLEASANT CHILDHOOD MEMORIES.
DESIGNED? MAN, YOU ARE JUST COPYING REAL MONSTERS.
HE A VEGETARIAN?
NO.
I'VE ONLY BEEN HERE A COUPLE OF HOURS AND ALREADY I DON'T LIKE THIS PLACE.

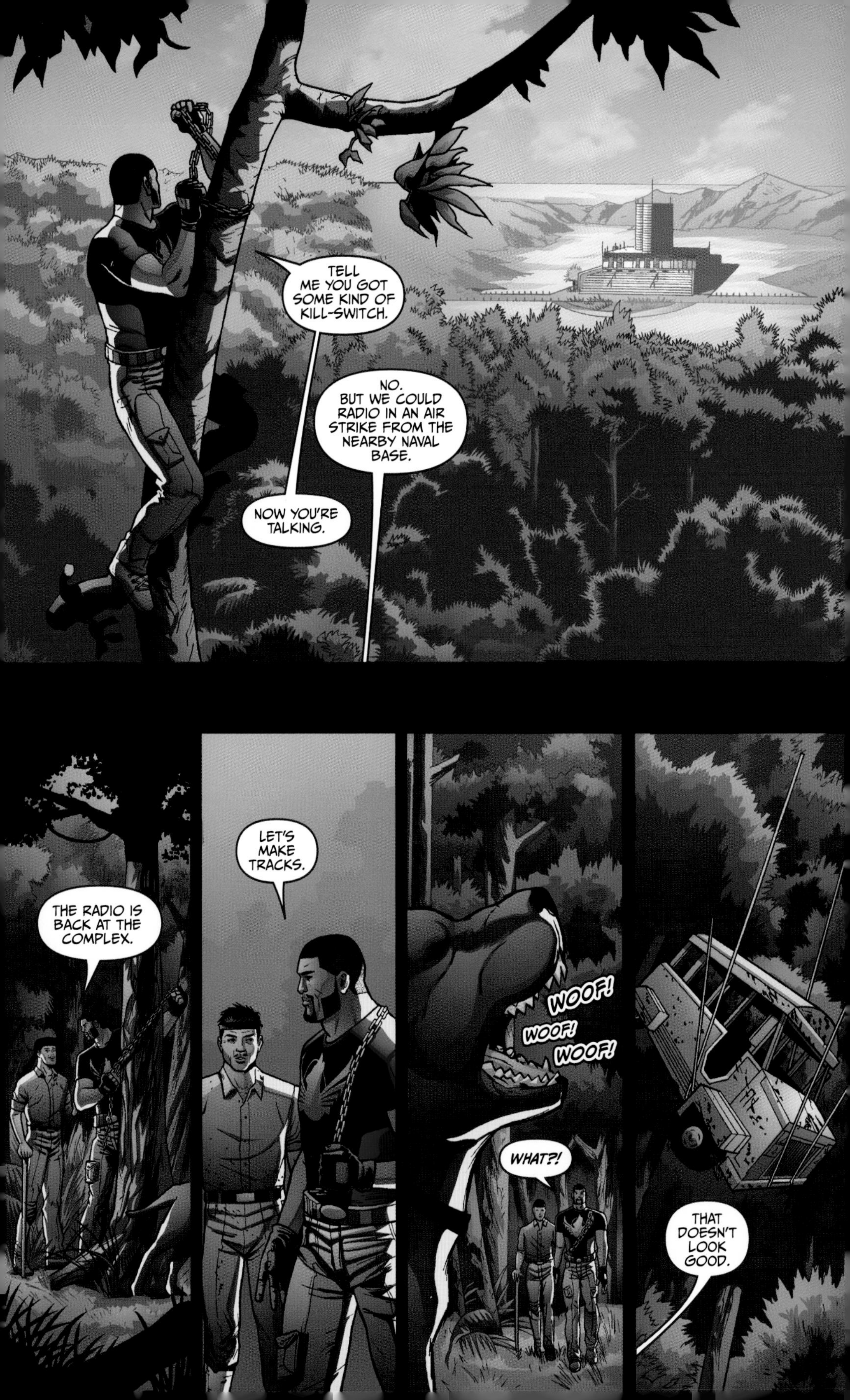
TELL ME YOU GOT SOME KIND OF KILL-SWITCH.
NO. BUT WE COULD RADIO IN AN AIR STRIKE FROM THE NEARBY NAVAL BASE.
NOW YOU'RE TALKING.
THE RADIO IS BACK AT THE COMPLEX.
LET'S MAKE TRACKS.
WOOF!
WOOF!
WOOF!
WHAT?!
THAT DOESN'T LOOK GOOD.

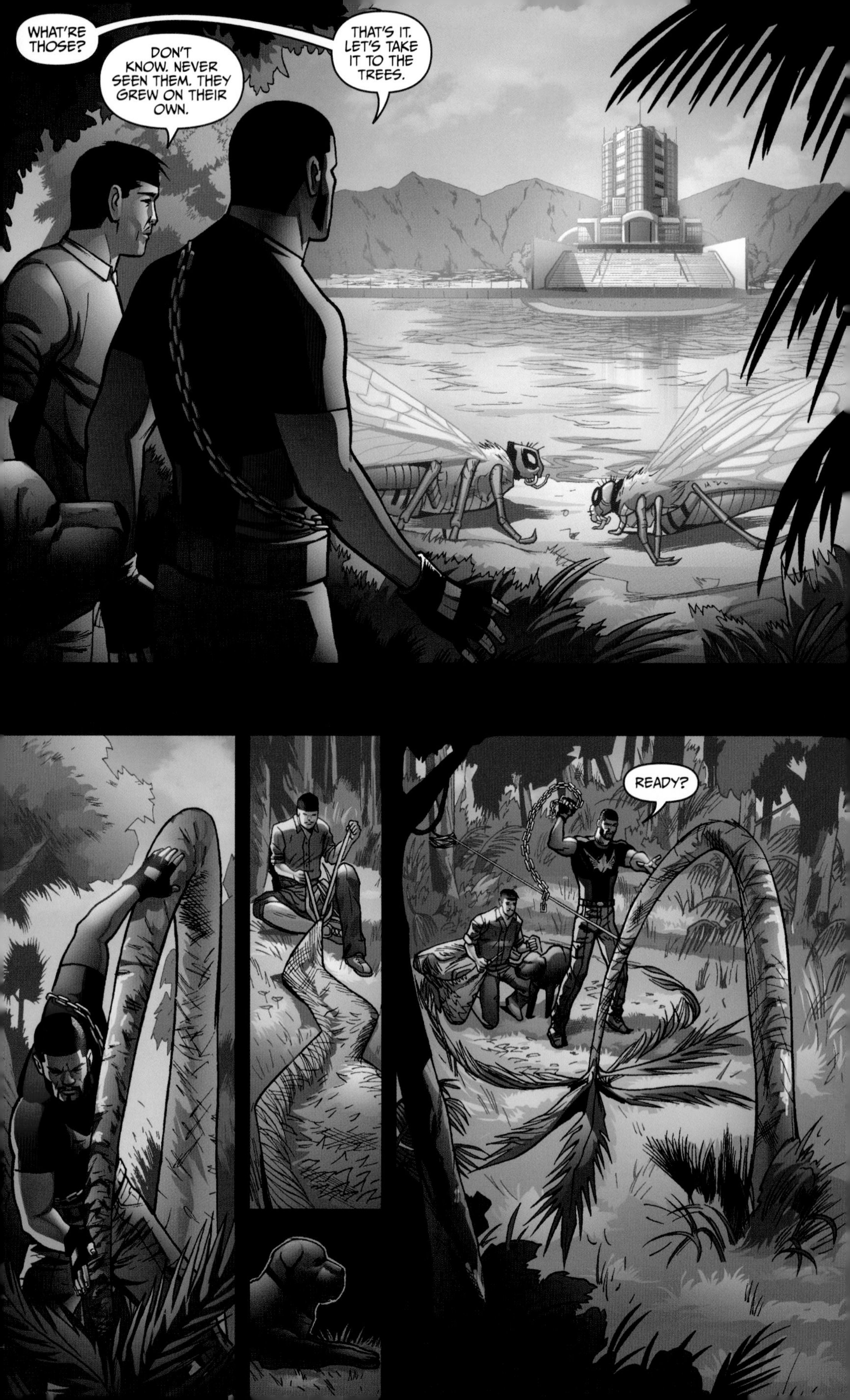
WHAT'RE THOSE?
DON'T KNOW. NEVER SEEN THEM. THEY GREW ON THEIR OWN.
THAT'S IT. LET'S TAKE IT TO THE TREES.
READY?

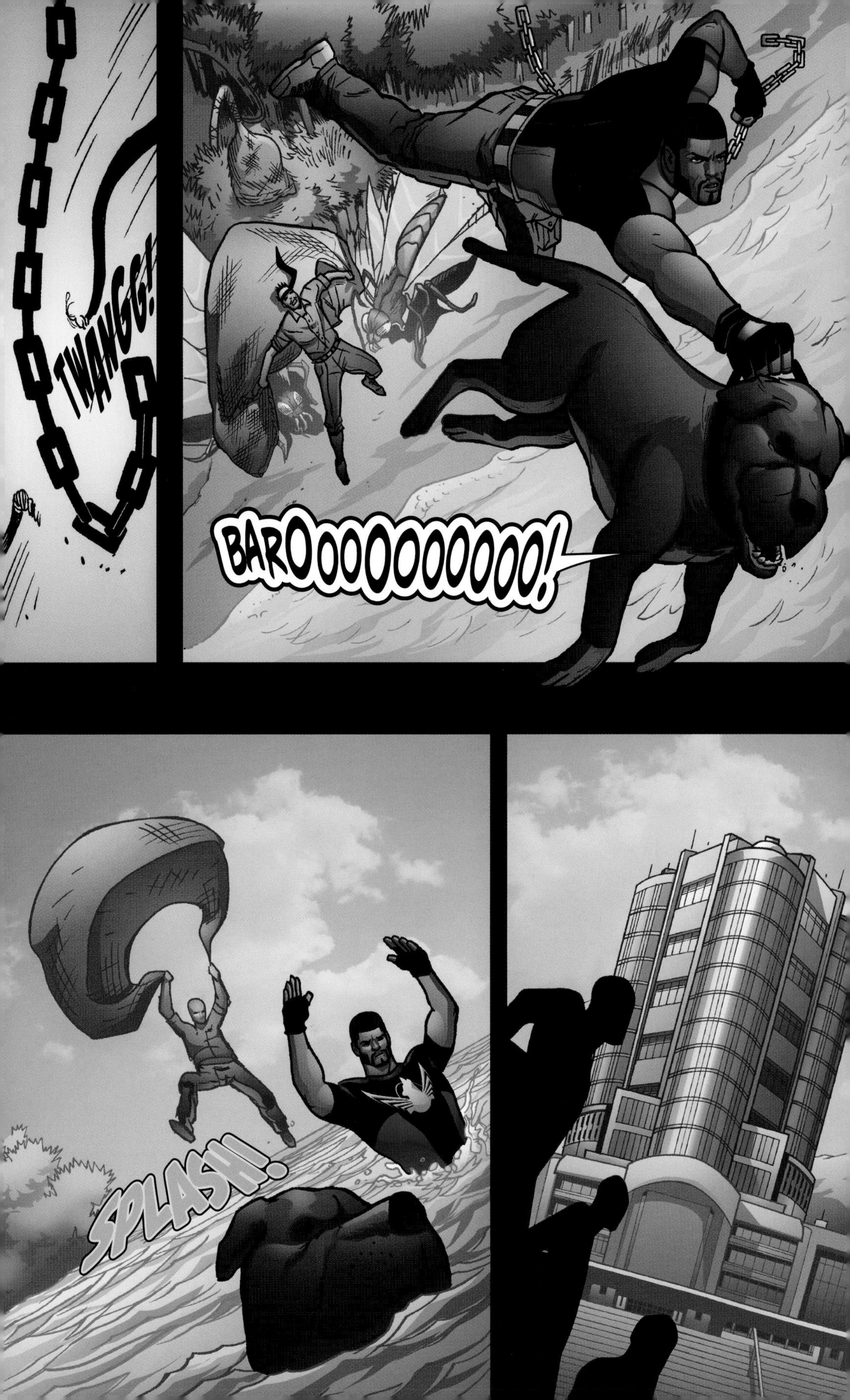
TWANGG!
BAROOOOOOOOOO!
SPLASH!

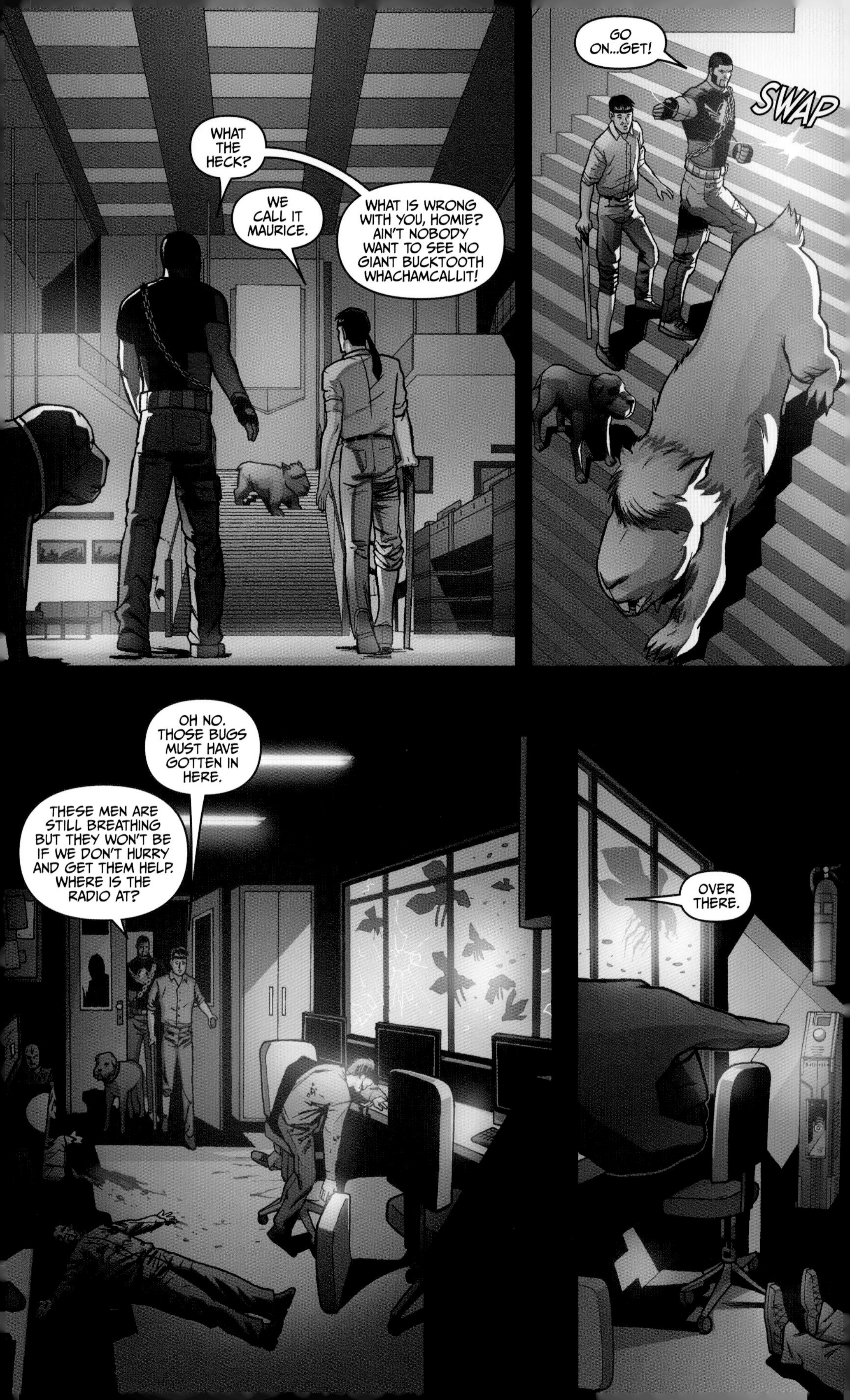
WHAT THE HECK?
WE CALL IT MAURICE.
WHAT IS WRONG WITH YOU, HOMIE? AIN'T NOBODY WANT TO SEE NO GIANT BUCKTOOTH WHACHAMCALLIT!
GO ON...GET!
SWAP
OH NO. THOSE BUGS MUST HAVE GOTTEN IN HERE.
THESE MEN ARE STILL BREATHING BUT THEY WON'T BE IF WE DON'T HURRY AND GET THEM HELP. WHERE IS THE RADIO AT?
OVER THERE.

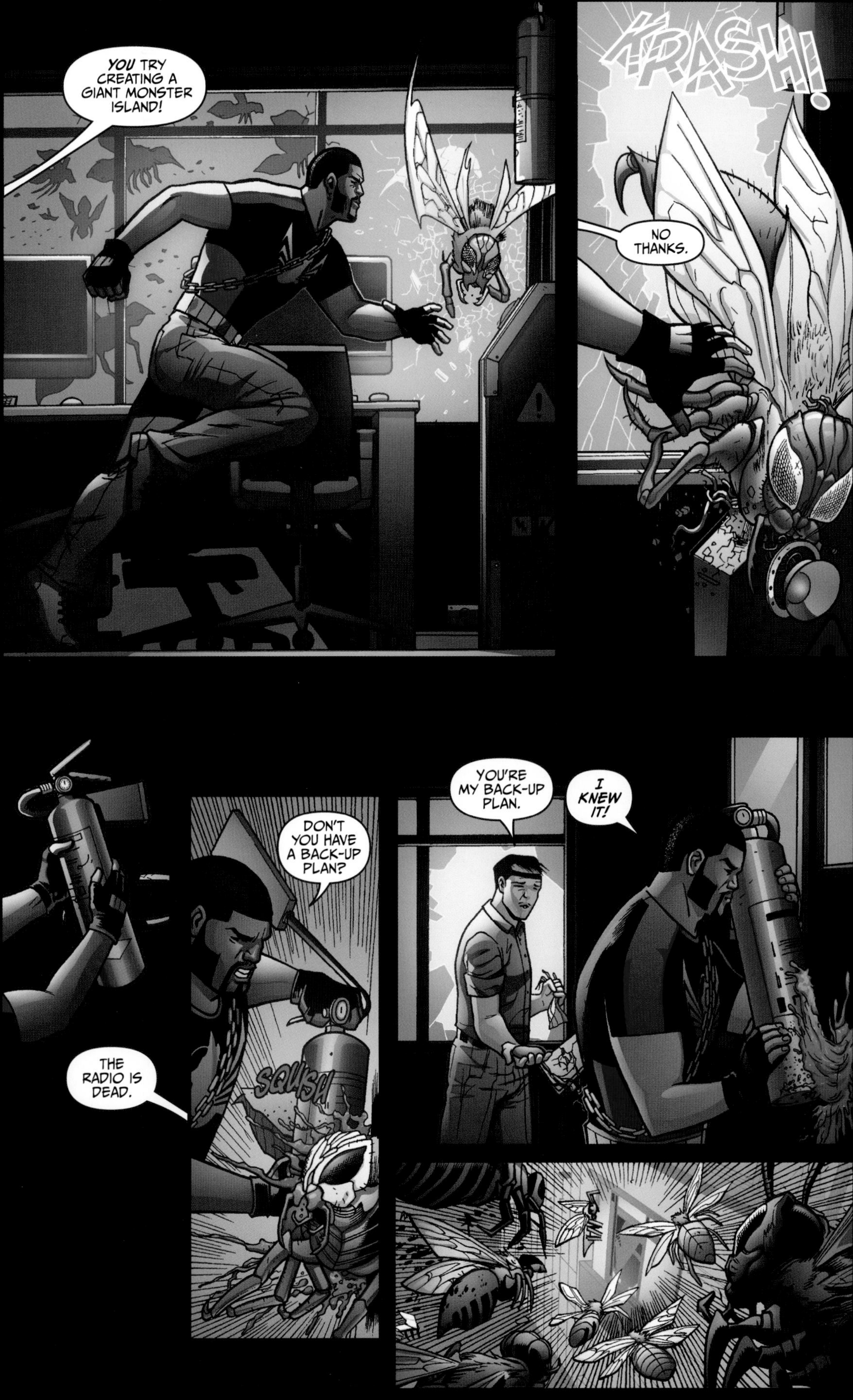
YOU TRY CREATING A GIANT MONSTER ISLAND!
KRASH!
NO THANKS.
DON'T YOU HAVE A BACK-UP PLAN?
THE RADIO IS DEAD.
SQUISH
YOU'RE MY BACK-UP PLAN.
I KNEW IT!

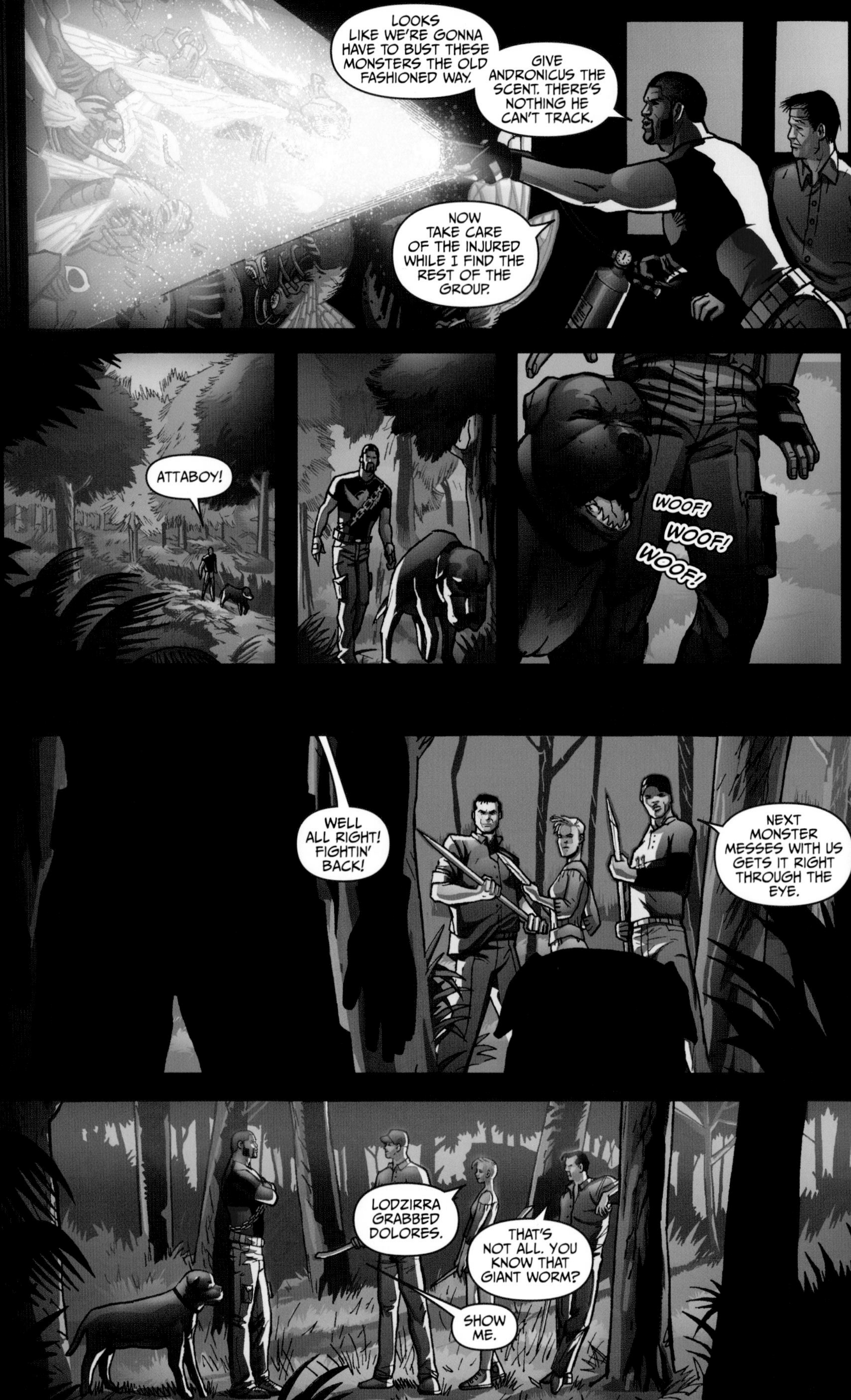
LOOKS LIKE WE'RE GONNA HAVE TO BUST THESE MONSTERS THE OLD FASHIONED WAY.
GIVE ANDRONICUS THE SCENT. THERE'S NOTHING HE CAN'T TRACK.
NOW TAKE CARE OF THE INJURED WHILE I FIND THE REST OF THE GROUP.
ATTABOY!
WOOF! WOOF! WOOF!
WELL ALL RIGHT! FIGHTIN' BACK!
NEXT MONSTER MESSES WITH US GETS IT RIGHT THROUGH THE EYE.
LODZIRRA GRABBED DOLORES.
THAT'S NOT ALL. YOU KNOW THAT GIANT WORM?
SHOW ME.

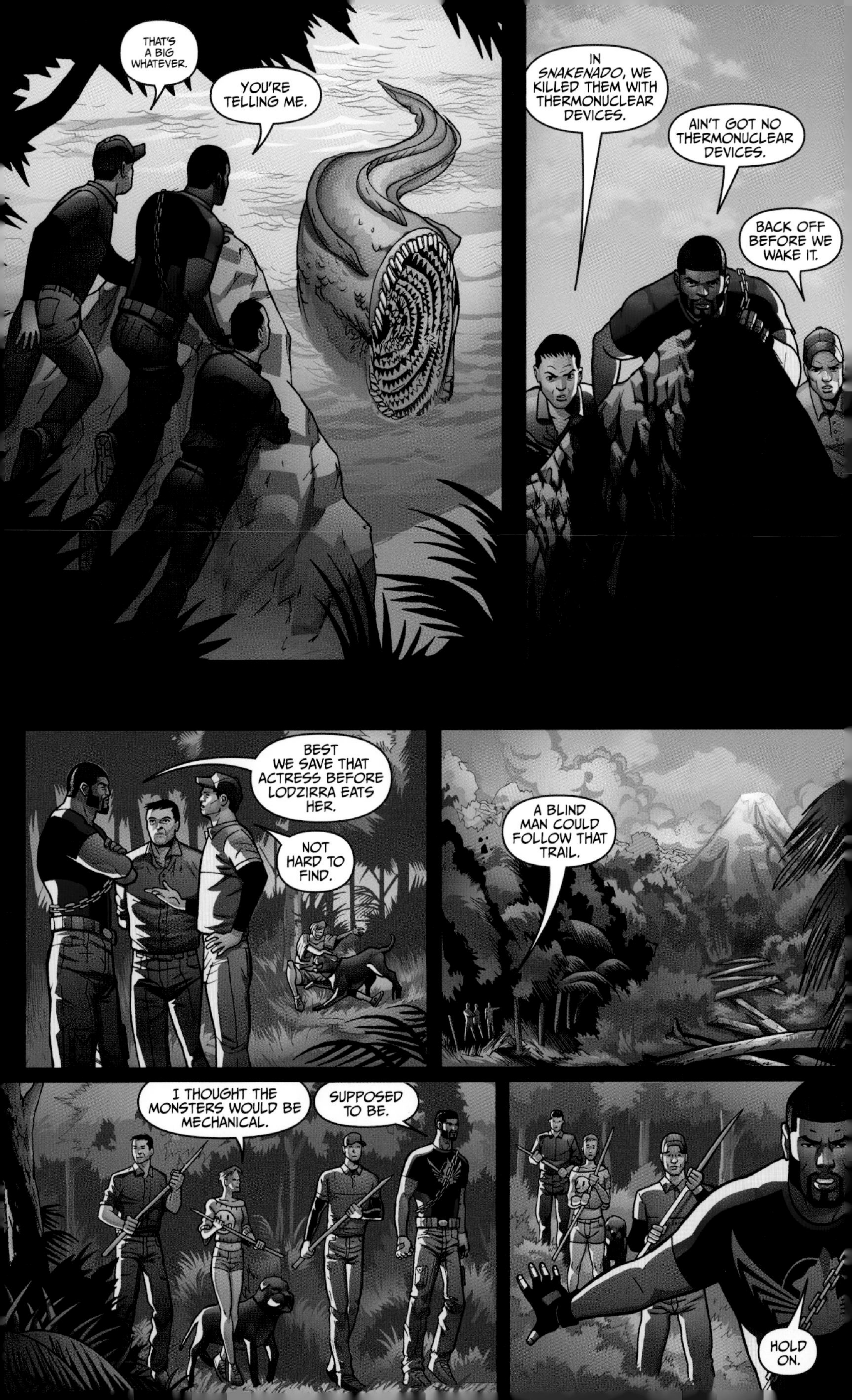
THAT'S A BIG WHATEVER.
YOU'RE TELLING ME.
IN SNAKENADO, WE KILLED THEM WITH THERMONUCLEAR DEVICES.
AIN'T GOT NO THERMONUCLEAR DEVICES.
BACK OFF BEFORE WE WAKE IT.
BEST WE SAVE THAT ACTRESS BEFORE LODZIRRA EATS HER.
NOT HARD TO FIND.
A BLIND MAN COULD FOLLOW THAT TRAIL.
I THOUGHT THE MONSTERS WOULD BE MECHANICAL.
SUPPOSED TO BE.
HOLD ON.

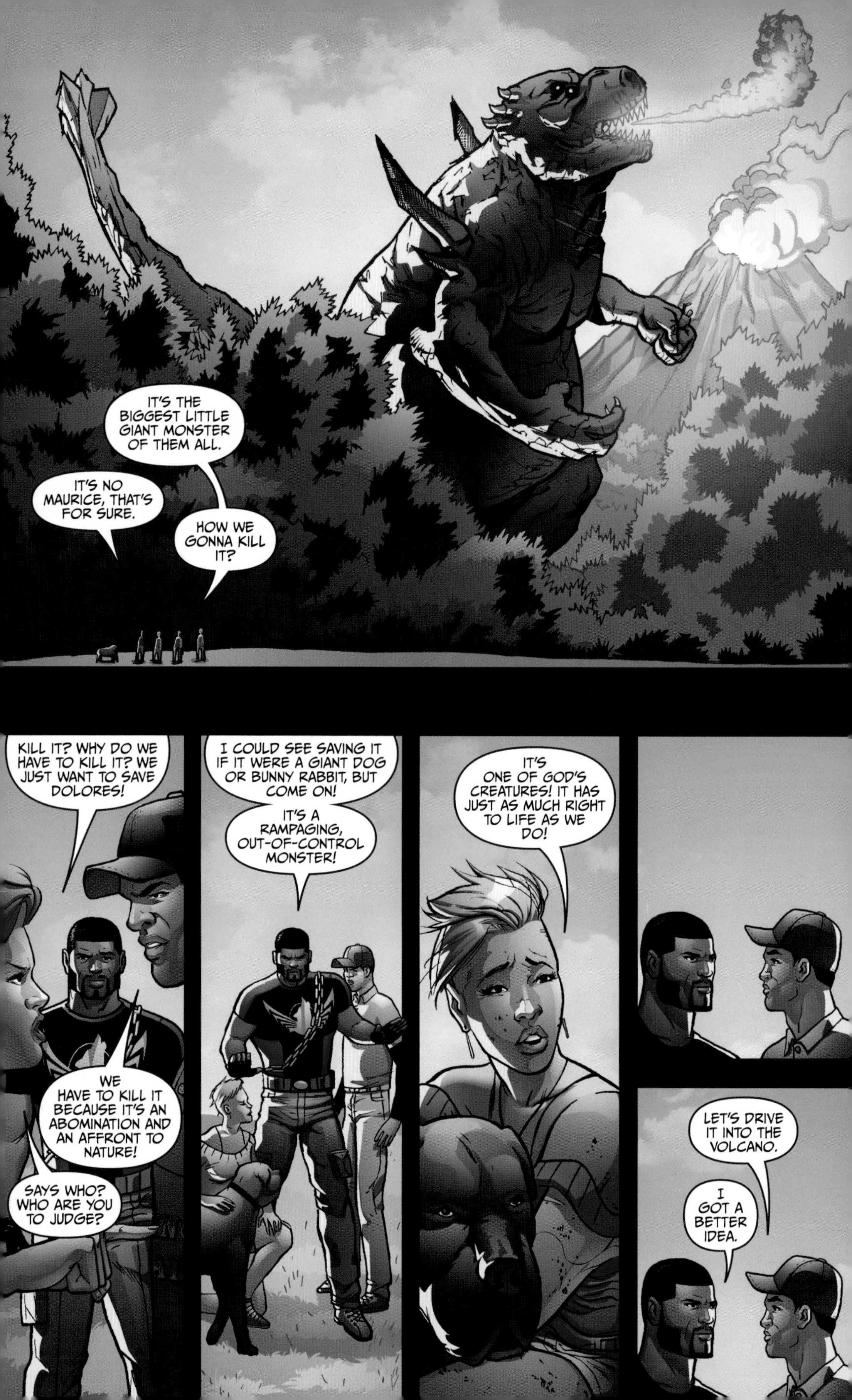
IT'S THE BIGGEST LITTLE GIANT MONSTER OF THEM ALL.
IT'S NO MAURICE, THAT'S FOR SURE.
HOW WE GONNA KILL IT?
KILL IT? WHY DO WE HAVE TO KILL IT? WE JUST WANT TO SAVE DOLORES!
WE HAVE TO KILL IT BECAUSE IT'S AN ABOMINATION AND AN AFFRONT TO NATURE!
SAYS WHO? WHO ARE YOU TO JUDGE?
I COULD SEE SAVING IT IF IT WERE A GIANT DOG OR BUNNY RABBIT, BUT COME ON!
IT'S A RAMPAGING, OUT-OF-CONTROL MONSTER!
IT'S ONE OF GOD'S CREATURES! IT HAS JUST AS MUCH RIGHT TO LIFE AS WE DO!
LET'S DRIVE IT INTO THE VOLCANO.
I GOT A BETTER IDEA.

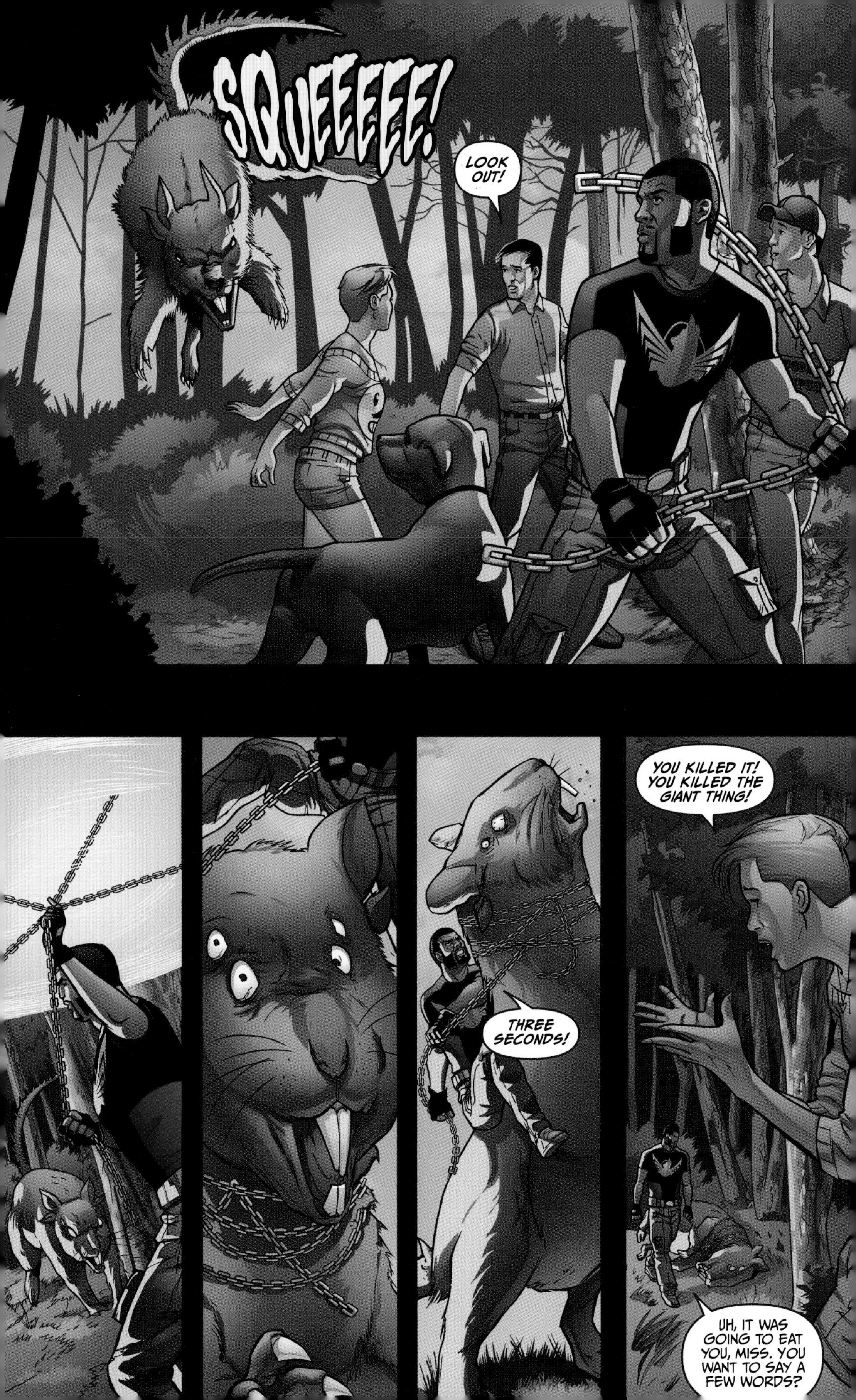
SQUEEEEE!
LOOK OUT!
THREE SECONDS!
YOU KILLED IT! YOU KILLED THE GIANT THING!
UH, IT WAS GOING TO EAT YOU, MISS. YOU WANT TO SAY A FEW WORDS?

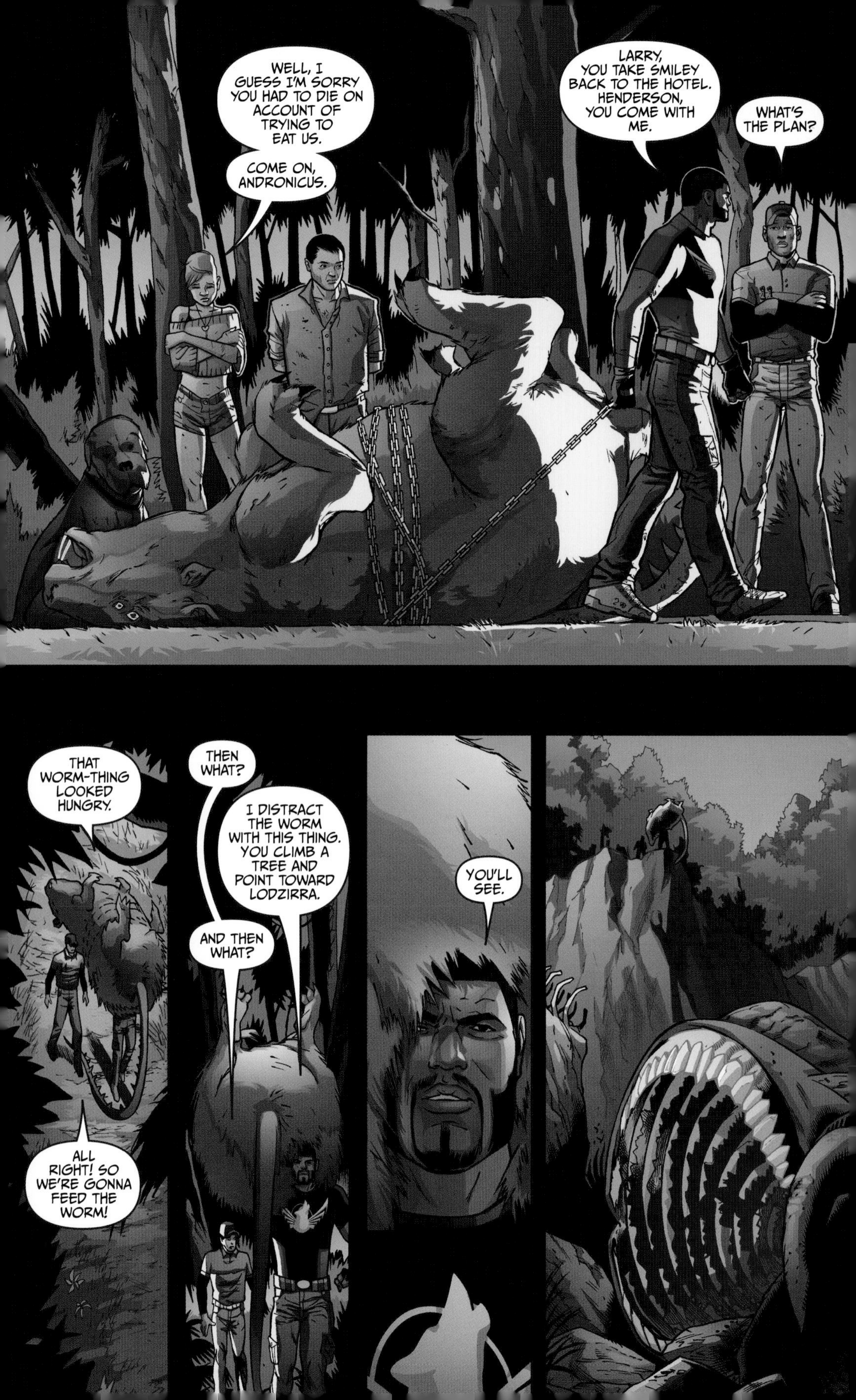
WELL, I GUESS I'M SORRY YOU HAD TO DIE ON ACCOUNT OF TRYING TO EAT US.
COME ON, ANDRONICUS.
LARRY, YOU TAKE SMILEY BACK TO THE HOTEL. HENDERSON, YOU COME WITH ME.
WHAT'S THE PLAN?
THAT WORM-THING LOOKED HUNGRY.
ALL RIGHT! SO WE'RE GONNA FEED THE WORM!
THEN WHAT?
I DISTRACT THE WORM WITH THIS THING. YOU CLIMB A TREE AND POINT TOWARD LODZIRRA.
AND THEN WHAT?
YOU'LL SEE.

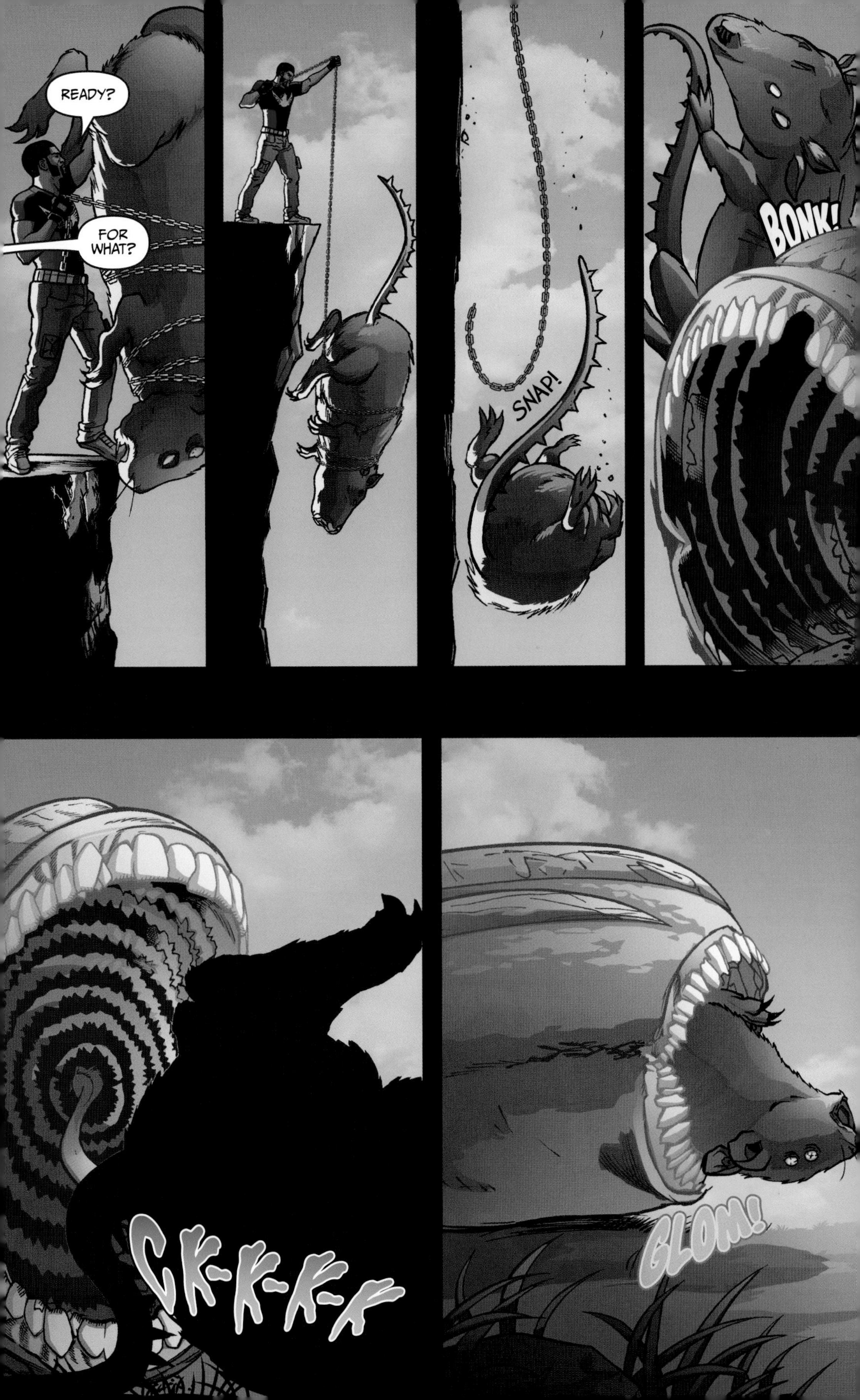
READY?
FOR WHAT?
SNAP!
BONK!
CK-K-K-K
GLOM!

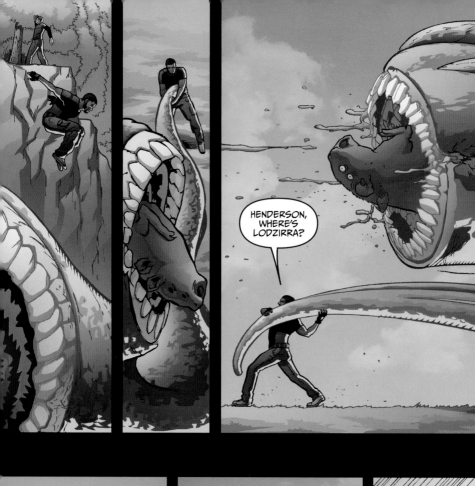

HENDERSON, WHERE'S LODZIRRA?

HE'S...

...THERE!

HERE WE GO!

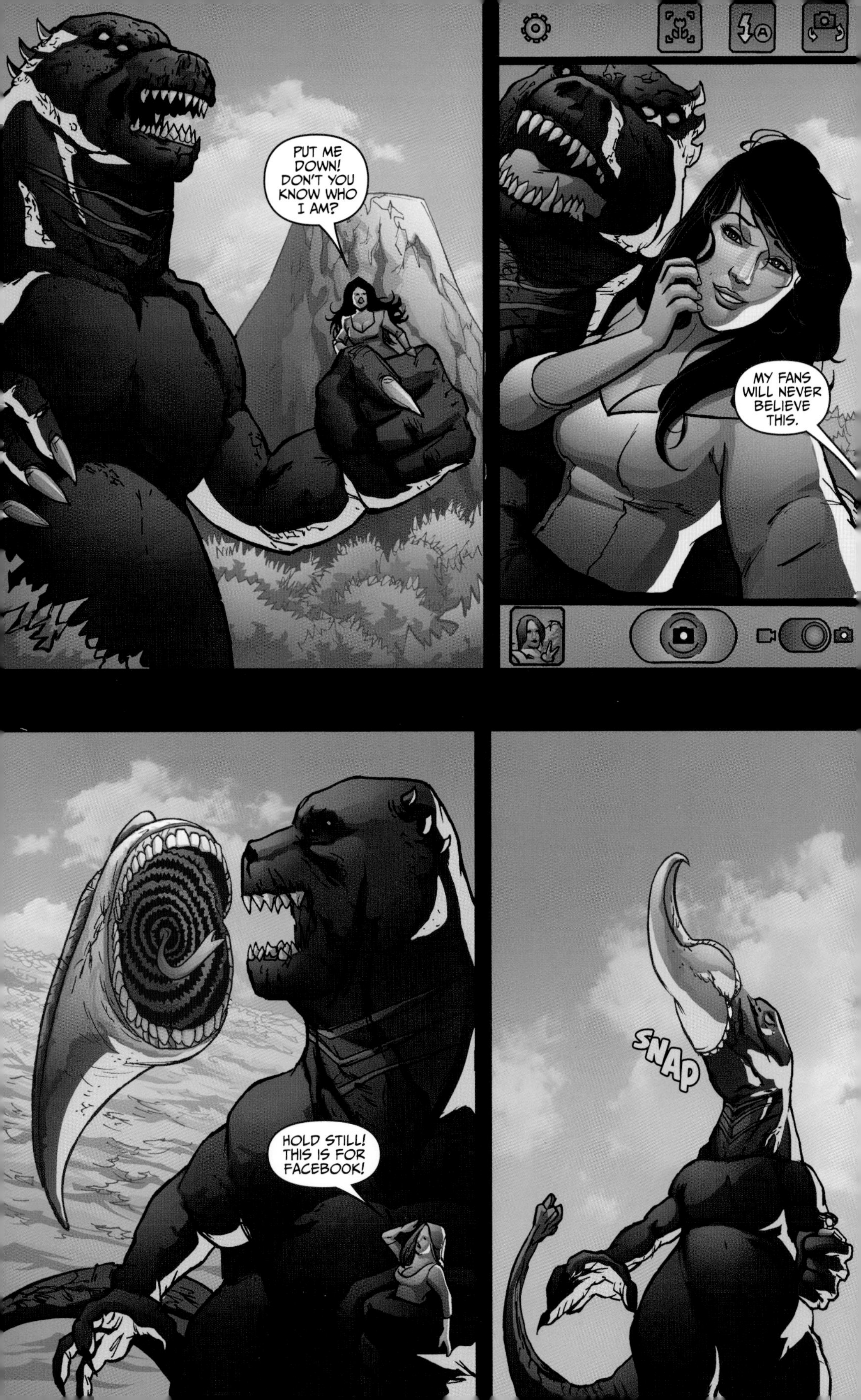
PUT ME DOWN! DON'T YOU KNOW WHO I AM?
MY FANS WILL NEVER BELIEVE THIS.
HOLD STILL! THIS IS FOR FACEBOOK!
SNAP

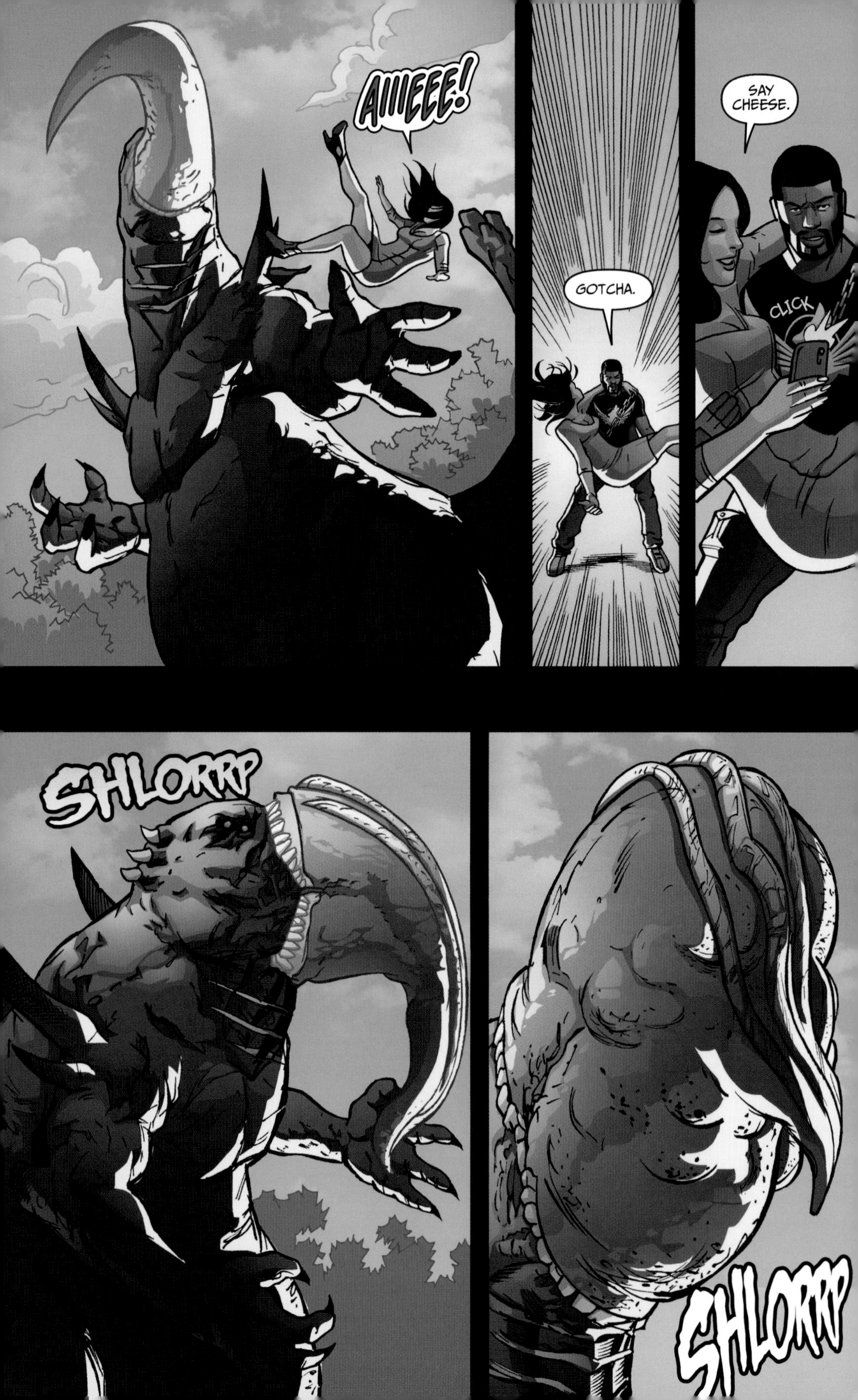
AIIIEEE!
GOTCHA.
SAY CHEESE.
CLICK
SHLORRP
SHLORRP

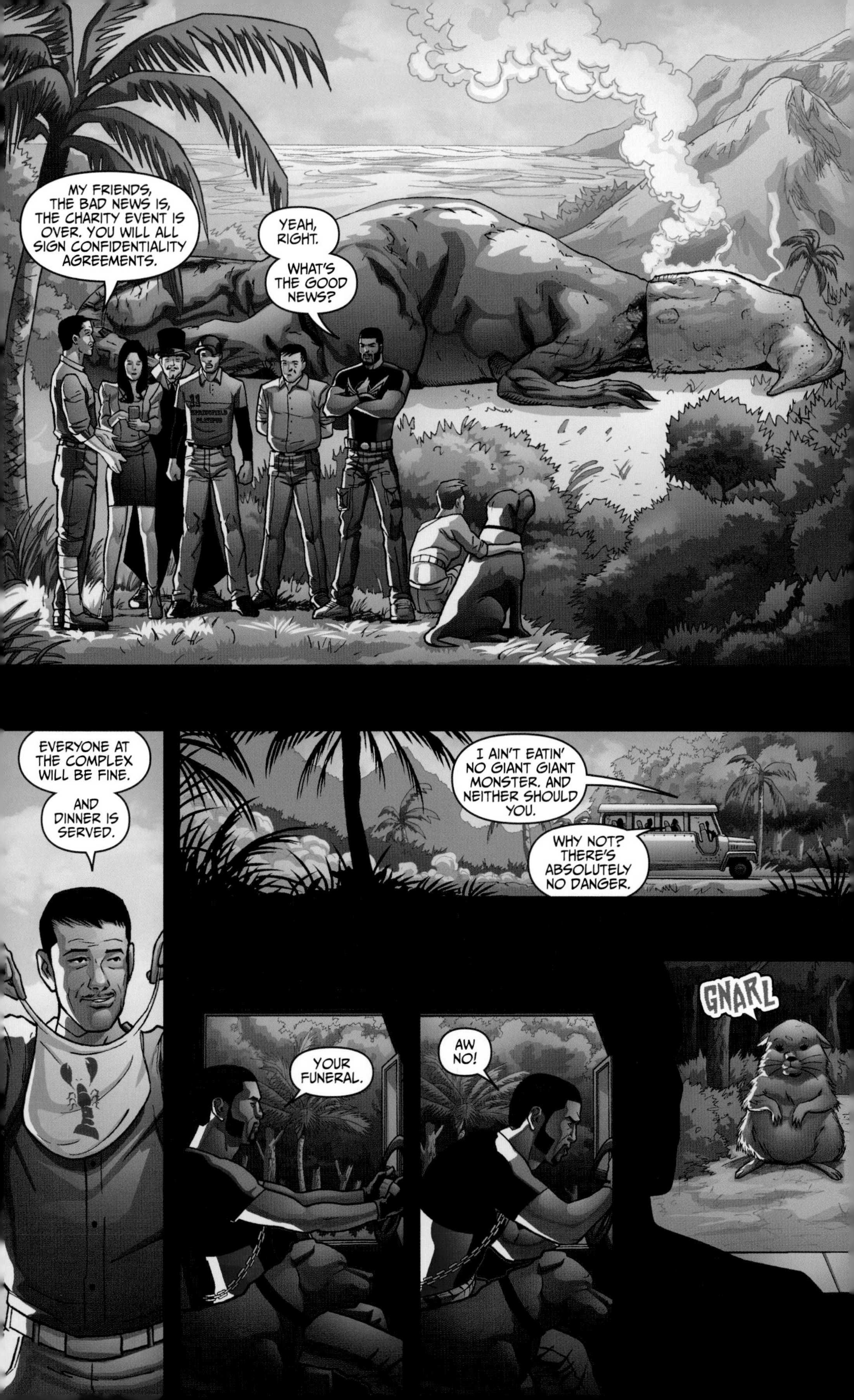
MY FRIENDS, THE BAD NEWS IS, THE CHARITY EVENT IS OVER. YOU WILL ALL SIGN CONFIDENTIALITY AGREEMENTS.
YEAH, RIGHT.
WHAT'S THE GOOD NEWS?
EVERYONE AT THE COMPLEX WILL BE FINE.
AND DINNER IS SERVED.
I AIN'T EATIN' NO GIANT GIANT MONSTER. AND NEITHER SHOULD YOU.
WHY NOT? THERE'S ABSOLUTELY NO DANGER.
YOUR FUNERAL.
AW NO!
GNARL

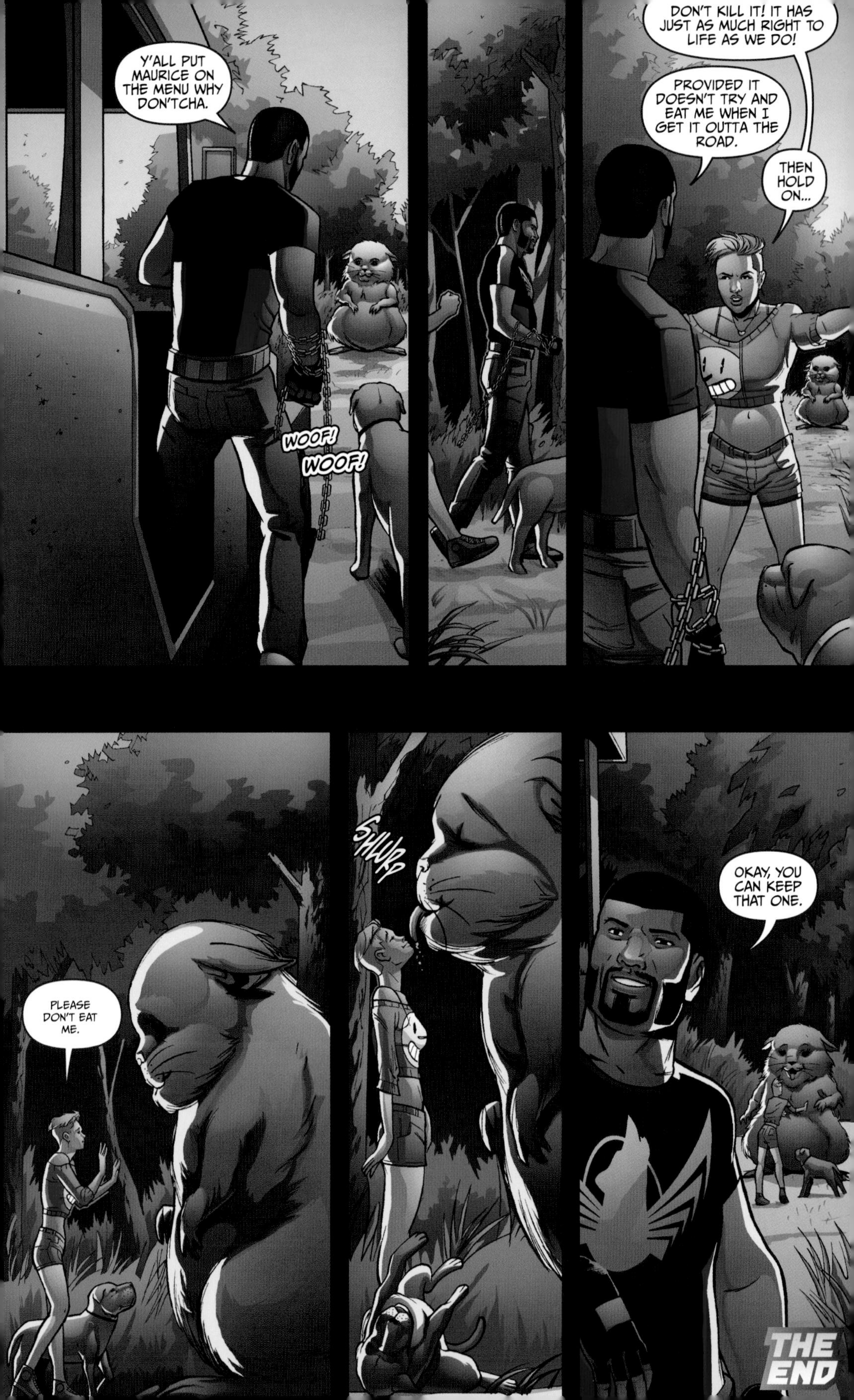
Y'ALL PUT MAURICE ON THE MENU WHY DON'TCHA.
WOOF! WOOF!
DON'T KILL IT! IT HAS JUST AS MUCH RIGHT TO LIFE AS WE DO!
PROVIDED IT DOESN'T TRY AND EAT ME WHEN I GET IT OUTTA THE ROAD.
THEN HOLD ON...
PLEASE DON'T EAT ME.
SHLURP
OKAY, YOU CAN KEEP THAT ONE.
THE END

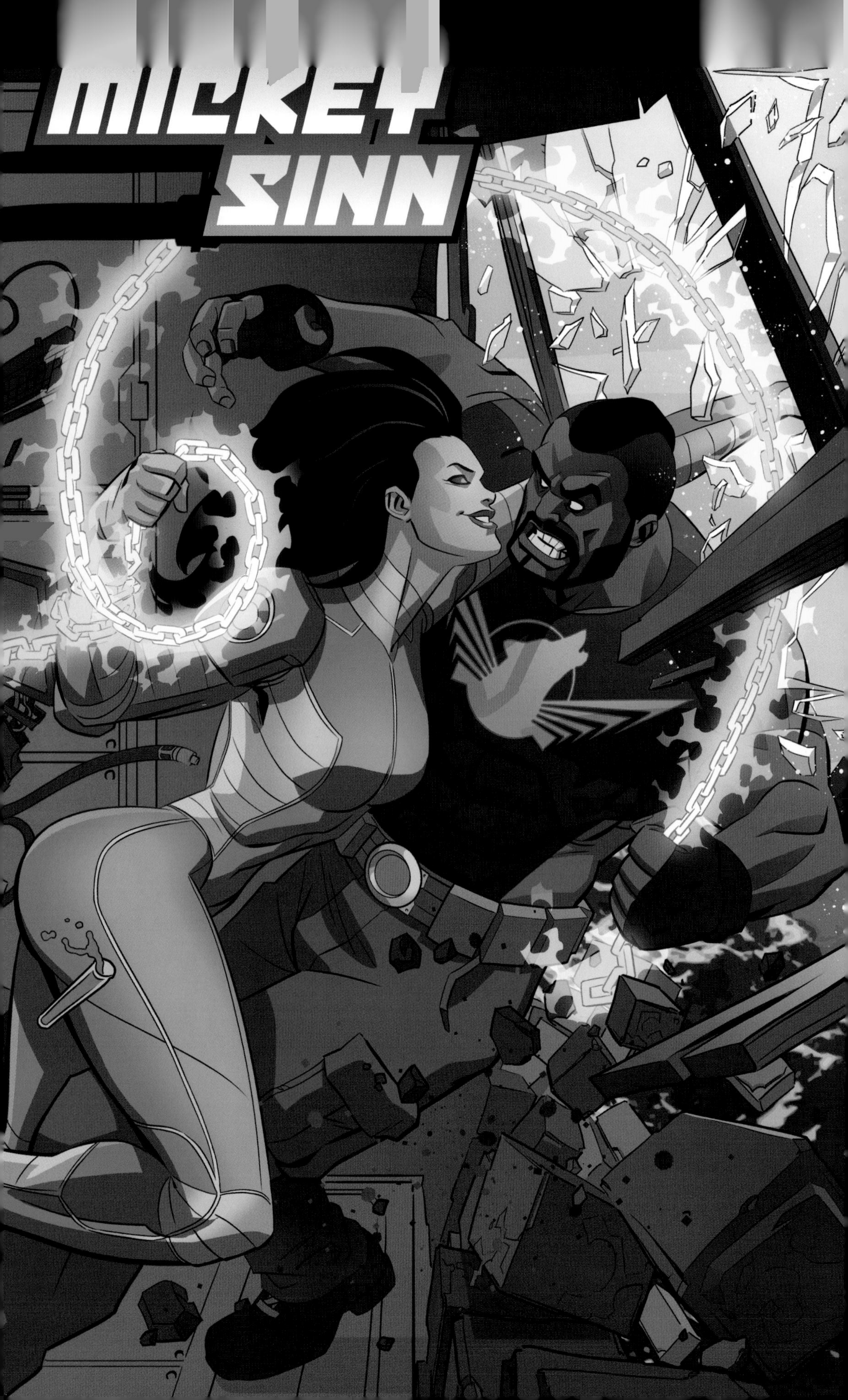
MICKEY
SINN

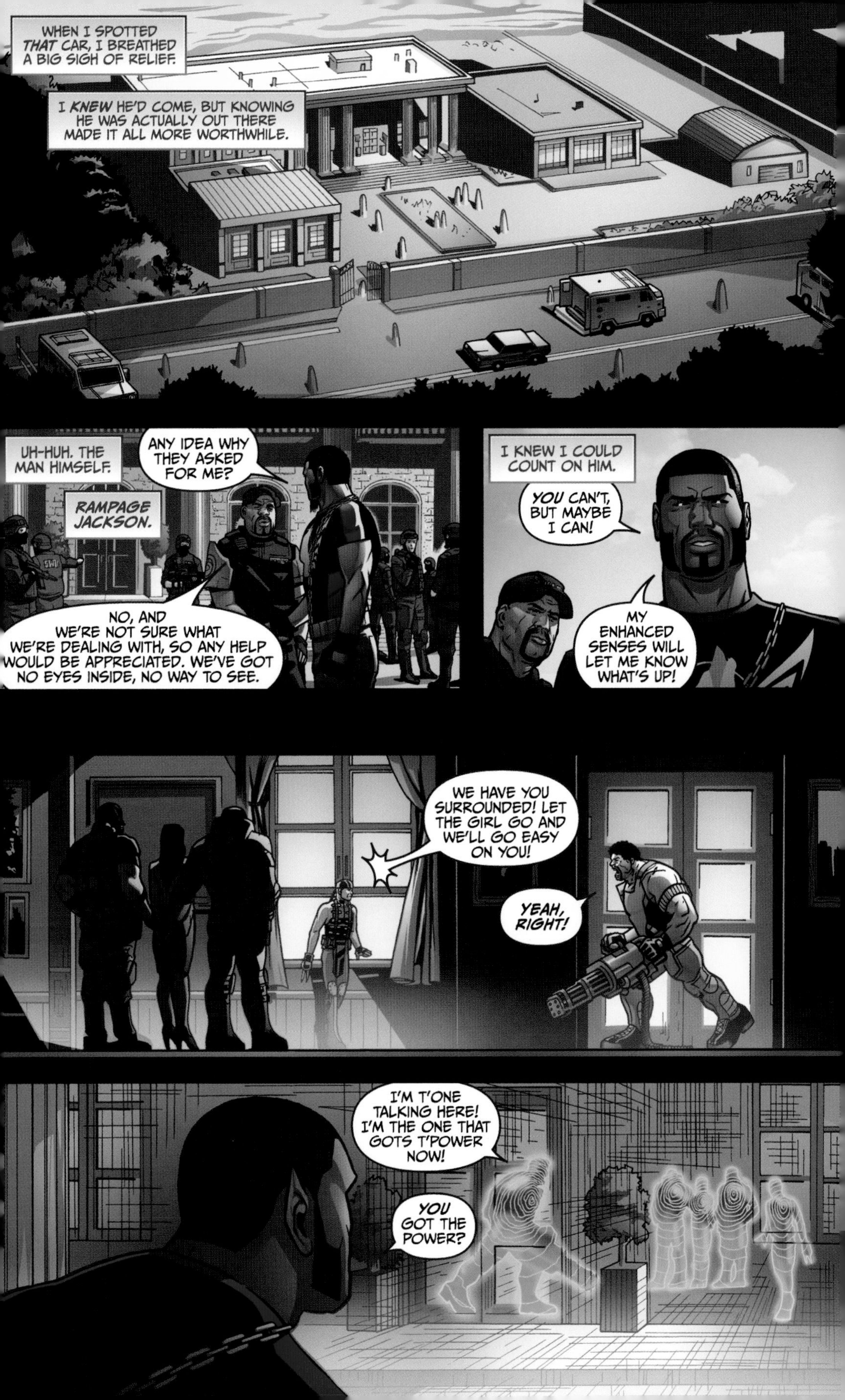
WHEN I SPOTTED THAT CAR, I BREATHED A BIG SIGH OF RELIEF.
I KNEW HE'D COME, BUT KNOWING HE WAS ACTUALLY OUT THERE MADE IT ALL MORE WORTHWHILE.
UH-HUH. THE MAN HIMSELF.
RAMPAGE JACKSON.
ANY IDEA WHY THEY ASKED FOR ME?
NO, AND WE'RE NOT SURE WHAT WE'RE DEALING WITH, SO ANY HELP WOULD BE APPRECIATED. WE'VE GOT NO EYES INSIDE, NO WAY TO SEE.
I KNEW I COULD COUNT ON HIM.
YOU CAN'T, BUT MAYBE I CAN!
MY ENHANCED SENSES WILL LET ME KNOW WHAT'S UP!
WE HAVE YOU SURROUNDED! LET THE GIRL GO AND WE'LL GO EASY ON YOU!
YEAH, RIGHT!
I'M T'ONE TALKING HERE! I'M THE ONE THAT GOTS T'POWER NOW!
YOU GOT THE POWER?

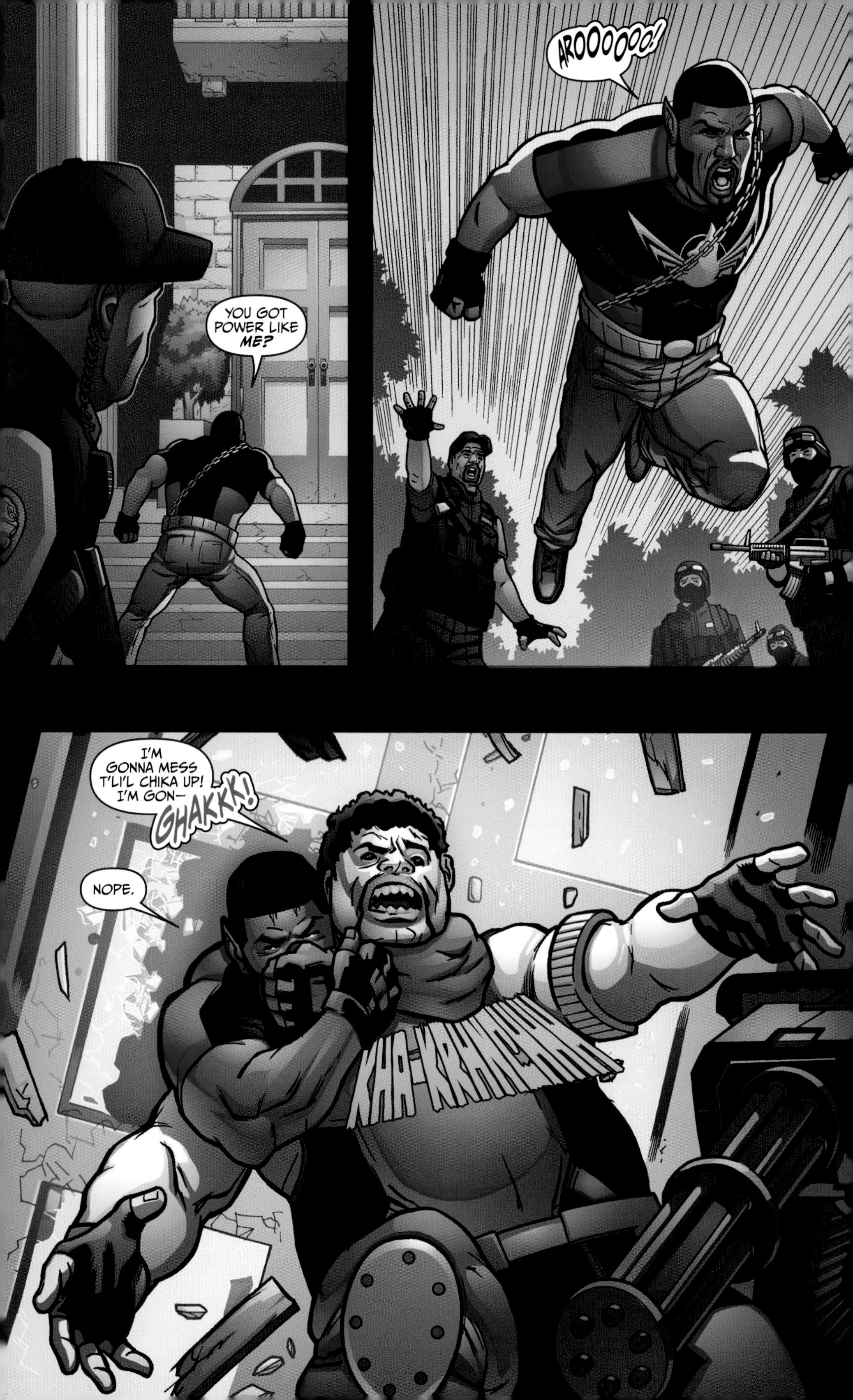
YOU GOT POWER LIKE ME?
AROOOOOO!
I'M GONNA MESS T'LI'L CHIKA UP! I'M GON—
GHAKKK!
NOPE.
KHA-KRHHHHH

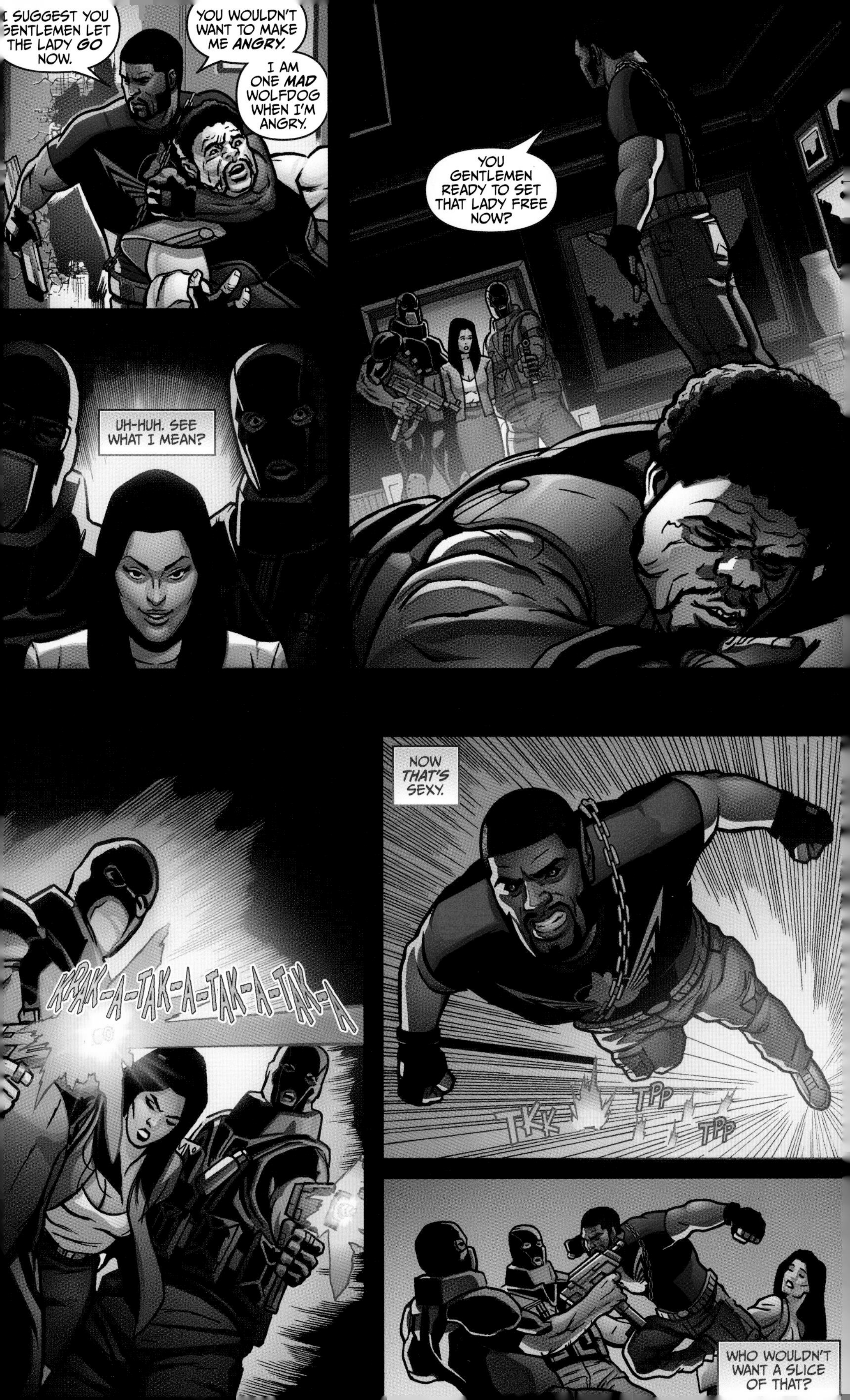
I SUGGEST YOU GENTLEMEN LET THE LADY GO NOW.
YOU WOULDN'T WANT TO MAKE ME ANGRY.
I AM ONE MAD WOLFDOG WHEN I'M ANGRY.
YOU GENTLEMEN READY TO SET THAT LADY FREE NOW?
UH-HUH. SEE WHAT I MEAN?
KRAK-A-TAK-A-TAK-A-TAK-A
NOW THAT'S SEXY.
TKK
TPP
TPP
WHO WOULDN'T WANT A SLICE OF THAT?

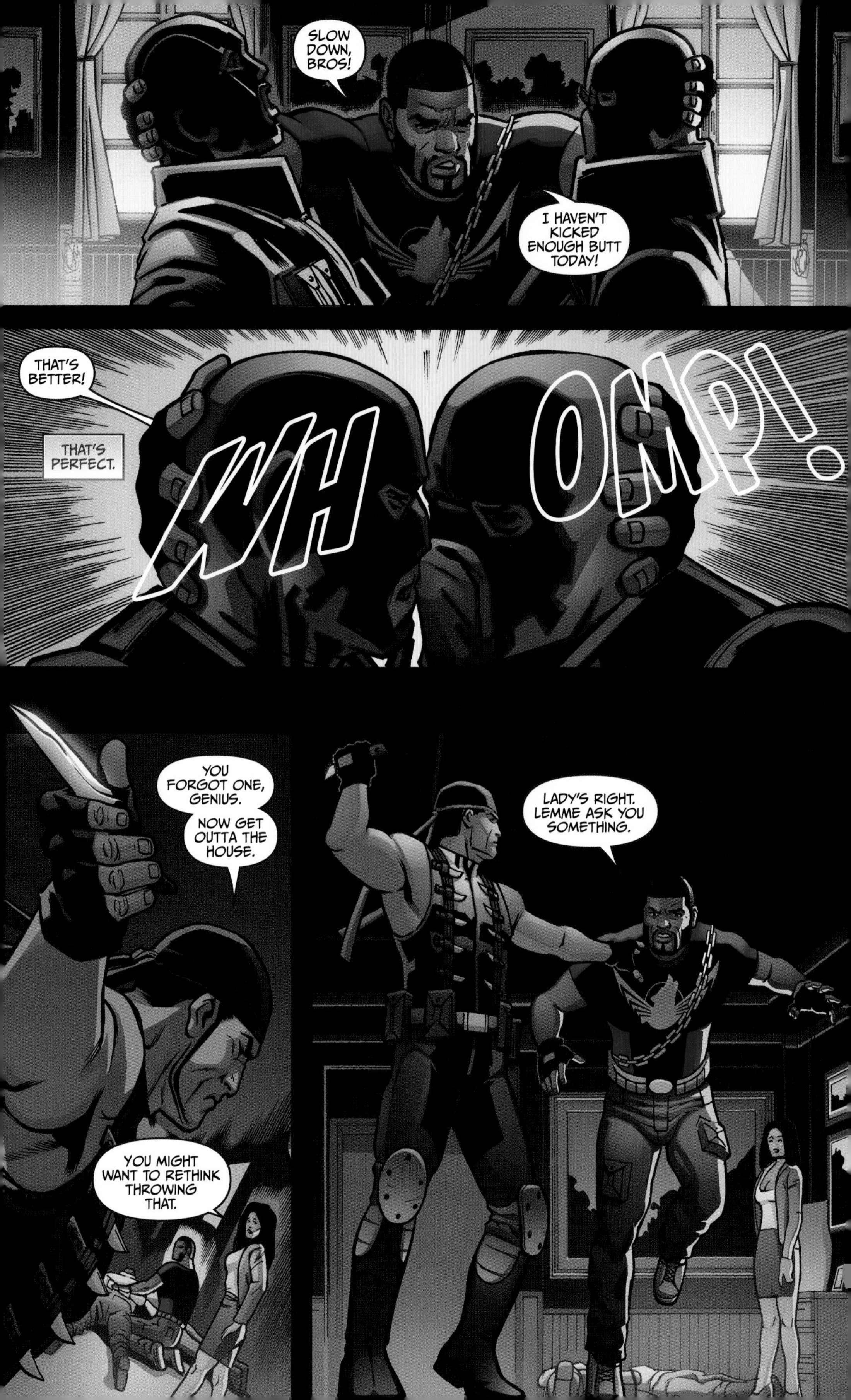
SLOW DOWN, BROS!
I HAVEN'T KICKED ENOUGH BUTT TODAY!
THAT'S BETTER!
THAT'S PERFECT.
WHOMP!
YOU FORGOT ONE, GENIUS.
NOW GET OUTTA THE HOUSE.
YOU MIGHT WANT TO RETHINK THROWING THAT.
LADY'S RIGHT. LEMME ASK YOU SOMETHING.

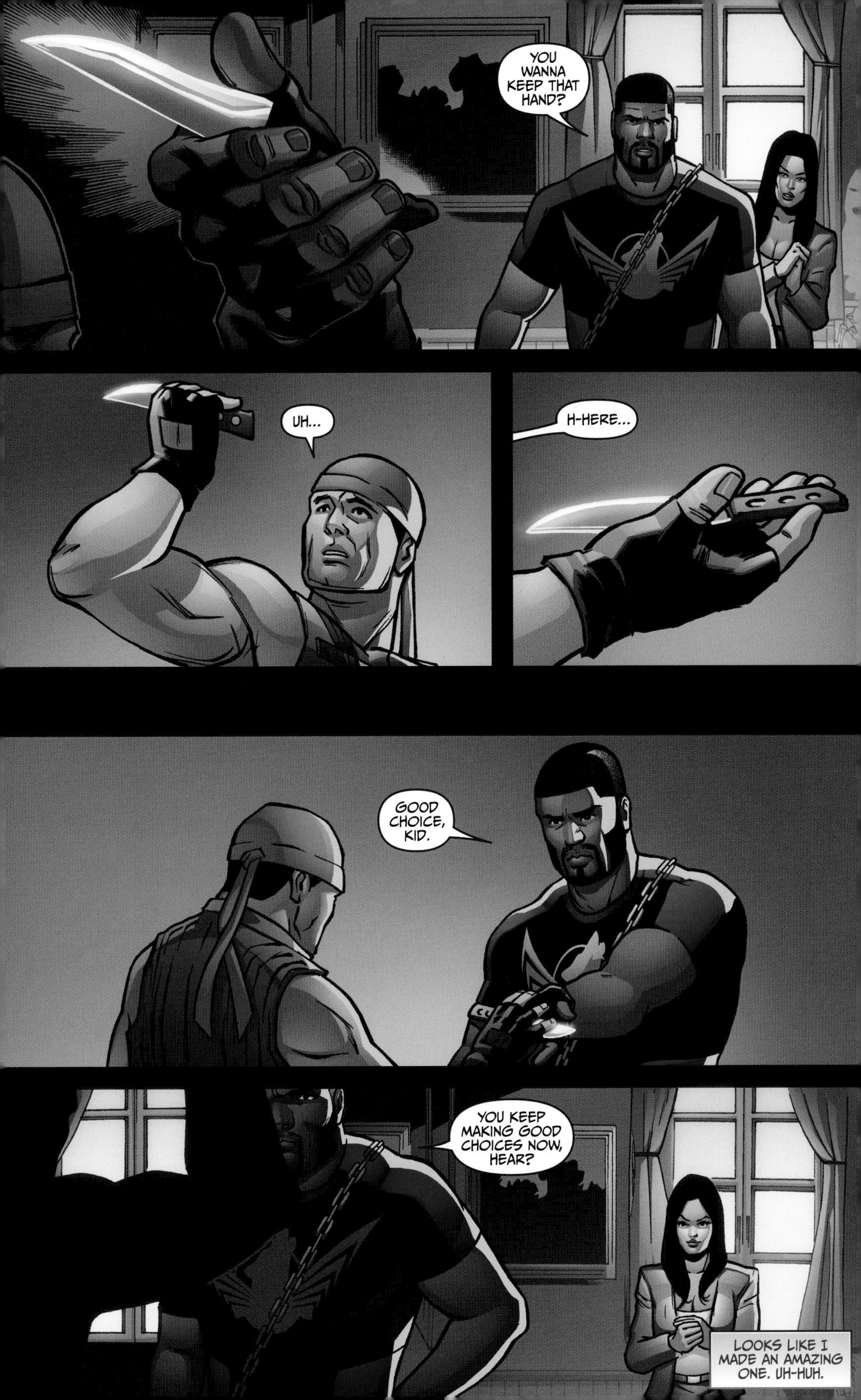
YOU WANNA KEEP THAT HAND?
UH...
H-HERE...
GOOD CHOICE, KID.
YOU KEEP MAKING GOOD CHOICES NOW, HEAR?
LOOKS LIKE I MADE AN AMAZING ONE. UH-HUH.

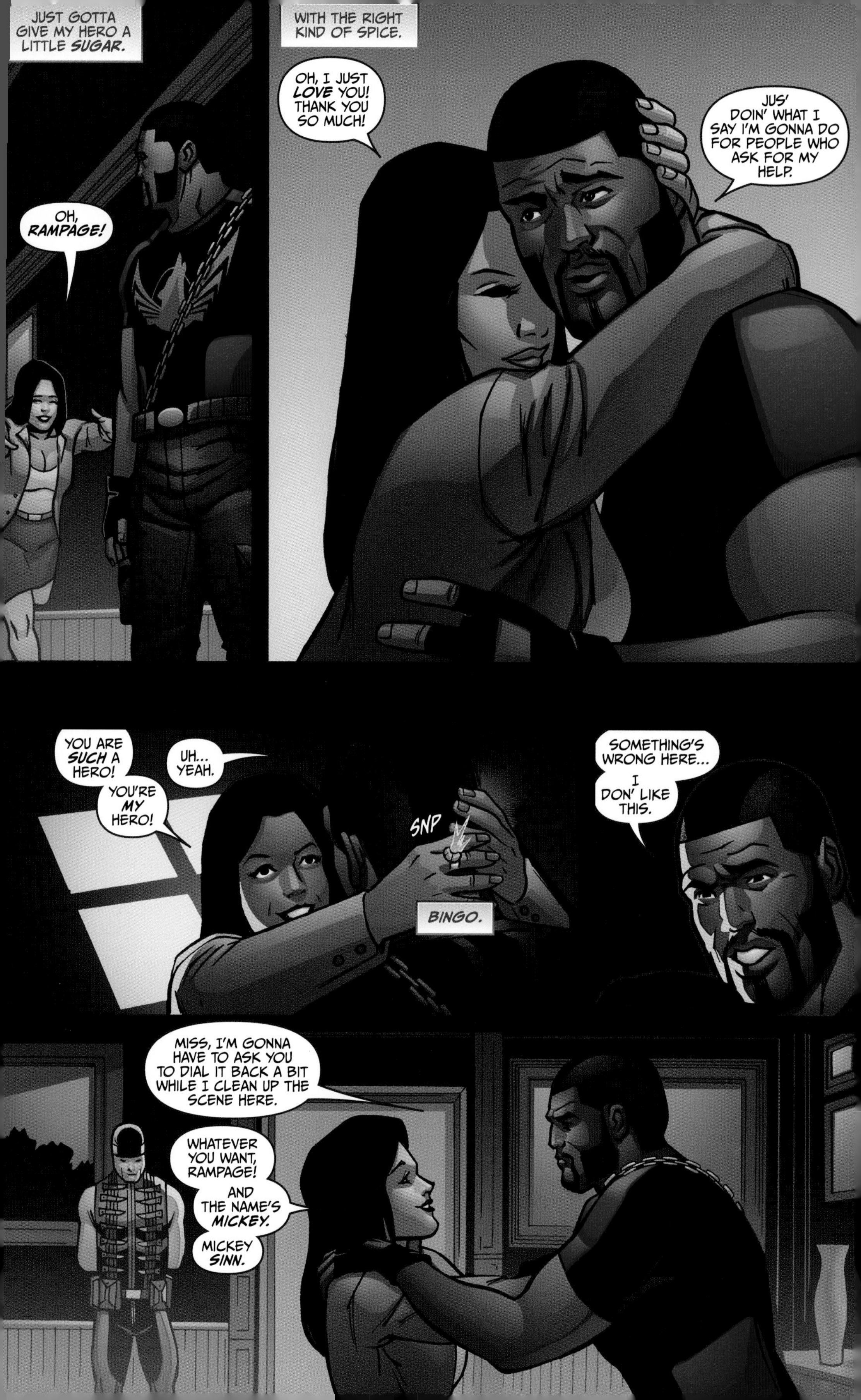
JUST GOTTA GIVE MY HERO A LITTLE SUGAR.
OH, RAMPAGE!
WITH THE RIGHT KIND OF SPICE.
OH, I JUST LOVE YOU! THANK YOU SO MUCH!
JUS' DOIN' WHAT I SAY I'M GONNA DO FOR PEOPLE WHO ASK FOR MY HELP.
YOU ARE SUCH A HERO!
YOU'RE MY HERO!
UH... YEAH.
SNP
BINGO.
SOMETHING'S WRONG HERE...
I DON' LIKE THIS.
MISS, I'M GONNA HAVE TO ASK YOU TO DIAL IT BACK A BIT WHILE I CLEAN UP THE SCENE HERE.
WHATEVER YOU WANT, RAMPAGE!
AND THE NAME'S MICKEY.
MICKEY SINN.

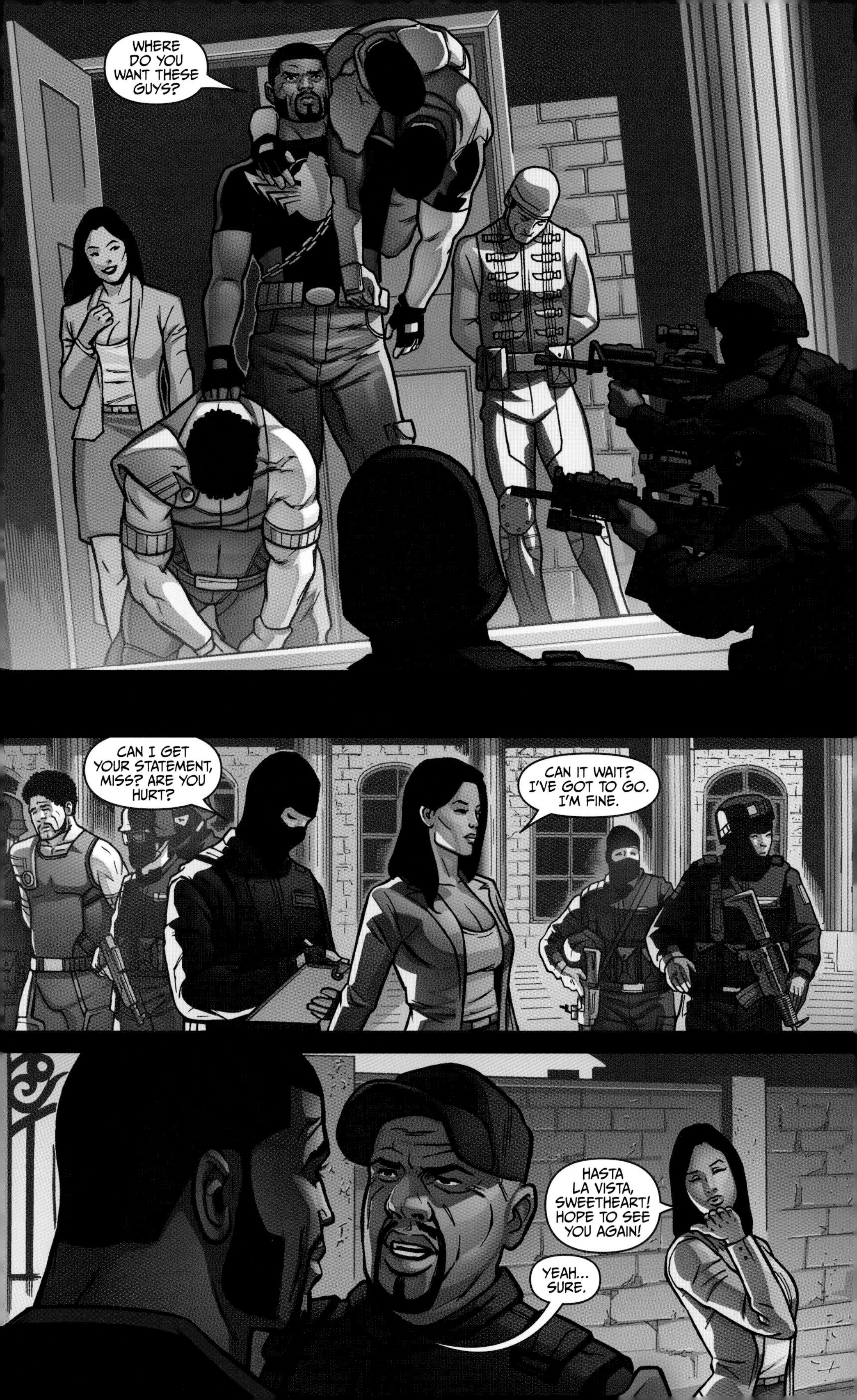
WHERE DO YOU WANT THESE GUYS?
CAN I GET YOUR STATEMENT, MISS? ARE YOU HURT?
CAN IT WAIT? I'VE GOT TO GO. I'M FINE.
HASTA LA VISTA, SWEETHEART! HOPE TO SEE YOU AGAIN!
YEAH... SURE.

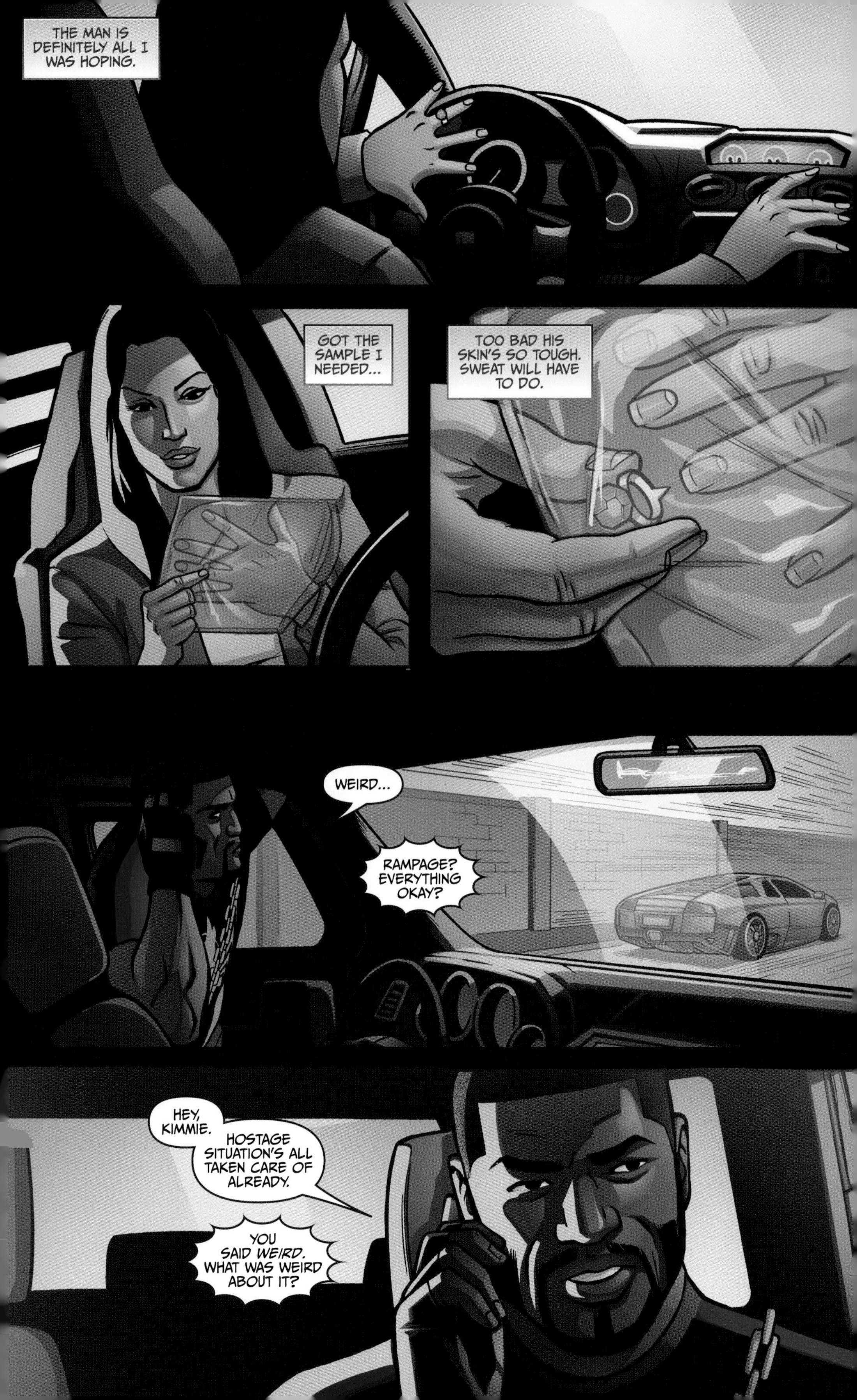
THE MAN IS DEFINITELY ALL I WAS HOPING.
GOT THE SAMPLE I NEEDED...
TOO BAD HIS SKIN'S SO TOUGH. SWEAT WILL HAVE TO DO.
WEIRD...
RAMPAGE? EVERYTHING OKAY?
HEY, KIMMIE.
HOSTAGE SITUATION'S ALL TAKEN CARE OF ALREADY.
YOU SAID *WEIRD*. WHAT WAS WEIRD ABOUT IT?

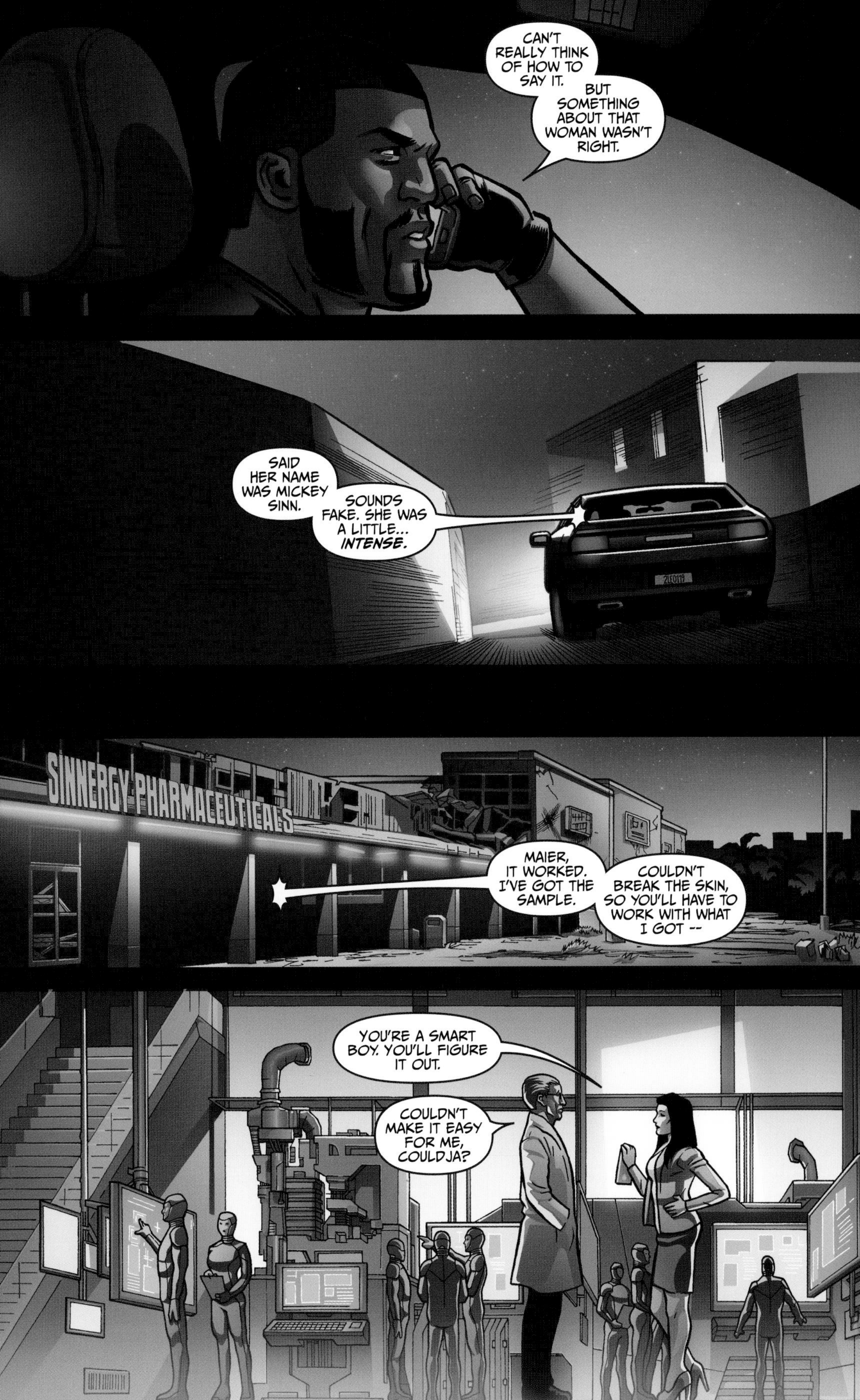
CAN'T REALLY THINK OF HOW TO SAY IT.
BUT SOMETHING ABOUT THAT WOMAN WASN'T RIGHT.
SAID HER NAME WAS MICKEY SINN.
SOUNDS FAKE. SHE WAS A LITTLE... *INTENSE*.
SINNERGY PHARMACEUTICALS
MAIER, IT WORKED. I'VE GOT THE SAMPLE.
COULDN'T BREAK THE SKIN, SO YOU'LL HAVE TO WORK WITH WHAT I GOT --
YOU'RE A SMART BOY. YOU'LL FIGURE IT OUT.
COULDN'T MAKE IT EASY FOR ME, COULDJA?

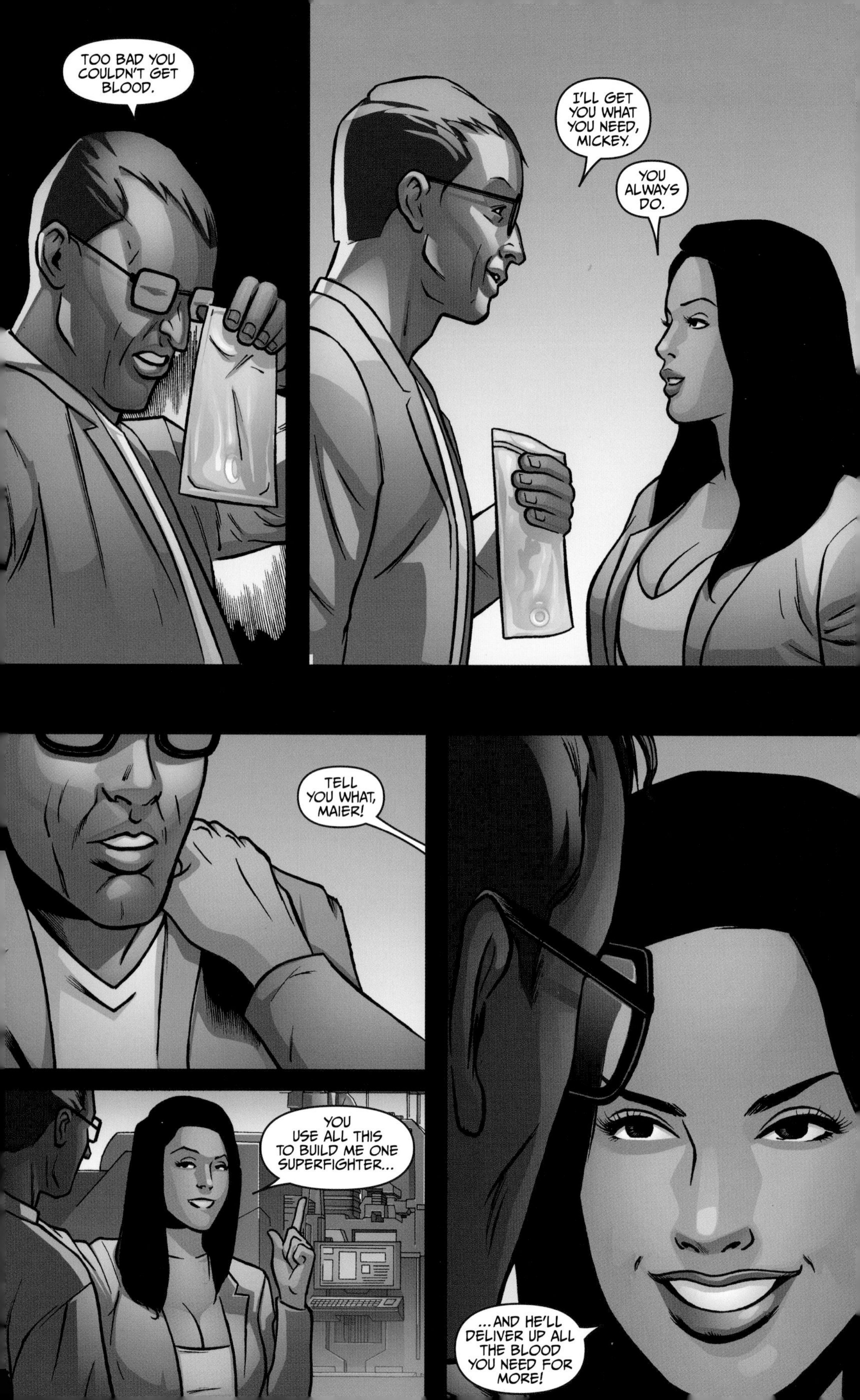
TOO BAD YOU COULDN'T GET BLOOD.
I'LL GET YOU WHAT YOU NEED, MICKEY.
YOU ALWAYS DO.
TELL YOU WHAT, MAIER!
YOU USE ALL THIS TO BUILD ME ONE SUPERFIGHTER...
...AND HE'LL DELIVER UP ALL THE BLOOD YOU NEED FOR MORE!

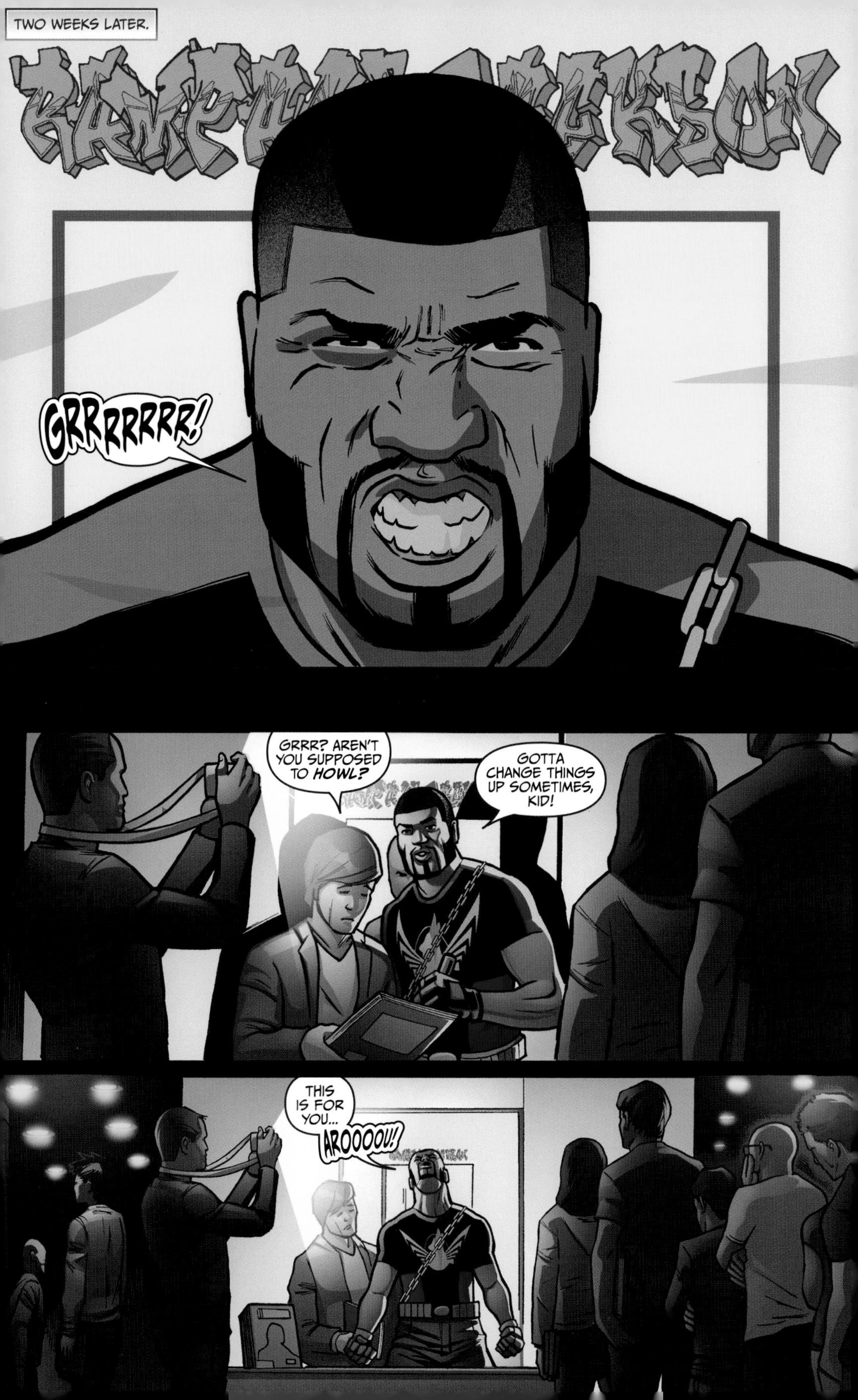
TWO WEEKS LATER.
GRRRRRRR!
GRRR? AREN'T YOU SUPPOSED TO *HOWL?*
GOTTA CHANGE THINGS UP SOMETIMES, KID!
THIS IS FOR YOU...
AROOOOU!

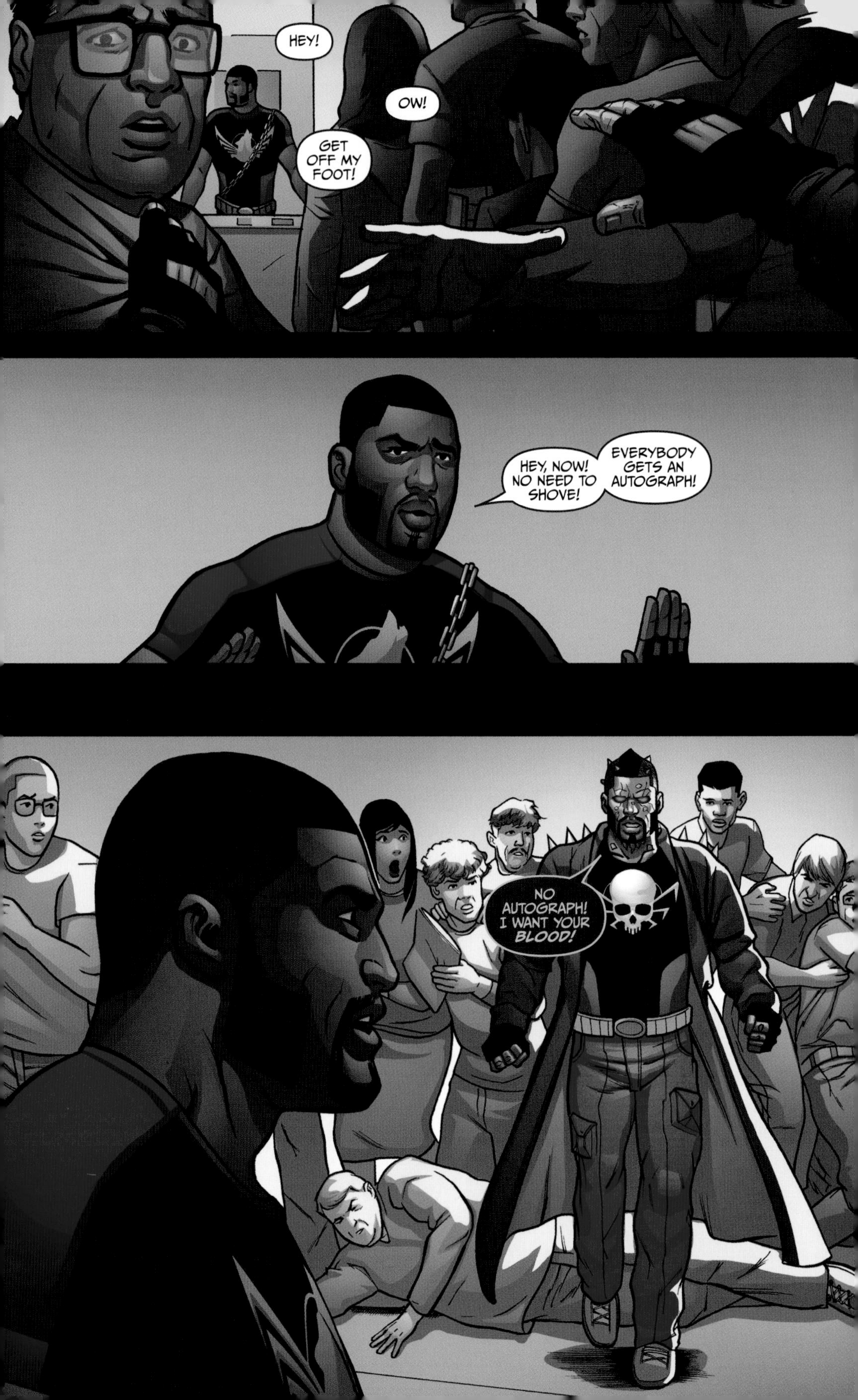
HEY!
OW!
GET OFF MY FOOT!
HEY, NOW! NO NEED TO SHOVE!
EVERYBODY GETS AN AUTOGRAPH!
NO AUTOGRAPH! I WANT YOUR *BLOOD!*

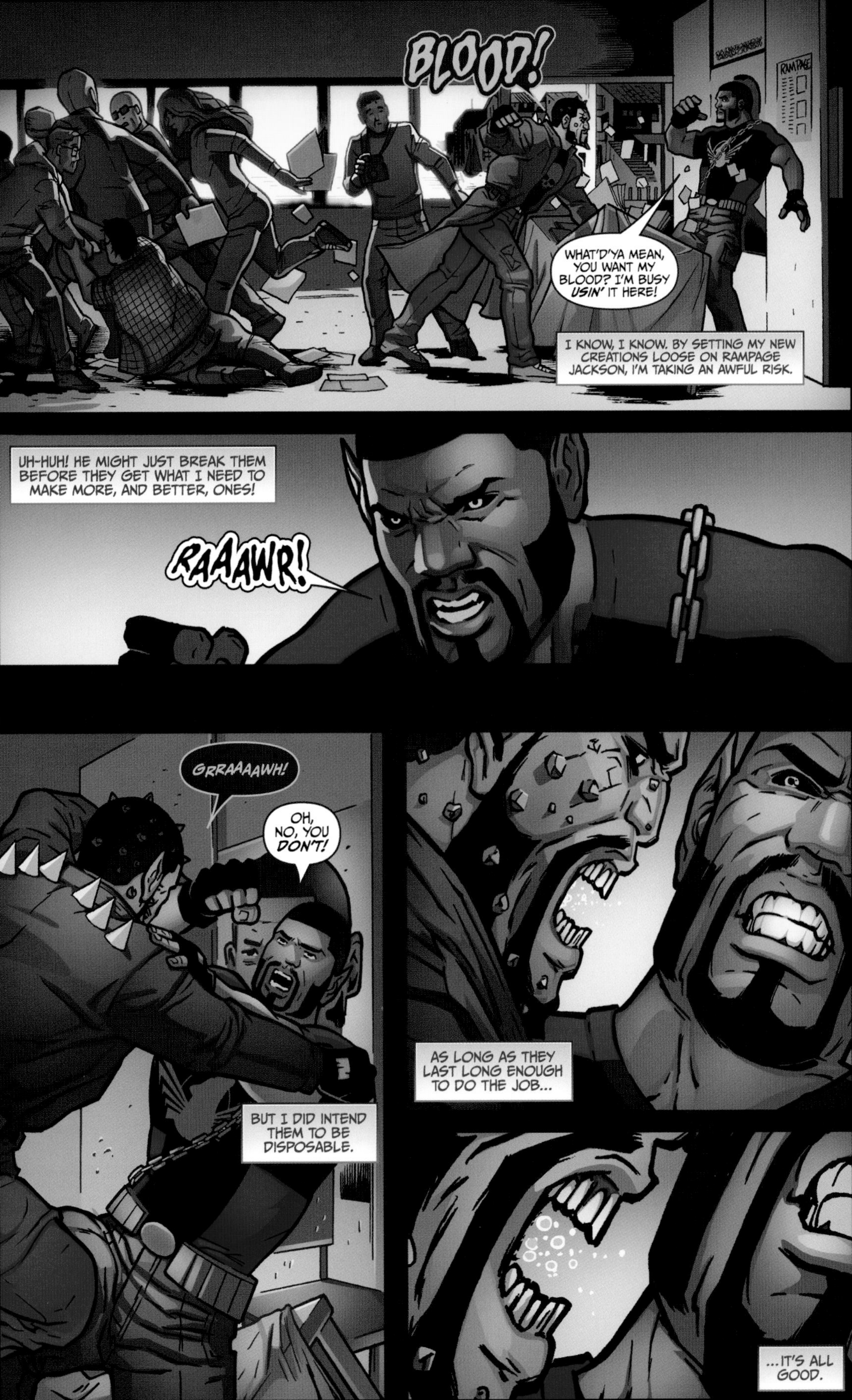
BLOOD!
RAMPAGE
WHAT'D'YA MEAN, YOU WANT MY BLOOD? I'M BUSY USIN' IT HERE!
I KNOW, I KNOW. BY SETTING MY NEW CREATIONS LOOSE ON RAMPAGE JACKSON, I'M TAKING AN AWFUL RISK.
UH-HUH! HE MIGHT JUST BREAK THEM BEFORE THEY GET WHAT I NEED TO MAKE MORE, AND BETTER, ONES!
RAAAWR!
GRRAAAAWH!
OH, NO, YOU DON'T!
BUT I DID INTEND THEM TO BE DISPOSABLE.
AS LONG AS THEY LAST LONG ENOUGH TO DO THE JOB...
...IT'S ALL GOOD.

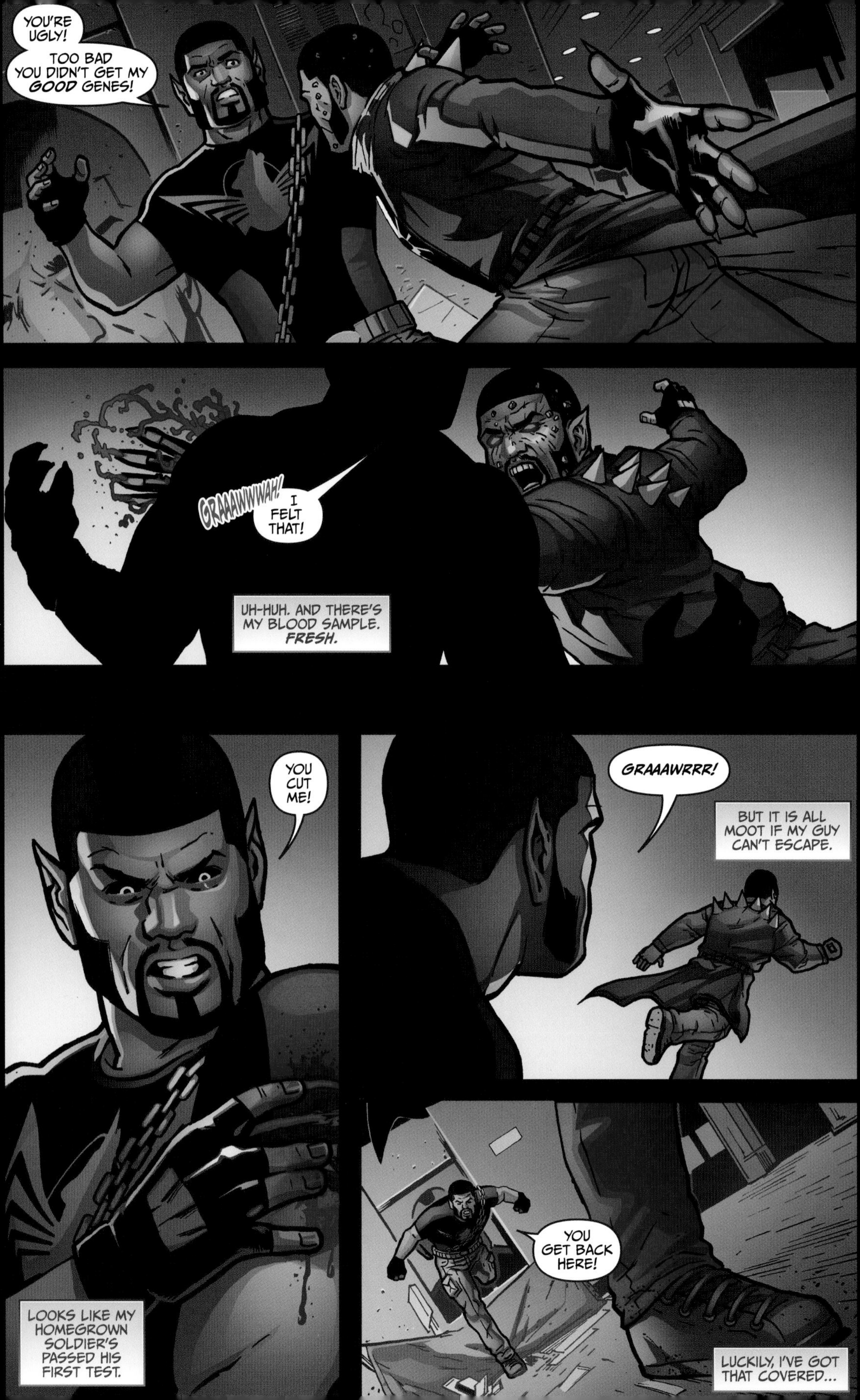
YOU'RE UGLY!
TOO BAD YOU DIDN'T GET MY GOOD GENES!
GRAAAWWWAH!
I FELT THAT!
UH-HUH. AND THERE'S MY BLOOD SAMPLE. FRESH.
YOU CUT ME!
LOOKS LIKE MY HOMEGROWN SOLDIER'S PASSED HIS FIRST TEST.
GRAAAWRRR!
BUT IT IS ALL MOOT IF MY GUY CAN'T ESCAPE.
YOU GET BACK HERE!
LUCKILY, I'VE GOT THAT COVERED...

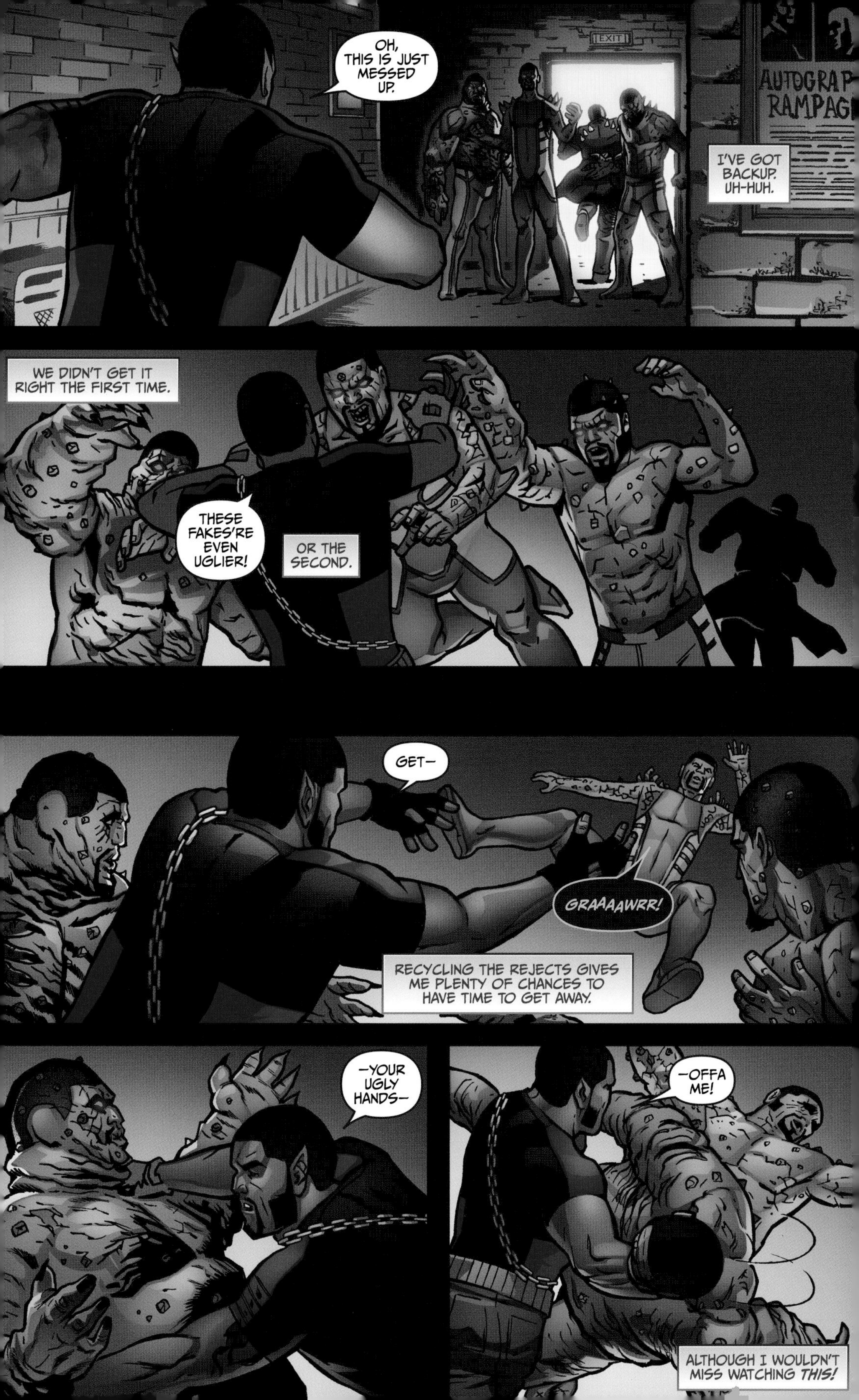
OH, THIS IS JUST MESSED UP.
EXIT
AUTOGRAP RAMPAG
I'VE GOT BACKUP. UH-HUH.
WE DIDN'T GET IT RIGHT THE FIRST TIME.
THESE FAKES'RE EVEN UGLIER!
OR THE SECOND.
GET—
GRAAAAWRR!
RECYCLING THE REJECTS GIVES ME PLENTY OF CHANCES TO HAVE TIME TO GET AWAY.
—YOUR UGLY HANDS—
—OFFA ME!
ALTHOUGH I WOULDN'T MISS WATCHING *THIS!*

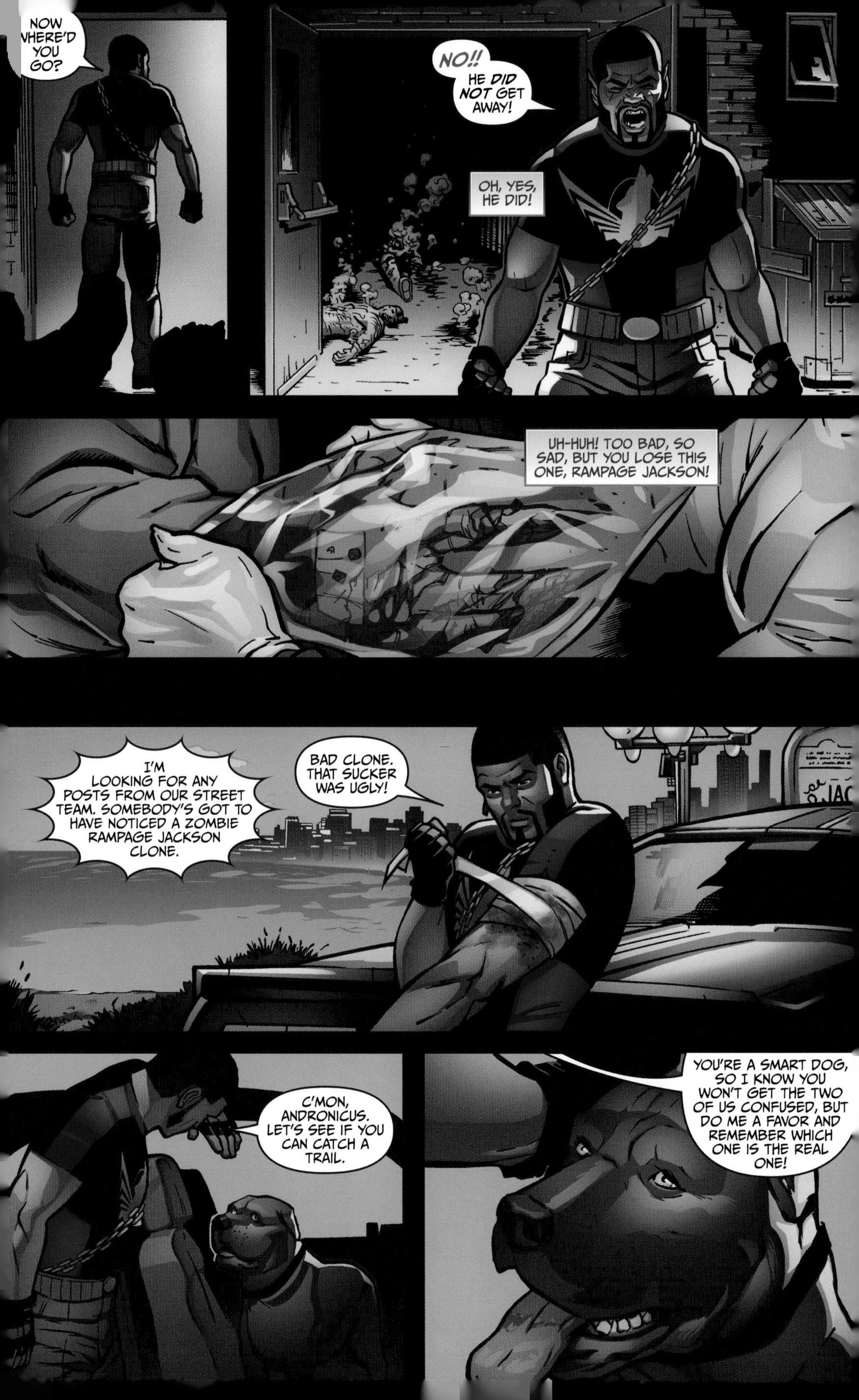
NOW WHERE'D YOU GO?
NO!! HE DID NOT GET AWAY!
OH, YES, HE DID!
UH-HUH! TOO BAD, SO SAD, BUT YOU LOSE THIS ONE, RAMPAGE JACKSON!
I'M LOOKING FOR ANY POSTS FROM OUR STREET TEAM. SOMEBODY'S GOT TO HAVE NOTICED A ZOMBIE RAMPAGE JACKSON CLONE.
BAD CLONE. THAT SUCKER WAS UGLY!
C'MON, ANDRONICUS. LET'S SEE IF YOU CAN CATCH A TRAIL.
YOU'RE A SMART DOG, SO I KNOW YOU WON'T GET THE TWO OF US CONFUSED, BUT DO ME A FAVOR AND REMEMBER WHICH ONE IS THE REAL ONE!

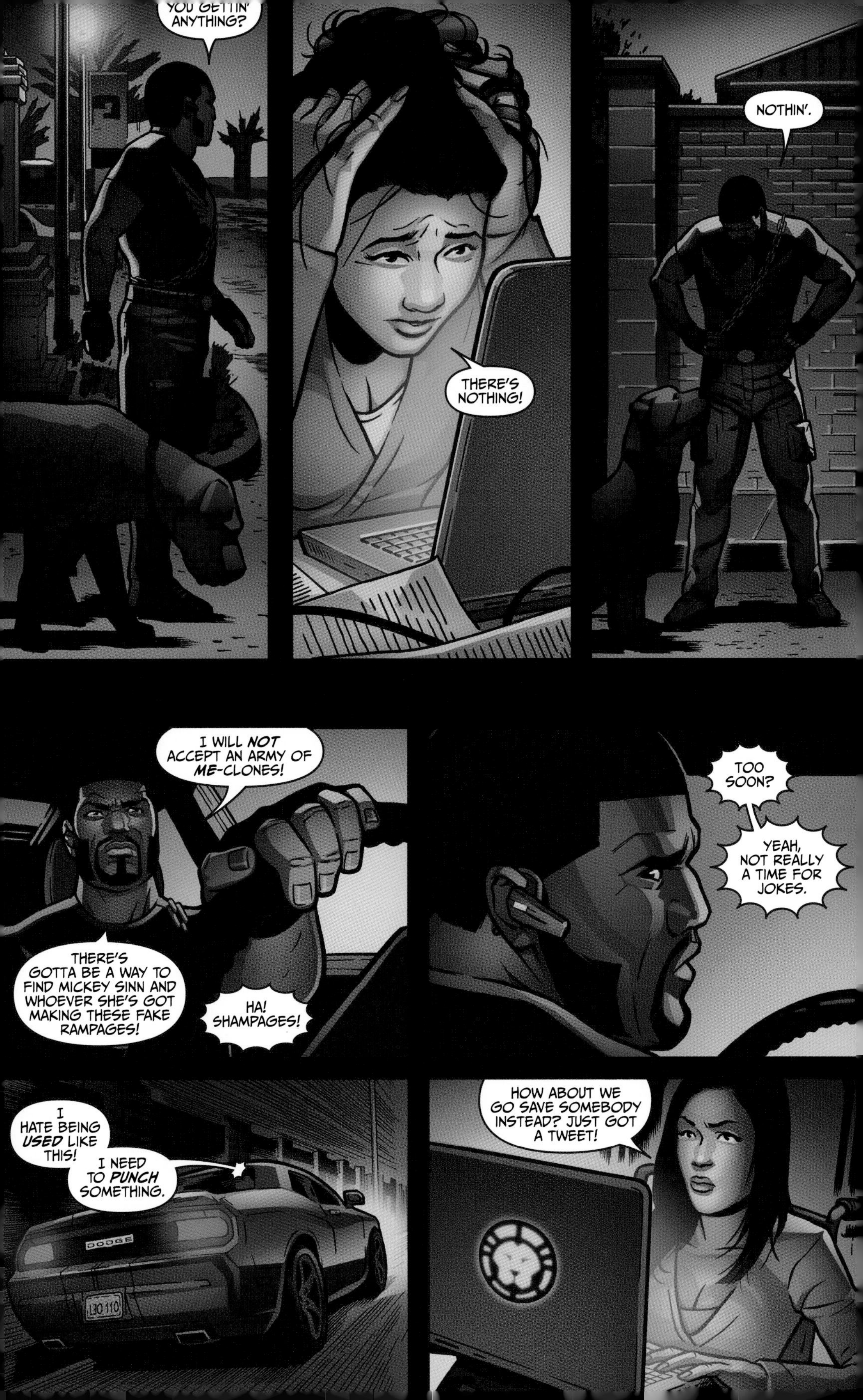
YOU GETTIN' ANYTHING?
THERE'S NOTHING!
NOTHIN'.
I WILL *NOT* ACCEPT AN ARMY OF *ME*-CLONES!
THERE'S GOTTA BE A WAY TO FIND MICKEY SINN AND WHOEVER SHE'S GOT MAKING THESE FAKE RAMPAGES!
HA! SHAMPAGES!
TOO SOON?
YEAH, NOT REALLY A TIME FOR JOKES.
I HATE BEING *USED* LIKE THIS!
I NEED TO *PUNCH* SOMETHING.
DODGE
HOW ABOUT WE GO SAVE SOMEBODY INSTEAD? JUST GOT A TWEET!

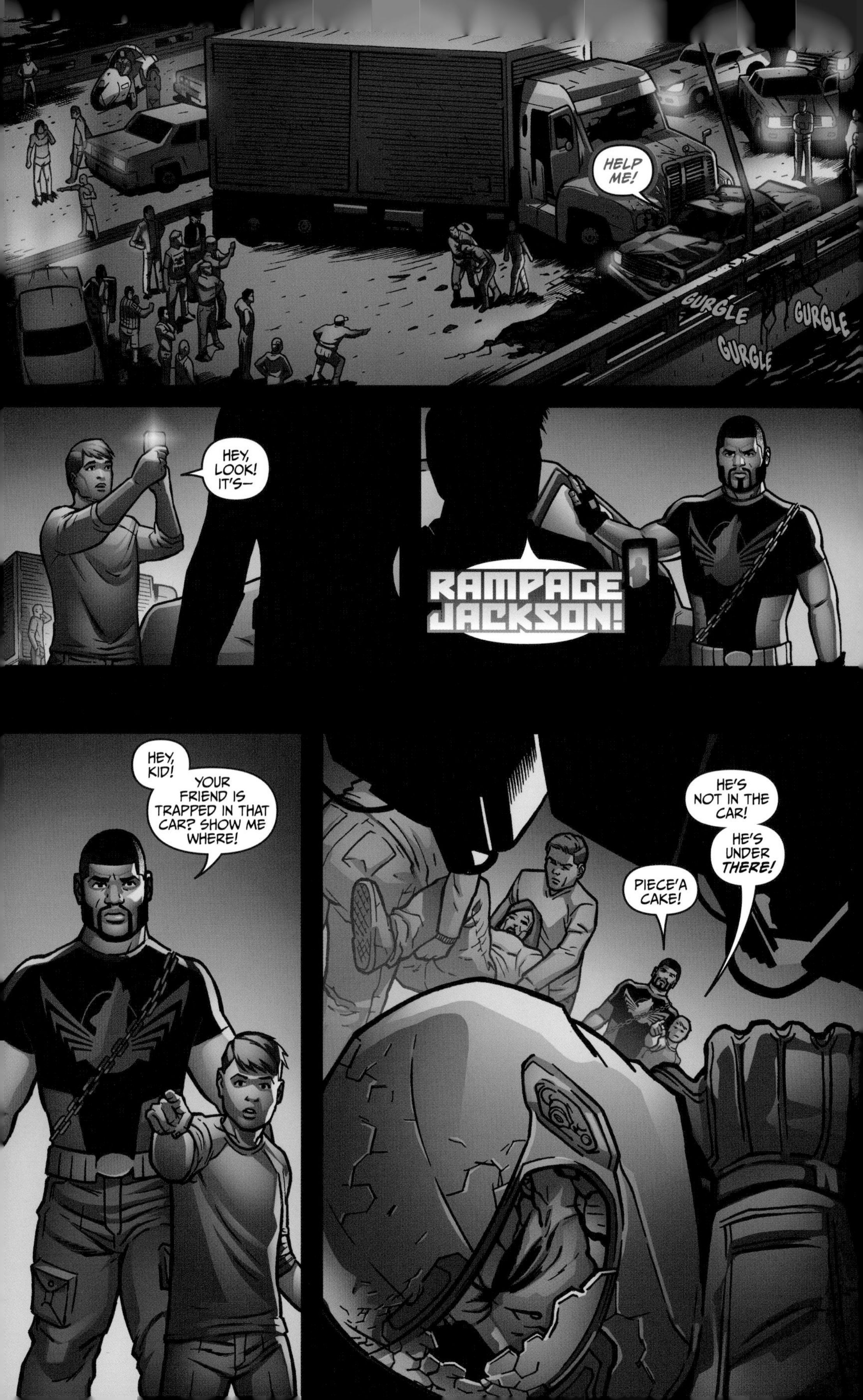
HELP ME!
GURGLE
GURGLE
GURGLE
HEY, LOOK! IT'S—
RAMPAGE JACKSON!
HEY, KID!
YOUR FRIEND IS TRAPPED IN THAT CAR? SHOW ME WHERE!
HE'S NOT IN THE CAR!
HE'S UNDER *THERE!*
PIECE'A CAKE!

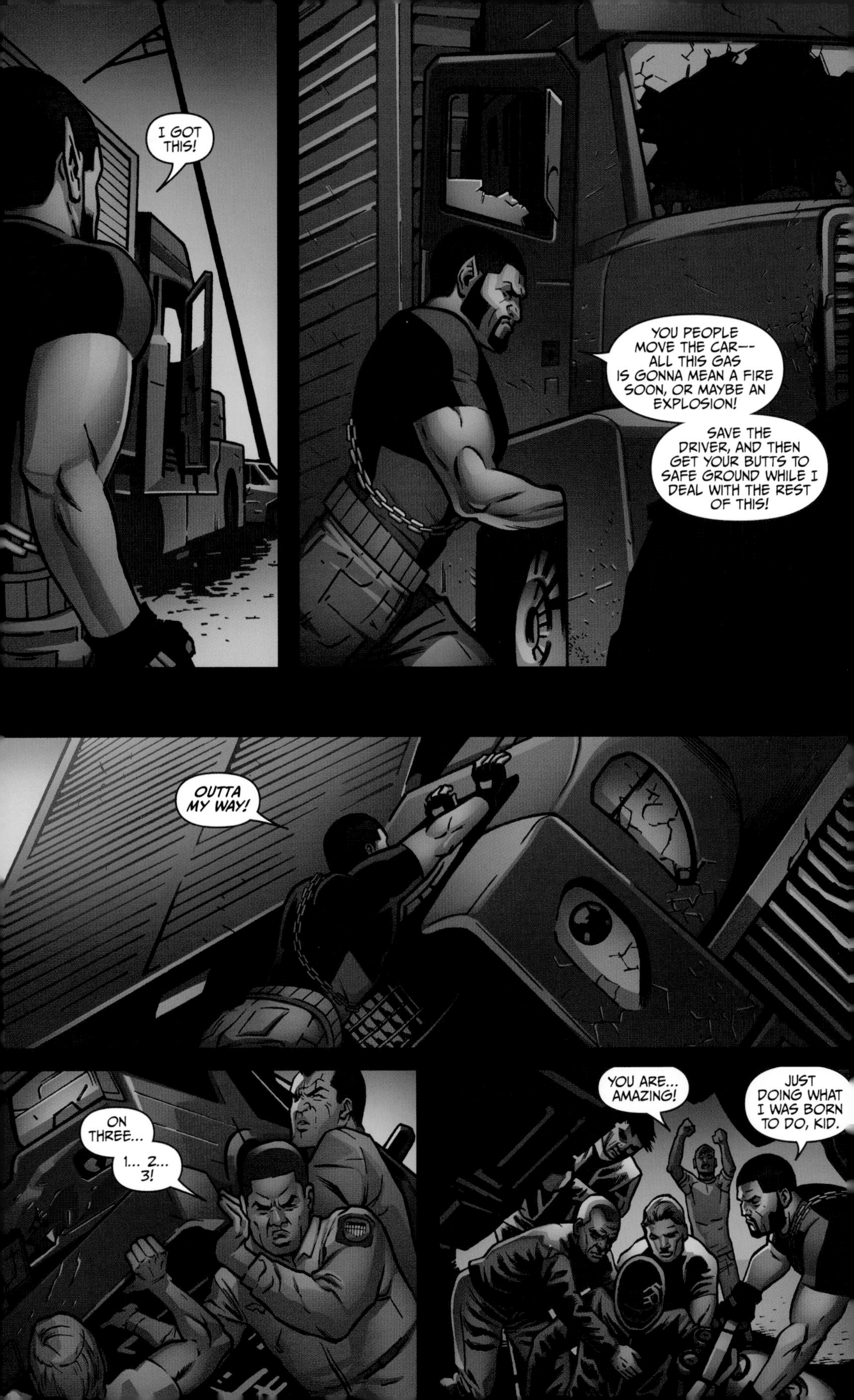
I GOT THIS!
YOU PEOPLE MOVE THE CAR-- ALL THIS GAS IS GONNA MEAN A FIRE SOON, OR MAYBE AN EXPLOSION!
SAVE THE DRIVER, AND THEN GET YOUR BUTTS TO SAFE GROUND WHILE I DEAL WITH THE REST OF THIS!
OUTTA MY WAY!
ON THREE...
1... 2... 3!
YOU ARE... AMAZING!
JUST DOING WHAT I WAS BORN TO DO, KID.

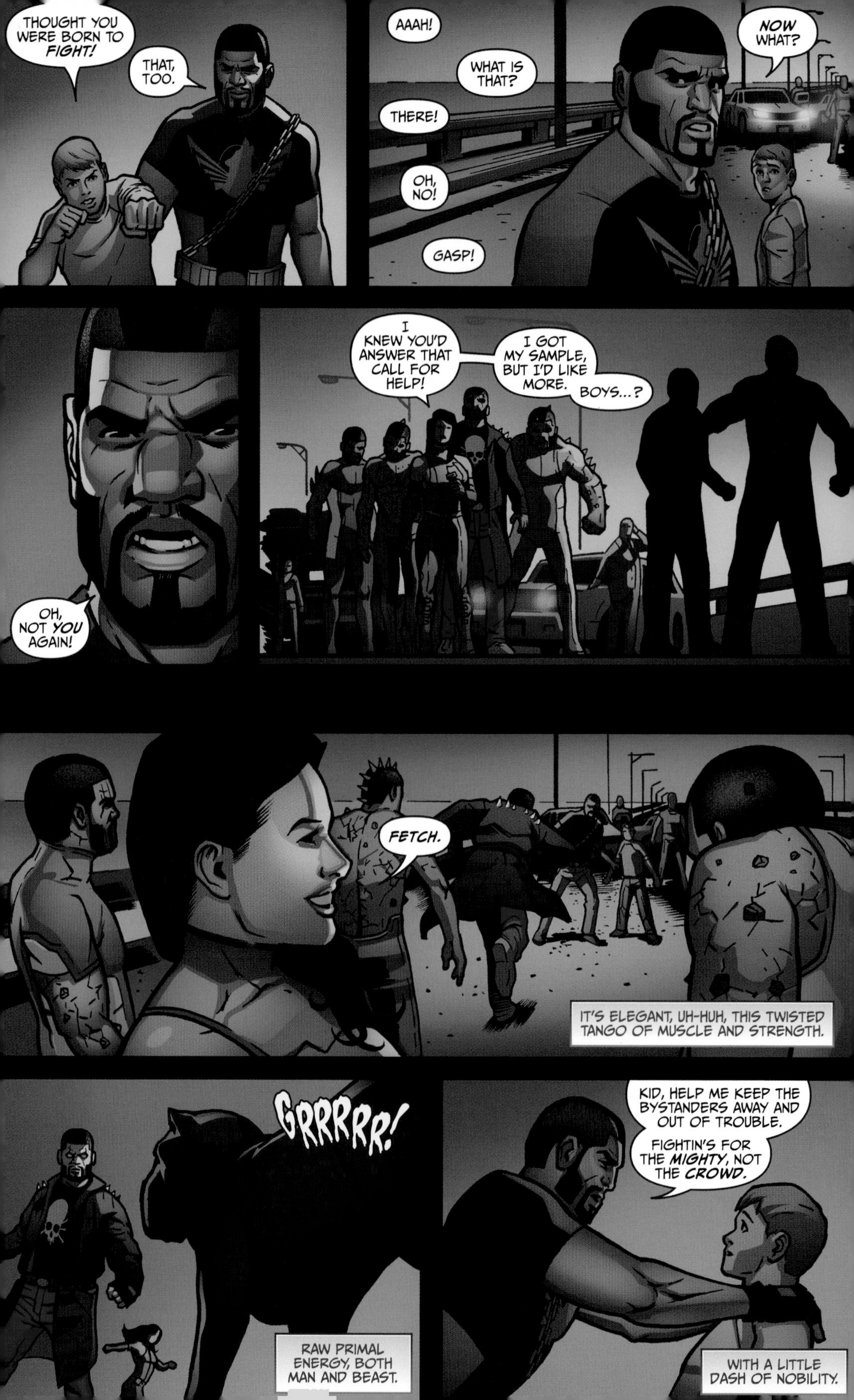
THOUGHT YOU WERE BORN TO *FIGHT!*
THAT, TOO.
AAAH!
WHAT IS THAT?
THERE!
OH, NO!
GASP!
NOW WHAT?
OH, NOT *YOU* AGAIN!
I KNEW YOU'D ANSWER THAT CALL FOR HELP!
I GOT MY SAMPLE, BUT I'D LIKE MORE.
BOYS...?
FETCH.
IT'S ELEGANT, UH-HUH, THIS TWISTED TANGO OF MUSCLE AND STRENGTH.
GRRRRR!
RAW PRIMAL ENERGY, BOTH MAN AND BEAST.
KID, HELP ME KEEP THE BYSTANDERS AWAY AND OUT OF TROUBLE.
FIGHTIN'S FOR THE *MIGHTY*, NOT THE *CROWD.*
WITH A LITTLE DASH OF NOBILITY.

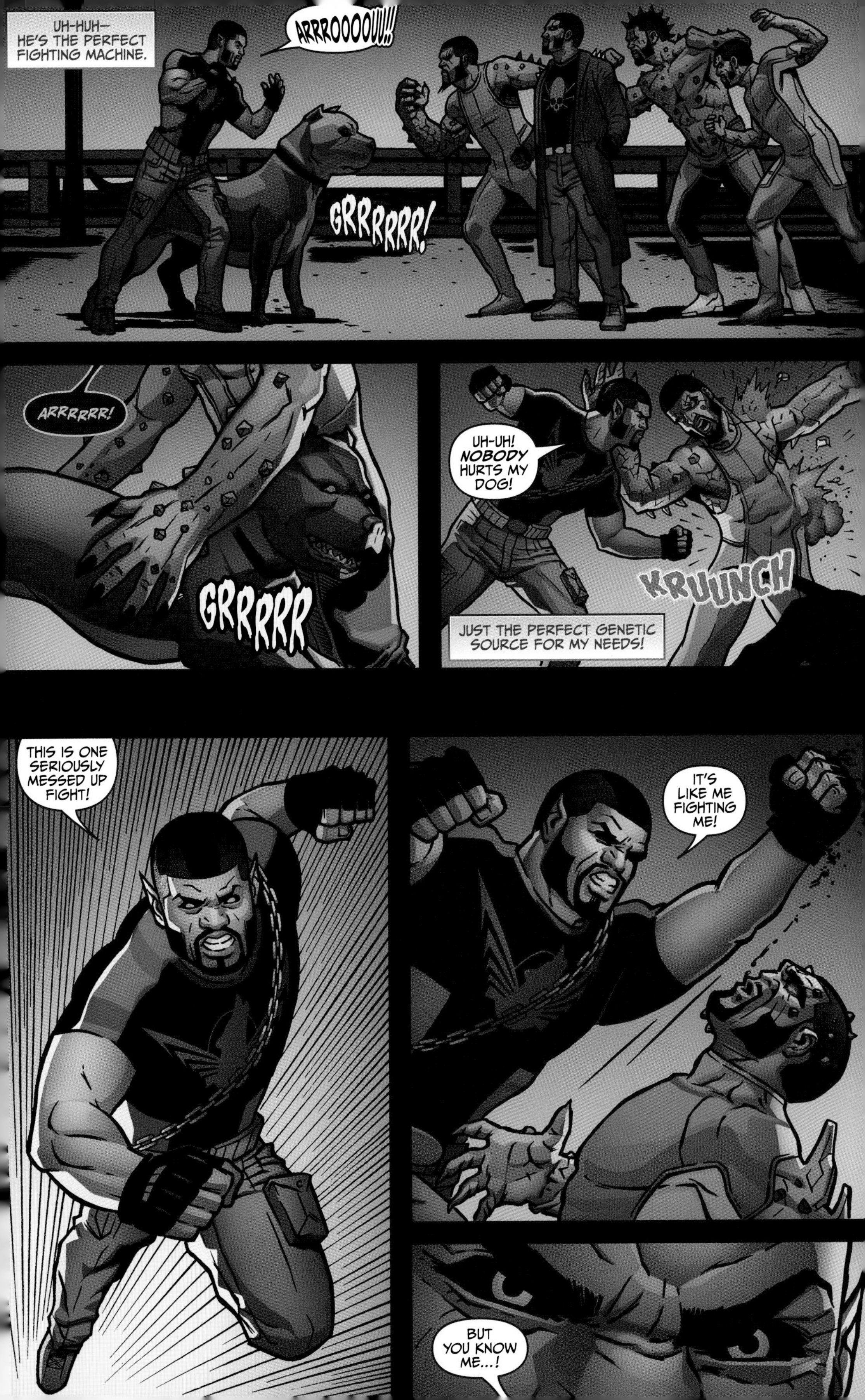
UH-HUH— HE'S THE PERFECT FIGHTING MACHINE.
ARRROOOOUU!!
GRRRRRR!
ARRRRRR!
GRRRRR
UH-UH! NOBODY HURTS MY DOG!
KRUUNCH
JUST THE PERFECT GENETIC SOURCE FOR MY NEEDS!
THIS IS ONE SERIOUSLY MESSED UP FIGHT!
IT'S LIKE ME FIGHTING ME!
BUT YOU KNOW ME...!

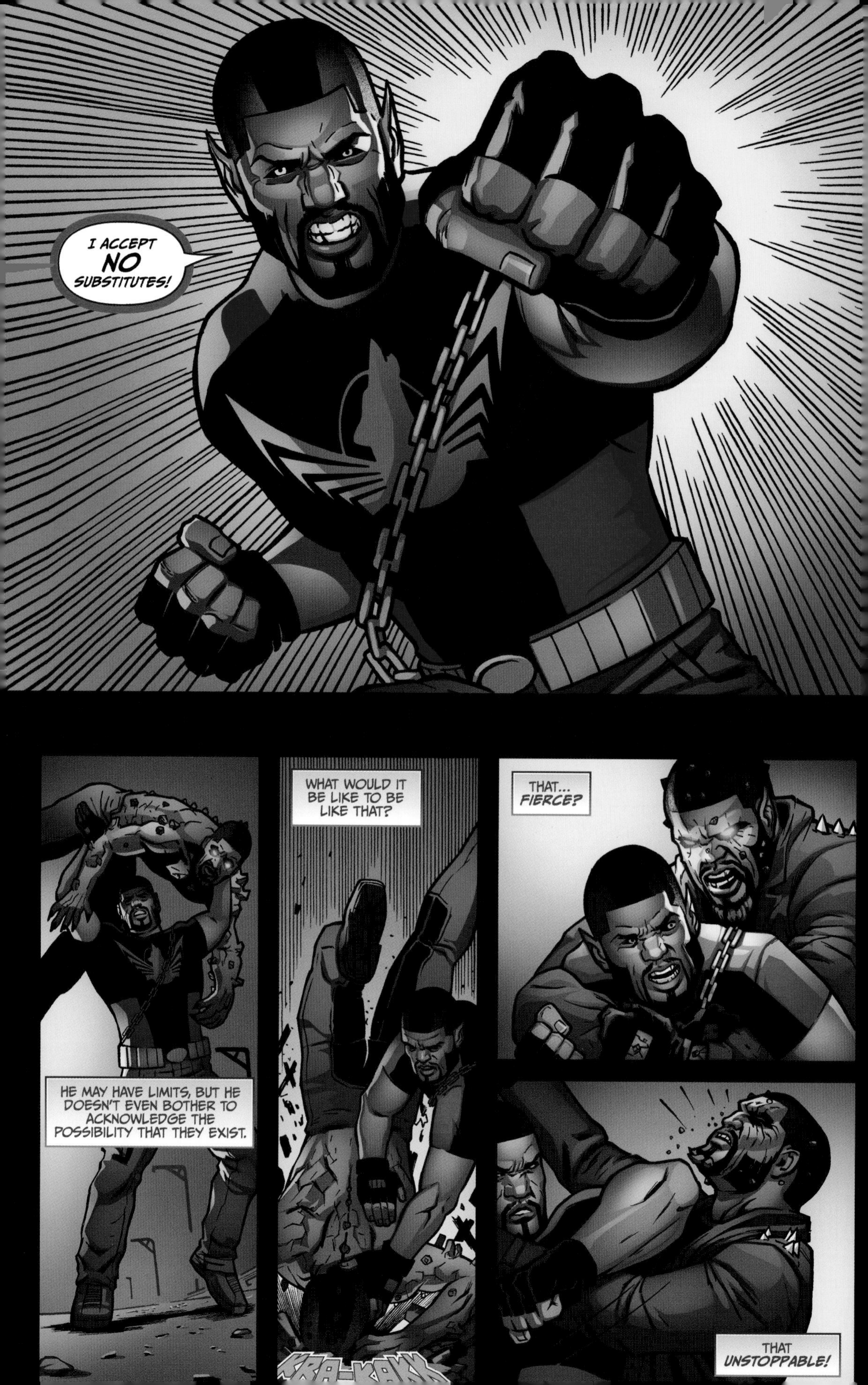
I ACCEPT NO SUBSTITUTES!
HE MAY HAVE LIMITS, BUT HE DOESN'T EVEN BOTHER TO ACKNOWLEDGE THE POSSIBILITY THAT THEY EXIST.
WHAT WOULD IT BE LIKE TO BE LIKE THAT?
KRA-KAKK
THAT... FIERCE?
THAT UNSTOPPABLE!

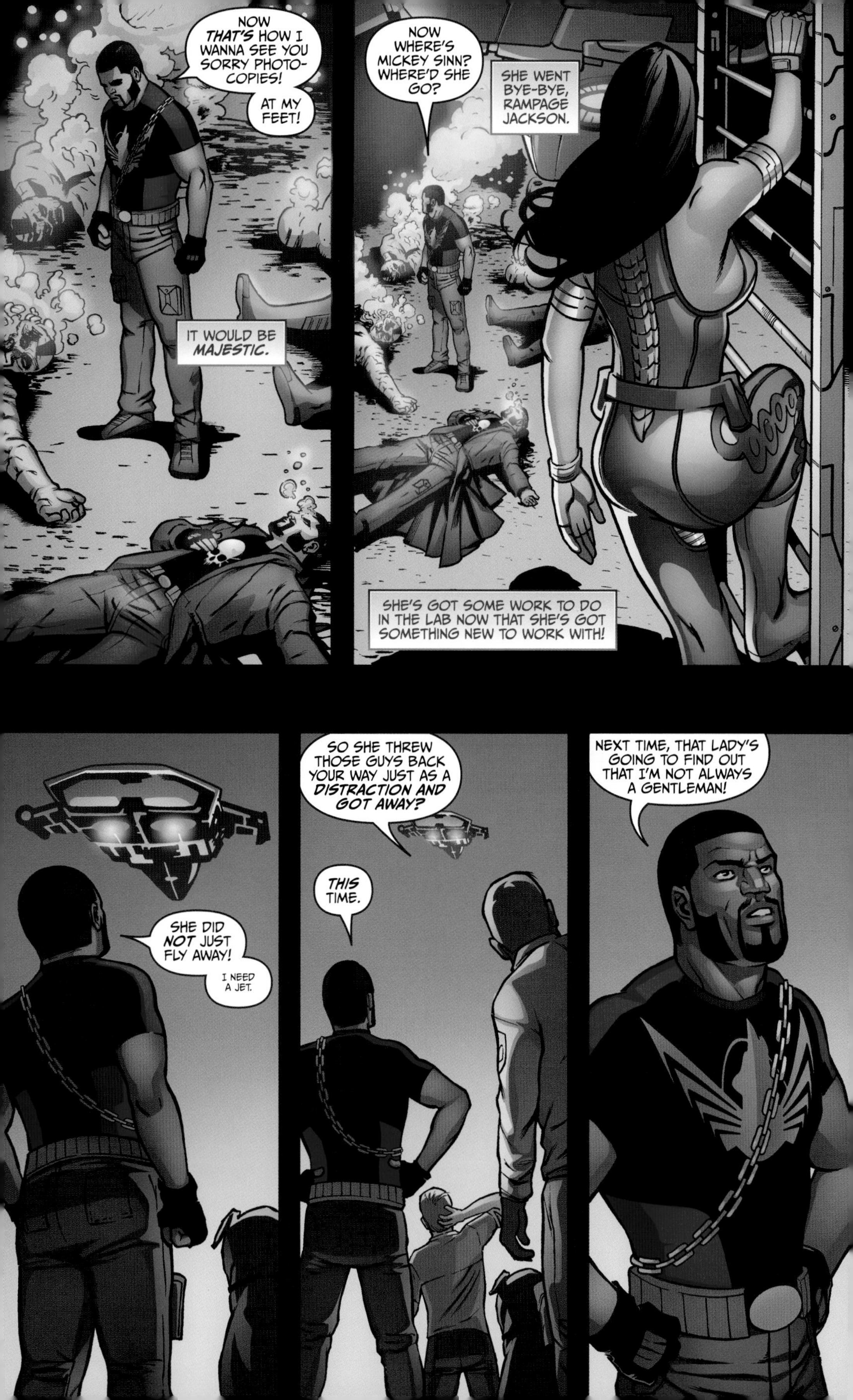
NOW THAT'S HOW I WANNA SEE YOU SORRY PHOTO-COPIES!
AT MY FEET!
IT WOULD BE MAJESTIC.
NOW WHERE'S MICKEY SINN? WHERE'D SHE GO?
SHE WENT BYE-BYE, RAMPAGE JACKSON.
SHE'S GOT SOME WORK TO DO IN THE LAB NOW THAT SHE'S GOT SOMETHING NEW TO WORK WITH!
SHE DID NOT JUST FLY AWAY!
I NEED A JET.
SO SHE THREW THOSE GUYS BACK YOUR WAY JUST AS A DISTRACTION AND GOT AWAY?
THIS TIME.
NEXT TIME, THAT LADY'S GOING TO FIND OUT THAT I'M NOT ALWAYS A GENTLEMAN!

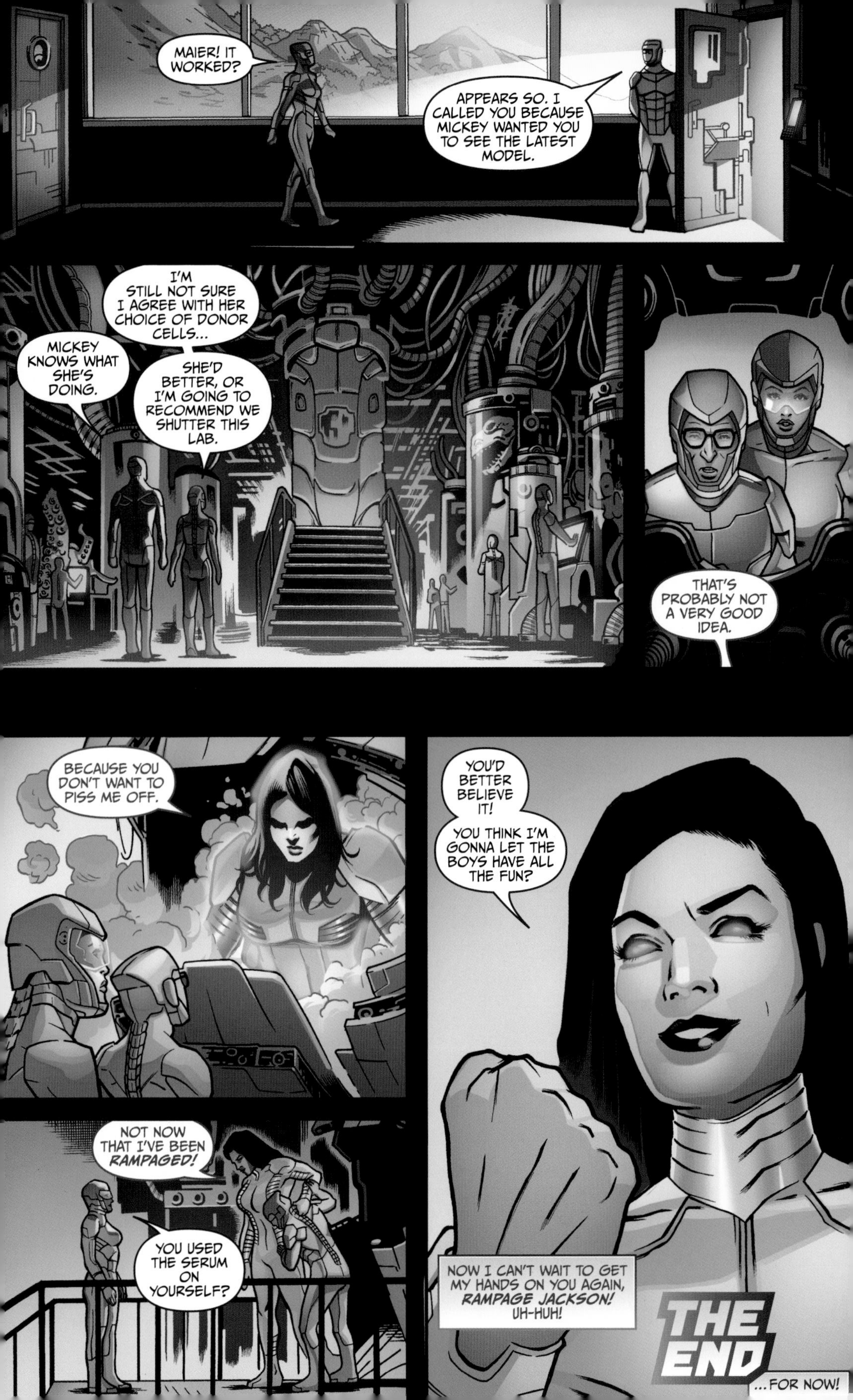
MAIER! IT WORKED?
APPEARS SO. I CALLED YOU BECAUSE MICKEY WANTED YOU TO SEE THE LATEST MODEL.
I'M STILL NOT SURE I AGREE WITH HER CHOICE OF DONOR CELLS...
MICKEY KNOWS WHAT SHE'S DOING.
SHE'D BETTER, OR I'M GOING TO RECOMMEND WE SHUTTER THIS LAB.
THAT'S PROBABLY NOT A VERY GOOD IDEA.
BECAUSE YOU DON'T WANT TO PISS ME OFF.
NOT NOW THAT I'VE BEEN *RAMPAGED!*
YOU USED THE SERUM ON YOURSELF?
YOU'D BETTER BELIEVE IT!
YOU THINK I'M GONNA LET THE BOYS HAVE ALL THE FUN?
NOW I CAN'T WAIT TO GET MY HANDS ON YOU AGAIN, *RAMPAGE JACKSON!* UH-HUH!
THE END
...FOR NOW!

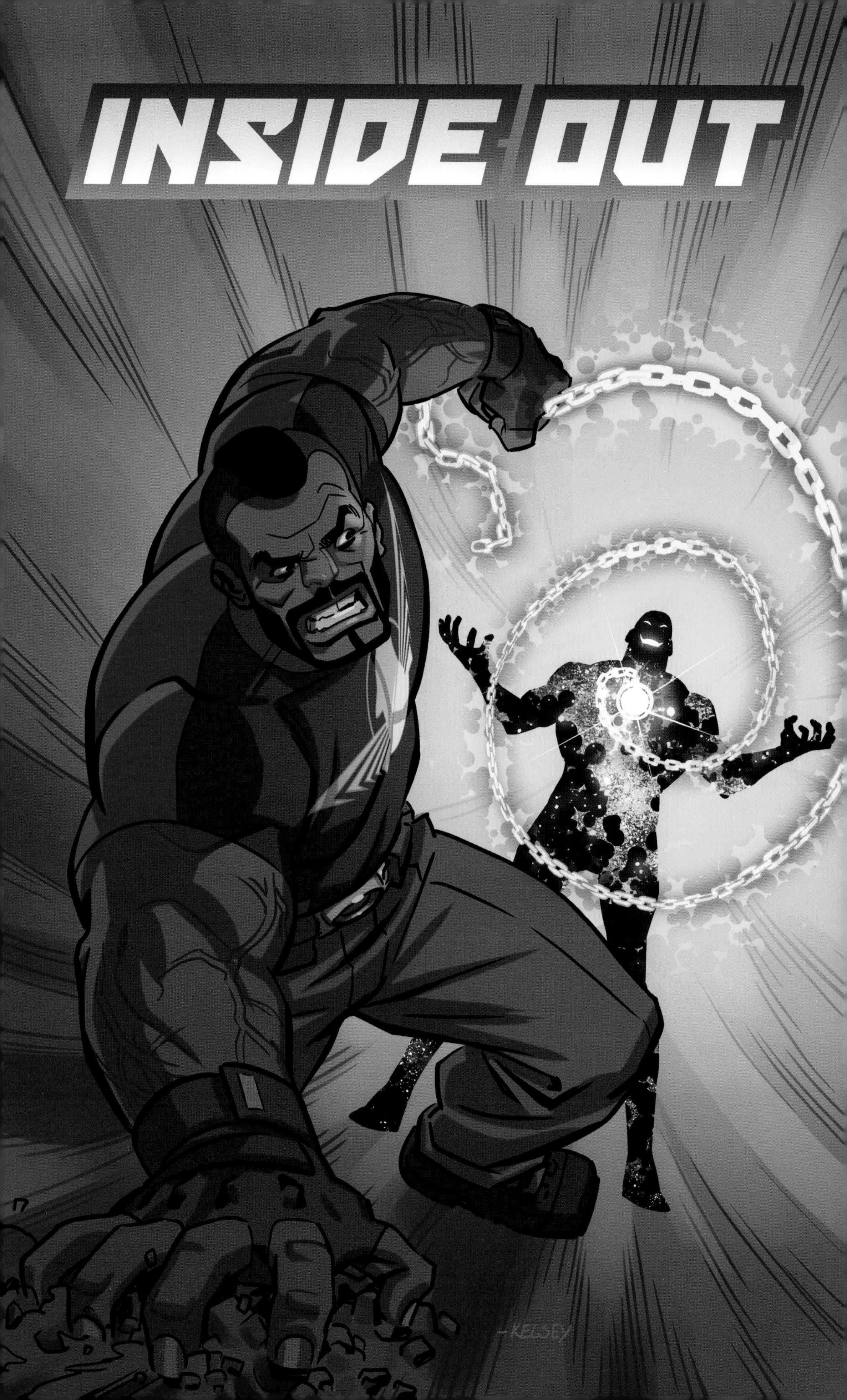
INSIDE OUT
-KELSEY

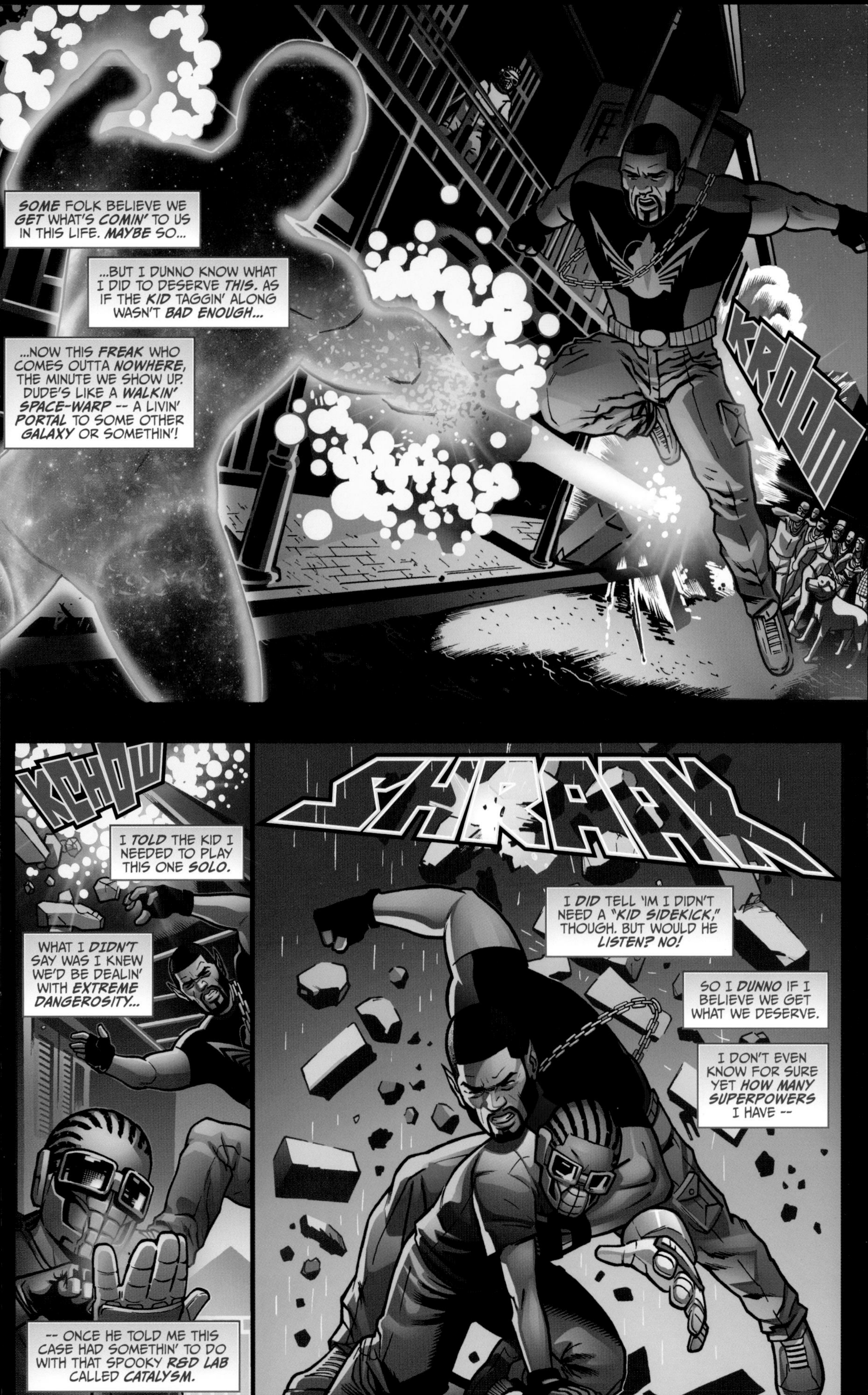
SOME FOLK BELIEVE WE GET WHAT'S COMIN' TO US IN THIS LIFE. MAYBE SO...
...BUT I DUNNO KNOW WHAT I DID TO DESERVE THIS. AS IF THE KID TAGGIN' ALONG WASN'T BAD ENOUGH...
...NOW THIS FREAK WHO COMES OUTTA NOWHERE, THE MINUTE WE SHOW UP. DUDE'S LIKE A WALKIN' SPACE-WARP -- A LIVIN' PORTAL TO SOME OTHER GALAXY OR SOMETHIN'!
KROOM
KCHOO
I TOLD THE KID I NEEDED TO PLAY THIS ONE SOLO.
WHAT I DIDN'T SAY WAS I KNEW WE'D BE DEALIN' WITH EXTREME DANGEROSITY...
-- ONCE HE TOLD ME THIS CASE HAD SOMETHIN' TO DO WITH THAT SPOOKY R&D LAB CALLED CATALYSM.
SHRAAK
I DID TELL 'IM I DIDN'T NEED A "KID SIDEKICK," THOUGH. BUT WOULD HE LISTEN? NO!
SO I DUNNO IF I BELIEVE WE GET WHAT WE DESERVE.
I DON'T EVEN KNOW FOR SURE YET HOW MANY SUPERPOWERS I HAVE --

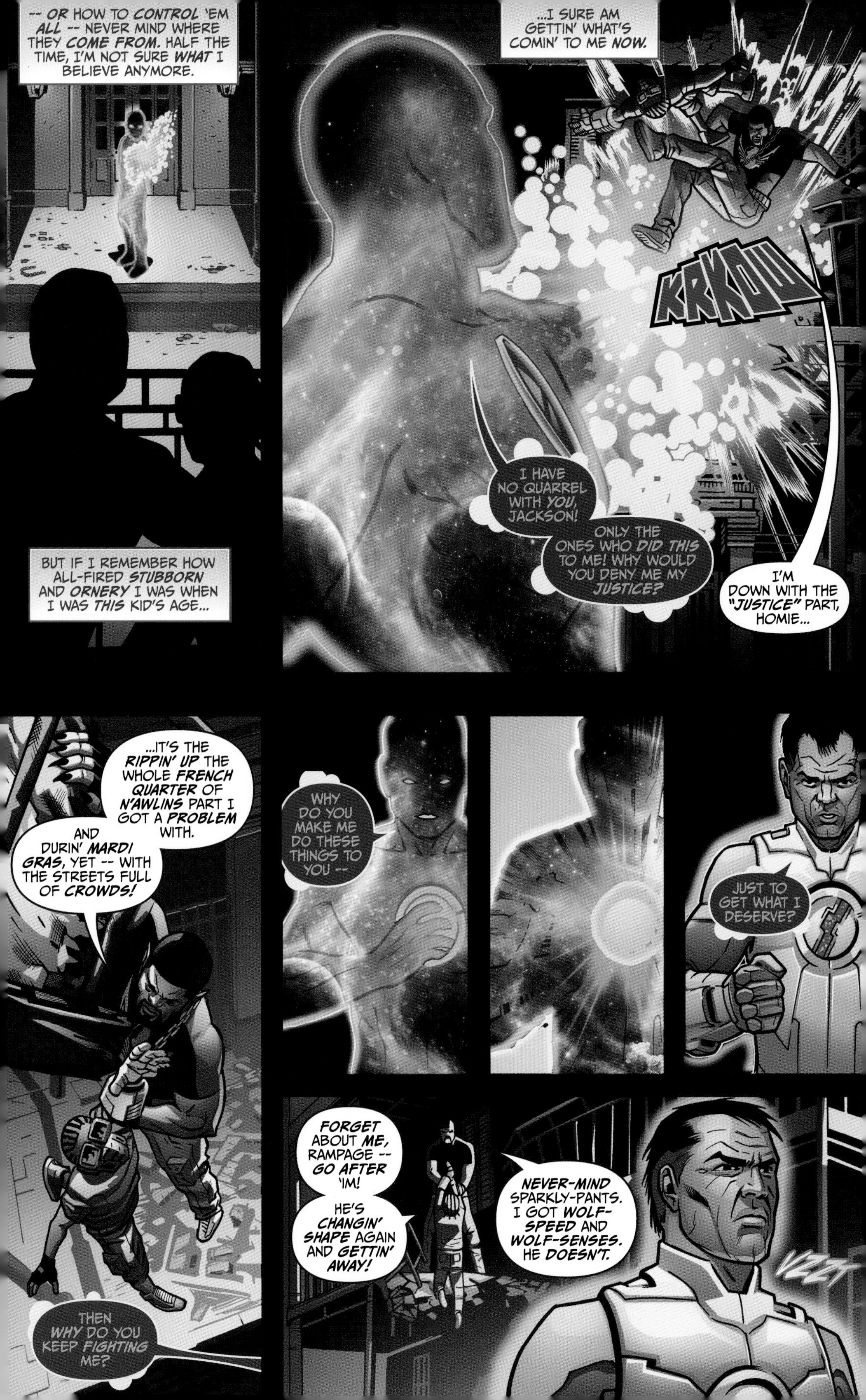

-- OR HOW TO CONTROL 'EM ALL -- NEVER MIND WHERE THEY COME FROM. HALF THE TIME, I'M NOT SURE WHAT I BELIEVE ANYMORE.
BUT IF I REMEMBER HOW ALL-FIRED STUBBORN AND ORNERY I WAS WHEN I WAS THIS KID'S AGE...
...I SURE AM GETTIN' WHAT'S COMIN' TO ME NOW.
KRKOOOM
I HAVE NO QUARREL WITH YOU, JACKSON!
ONLY THE ONES WHO DID THIS TO ME! WHY WOULD YOU DENY ME MY JUSTICE?
I'M DOWN WITH THE "JUSTICE" PART, HOMIE...
...IT'S THE RIPPIN' UP THE WHOLE FRENCH QUARTER OF N'AWLINS PART I GOT A PROBLEM WITH.
AND DURIN' MARDI GRAS, YET -- WITH THE STREETS FULL OF CROWDS!
THEN WHY DO YOU KEEP FIGHTING ME?
WHY DO YOU MAKE ME DO THESE THINGS TO YOU --
JUST TO GET WHAT I DESERVE?
FORGET ABOUT ME, RAMPAGE -- GO AFTER 'IM!
HE'S CHANGIN' SHAPE AGAIN AND GETTIN' AWAY!
NEVER-MIND SPARKLY-PANTS. I GOT WOLF-SPEED AND WOLF-SENSES. HE DOESN'T.
VZZT

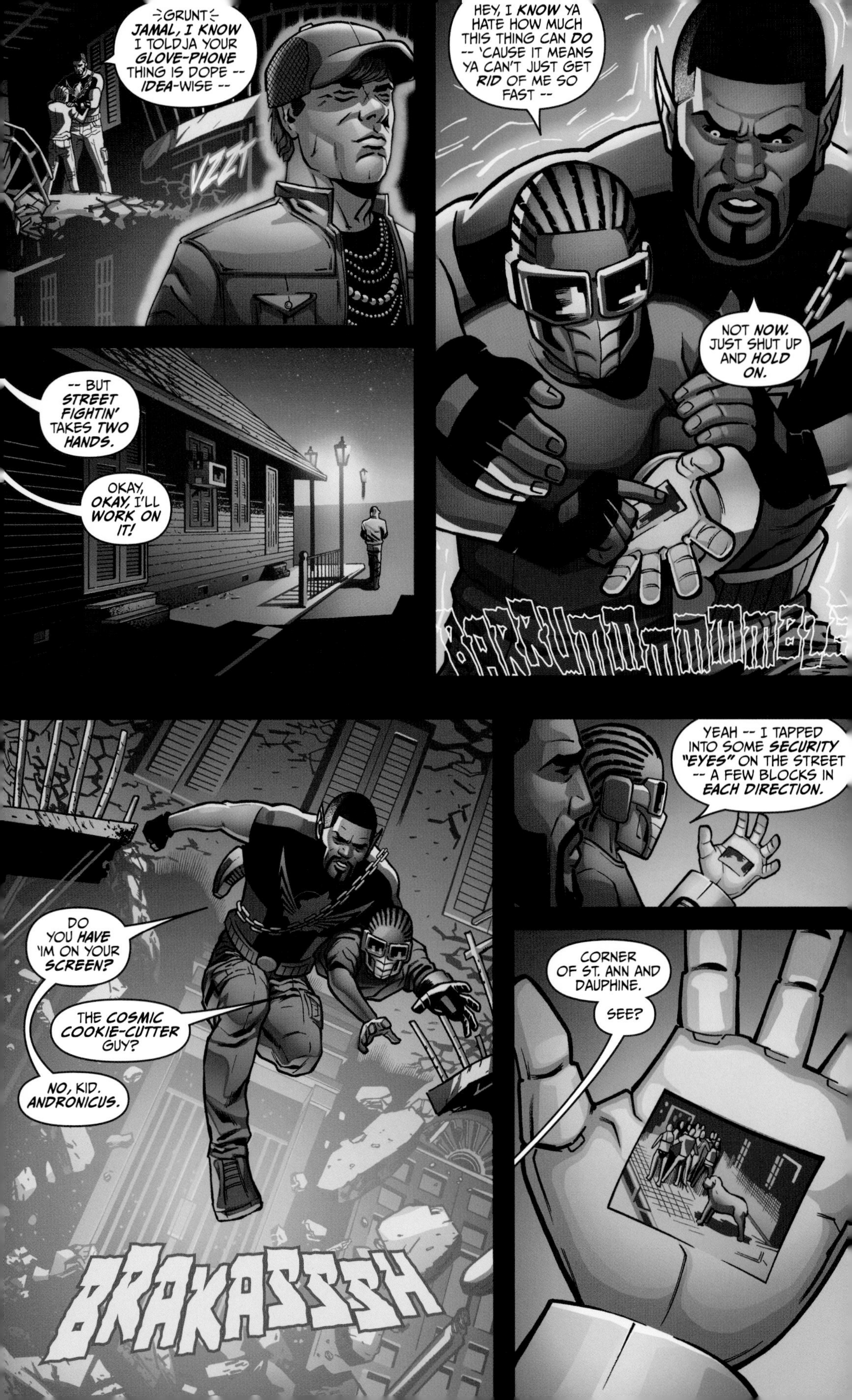

GRUNT JAMAL, I KNOW I TOLDJA YOUR GLOVE-PHONE THING IS DOPE -- IDEA-WISE --
VZZT
HEY, I KNOW YA HATE HOW MUCH THIS THING CAN DO -- 'CAUSE IT MEANS YA CAN'T JUST GET RID OF ME SO FAST --
-- BUT STREET FIGHTIN' TAKES TWO HANDS.
OKAY, OKAY, I'LL WORK ON IT!
NOT NOW. JUST SHUT UP AND HOLD ON.
DO YOU HAVE 'IM ON YOUR SCREEN?
THE COSMIC COOKIE-CUTTER GUY?
NO, KID. ANDRONICUS.
BRAKASSSH
YEAH -- I TAPPED INTO SOME SECURITY "EYES" ON THE STREET -- A FEW BLOCKS IN EACH DIRECTION.
CORNER OF ST. ANN AND DAUPHINE.
SEE?

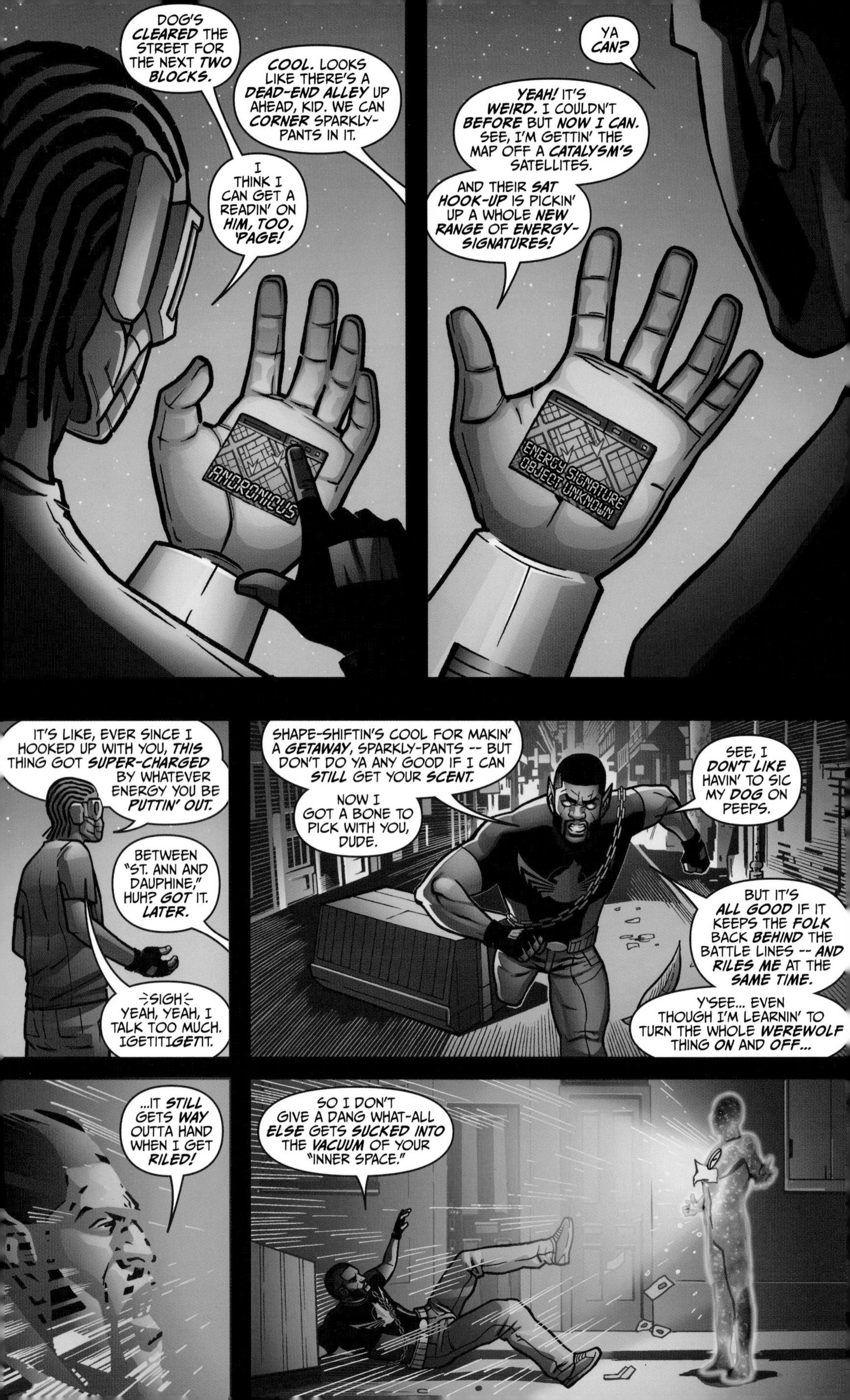
DOG'S CLEARED THE STREET FOR THE NEXT TWO BLOCKS.
COOL. LOOKS LIKE THERE'S A DEAD-END ALLEY UP AHEAD, KID. WE CAN CORNER SPARKLY-PANTS IN IT.
I THINK I CAN GET A READIN' ON HIM, TOO, 'PAGE!
ANDRONICUS
YA CAN?
YEAH! IT'S WEIRD. I COULDN'T BEFORE BUT NOW I CAN. SEE, I'M GETTIN' THE MAP OFF A CATALYSM'S SATELLITES.
AND THEIR SAT HOOK-UP IS PICKIN' UP A WHOLE NEW RANGE OF ENERGY-SIGNATURES!
ENERGY SIGNATURE OBJECT UNKNOWN
IT'S LIKE, EVER SINCE I HOOKED UP WITH YOU, THIS THING GOT SUPER-CHARGED BY WHATEVER ENERGY YOU BE PUTTIN' OUT.
BETWEEN "ST. ANN AND DAUPHINE," HUH? GOT IT. LATER.
SIGH YEAH, YEAH, I TALK TOO MUCH. IGETITIGETIT.
SHAPE-SHIFTIN'S COOL FOR MAKIN' A GETAWAY, SPARKLY-PANTS -- BUT DON'T DO YA ANY GOOD IF I CAN STILL GET YOUR SCENT.
NOW I GOT A BONE TO PICK WITH YOU, DUDE.
SEE, I DON'T LIKE HAVIN' TO SIC MY DOG ON PEEPS.
BUT IT'S ALL GOOD IF IT KEEPS THE FOLK BACK BEHIND THE BATTLE LINES -- AND RILES ME AT THE SAME TIME.
Y'SEE... EVEN THOUGH I'M LEARNIN' TO TURN THE WHOLE WEREWOLF THING ON AND OFF...
...IT STILL GETS WAY OUTTA HAND WHEN I GET RILED!
SO I DON'T GIVE A DANG WHAT-ALL ELSE GETS SUCKED INTO THE VACUUM OF YOUR "INNER SPACE."

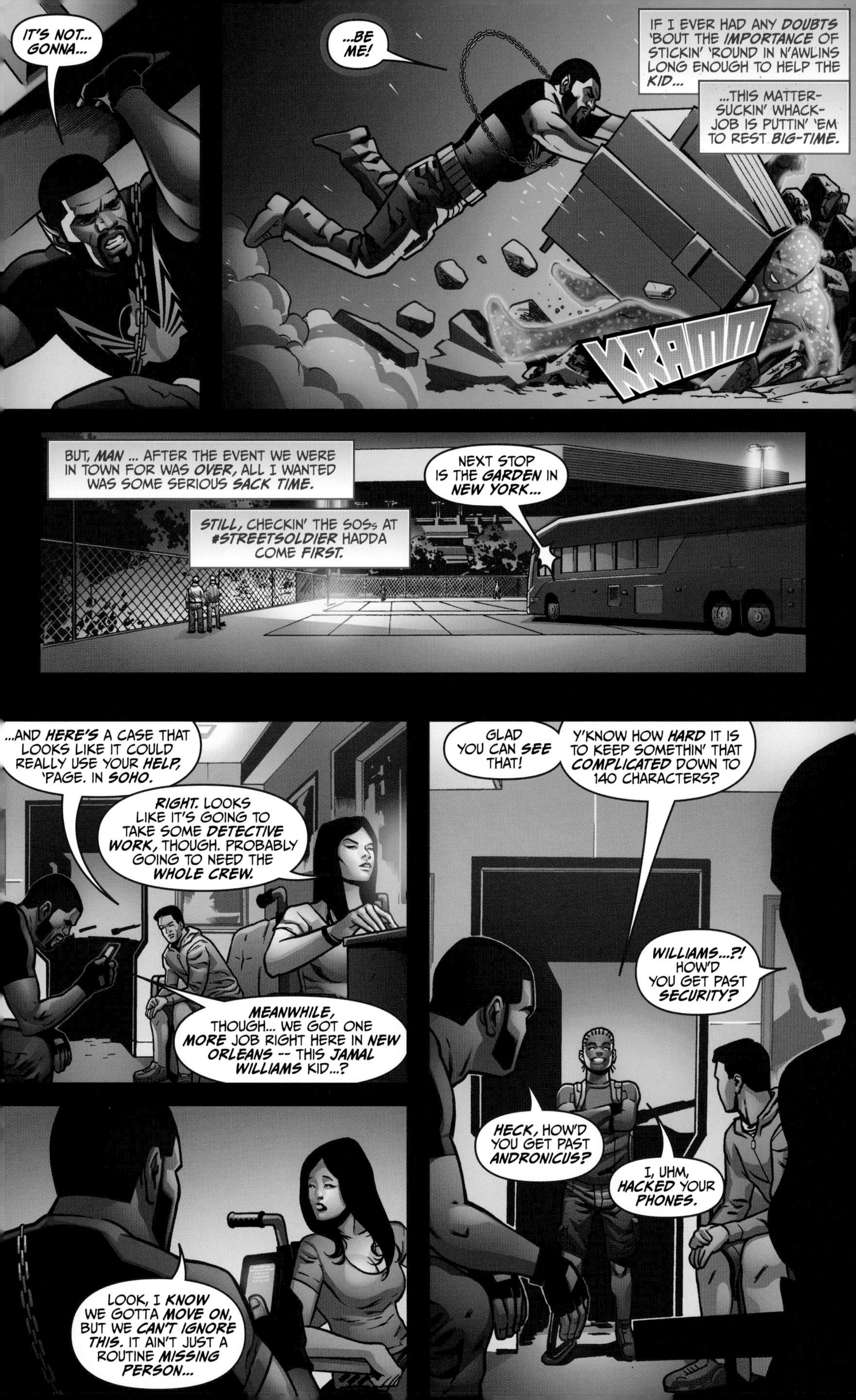
IT'S NOT... GONNA...
...BE ME!
IF I EVER HAD ANY DOUBTS 'BOUT THE IMPORTANCE OF STICKIN' 'ROUND IN N'AWLINS LONG ENOUGH TO HELP THE KID...
...THIS MATTER-SUCKIN' WHACK-JOB IS PUTTIN' 'EM TO REST BIG-TIME.
KRAMM
BUT, MAN ... AFTER THE EVENT WE WERE IN TOWN FOR WAS OVER, ALL I WANTED WAS SOME SERIOUS SACK TIME.
STILL, CHECKIN' THE SOSs AT #STREETSOLDIER HADDA COME FIRST.
NEXT STOP IS THE GARDEN IN NEW YORK...
...AND HERE'S A CASE THAT LOOKS LIKE IT COULD REALLY USE YOUR HELP, 'PAGE. IN SOHO.
RIGHT. LOOKS LIKE IT'S GOING TO TAKE SOME DETECTIVE WORK, THOUGH. PROBABLY GOING TO NEED THE WHOLE CREW.
MEANWHILE, THOUGH... WE GOT ONE MORE JOB RIGHT HERE IN NEW ORLEANS -- THIS JAMAL WILLIAMS KID...?
LOOK, I KNOW WE GOTTA MOVE ON, BUT WE CAN'T IGNORE THIS. IT AIN'T JUST A ROUTINE MISSING PERSON...
GLAD YOU CAN SEE THAT!
Y'KNOW HOW HARD IT IS TO KEEP SOMETHIN' THAT COMPLICATED DOWN TO 140 CHARACTERS?
WILLIAMS...?! HOW'D YOU GET PAST SECURITY?
HECK, HOW'D YOU GET PAST ANDRONICUS?
I, UHM, HACKED YOUR PHONES.

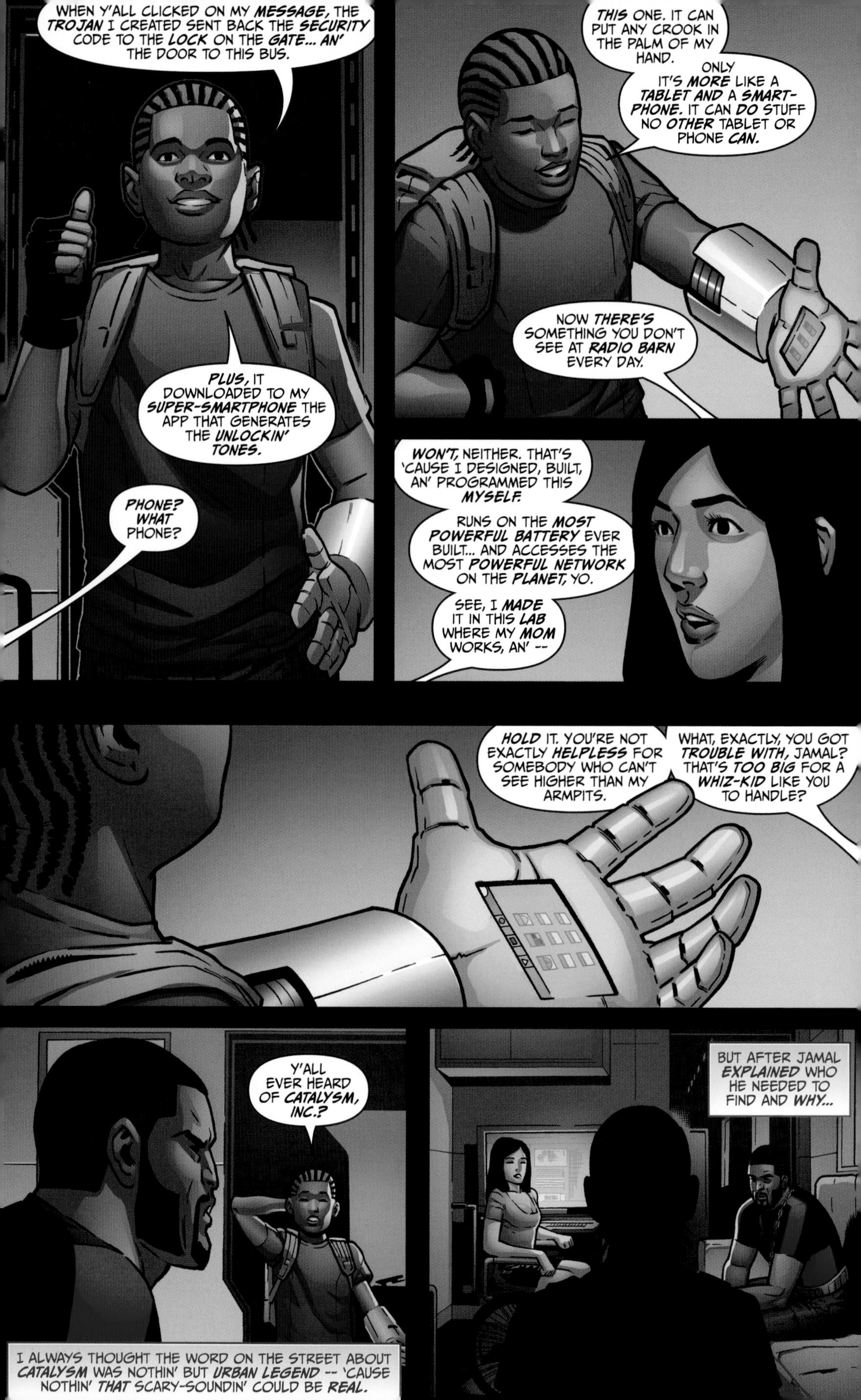
WHEN Y'ALL CLICKED ON MY MESSAGE, THE TROJAN I CREATED SENT BACK THE SECURITY CODE TO THE LOCK ON THE GATE... AN' THE DOOR TO THIS BUS.
PLUS, IT DOWNLOADED TO MY SUPER-SMARTPHONE THE APP THAT GENERATES THE UNLOCKIN' TONES.
PHONE? WHAT PHONE?
THIS ONE. IT CAN PUT ANY CROOK IN THE PALM OF MY HAND.
ONLY IT'S MORE LIKE A TABLET AND A SMART-PHONE. IT CAN DO STUFF NO OTHER TABLET OR PHONE CAN.
NOW THERE'S SOMETHING YOU DON'T SEE AT RADIO BARN EVERY DAY.
WON'T, NEITHER. THAT'S 'CAUSE I DESIGNED, BUILT, AN' PROGRAMMED THIS MYSELF.
RUNS ON THE MOST POWERFUL BATTERY EVER BUILT... AND ACCESSES THE MOST POWERFUL NETWORK ON THE PLANET, YO.
SEE, I MADE IT IN THIS LAB WHERE MY MOM WORKS, AN' --
HOLD IT. YOU'RE NOT EXACTLY HELPLESS FOR SOMEBODY WHO CAN'T SEE HIGHER THAN MY ARMPITS.
WHAT, EXACTLY, YOU GOT TROUBLE WITH, JAMAL? THAT'S TOO BIG FOR A WHIZ-KID LIKE YOU TO HANDLE?
Y'ALL EVER HEARD OF CATALYSM, INC.?
I ALWAYS THOUGHT THE WORD ON THE STREET ABOUT CATALYSM WAS NOTHIN' BUT URBAN LEGEND -- 'CAUSE NOTHIN' THAT SCARY-SOUNDIN' COULD BE REAL.
BUT AFTER JAMAL EXPLAINED WHO HE NEEDED TO FIND AND WHY...

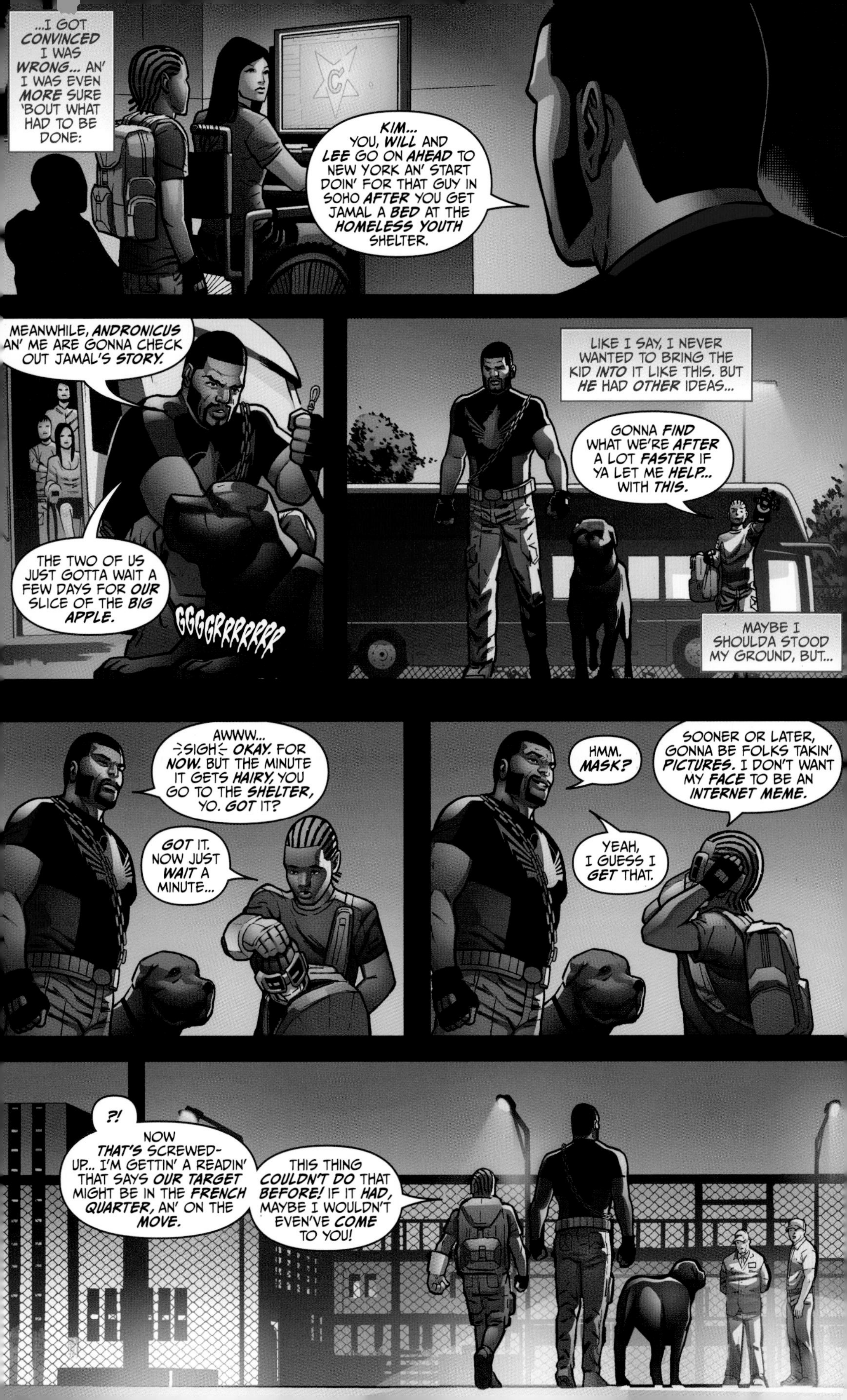

...I GOT CONVINCED I WAS WRONG... AN' I WAS EVEN MORE SURE 'BOUT WHAT HAD TO BE DONE:
KIM... YOU, WILL AND LEE GO ON AHEAD TO NEW YORK AN' START DOIN' FOR THAT GUY IN SOHO AFTER YOU GET JAMAL A BED AT THE HOMELESS YOUTH SHELTER.
MEANWHILE, ANDRONICUS AN' ME ARE GONNA CHECK OUT JAMAL'S STORY.
THE TWO OF US JUST GOTTA WAIT A FEW DAYS FOR OUR SLICE OF THE BIG APPLE.
GGGGRRRRRRR
LIKE I SAY, I NEVER WANTED TO BRING THE KID INTO IT LIKE THIS. BUT HE HAD OTHER IDEAS...
GONNA FIND WHAT WE'RE AFTER A LOT FASTER IF YA LET ME HELP... WITH THIS.
MAYBE I SHOULDA STOOD MY GROUND, BUT...
AWWW... ⇒SIGH⇐ OKAY. FOR NOW. BUT THE MINUTE IT GETS HAIRY, YOU GO TO THE SHELTER, YO. GOT IT?
GOT IT. NOW JUST WAIT A MINUTE...
HMM. MASK?
SOONER OR LATER, GONNA BE FOLKS TAKIN' PICTURES. I DON'T WANT MY FACE TO BE AN INTERNET MEME.
YEAH, I GUESS I GET THAT.
?!
NOW THAT'S SCREWED-UP... I'M GETTIN' A READIN' THAT SAYS OUR TARGET MIGHT BE IN THE FRENCH QUARTER, AN' ON THE MOVE.
THIS THING COULDN'T DO THAT BEFORE! IF IT HAD, MAYBE I WOULDN'T EVEN'VE COME TO YOU!

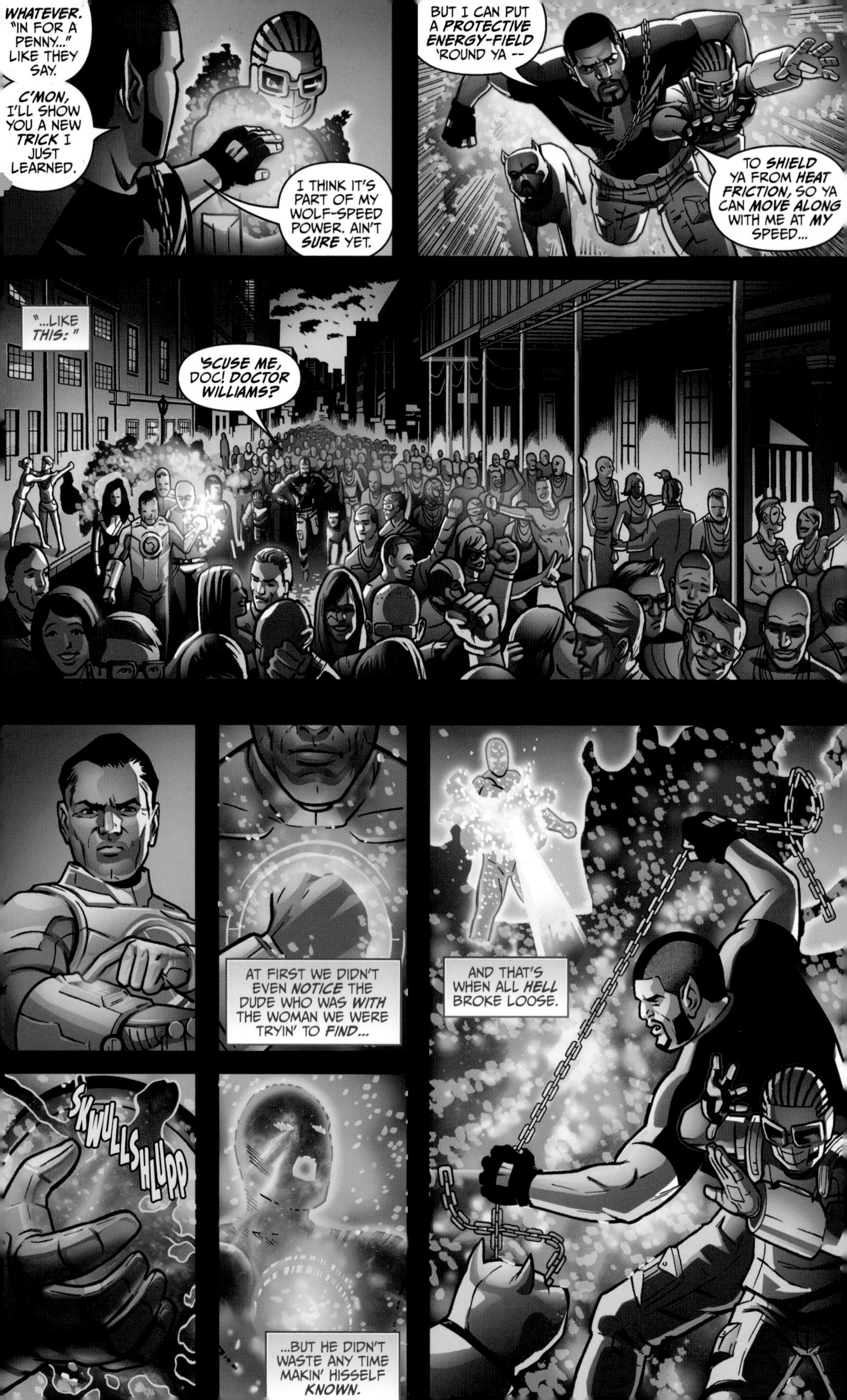
WHATEVER. "IN FOR A PENNY..." LIKE THEY SAY.
C'MON, I'LL SHOW YOU A NEW TRICK I JUST LEARNED.
I THINK IT'S PART OF MY WOLF-SPEED POWER. AIN'T SURE YET.
BUT I CAN PUT A PROTECTIVE ENERGY-FIELD 'ROUND YA --
TO SHIELD YA FROM HEAT FRICTION, SO YA CAN MOVE ALONG WITH ME AT MY SPEED...
"...LIKE THIS:"
'SCUSE ME, DOC! DOCTOR WILLIAMS?
AT FIRST WE DIDN'T EVEN NOTICE THE DUDE WHO WAS WITH THE WOMAN WE WERE TRYIN' TO FIND...
AND THAT'S WHEN ALL HELL BROKE LOOSE.
SKWULLSHLUPP
...BUT HE DIDN'T WASTE ANY TIME MAKIN' HISSELF KNOWN.

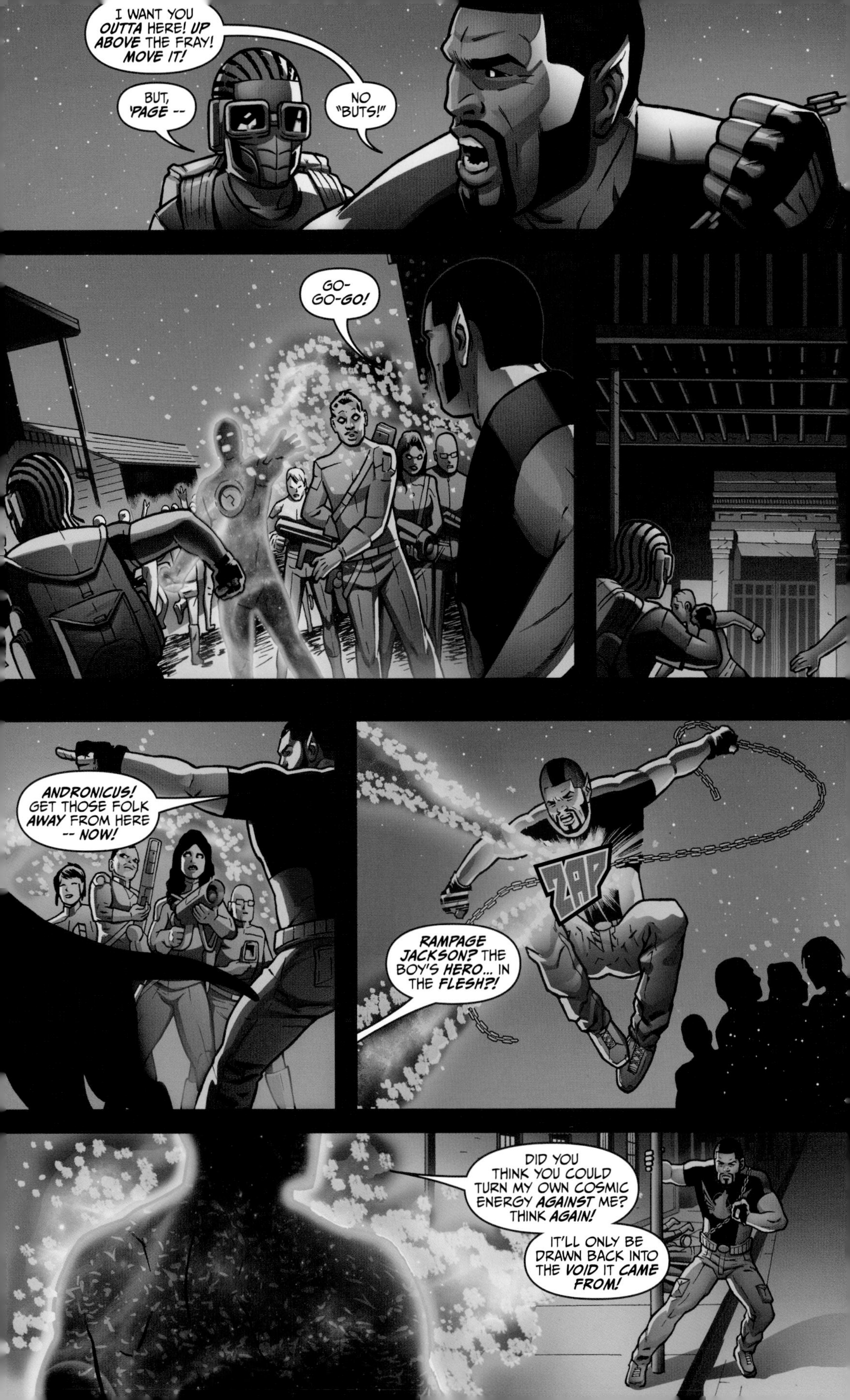
I WANT YOU OUTTA HERE! UP ABOVE THE FRAY! MOVE IT!
BUT, 'PAGE --
NO "BUTS!"
GO-GO-GO!
ANDRONICUS! GET THOSE FOLK AWAY FROM HERE -- NOW!
ZAP
RAMPAGE JACKSON? THE BOY'S HERO... IN THE FLESH?!
DID YOU THINK YOU COULD TURN MY OWN COSMIC ENERGY AGAINST ME? THINK AGAIN!
IT'LL ONLY BE DRAWN BACK INTO THE VOID IT CAME FROM!

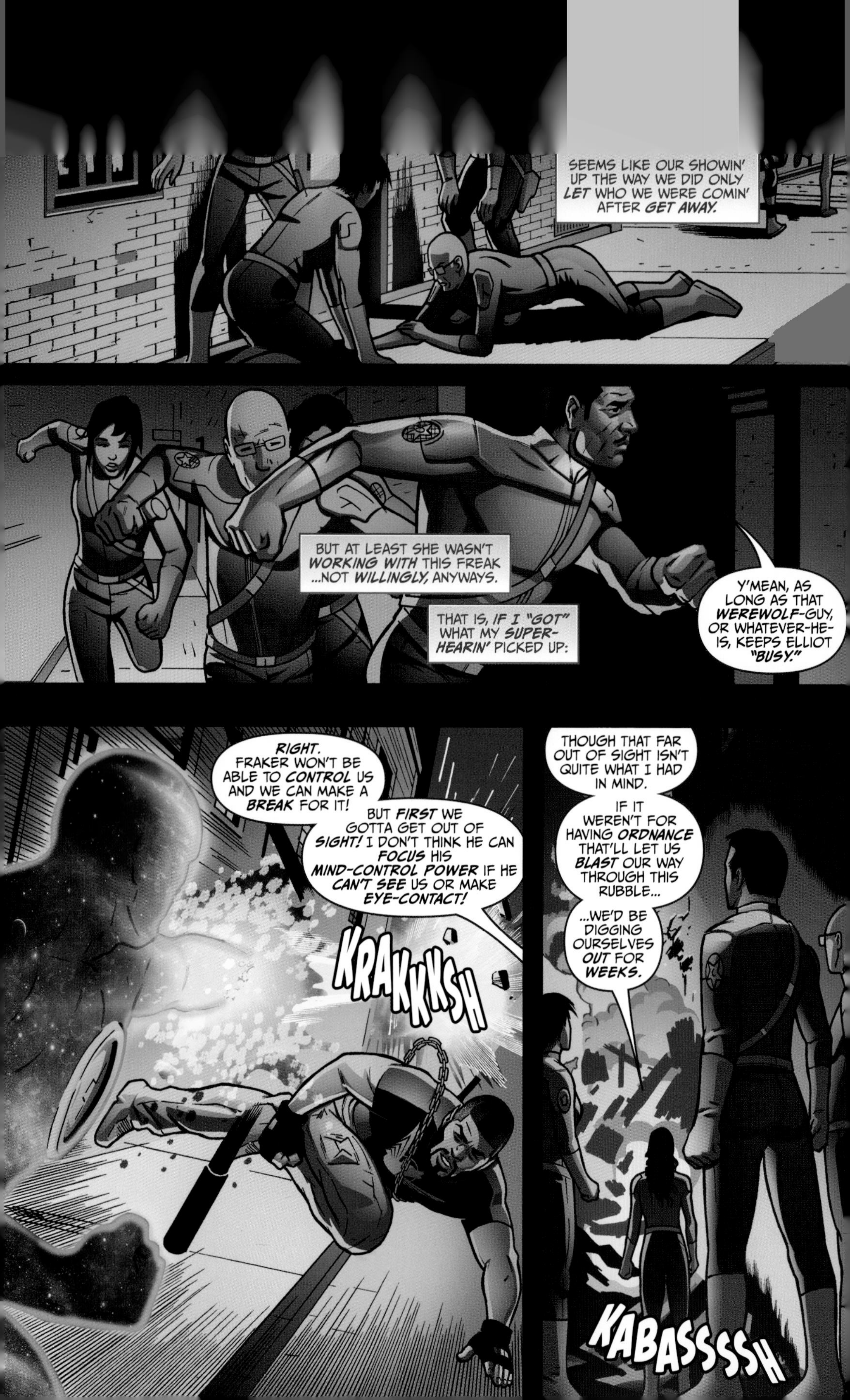
SEEMS LIKE OUR SHOWIN' UP THE WAY WE DID ONLY LET WHO WE WERE COMIN' AFTER GET AWAY.
BUT AT LEAST SHE WASN'T WORKING WITH THIS FREAK ...NOT WILLINGLY, ANYWAYS.
THAT IS, IF I "GOT" WHAT MY SUPER-HEARIN' PICKED UP:
Y'MEAN, AS LONG AS THAT WEREWOLF-GUY, OR WHATEVER-HE-IS, KEEPS ELLIOT "BUSY."
RIGHT. FRAKER WON'T BE ABLE TO CONTROL US AND WE CAN MAKE A BREAK FOR IT!
BUT FIRST WE GOTTA GET OUT OF SIGHT! I DON'T THINK HE CAN FOCUS HIS MIND-CONTROL POWER IF HE CAN'T SEE US OR MAKE EYE-CONTACT!
KRAKKKSH
THOUGH THAT FAR OUT OF SIGHT ISN'T QUITE WHAT I HAD IN MIND.
IF IT WEREN'T FOR HAVING ORDNANCE THAT'LL LET US BLAST OUR WAY THROUGH THIS RUBBLE...
...WE'D BE DIGGING OURSELVES OUT FOR WEEKS.
KABASSSSH

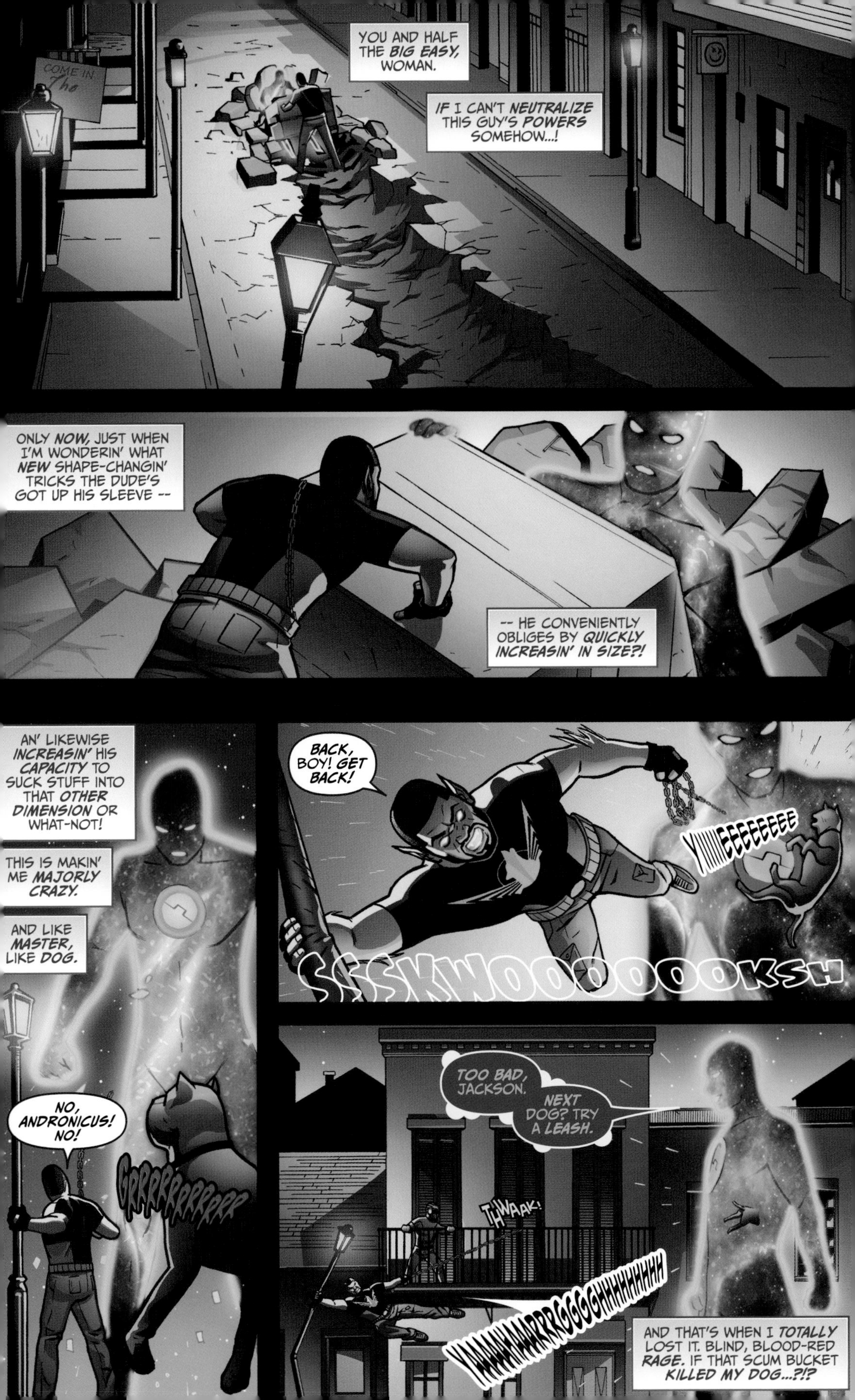

COME IN
YOU AND HALF THE *BIG EASY,* WOMAN.
IF I CAN'T *NEUTRALIZE* THIS GUY'S *POWERS* SOMEHOW...!
ONLY *NOW,* JUST WHEN I'M WONDERIN' WHAT *NEW* SHAPE-CHANGIN' TRICKS THE DUDE'S GOT UP HIS SLEEVE --
-- HE CONVENIENTLY OBLIGES BY *QUICKLY INCREASIN' IN SIZE?!*
AN' LIKEWISE *INCREASIN'* HIS *CAPACITY* TO SUCK STUFF INTO THAT *OTHER DIMENSION* OR WHAT-NOT!
THIS IS MAKIN' ME *MAJORLY CRAZY.*
AND LIKE *MASTER,* LIKE *DOG.*
NO, *ANDRONICUS!* NO!
GRRRRRRRRRRR
BACK, BOY! GET BACK!
YIIIIIIEEEEEEEE
SSSKWOOOOOOOOKSH
TOO BAD, JACKSON.
NEXT DOG? TRY A *LEASH.*
THWAAK!
YAAAAHAARRRGGGGHHHHHHHH
AND THAT'S WHEN I *TOTALLY* LOST IT. BLIND, BLOOD-RED *RAGE.* IF THAT SCUM BUCKET *KILLED MY DOG...?!?*

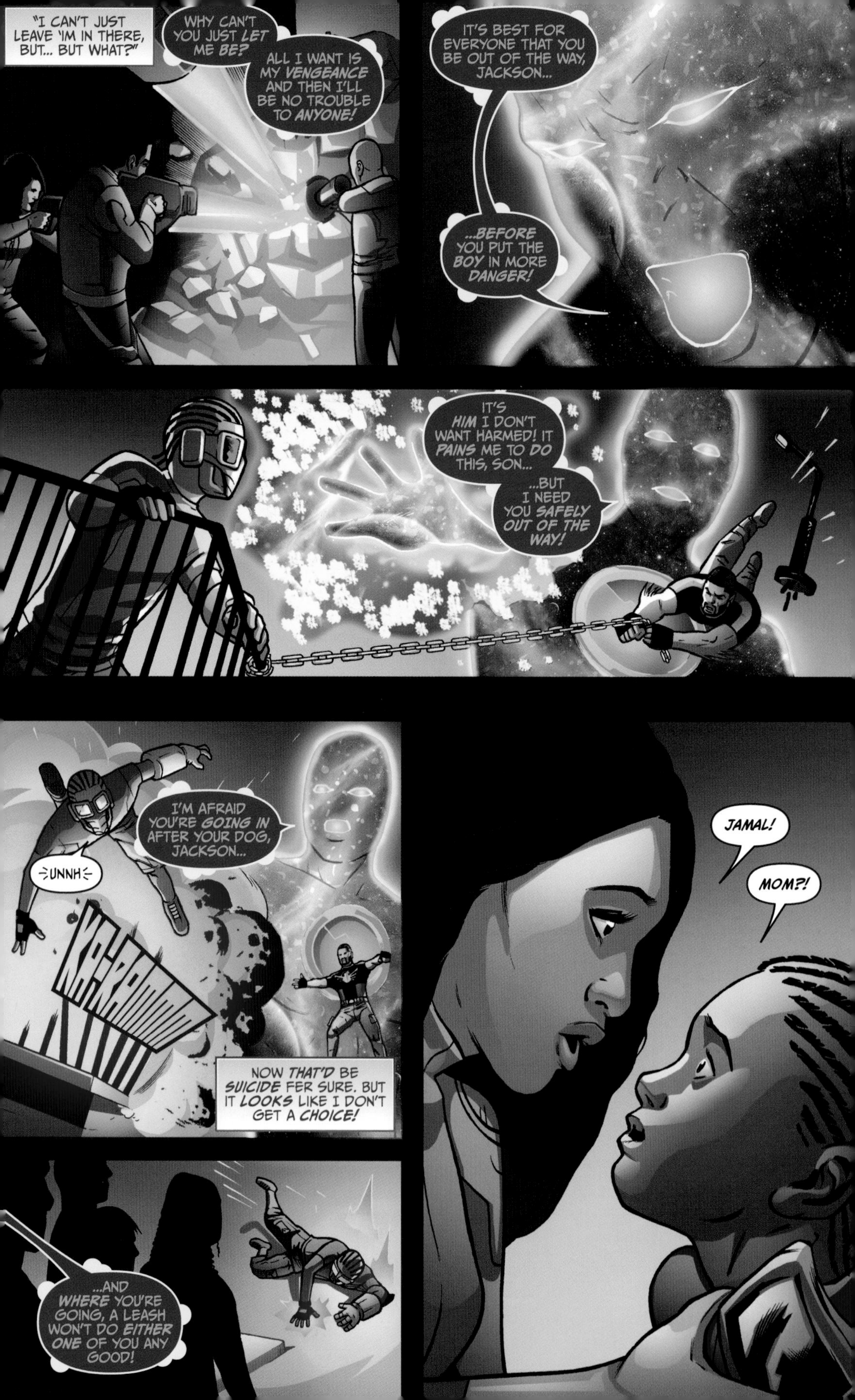
"I CAN'T JUST LEAVE 'IM IN THERE, BUT... BUT WHAT?"
WHY CAN'T YOU JUST LET ME BE?
ALL I WANT IS MY VENGEANCE AND THEN I'LL BE NO TROUBLE TO ANYONE!
IT'S BEST FOR EVERYONE THAT YOU BE OUT OF THE WAY, JACKSON...
...BEFORE YOU PUT THE BOY IN MORE DANGER!
IT'S HIM I DON'T WANT HARMED! IT PAINS ME TO DO THIS, SON...
...BUT I NEED YOU SAFELY OUT OF THE WAY!
I'M AFRAID YOU'RE GOING IN AFTER YOUR DOG, JACKSON...
UNNH
KA-BOOM
NOW THAT'D BE SUICIDE FER SURE. BUT IT LOOKS LIKE I DON'T GET A CHOICE!
...AND WHERE YOU'RE GOING, A LEASH WON'T DO EITHER ONE OF YOU ANY GOOD!
JAMAL!
MOM?!

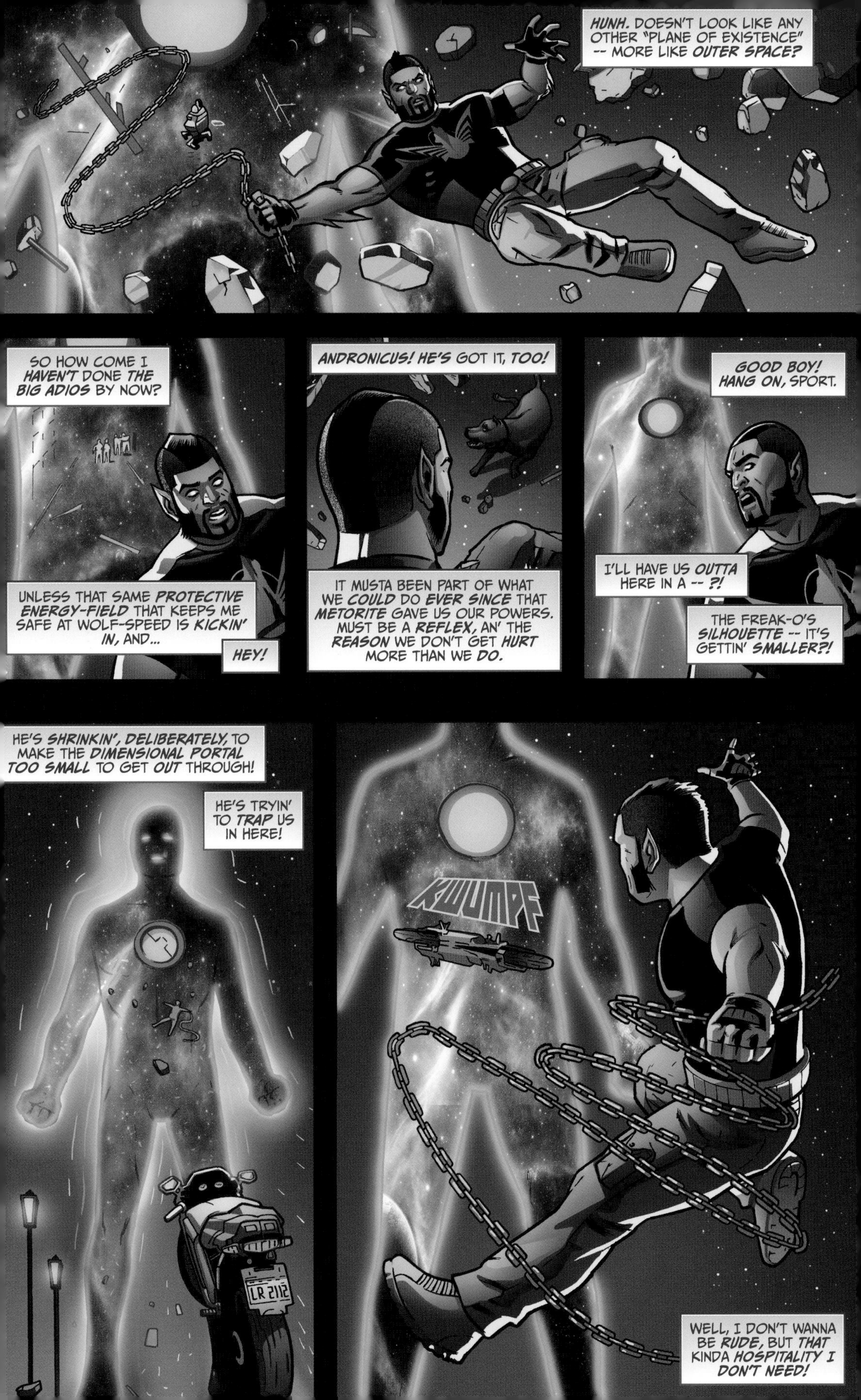

HUNH. DOESN'T LOOK LIKE ANY OTHER "PLANE OF EXISTENCE" -- MORE LIKE OUTER SPACE?
SO HOW COME I HAVEN'T DONE THE BIG ADIOS BY NOW?
UNLESS THAT SAME PROTECTIVE ENERGY-FIELD THAT KEEPS ME SAFE AT WOLF-SPEED IS KICKIN' IN, AND...
HEY!
ANDRONICUS! HE'S GOT IT, TOO!
IT MUSTA BEEN PART OF WHAT WE COULD DO EVER SINCE THAT METORITE GAVE US OUR POWERS. MUST BE A REFLEX, AN' THE REASON WE DON'T GET HURT MORE THAN WE DO.
GOOD BOY! HANG ON, SPORT.
I'LL HAVE US OUTTA HERE IN A -- ?!
THE FREAK-O'S SILHOUETTE -- IT'S GETTIN' SMALLER?!
HE'S SHRINKIN', DELIBERATELY, TO MAKE THE DIMENSIONAL PORTAL TOO SMALL TO GET OUT THROUGH!
HE'S TRYIN' TO TRAP US IN HERE!
LR 2112
KWUMPF
WELL, I DON'T WANNA BE RUDE, BUT THAT KINDA HOSPITALITY I DON'T NEED!

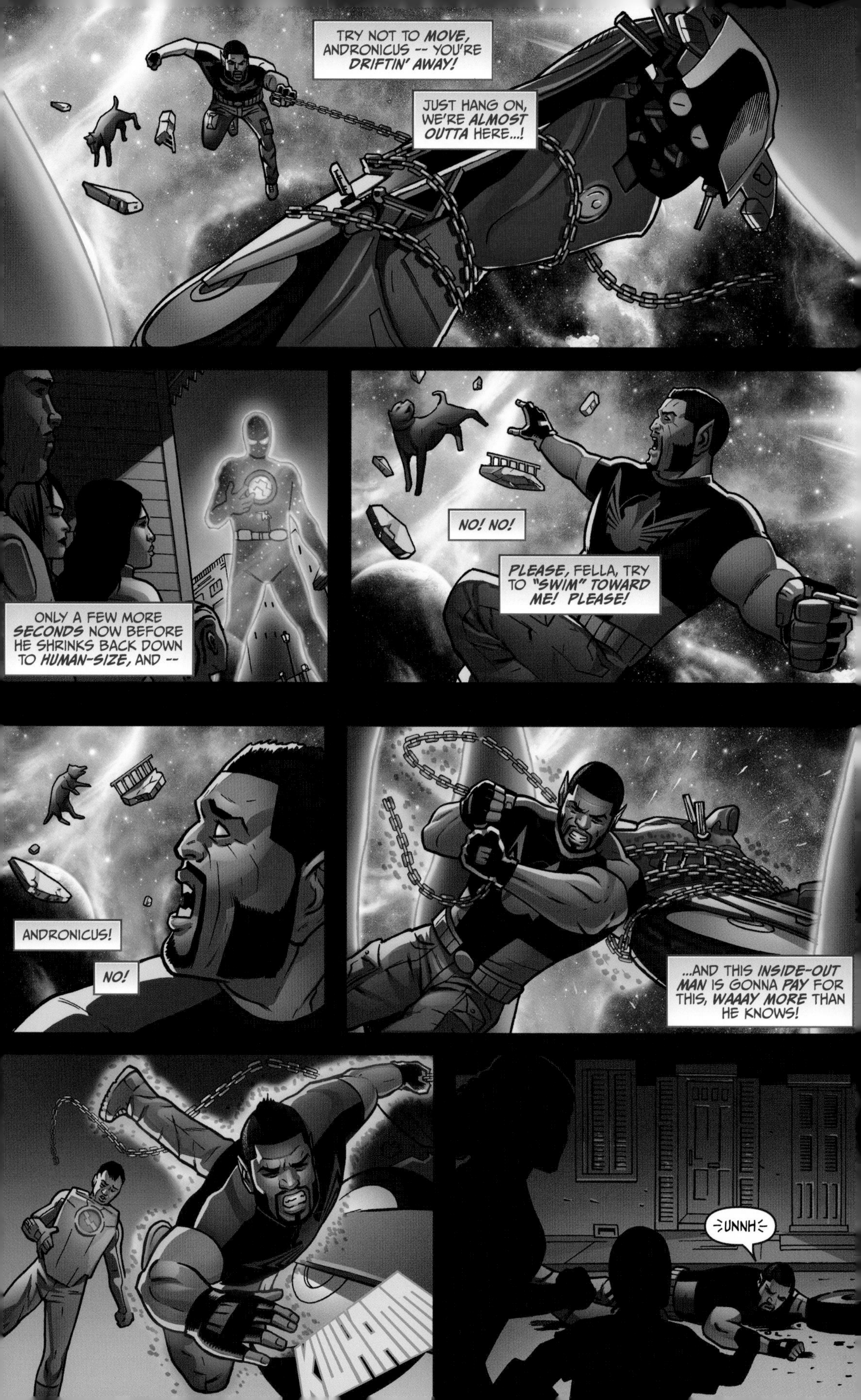
TRY NOT TO MOVE, ANDRONICUS -- YOU'RE DRIFTIN' AWAY!
JUST HANG ON, WE'RE ALMOST OUTTA HERE...!
ONLY A FEW MORE SECONDS NOW BEFORE HE SHRINKS BACK DOWN TO HUMAN-SIZE, AND --
NO! NO!
PLEASE, FELLA, TRY TO "SWIM" TOWARD ME! PLEASE!
ANDRONICUS!
NO!
...AND THIS INSIDE-OUT MAN IS GONNA PAY FOR THIS, WAAAY MORE THAN HE KNOWS!
UNNH

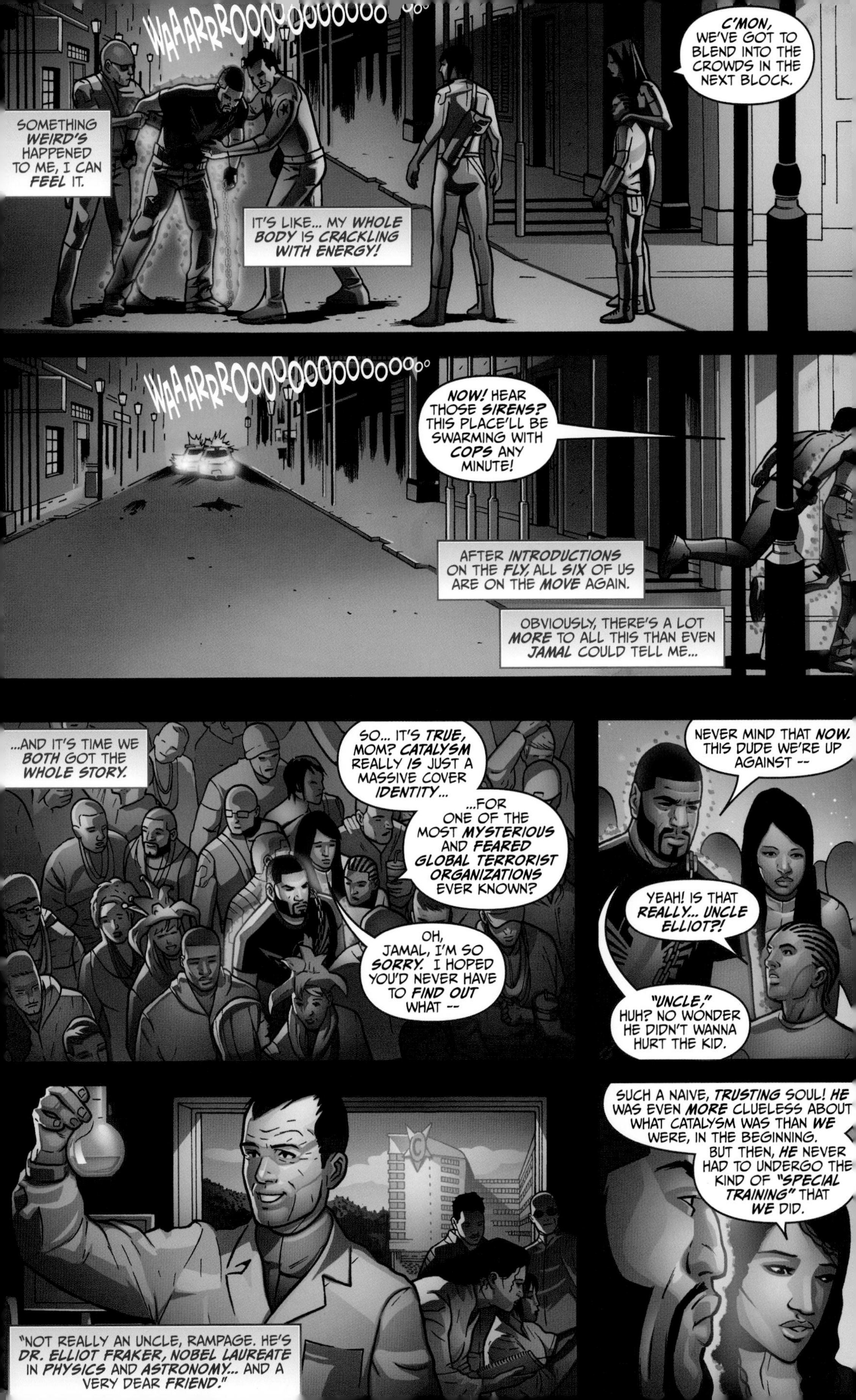

WAAARRROOOOOOOOOOOO
SOMETHING WEIRD'S HAPPENED TO ME, I CAN FEEL IT.
IT'S LIKE... MY WHOLE BODY IS CRACKLING WITH ENERGY!
C'MON, WE'VE GOT TO BLEND INTO THE CROWDS IN THE NEXT BLOCK.
WAAARRROOOOOOOOOOOOOO
NOW! HEAR THOSE SIRENS? THIS PLACE'LL BE SWARMING WITH COPS ANY MINUTE!
AFTER INTRODUCTIONS ON THE FLY, ALL SIX OF US ARE ON THE MOVE AGAIN.
OBVIOUSLY, THERE'S A LOT MORE TO ALL THIS THAN EVEN JAMAL COULD TELL ME...
...AND IT'S TIME WE BOTH GOT THE WHOLE STORY.
SO... IT'S TRUE, MOM? CATALYSM REALLY IS JUST A MASSIVE COVER IDENTITY...
...FOR ONE OF THE MOST MYSTERIOUS AND FEARED GLOBAL TERRORIST ORGANIZATIONS EVER KNOWN?
OH, JAMAL, I'M SO SORRY. I HOPED YOU'D NEVER HAVE TO FIND OUT WHAT --
NEVER MIND THAT NOW. THIS DUDE WE'RE UP AGAINST --
YEAH! IS THAT REALLY... UNCLE ELLIOT?!
"UNCLE," HUH? NO WONDER HE DIDN'T WANNA HURT THE KID.
"NOT REALLY AN UNCLE, RAMPAGE. HE'S DR. ELLIOT FRAKER, NOBEL LAUREATE IN PHYSICS AND ASTRONOMY... AND A VERY DEAR FRIEND."
SUCH A NAIVE, TRUSTING SOUL! HE WAS EVEN MORE CLUELESS ABOUT WHAT CATALYSM WAS THAN WE WERE, IN THE BEGINNING.
BUT THEN, HE NEVER HAD TO UNDERGO THE KIND OF "SPECIAL TRAINING" THAT WE DID.

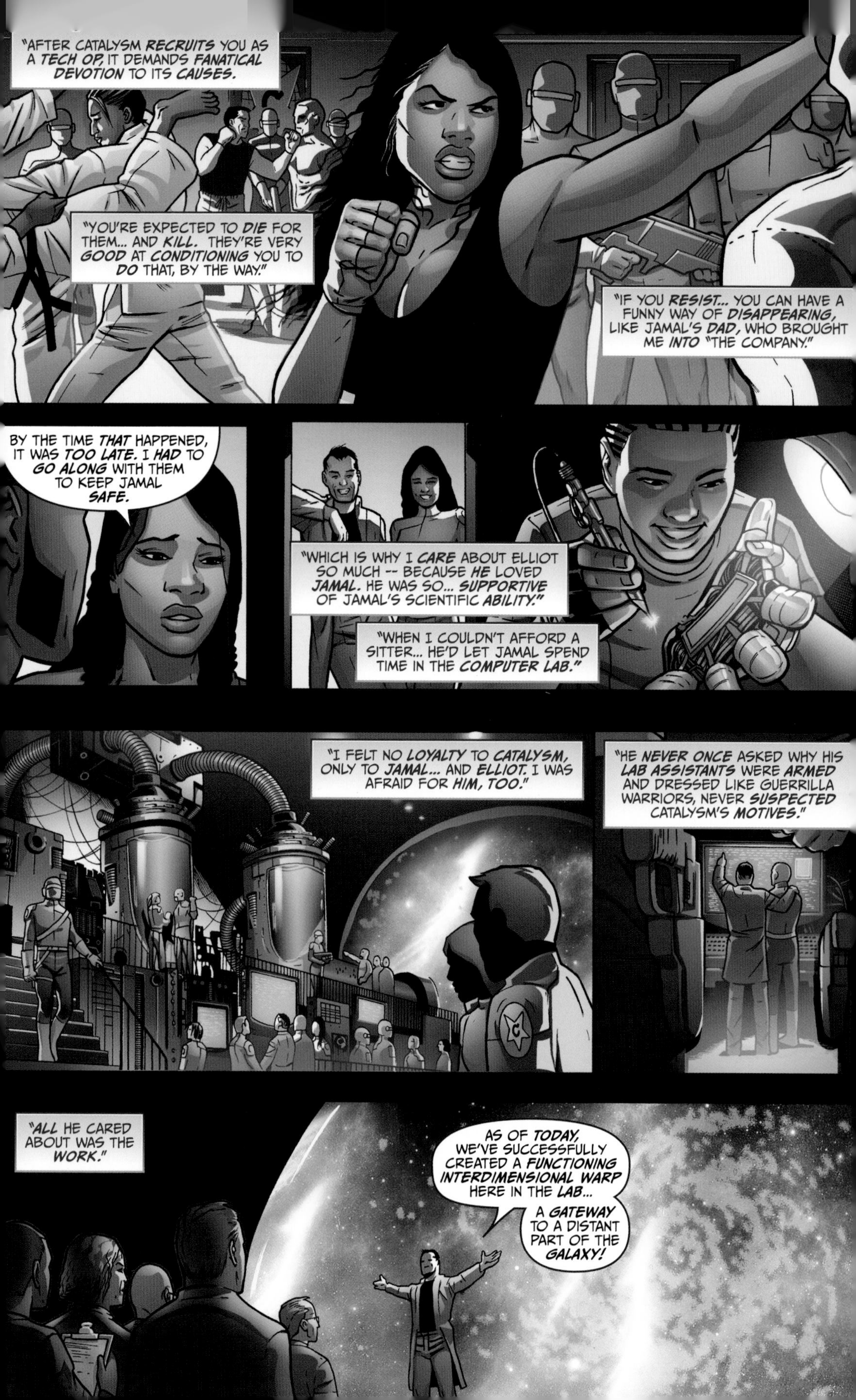
"AFTER CATALYSM RECRUITS YOU AS A TECH OP, IT DEMANDS FANATICAL DEVOTION TO ITS CAUSES.
"YOU'RE EXPECTED TO DIE FOR THEM... AND KILL. THEY'RE VERY GOOD AT CONDITIONING YOU TO DO THAT, BY THE WAY."
"IF YOU RESIST... YOU CAN HAVE A FUNNY WAY OF DISAPPEARING, LIKE JAMAL'S DAD, WHO BROUGHT ME INTO "THE COMPANY."
BY THE TIME THAT HAPPENED, IT WAS TOO LATE. I HAD TO GO ALONG WITH THEM TO KEEP JAMAL SAFE.
"WHICH IS WHY I CARE ABOUT ELLIOT SO MUCH -- BECAUSE HE LOVED JAMAL. HE WAS SO... SUPPORTIVE OF JAMAL'S SCIENTIFIC ABILITY."
"WHEN I COULDN'T AFFORD A SITTER... HE'D LET JAMAL SPEND TIME IN THE COMPUTER LAB."
"I FELT NO LOYALTY TO CATALYSM, ONLY TO JAMAL... AND ELLIOT. I WAS AFRAID FOR HIM, TOO."
"HE NEVER ONCE ASKED WHY HIS LAB ASSISTANTS WERE ARMED AND DRESSED LIKE GUERRILLA WARRIORS, NEVER SUSPECTED CATALYSM'S MOTIVES."
"ALL HE CARED ABOUT WAS THE WORK."
AS OF TODAY, WE'VE SUCCESSFULLY CREATED A FUNCTIONING INTERDIMENSIONAL WARP HERE IN THE LAB...
A GATEWAY TO A DISTANT PART OF THE GALAXY!

ANY POINT TO ANOTHER IS THROUGH *MOLECULAR DISINTEGRATION* AND *REMOTE INTEGRATION.*

IN OTHER WORDS, *TELEPORTATION* -- WHICH WE'RE *ALSO* PERFECTING HERE. IN THEORY...

...WE SHOULD BE ABLE TO CONSTRUCT A *SPACE STATION* IN THE DISTANT REACHES OF SPACE.

WE'LL BE ABLE TO TELEPORT PEOPLE HERE TO THE *LAB* FROM *ANYWHERE* ON *EARTH...*

...*THEN* SEND THEM *THROUGH THE WARP* TO THE SPACE STATION!

JUST *THINK* HOW WE MIGHT EASE *OVERPOPULATION* BY *COLONIZING OTHER DIMENSIONS...*

...OR REDUCE *PRISON OVERCROWDING...* OR *EVACUATE DISASTER AREAS!*

THE APPLICATIONS FOR THE BETTERMENT OF HUMANKIND ARE *LIMITLESS!*

"BUT *I'D* BEEN BRIEFED ON WHAT CATALYSM *REALLY* WANTED THIS STUFF FOR... AND I KNEW ELLIOT WOULD WANT NO *PART* OF IT."

"HE *HAD* TO BE *TOLD...*"

ANOTHER DIMENSION WOULD BE THE PERFECT *TERRORIST STRONGHOLD...* A PLACE TO STASH *KIDNAP* VICTIMS...

...OR THE ULTIMATE WAY FOR CATALYSM TO *"DISAPPEAR"* ITS ENEMIES.

AS IF EVERYTHING THAT WENT ON IN THAT LAB *WASN'T* BEING *MONITORED CONSTANTLY.* AN *ASSASSINATION SQUAD* CAME FOR HIM WHILE THE FOUR OF US WERE IN ANOTHER PART OF THE LAB.

WHAT I *DIDN'T* EXPECT WAS THAT ELLIOT WOULD GO *BERSERK* WITH *RAGE* -- AND TRY TO *DESTROY* HIS OWN HANDIWORK SO IT COULDN'T BE *PERVERTED.*

"WE TOOK THEM OUT... *SHOT OUT* THE SECURITY CAMERAS... LOCKED OURSELVES IN... AND STARTED LOOKING FOR FRAKER."

EEEOOOW

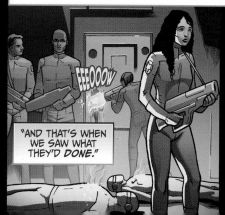

"AND THAT'S WHEN WE SAW WHAT THEY'D *DONE.*"

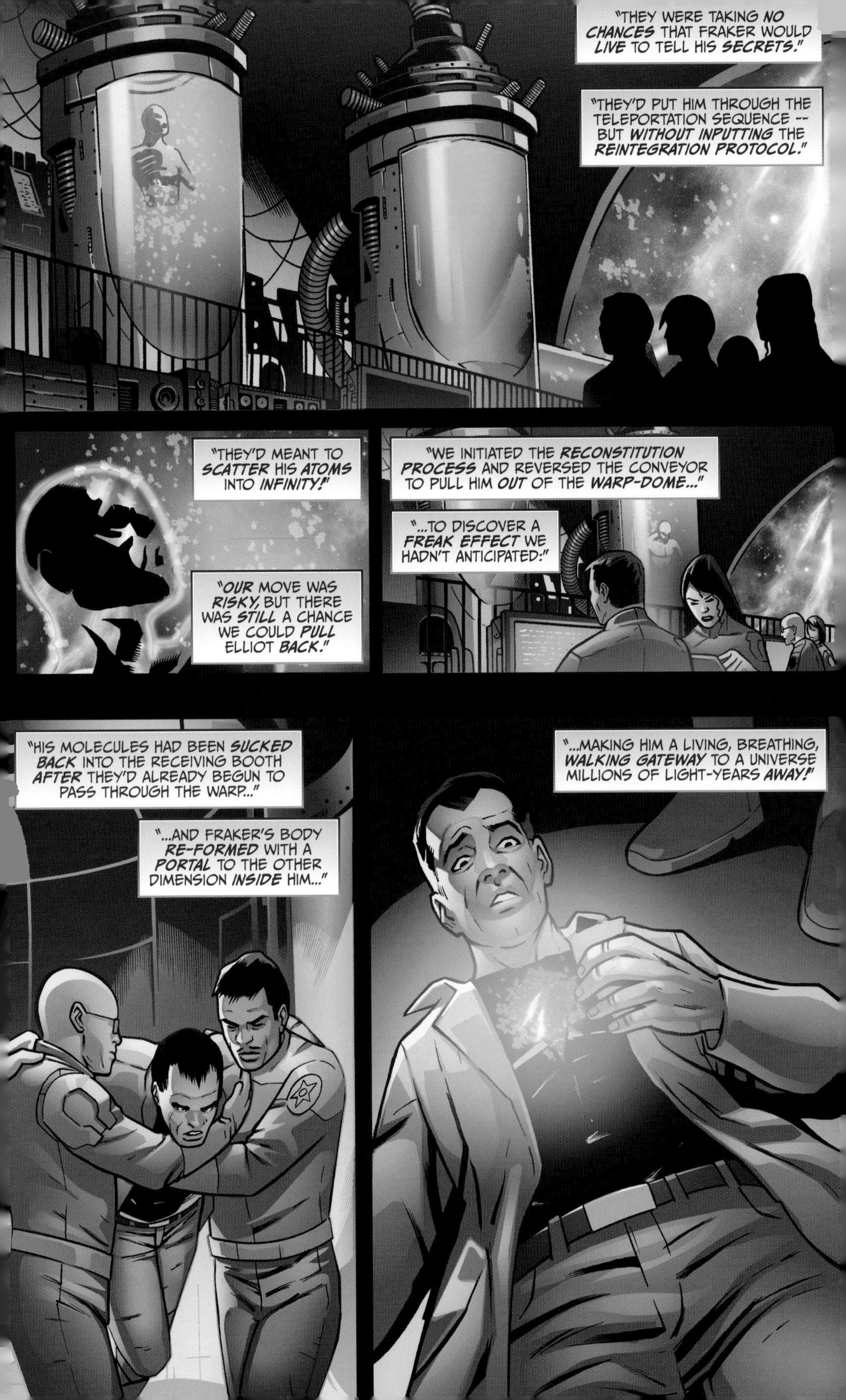
"THEY WERE TAKING NO CHANCES THAT FRAKER WOULD LIVE TO TELL HIS SECRETS."
"THEY'D PUT HIM THROUGH THE TELEPORTATION SEQUENCE -- BUT WITHOUT INPUTTING THE REINTEGRATION PROTOCOL."
"THEY'D MEANT TO SCATTER HIS ATOMS INTO INFINITY!"
"OUR MOVE WAS RISKY, BUT THERE WAS STILL A CHANCE WE COULD PULL ELLIOT BACK."
"WE INITIATED THE RECONSTITUTION PROCESS AND REVERSED THE CONVEYOR TO PULL HIM OUT OF THE WARP-DOME..."
"...TO DISCOVER A FREAK EFFECT WE HADN'T ANTICIPATED:"
"HIS MOLECULES HAD BEEN SUCKED BACK INTO THE RECEIVING BOOTH AFTER THEY'D ALREADY BEGUN TO PASS THROUGH THE WARP..."
"...AND FRAKER'S BODY RE-FORMED WITH A PORTAL TO THE OTHER DIMENSION INSIDE HIM..."
"...MAKING HIM A LIVING, BREATHING, WALKING GATEWAY TO A UNIVERSE MILLIONS OF LIGHT-YEARS AWAY!"

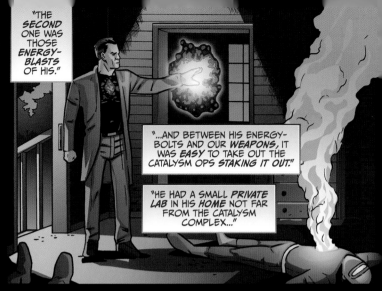

"IT DIDN'T TAKE LONG FOR ELLIOT TO DISCOVER THE *NEW POWERS* HE'D BEEN IMBUED WITH, PROBABLY DUE TO EXPOSURE TO *COSMIC RADIATION.*"

"THE *SECOND ONE* WAS THOSE *ENERGY-BLASTS* OF HIS."

"...AND BETWEEN HIS ENERGY-BOLTS AND OUR *WEAPONS,* IT WAS *EASY* TO TAKE OUT THE CATALYSM OPS *STAKING IT OUT.*"

"HE HAD A SMALL *PRIVATE LAB* IN HIS *HOME* NOT FAR FROM THE CATALYSM COMPLEX..."

"HIS POWER TO *CONTROL* OUR *MINDS* AND MAKE US HIS *PUPPETS* WAS THE *FIRST* ONE."

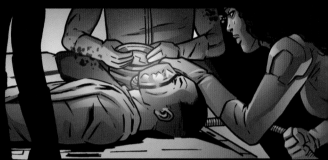

"SOON WE'D CREATED THE SPECIAL *DEVICES* WHICH HELP HIM *CONTROL* THE WARP..."

"...AND SINCE THEN, HE'S BEEN MAKING HIS WAY -- WITH OUR *FORCED HELP* -- TO THE *CATALYSM HQ* NEAR *TULANE.*"

THERE'S JUST *ONE* THING I DON'T *UNDERSTAND,* JAMAL:

WHY YOU'D RISK *COMING AFTER US* AFTER I'D *LEFT WORD* FOR YOU TO --

NOBODY TOLD ME *SQUAT,* MOM. YESTERDAY MORNING, OUR *BARRACKS* WAS *DESERTED*... THE *LAB* WAS *SHUT DOWN* AND *LOCKED*...

THAT'S NOT GOOD. IT *SOUNDS* LIKE THEY'RE GETTIN' READY TO *KICK OVER THE TRACES.*

BUT I THINK I CAN *TAKE* FRAKER NOW THAT I'VE HAD A *"COSMIC ENERGY BATH"* OF MY OWN. IT FEELS LIKE I'M MORE *POWERFUL*...

KROOM

...MAYBE EVEN MORE THAN *HIM.* AND IF I CAN *DO* THIS, THE PLAYING FIELD JUST GOT *LEVELER.*

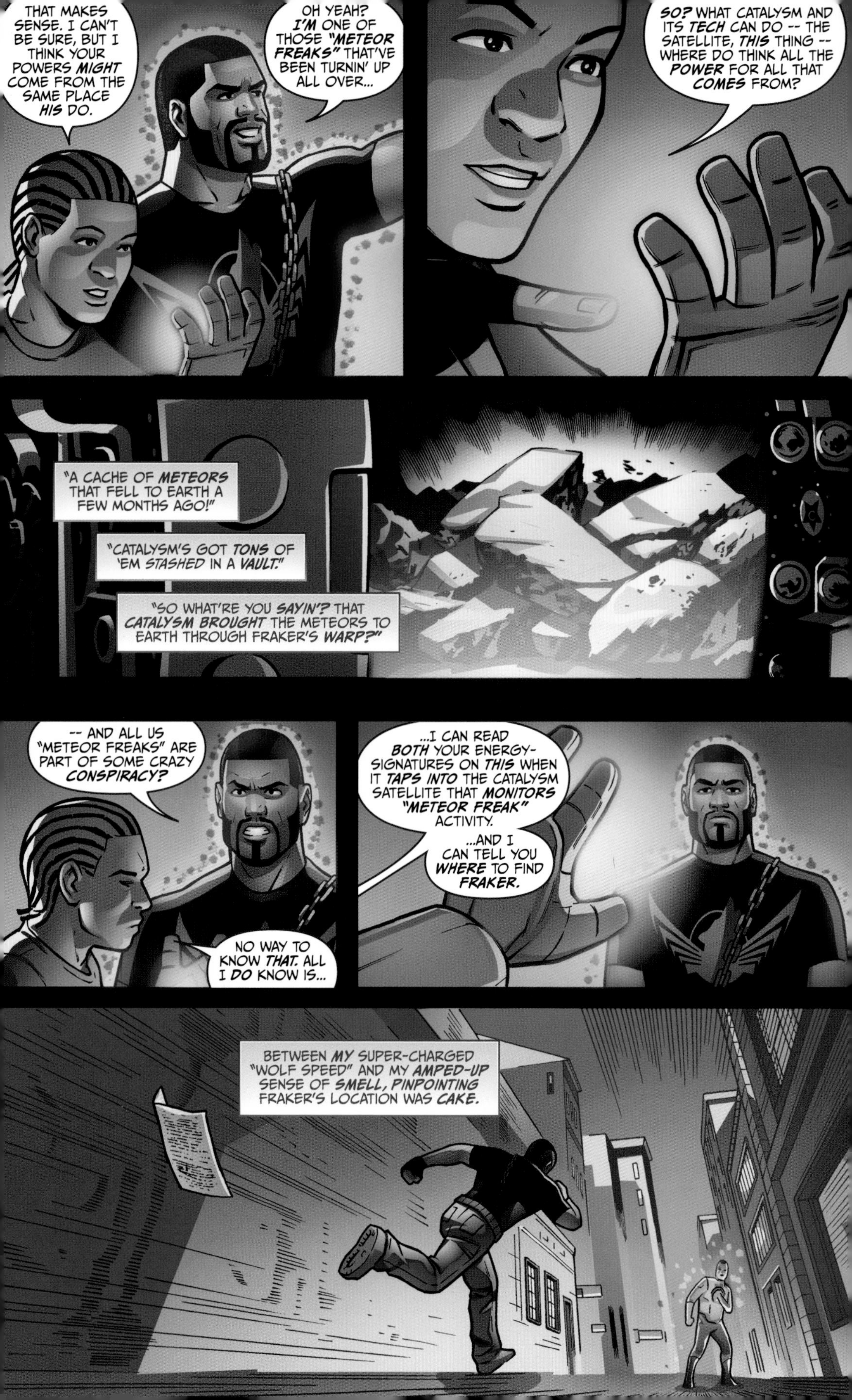
THAT MAKES SENSE. I CAN'T BE SURE, BUT I THINK YOUR POWERS MIGHT COME FROM THE SAME PLACE HIS DO.
OH YEAH? I'M ONE OF THOSE "METEOR FREAKS" THAT'VE BEEN TURNIN' UP ALL OVER...
SO? WHAT CATALYSM AND ITS TECH CAN DO -- THE SATELLITE, THIS THING -- WHERE DO THINK ALL THE POWER FOR ALL THAT COMES FROM?
"A CACHE OF METEORS THAT FELL TO EARTH A FEW MONTHS AGO!"
"CATALYSM'S GOT TONS OF 'EM STASHED IN A VAULT."
"SO WHAT'RE YOU SAYIN'? THAT CATALYSM BROUGHT THE METEORS TO EARTH THROUGH FRAKER'S WARP?"
-- AND ALL US "METEOR FREAKS" ARE PART OF SOME CRAZY CONSPIRACY?
NO WAY TO KNOW THAT. ALL I DO KNOW IS...
...I CAN READ BOTH YOUR ENERGY-SIGNATURES ON THIS WHEN IT TAPS INTO THE CATALYSM SATELLITE THAT MONITORS "METEOR FREAK" ACTIVITY.
...AND I CAN TELL YOU WHERE TO FIND FRAKER.
BETWEEN MY SUPER-CHARGED "WOLF SPEED" AND MY AMPED-UP SENSE OF SMELL, PINPOINTING FRAKER'S LOCATION WAS CAKE.

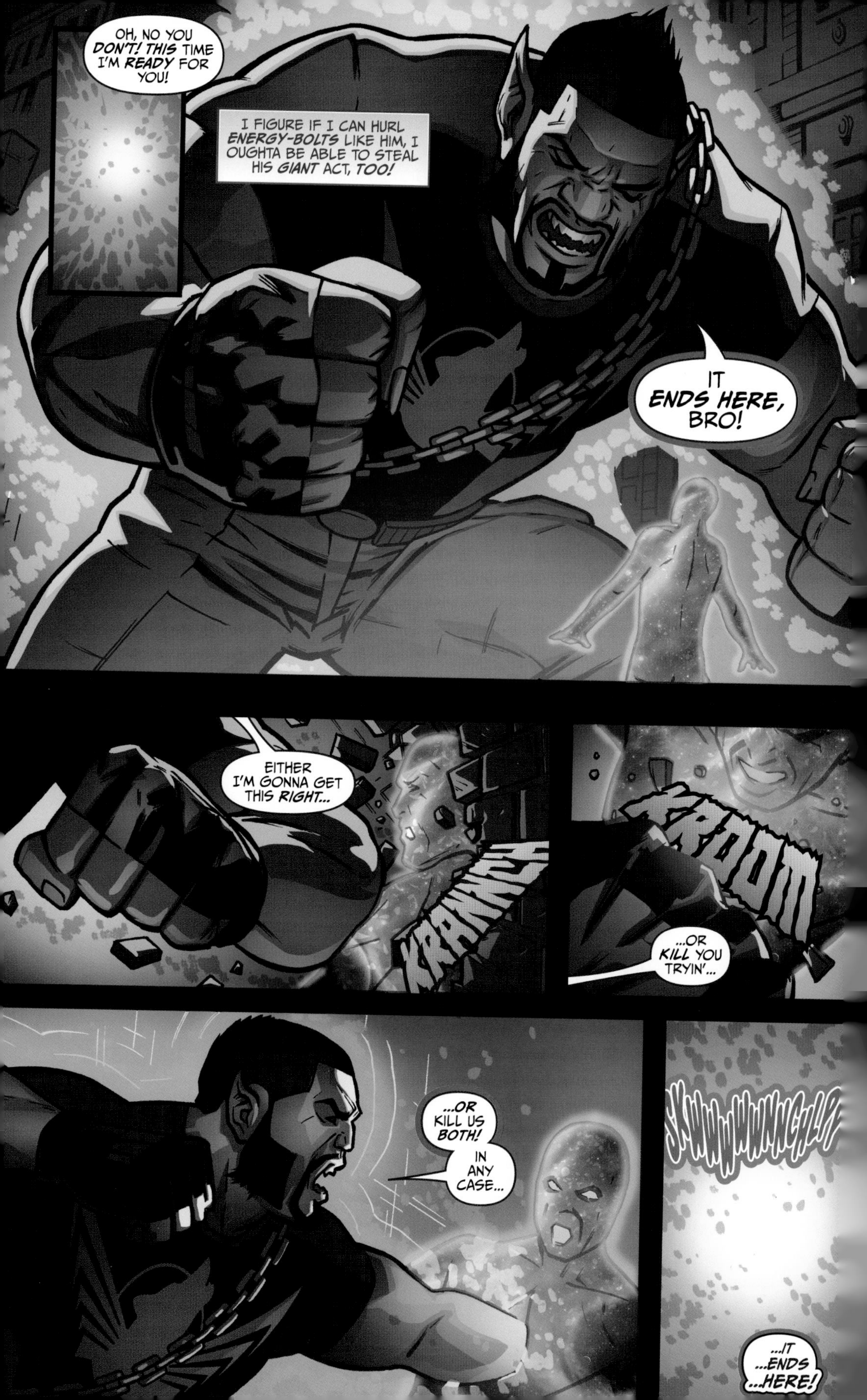
OH, NO YOU DON'T! THIS TIME I'M READY FOR YOU!
I FIGURE IF I CAN HURL ENERGY-BOLTS LIKE HIM, I OUGHTA BE ABLE TO STEAL HIS GIANT ACT, TOO!
IT ENDS HERE, BRO!
EITHER I'M GONNA GET THIS RIGHT...
KRANNCH
KROOM
...OR KILL YOU TRYIN'...
...OR KILL US BOTH!
IN ANY CASE...
SKWWWWWWNCHLR
...IT ...ENDS ...HERE!

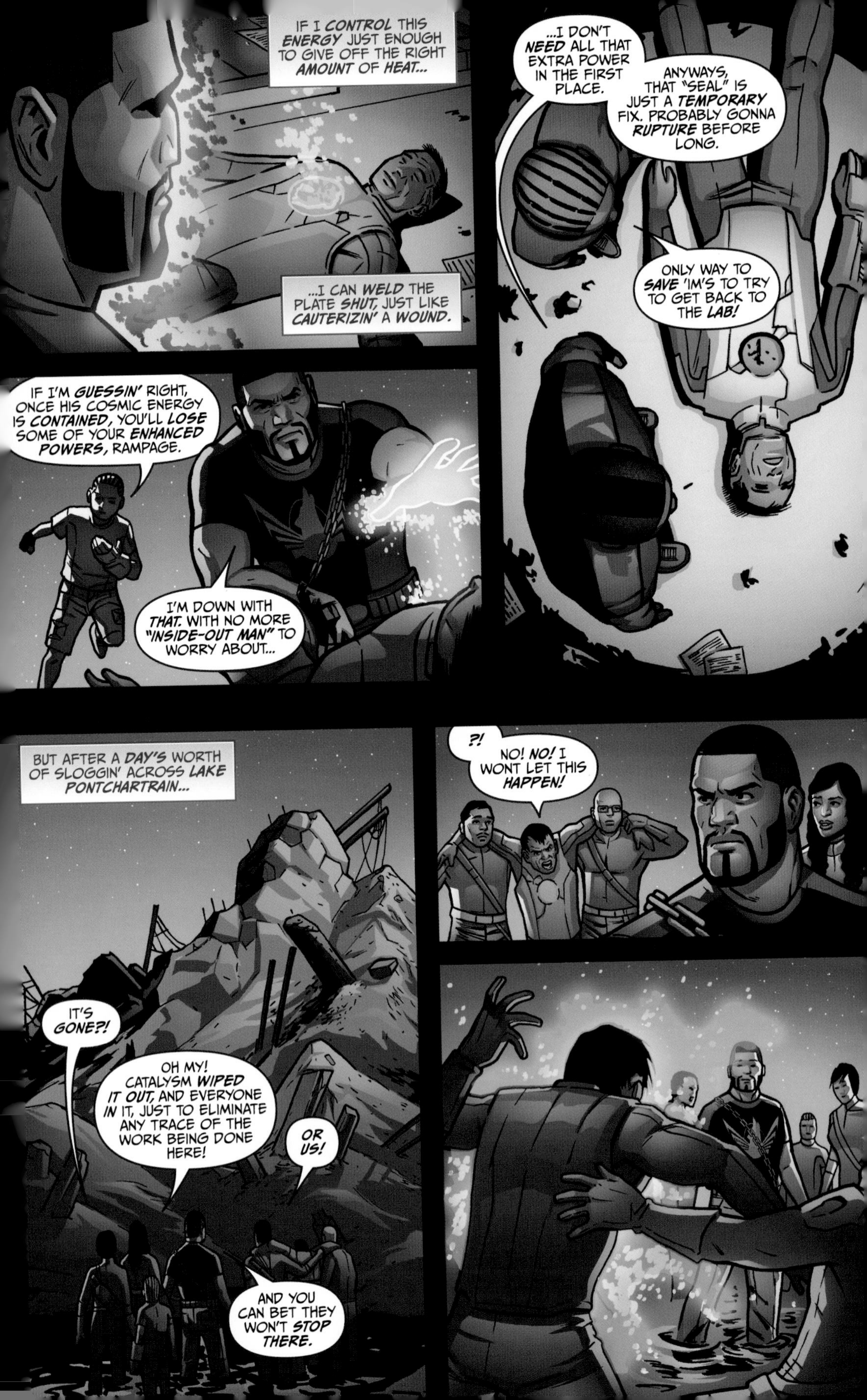
IF I CONTROL THIS ENERGY JUST ENOUGH TO GIVE OFF THE RIGHT AMOUNT OF HEAT...
...I CAN WELD THE PLATE SHUT, JUST LIKE CAUTERIZIN' A WOUND.
IF I'M GUESSIN' RIGHT, ONCE HIS COSMIC ENERGY IS CONTAINED, YOU'LL LOSE SOME OF YOUR ENHANCED POWERS, RAMPAGE.
I'M DOWN WITH THAT. WITH NO MORE "INSIDE-OUT MAN" TO WORRY ABOUT...
...I DON'T NEED ALL THAT EXTRA POWER IN THE FIRST PLACE.
ANYWAYS, THAT "SEAL" IS JUST A TEMPORARY FIX. PROBABLY GONNA RUPTURE BEFORE LONG.
ONLY WAY TO SAVE 'IM'S TO TRY TO GET BACK TO THE LAB!
BUT AFTER A DAY'S WORTH OF SLOGGIN' ACROSS LAKE PONTCHARTRAIN...
IT'S GONE?!
OH MY! CATALYSM WIPED IT OUT, AND EVERYONE IN IT, JUST TO ELIMINATE ANY TRACE OF THE WORK BEING DONE HERE!
OR US!
AND YOU CAN BET THEY WON'T STOP THERE.
?!
NO! NO! I WONT LET THIS HAPPEN!

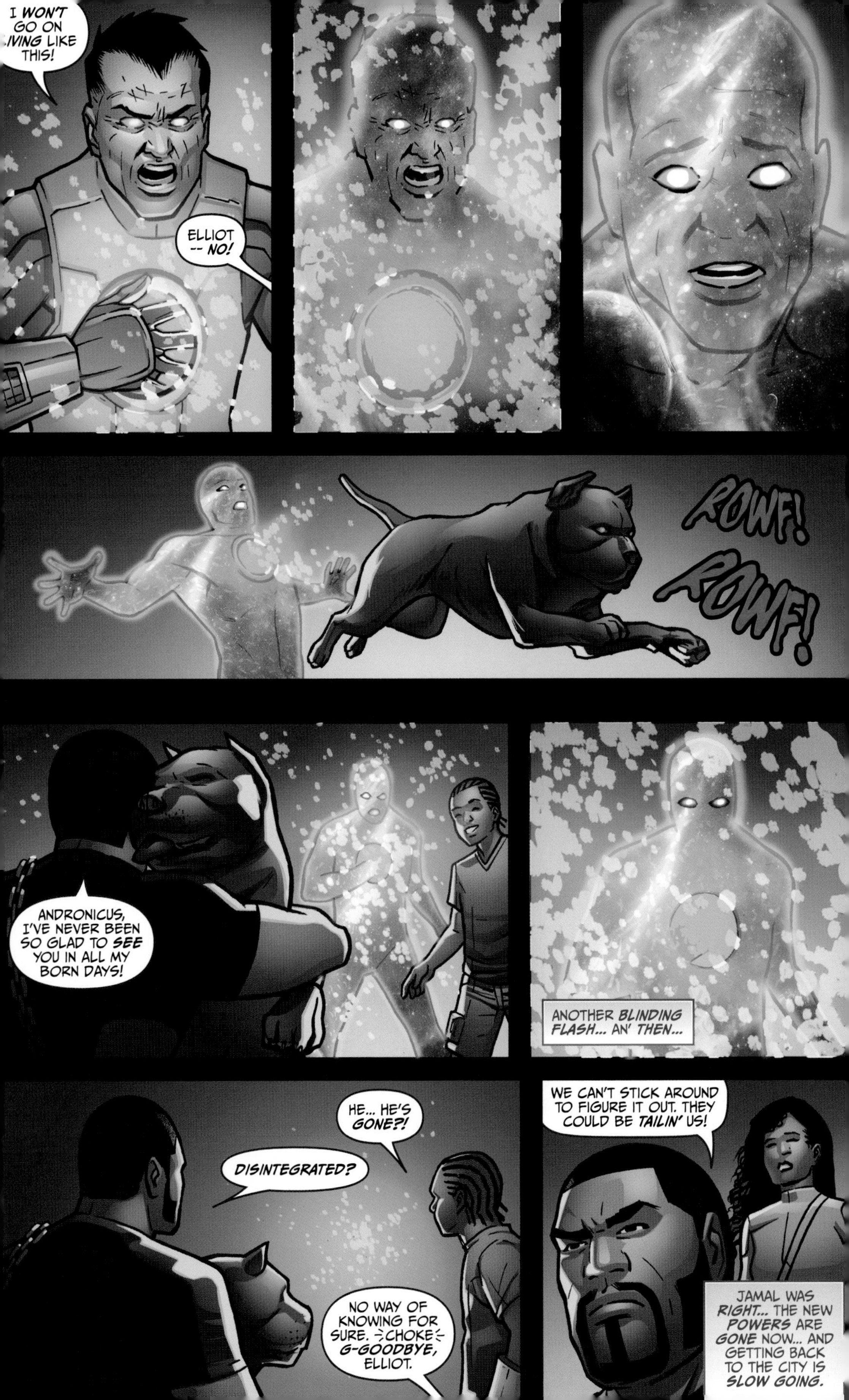
I WON'T GO ON LIVING LIKE THIS!
ELLIOT -- NO!
ROWF!
ROWF!
ANDRONICUS, I'VE NEVER BEEN SO GLAD TO SEE YOU IN ALL MY BORN DAYS!
ANOTHER BLINDING FLASH... AN' THEN...
HE... HE'S GONE?!
DISINTEGRATED?
NO WAY OF KNOWING FOR SURE. ⸗CHOKE⸗ G-GOODBYE, ELLIOT.
WE CAN'T STICK AROUND TO FIGURE IT OUT. THEY COULD BE TAILIN' US!
JAMAL WAS RIGHT... THE NEW POWERS ARE GONE NOW... AND GETTING BACK TO THE CITY IS SLOW GOING.

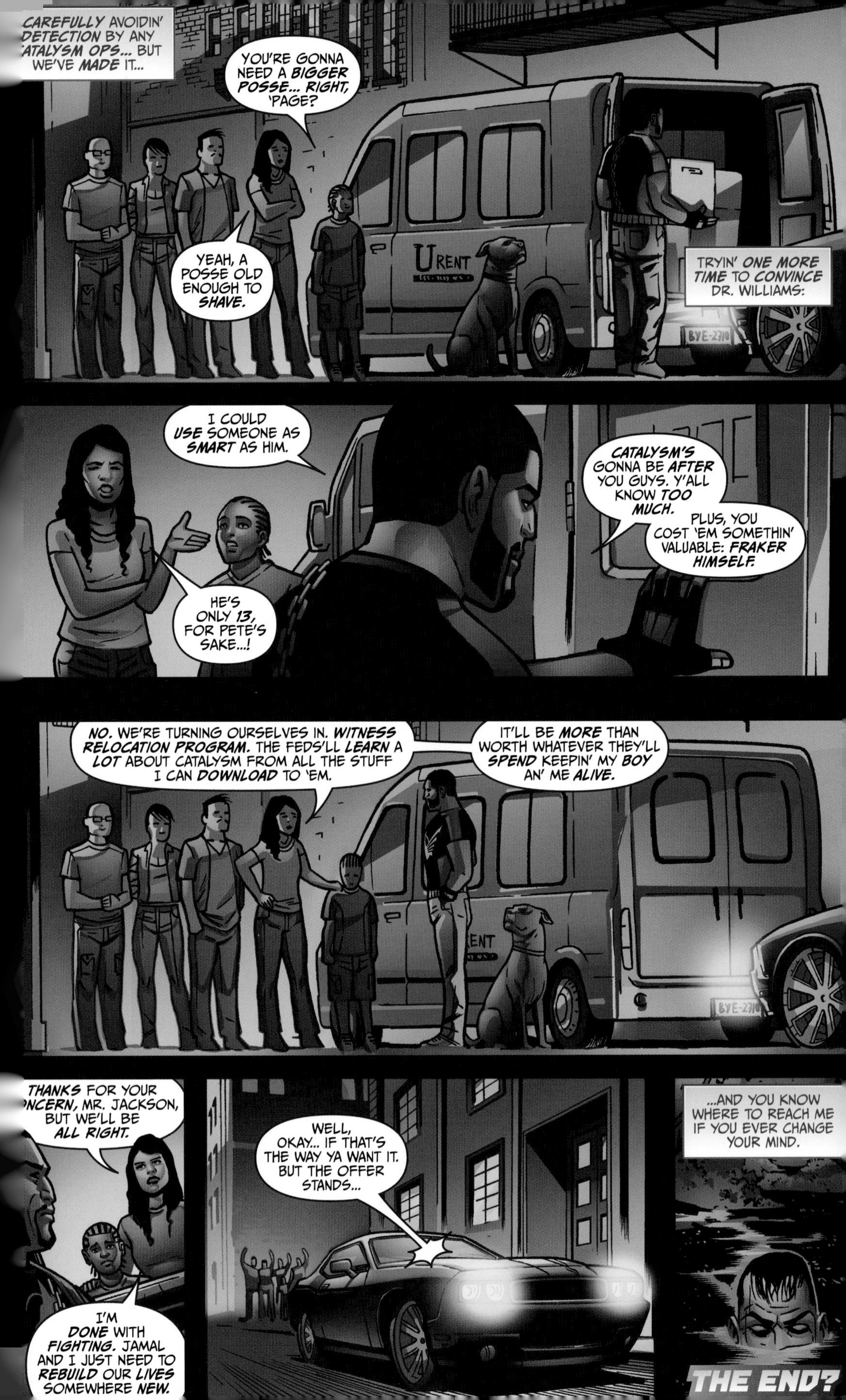
CAREFULLY AVOIDIN' DETECTION BY ANY CATALYSM OPS... BUT WE'VE MADE IT...
YOU'RE GONNA NEED A BIGGER POSSE... RIGHT, 'PAGE?
YEAH, A POSSE OLD ENOUGH TO SHAVE.
URENT
BYE-2710
TRYIN' ONE MORE TIME TO CONVINCE DR. WILLIAMS:
I COULD USE SOMEONE AS SMART AS HIM.
CATALYSM'S GONNA BE AFTER YOU GUYS. Y'ALL KNOW TOO MUCH.
PLUS, YOU COST 'EM SOMETHIN' VALUABLE: FRAKER HIMSELF.
HE'S ONLY 13, FOR PETE'S SAKE...!
NO. WE'RE TURNING OURSELVES IN. WITNESS RELOCATION PROGRAM. THE FEDS'LL LEARN A LOT ABOUT CATALYSM FROM ALL THE STUFF I CAN DOWNLOAD TO 'EM.
IT'LL BE MORE THAN WORTH WHATEVER THEY'LL SPEND KEEPIN' MY BOY AN' ME ALIVE.
BYE-2710
THANKS FOR YOUR CONCERN, MR. JACKSON, BUT WE'LL BE ALL RIGHT.
I'M DONE WITH FIGHTING. JAMAL AND I JUST NEED TO REBUILD OUR LIVES SOMEWHERE NEW.
WELL, OKAY... IF THAT'S THE WAY YA WANT IT. BUT THE OFFER STANDS...
...AND YOU KNOW WHERE TO REACH ME IF YOU EVER CHANGE YOUR MIND.
THE END?

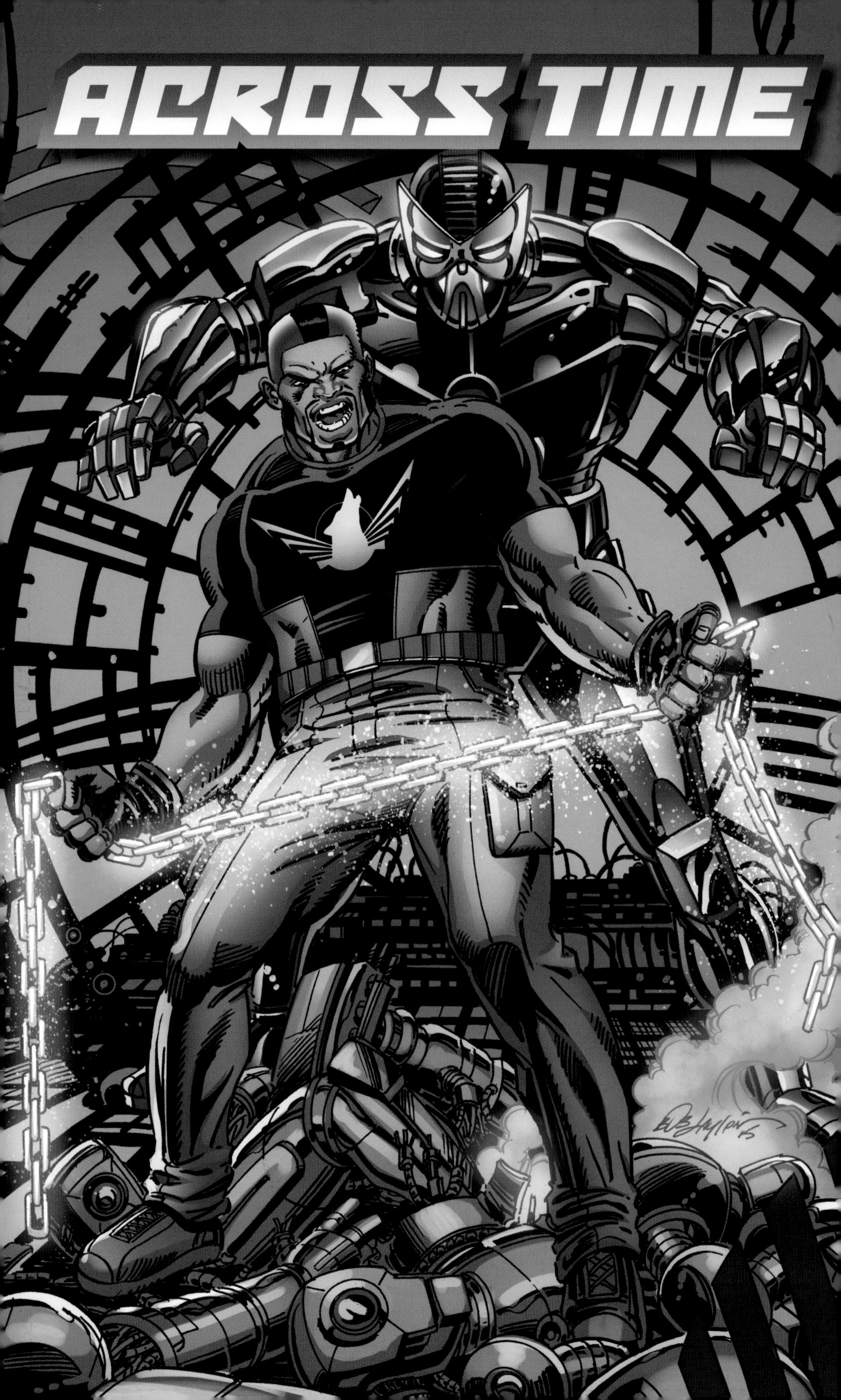
ACROSS TIME

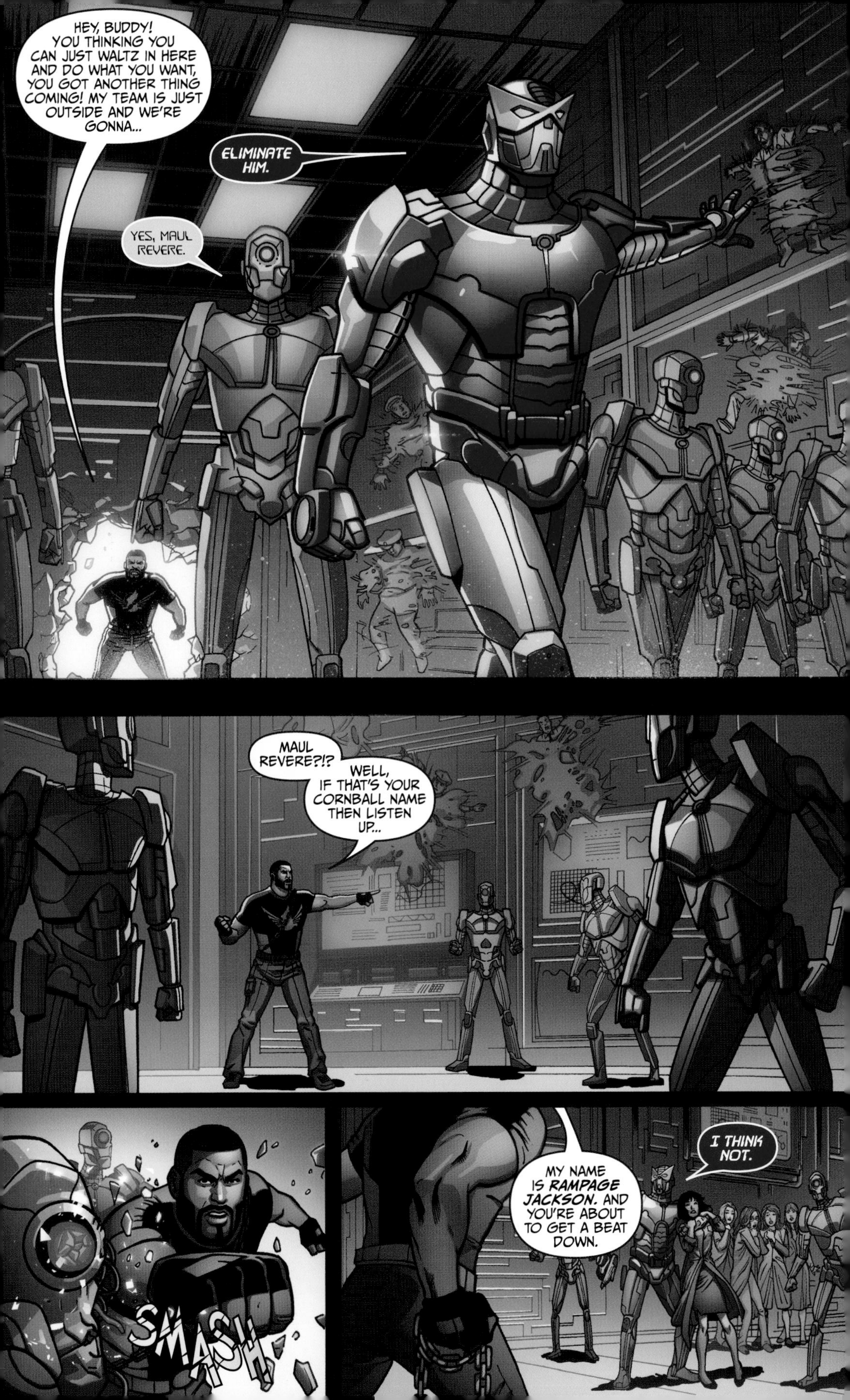
HEY, BUDDY! YOU THINKING YOU CAN JUST WALTZ IN HERE AND DO WHAT YOU WANT, YOU GOT ANOTHER THING COMING! MY TEAM IS JUST OUTSIDE AND WE'RE GONNA...
ELIMINATE HIM.
YES, MAUL REVERE.
MAUL REVERE?!? WELL, IF THAT'S YOUR CORNBALL NAME THEN LISTEN UP...
SMASH
MY NAME IS RAMPAGE JACKSON. AND YOU'RE ABOUT TO GET A BEAT DOWN.
I THINK NOT.

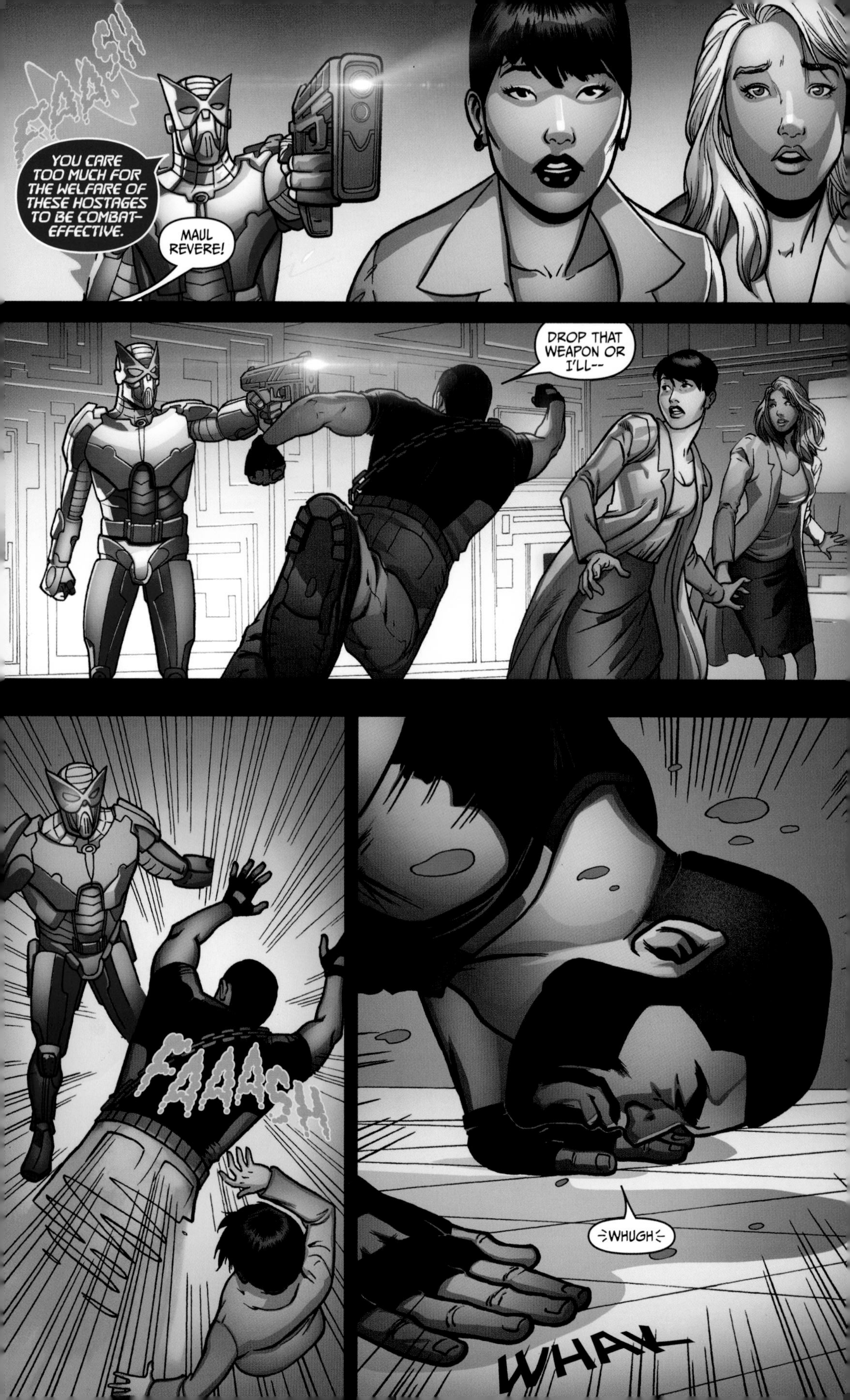
FAAASH
YOU CARE TOO MUCH FOR THE WELFARE OF THESE HOSTAGES TO BE COMBAT-EFFECTIVE.
MAUL REVERE!
DROP THAT WEAPON OR I'LL--
FAAASH
WHUGH
WHAK

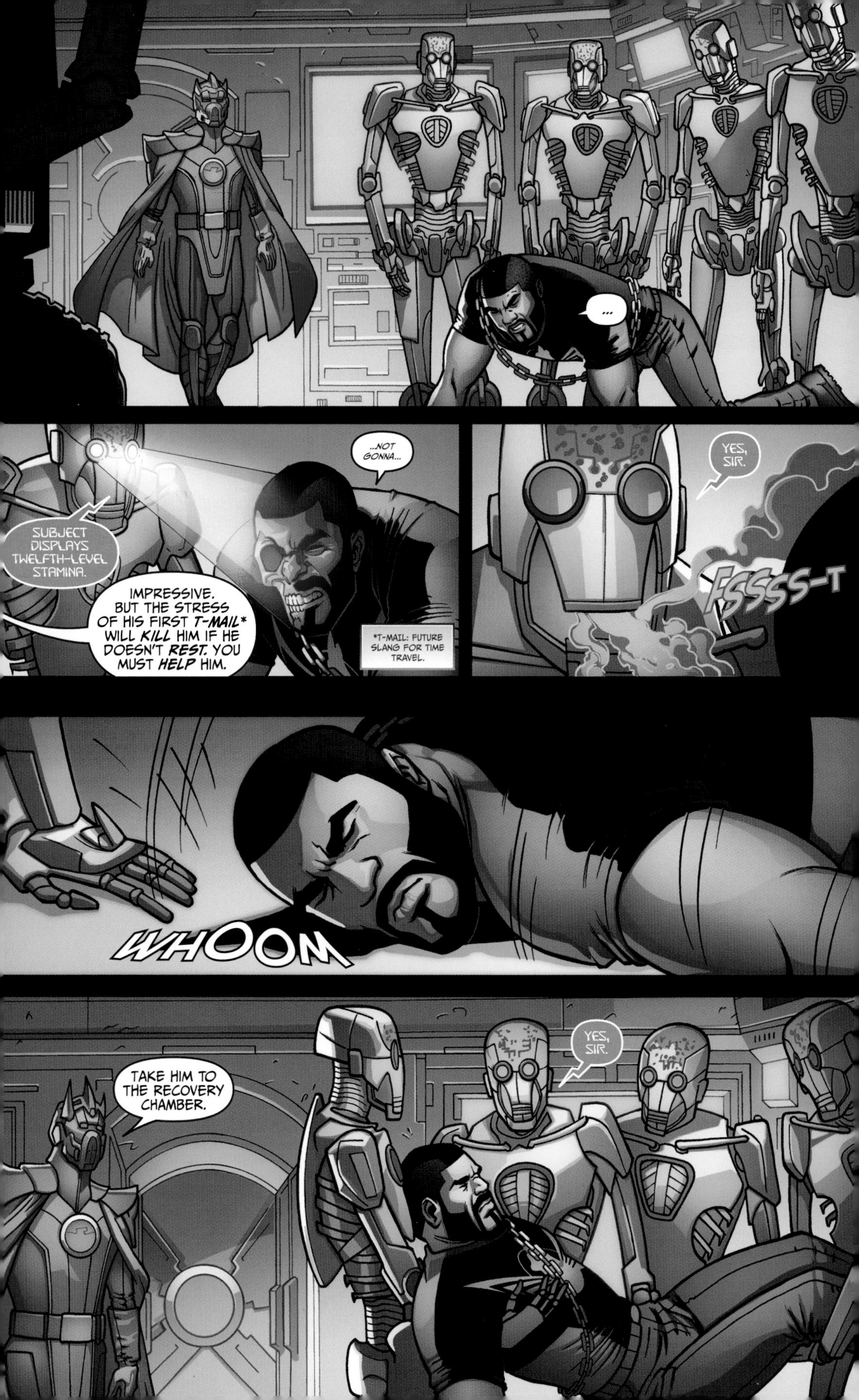
...
...NOT GONNA...
SUBJECT DISPLAYS TWELFTH-LEVEL STAMINA.
IMPRESSIVE. BUT THE STRESS OF HIS FIRST T-MAIL* WILL KILL HIM IF HE DOESN'T REST. YOU MUST HELP HIM.
*T-MAIL: FUTURE SLANG FOR TIME TRAVEL.
YES, SIR.
FSSSS-T
WHOOM
TAKE HIM TO THE RECOVERY CHAMBER.
YES, SIR.

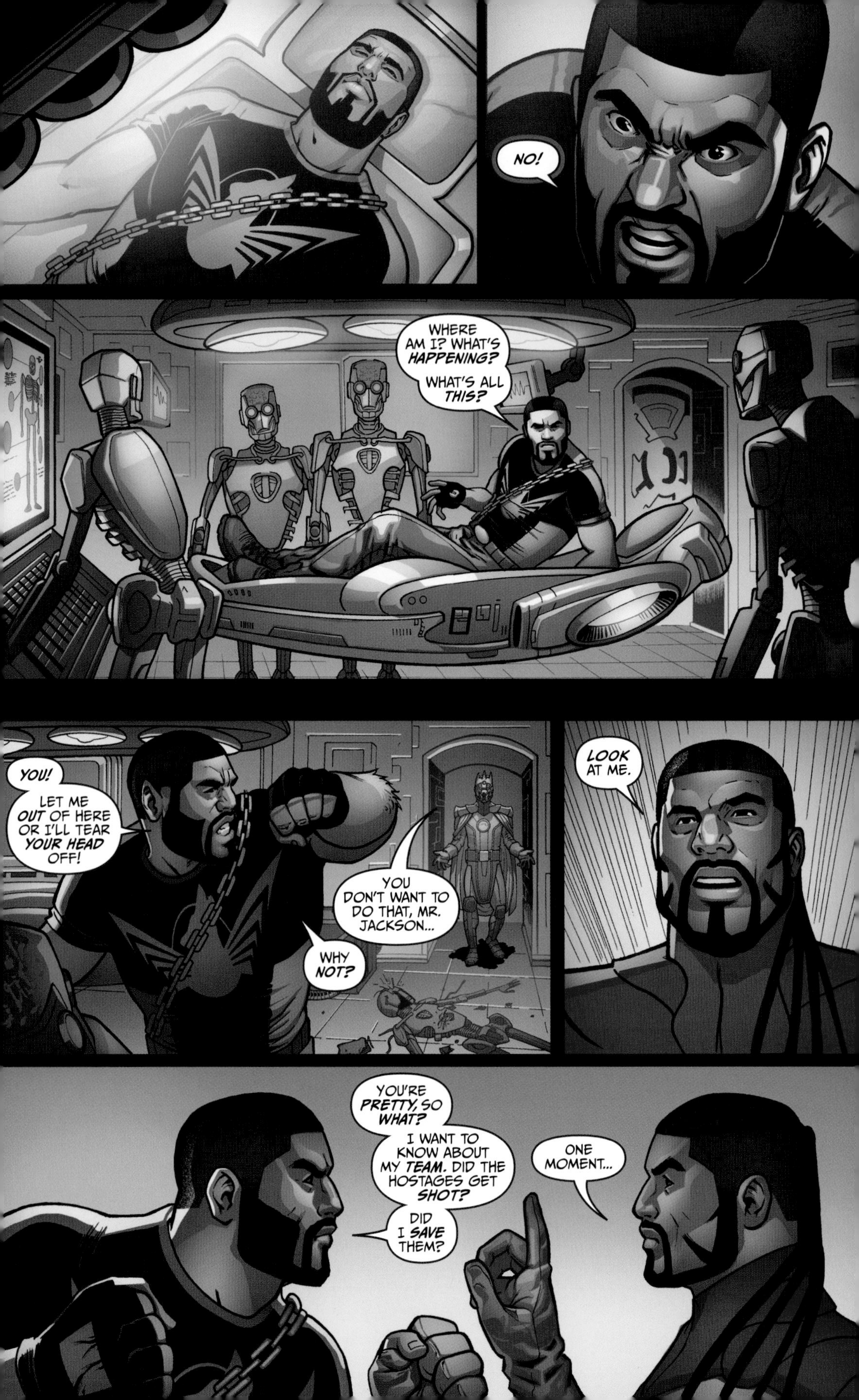
NO!
WHERE AM I? WHAT'S HAPPENING?
WHAT'S ALL THIS?
YOU!
LET ME OUT OF HERE OR I'LL TEAR YOUR HEAD OFF!
YOU DON'T WANT TO DO THAT, MR. JACKSON...
WHY NOT?
LOOK AT ME.
YOU'RE PRETTY, SO WHAT?
I WANT TO KNOW ABOUT MY TEAM. DID THE HOSTAGES GET SHOT?
DID I SAVE THEM?
ONE MOMENT...

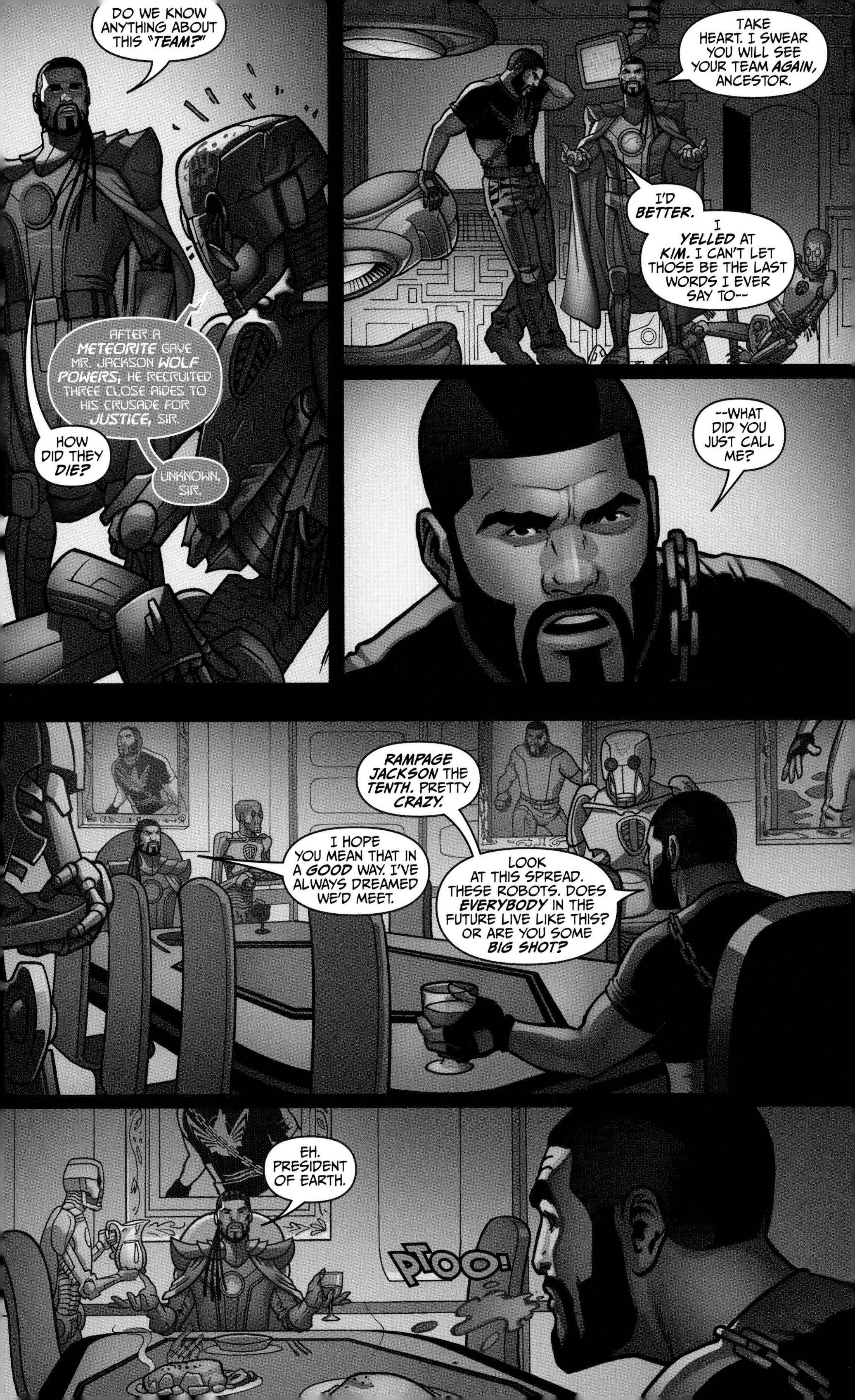
DO WE KNOW ANYTHING ABOUT THIS "TEAM?"
AFTER A METEORITE GAVE MR. JACKSON WOLF POWERS, HE RECRUITED THREE CLOSE AIDES TO HIS CRUSADE FOR JUSTICE, SIR.
HOW DID THEY DIE?
UNKNOWN, SIR.
TAKE HEART. I SWEAR YOU WILL SEE YOUR TEAM AGAIN, ANCESTOR.
I'D BETTER.
I YELLED AT KIM. I CAN'T LET THOSE BE THE LAST WORDS I EVER SAY TO--
--WHAT DID YOU JUST CALL ME?
RAMPAGE JACKSON THE TENTH. PRETTY CRAZY.
I HOPE YOU MEAN THAT IN A GOOD WAY. I'VE ALWAYS DREAMED WE'D MEET.
LOOK AT THIS SPREAD. THESE ROBOTS. DOES EVERYBODY IN THE FUTURE LIVE LIKE THIS? OR ARE YOU SOME BIG SHOT?
EH. PRESIDENT OF EARTH.
PTOO!

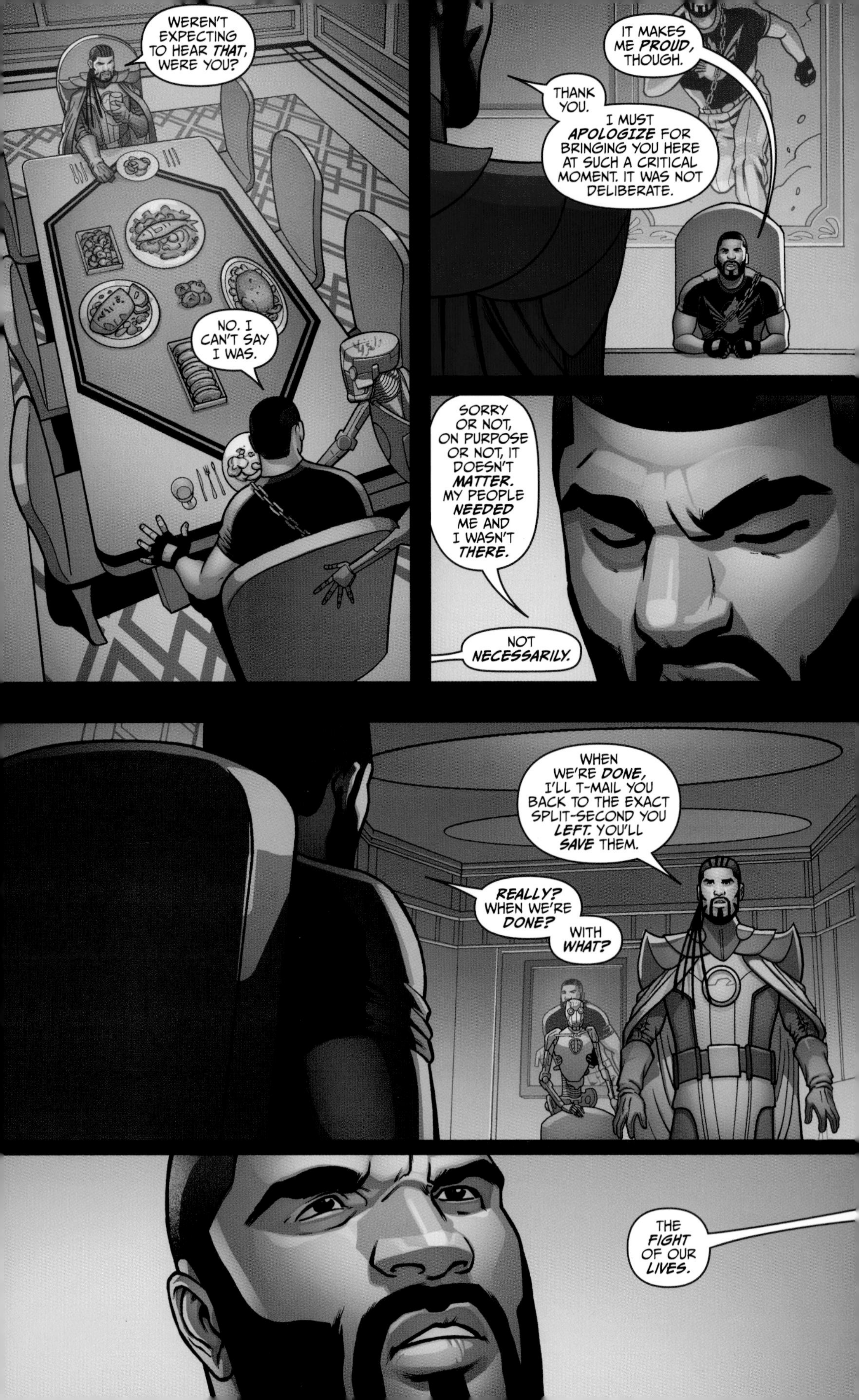
WEREN'T EXPECTING TO HEAR THAT, WERE YOU?
NO. I CAN'T SAY I WAS.
IT MAKES ME PROUD, THOUGH.
THANK YOU.
I MUST APOLOGIZE FOR BRINGING YOU HERE AT SUCH A CRITICAL MOMENT. IT WAS NOT DELIBERATE.
SORRY OR NOT, ON PURPOSE OR NOT, IT DOESN'T MATTER. MY PEOPLE NEEDED ME AND I WASN'T THERE.
NOT NECESSARILY.
WHEN WE'RE DONE, I'LL T-MAIL YOU BACK TO THE EXACT SPLIT-SECOND YOU LEFT. YOU'LL SAVE THEM.
REALLY? WHEN WE'RE DONE?
WITH WHAT?
THE FIGHT OF OUR LIVES.

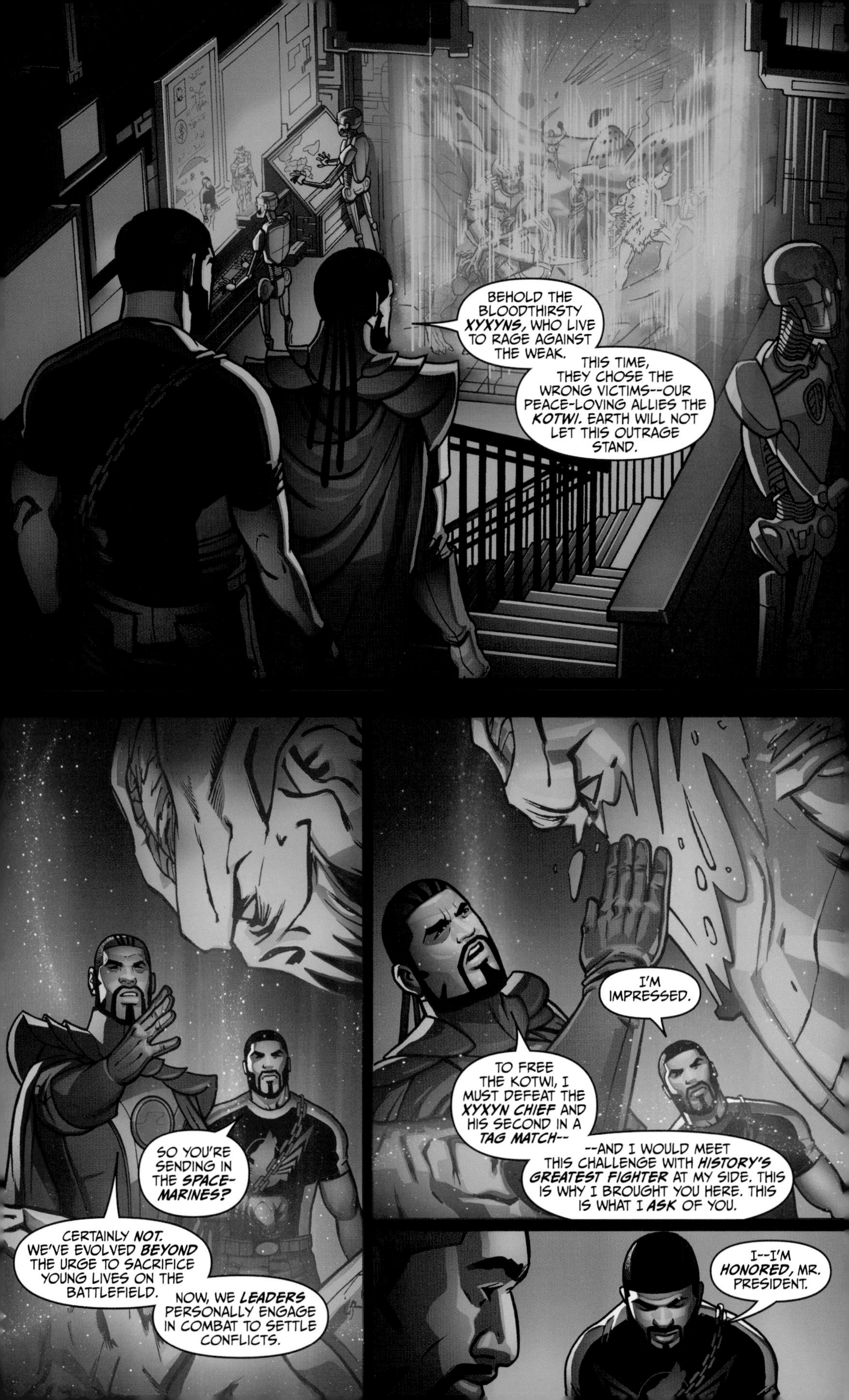
BEHOLD THE BLOODTHIRSTY XYXYNS, WHO LIVE TO RAGE AGAINST THE WEAK.
THIS TIME, THEY CHOSE THE WRONG VICTIMS--OUR PEACE-LOVING ALLIES THE KOTWI. EARTH WILL NOT LET THIS OUTRAGE STAND.
SO YOU'RE SENDING IN THE SPACE-MARINES?
CERTAINLY NOT. WE'VE EVOLVED BEYOND THE URGE TO SACRIFICE YOUNG LIVES ON THE BATTLEFIELD.
NOW, WE LEADERS PERSONALLY ENGAGE IN COMBAT TO SETTLE CONFLICTS.
I'M IMPRESSED.
TO FREE THE KOTWI, I MUST DEFEAT THE XYXYN CHIEF AND HIS SECOND IN A TAG MATCH--
--AND I WOULD MEET THIS CHALLENGE WITH HISTORY'S GREATEST FIGHTER AT MY SIDE. THIS IS WHY I BROUGHT YOU HERE. THIS IS WHAT I ASK OF YOU.
I--I'M HONORED, MR. PRESIDENT.

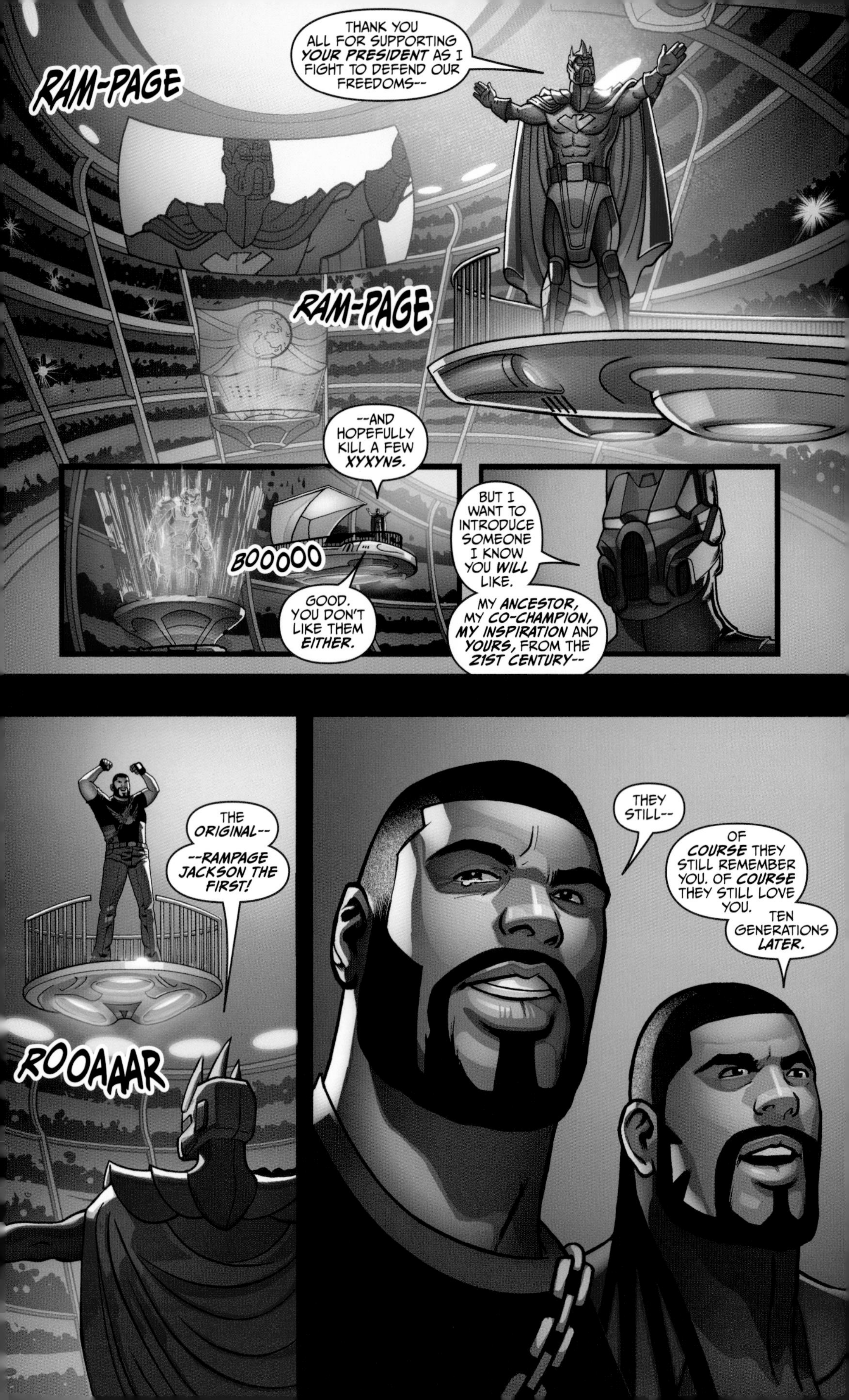
RAM-PAGE
THANK YOU ALL FOR SUPPORTING YOUR PRESIDENT AS I FIGHT TO DEFEND OUR FREEDOMS--
RAM-PAGE
--AND HOPEFULLY KILL A FEW XYXYNS.
BOOOOO
GOOD. YOU DON'T LIKE THEM EITHER.
BUT I WANT TO INTRODUCE SOMEONE I KNOW YOU WILL LIKE.
MY ANCESTOR, MY CO-CHAMPION, MY INSPIRATION AND YOURS, FROM THE 21ST CENTURY--
THE ORIGINAL--
--RAMPAGE JACKSON THE FIRST!
ROOAAAR
THEY STILL--
OF COURSE THEY STILL REMEMBER YOU. OF COURSE THEY STILL LOVE YOU.
TEN GENERATIONS LATER.

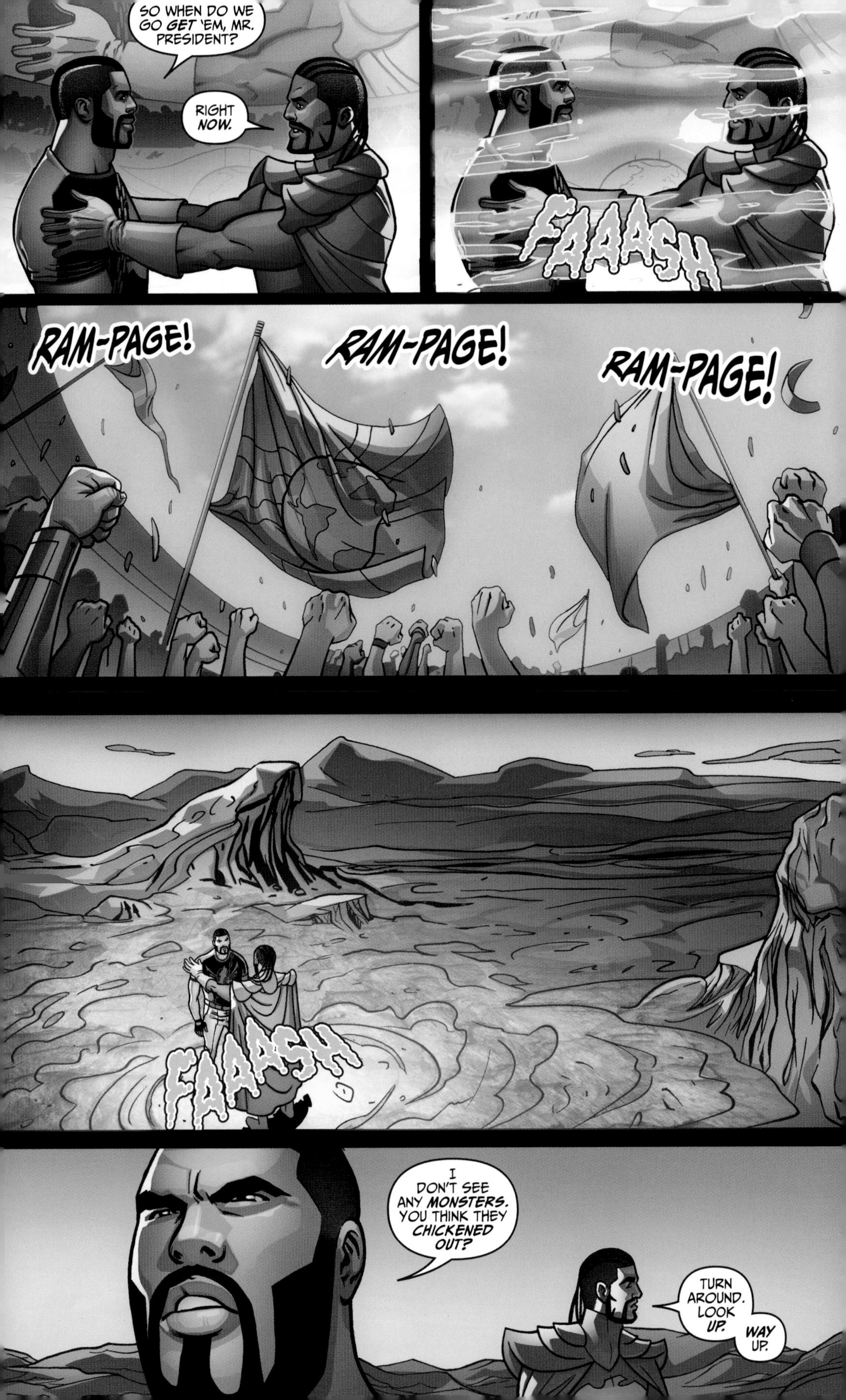
SO WHEN DO WE GO GET 'EM, MR. PRESIDENT?
RIGHT NOW.
FAAASH
RAM-PAGE!
RAM-PAGE!
RAM-PAGE!
FAAASH
I DON'T SEE ANY MONSTERS. YOU THINK THEY CHICKENED OUT?
TURN AROUND. LOOK UP.
WAY UP.

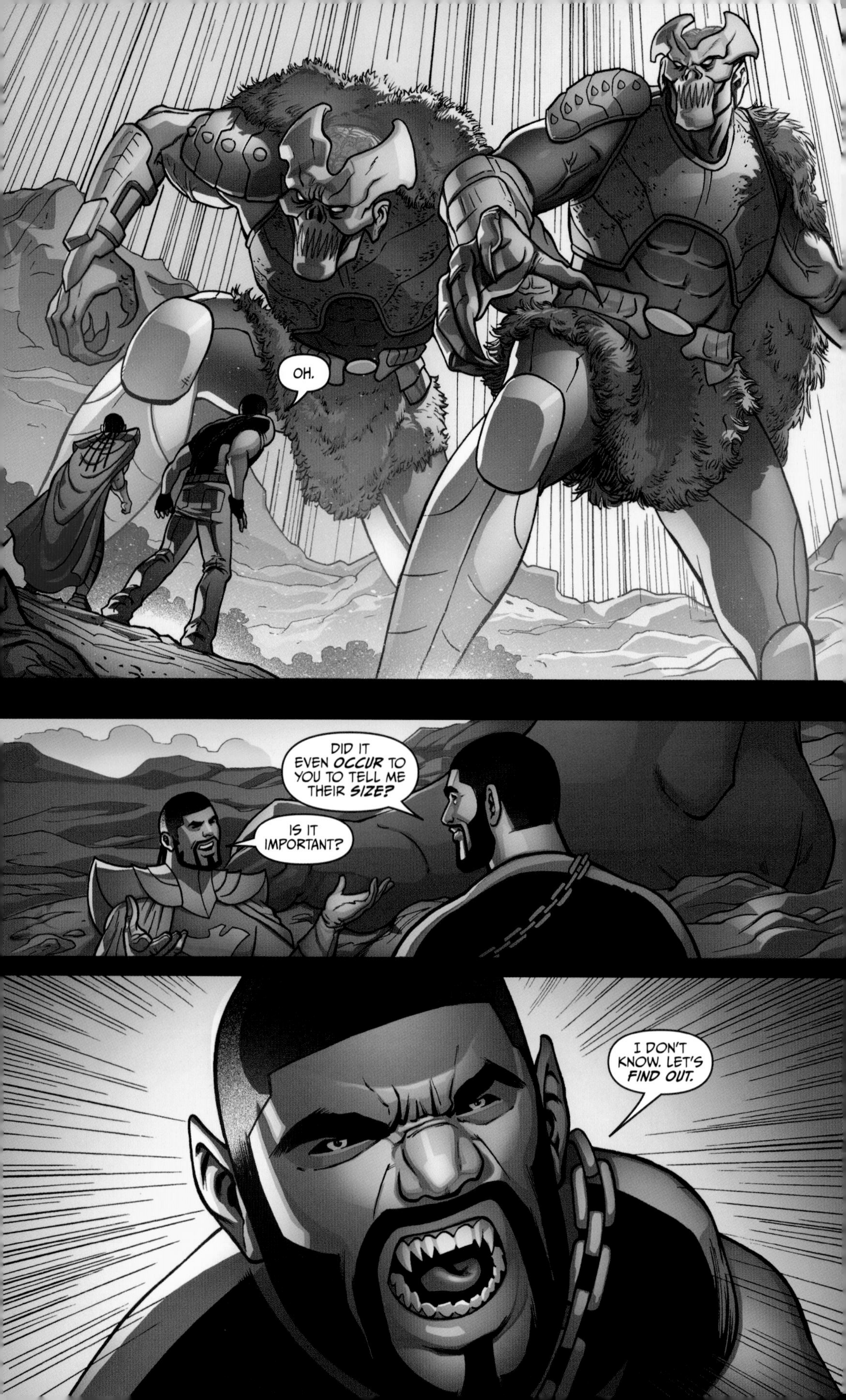
OH.
DID IT EVEN OCCUR TO YOU TO TELL ME THEIR SIZE?
IS IT IMPORTANT?
I DON'T KNOW. LET'S FIND OUT.

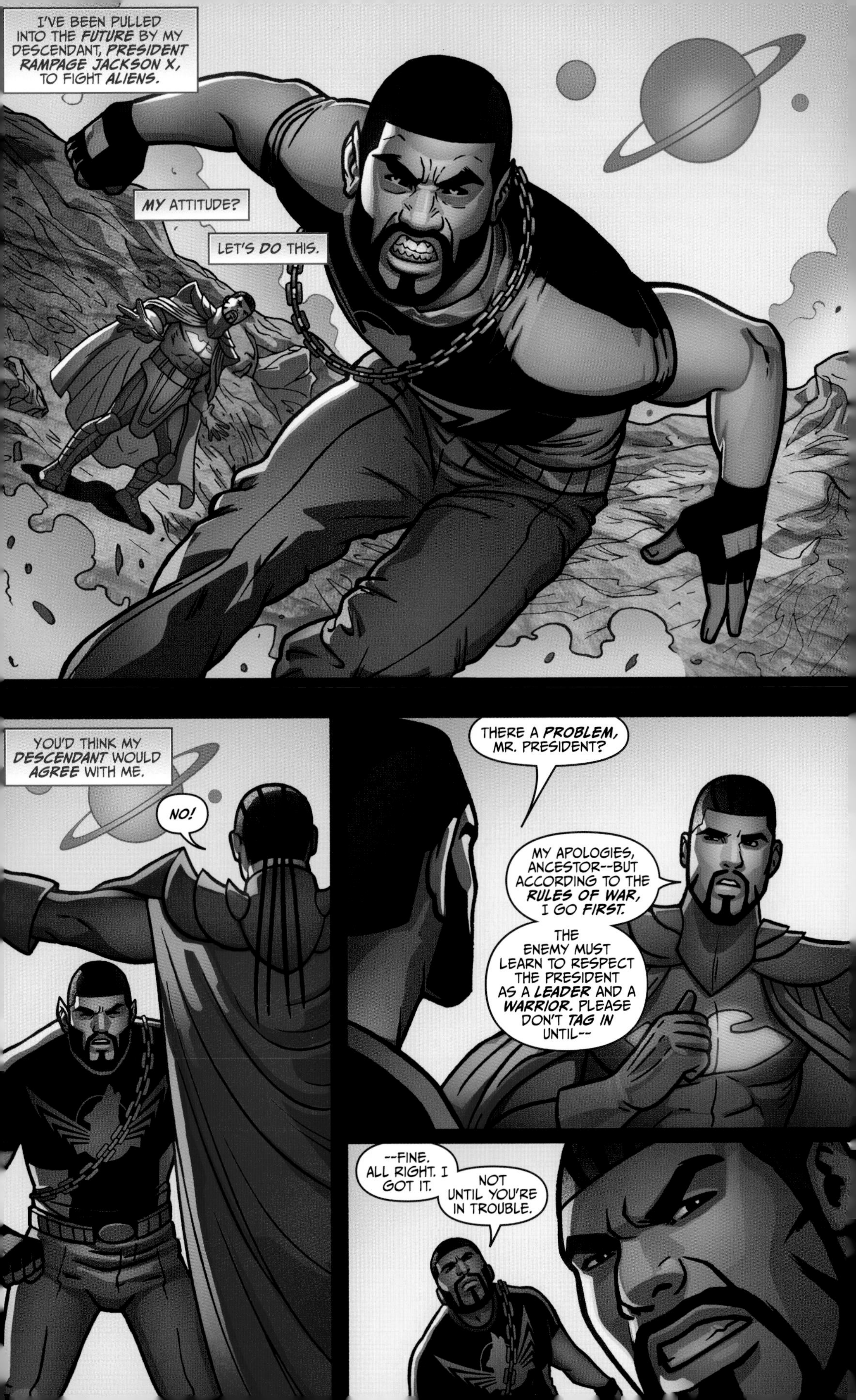

I'VE BEEN PULLED INTO THE FUTURE BY MY DESCENDANT, PRESIDENT RAMPAGE JACKSON X, TO FIGHT ALIENS.
MY ATTITUDE?
LET'S DO THIS.
YOU'D THINK MY DESCENDANT WOULD AGREE WITH ME.
NO!
THERE A PROBLEM, MR. PRESIDENT?
MY APOLOGIES, ANCESTOR--BUT ACCORDING TO THE RULES OF WAR, I GO FIRST.
THE ENEMY MUST LEARN TO RESPECT THE PRESIDENT AS A LEADER AND A WARRIOR. PLEASE DON'T TAG IN UNTIL--
--FINE. ALL RIGHT. I GOT IT.
NOT UNTIL YOU'RE IN TROUBLE.

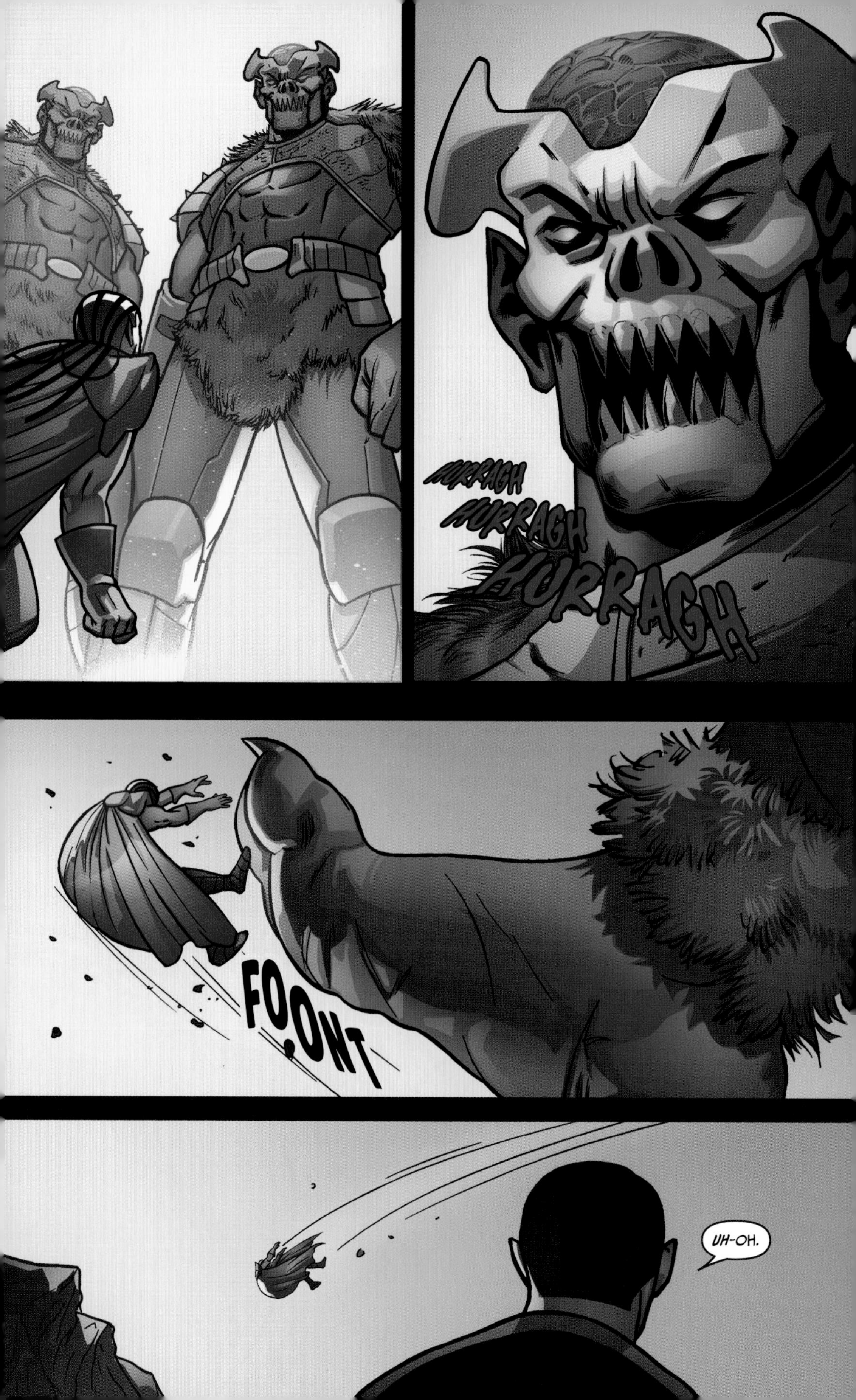
HURRAGH
HURRAGH
HURRAGH
FOOOMT
UH-OH.

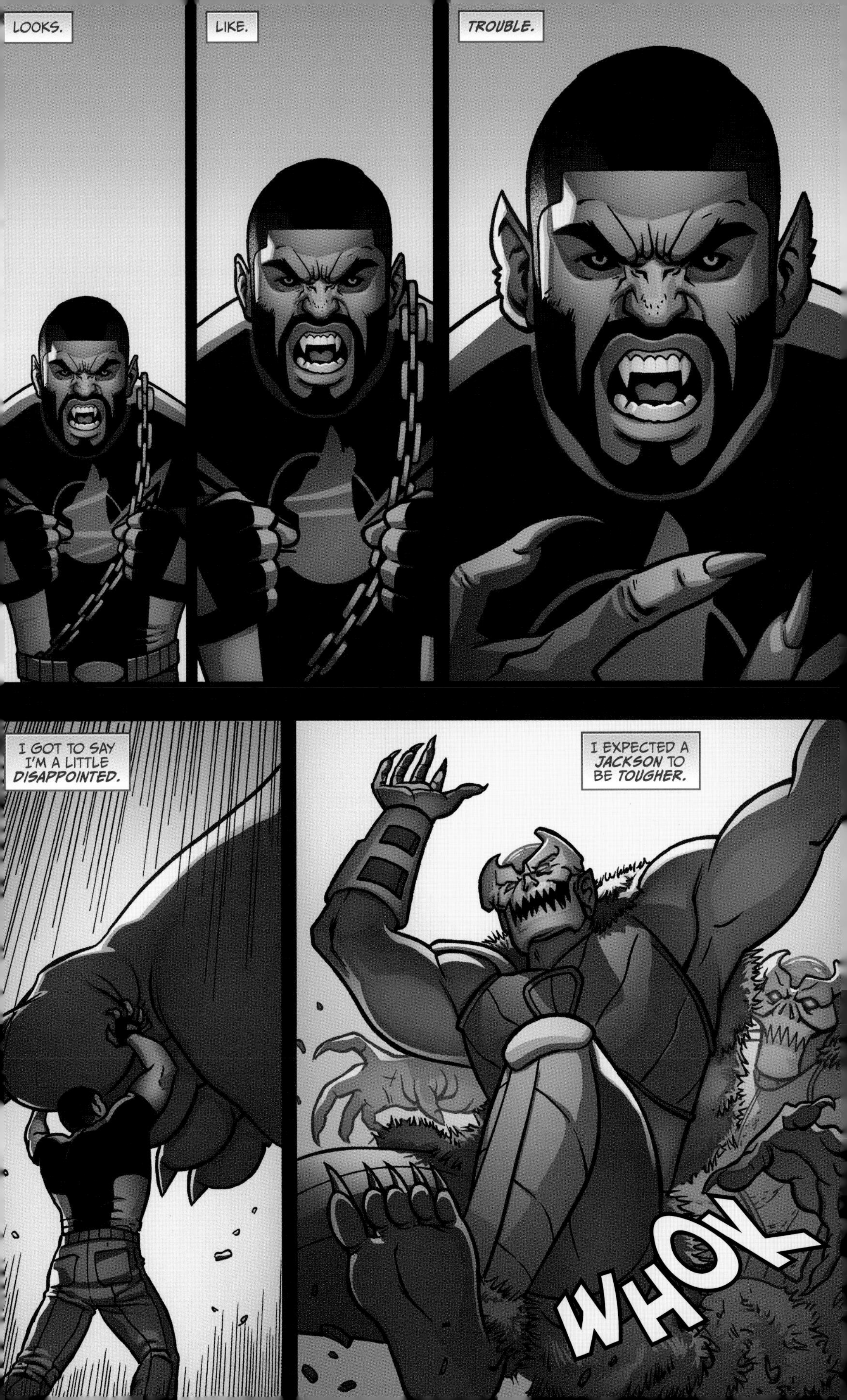

LOOKS.
LIKE.
TROUBLE.
I GOT TO SAY I'M A LITTLE DISAPPOINTED.
I EXPECTED A JACKSON TO BE TOUGHER.
WHOK

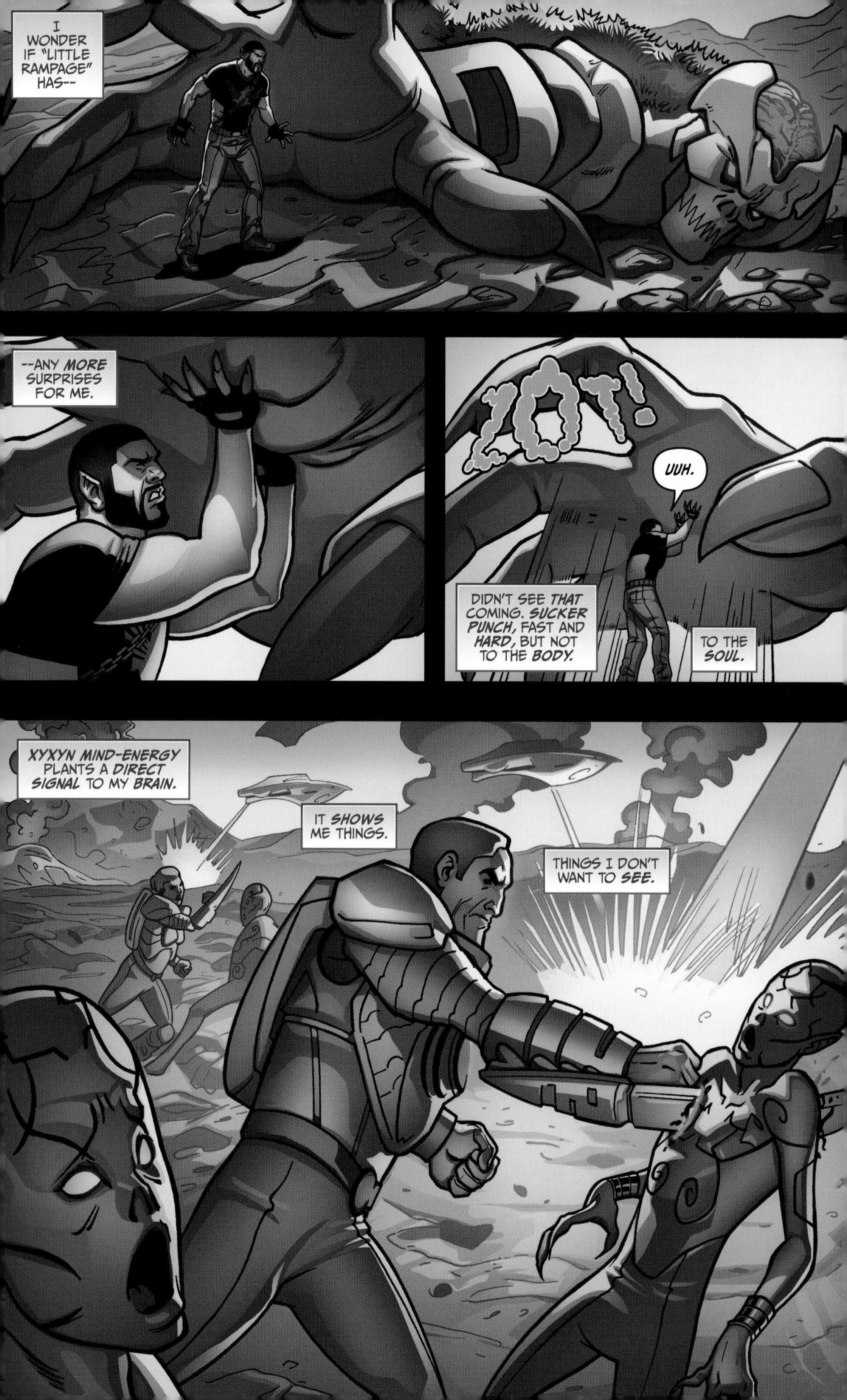
I WONDER IF "LITTLE RAMPAGE" HAS--
--ANY MORE SURPRISES FOR ME.
ZOT!
UUH.
DIDN'T SEE THAT COMING. SUCKER PUNCH, FAST AND HARD, BUT NOT TO THE BODY.
TO THE SOUL.
XYXYN MIND-ENERGY PLANTS A DIRECT SIGNAL TO MY BRAIN.
IT SHOWS ME THINGS.
THINGS I DON'T WANT TO SEE.

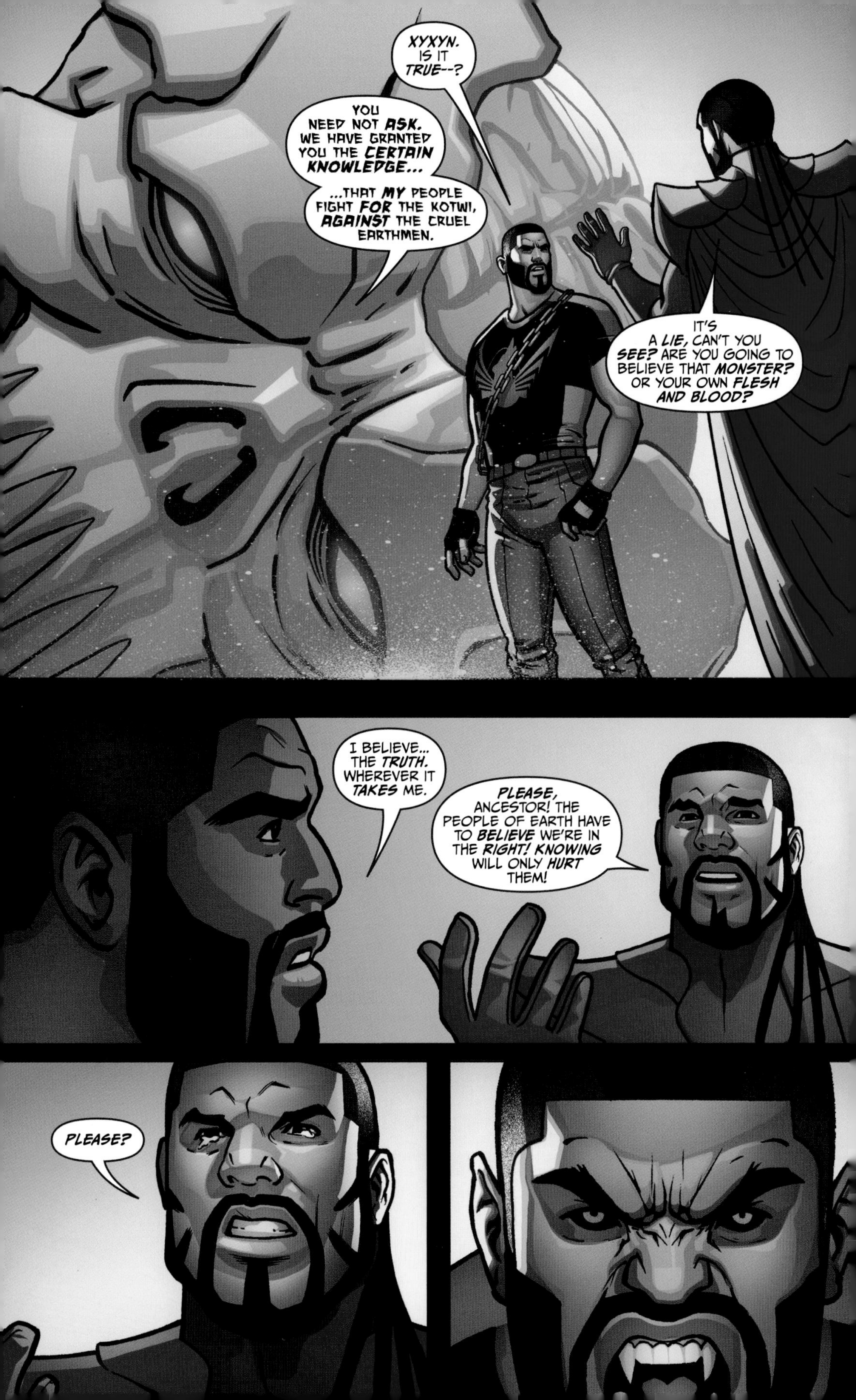
XYXYN. IS IT TRUE--?
YOU NEED NOT ASK. WE HAVE GRANTED YOU THE CERTAIN KNOWLEDGE...
...THAT MY PEOPLE FIGHT FOR THE KOTWI, AGAINST THE CRUEL EARTHMEN.
IT'S A LIE, CAN'T YOU SEE? ARE YOU GOING TO BELIEVE THAT MONSTER? OR YOUR OWN FLESH AND BLOOD?
I BELIEVE... THE TRUTH. WHEREVER IT TAKES ME.
PLEASE, ANCESTOR! THE PEOPLE OF EARTH HAVE TO BELIEVE WE'RE IN THE RIGHT! KNOWING WILL ONLY HURT THEM!
PLEASE?

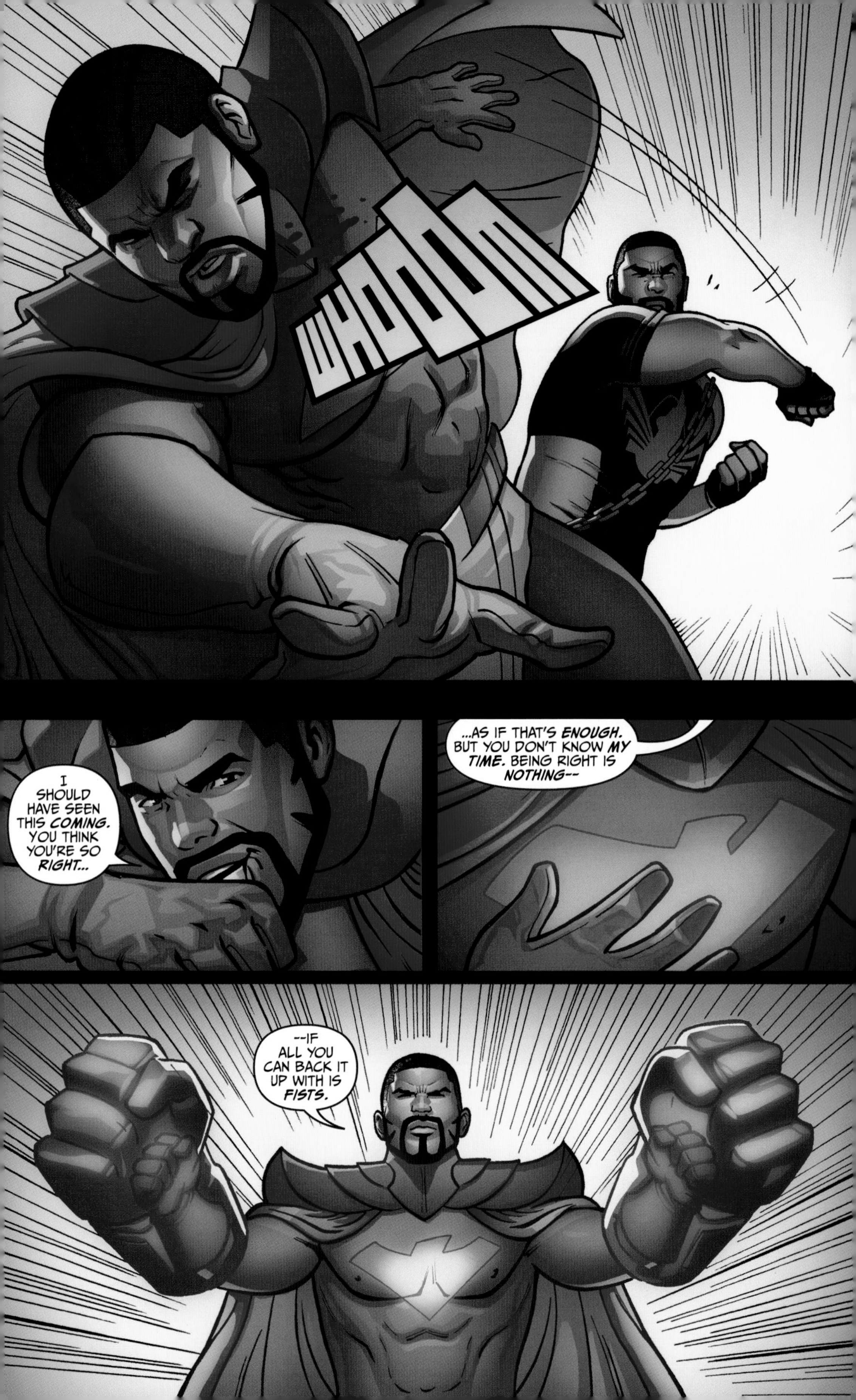
WHOOM
I SHOULD HAVE SEEN THIS COMING. YOU THINK YOU'RE SO RIGHT...
...AS IF THAT'S ENOUGH. BUT YOU DON'T KNOW MY TIME. BEING RIGHT IS NOTHING--
--IF ALL YOU CAN BACK IT UP WITH IS FISTS.

I HAVE OTHER METHODS --LIKE THESE EARTHQUAKE GLOVES!

SK-RAAK

THIS IS HOW YOU FIGHT AN UNARMED MAN?

I DO WHAT IT TAKES TO WIN, GRANDPA.

RUUMBL

NEVER THOUGHT I'D SEE A JACKSON CHEAT.

RUUMBL

AND I SURE NEVER THOUGHT TO DIE THIS WAY...

...GASPING FOR BREATH UNDER AN ALIEN BATTLEFIELD...

RAMPAGE JACKSON THE FIRST!

...HUNDREDS OF YEARS PAST MY FRESHNESS DATE.

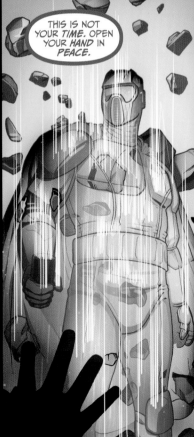

THIS IS NOT YOUR TIME. OPEN YOUR HAND IN PEACE.

NOW CLOSE YOUR FIST IN DEFIANCE.

THE SHOCK POD WILL HELP YOU DO WHAT MUST BE DONE.

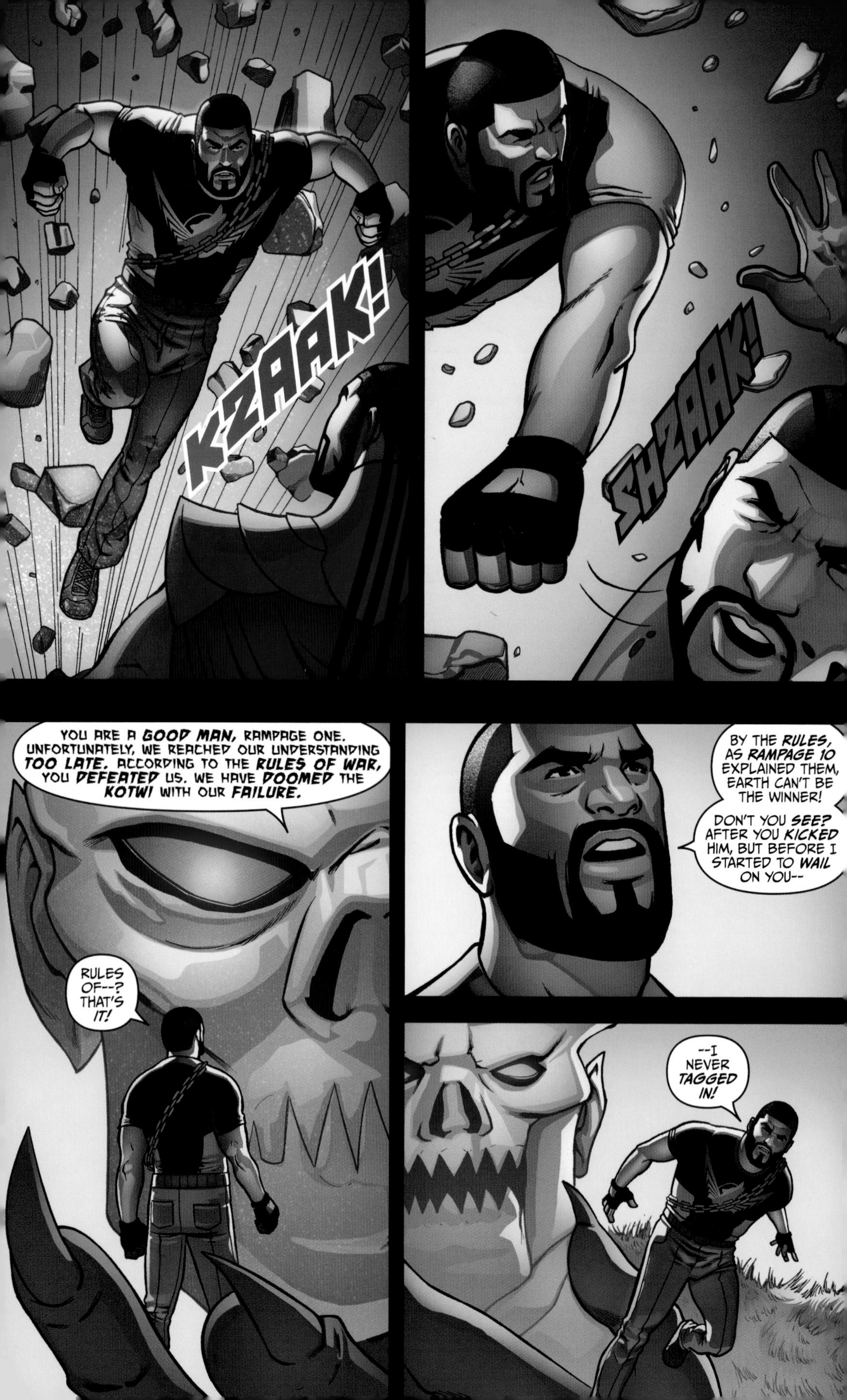
KZAAK!
SHZAAK!
YOU ARE A GOOD MAN, RAMPAGE ONE. UNFORTUNATELY, WE REACHED OUR UNDERSTANDING TOO LATE. ACCORDING TO THE RULES OF WAR, YOU DEFEATED US. WE HAVE DOOMED THE KOTWI WITH OUR FAILURE.
RULES OF--? THAT'S IT!
BY THE RULES, AS RAMPAGE 10 EXPLAINED THEM, EARTH CAN'T BE THE WINNER!
DON'T YOU SEE? AFTER YOU KICKED HIM, BUT BEFORE I STARTED TO WAIL ON YOU--
--I NEVER TAGGED IN!

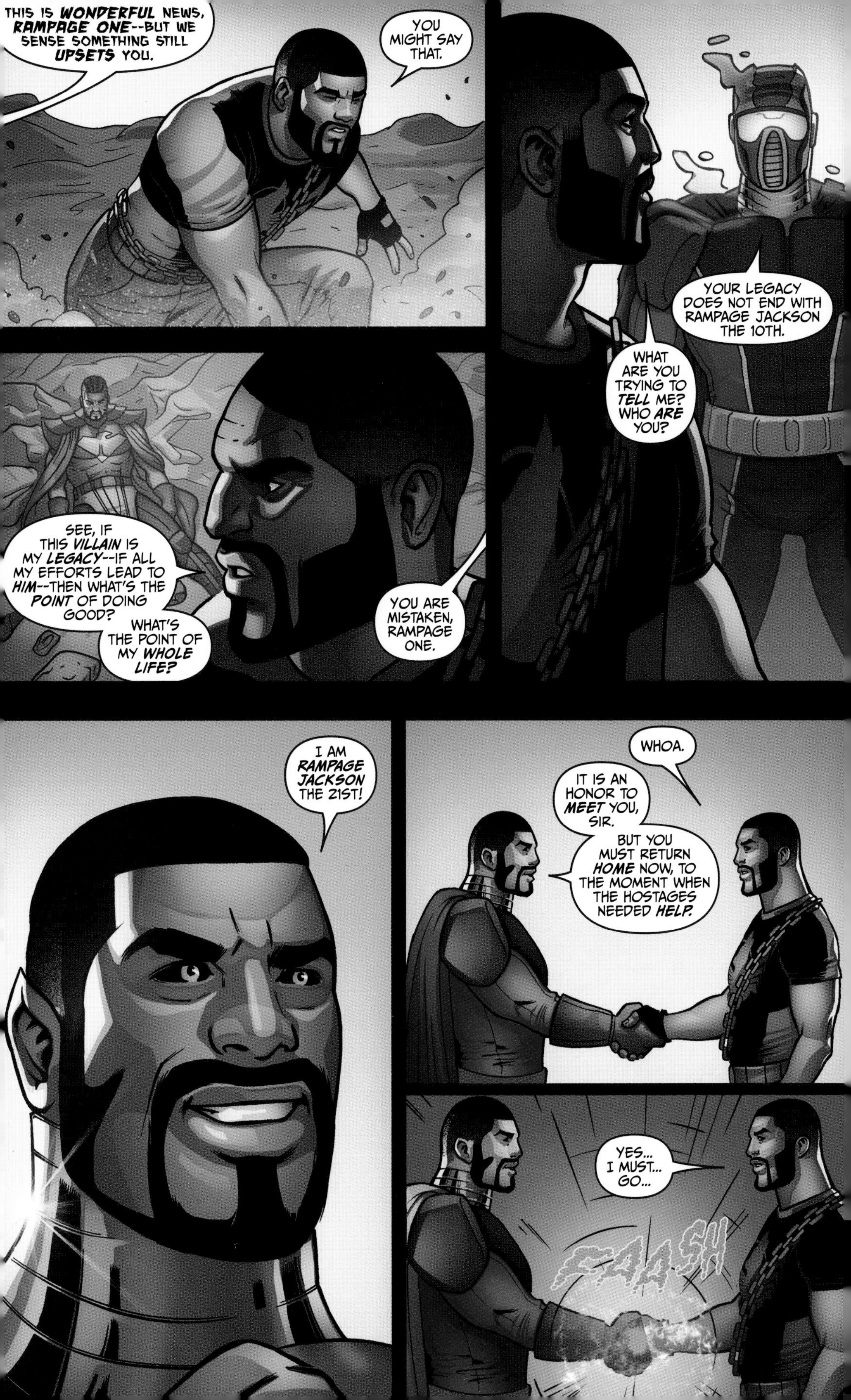

THIS IS WONDERFUL NEWS, RAMPAGE ONE--BUT WE SENSE SOMETHING STILL UPSETS YOU.
YOU MIGHT SAY THAT.
YOUR LEGACY DOES NOT END WITH RAMPAGE JACKSON THE 10TH.
WHAT ARE YOU TRYING TO TELL ME? WHO ARE YOU?
SEE, IF THIS VILLAIN IS MY LEGACY--IF ALL MY EFFORTS LEAD TO HIM--THEN WHAT'S THE POINT OF DOING GOOD?
WHAT'S THE POINT OF MY WHOLE LIFE?
YOU ARE MISTAKEN, RAMPAGE ONE.
I AM RAMPAGE JACKSON THE 21ST!
WHOA.
IT IS AN HONOR TO MEET YOU, SIR.
BUT YOU MUST RETURN HOME NOW, TO THE MOMENT WHEN THE HOSTAGES NEEDED HELP.
YES... I MUST... GO...
FAASH

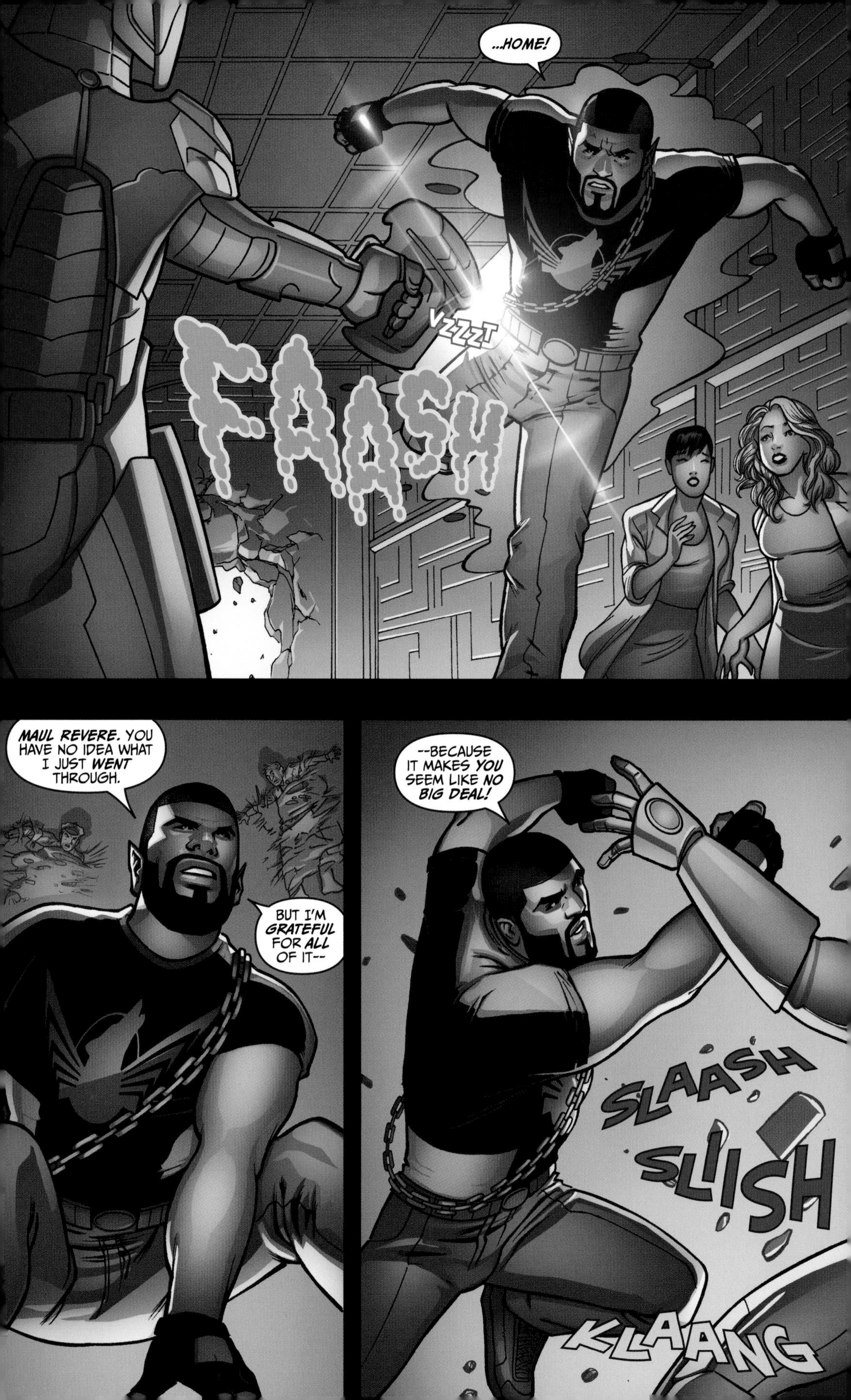
...HOME!
VZZZT
FAASH
MAUL REVERE. YOU HAVE NO IDEA WHAT I JUST WENT THROUGH.
BUT I'M GRATEFUL FOR ALL OF IT--
--BECAUSE IT MAKES YOU SEEM LIKE NO BIG DEAL!
SLAASH
SLISH
KLAAANG

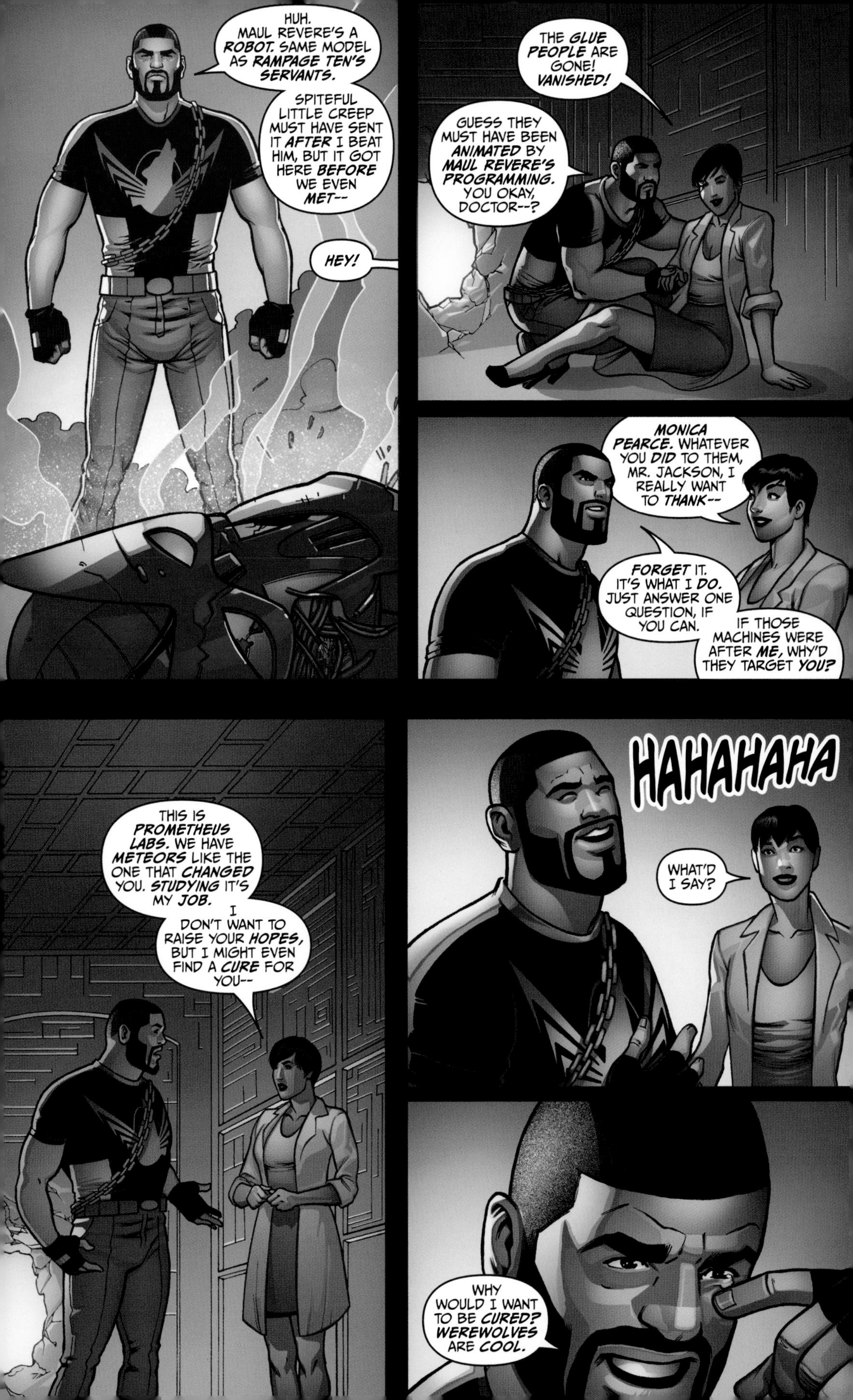

HUH. MAUL REVERE'S A ROBOT. SAME MODEL AS RAMPAGE TEN'S SERVANTS.
SPITEFUL LITTLE CREEP MUST HAVE SENT IT AFTER I BEAT HIM, BUT IT GOT HERE BEFORE WE EVEN MET--
HEY!
THE GLUE PEOPLE ARE GONE! VANISHED!
GUESS THEY MUST HAVE BEEN ANIMATED BY MAUL REVERE'S PROGRAMMING. YOU OKAY, DOCTOR--?
MONICA PEARCE. WHATEVER YOU DID TO THEM, MR. JACKSON, I REALLY WANT TO THANK--
FORGET IT. IT'S WHAT I DO. JUST ANSWER ONE QUESTION, IF YOU CAN.
IF THOSE MACHINES WERE AFTER ME, WHY'D THEY TARGET YOU?
THIS IS PROMETHEUS LABS. WE HAVE METEORS LIKE THE ONE THAT CHANGED YOU. STUDYING IT'S MY JOB.
I DON'T WANT TO RAISE YOUR HOPES, BUT I MIGHT EVEN FIND A CURE FOR YOU--
HAHAHAHA
WHAT'D I SAY?
WHY WOULD I WANT TO BE CURED? WEREWOLVES ARE COOL.

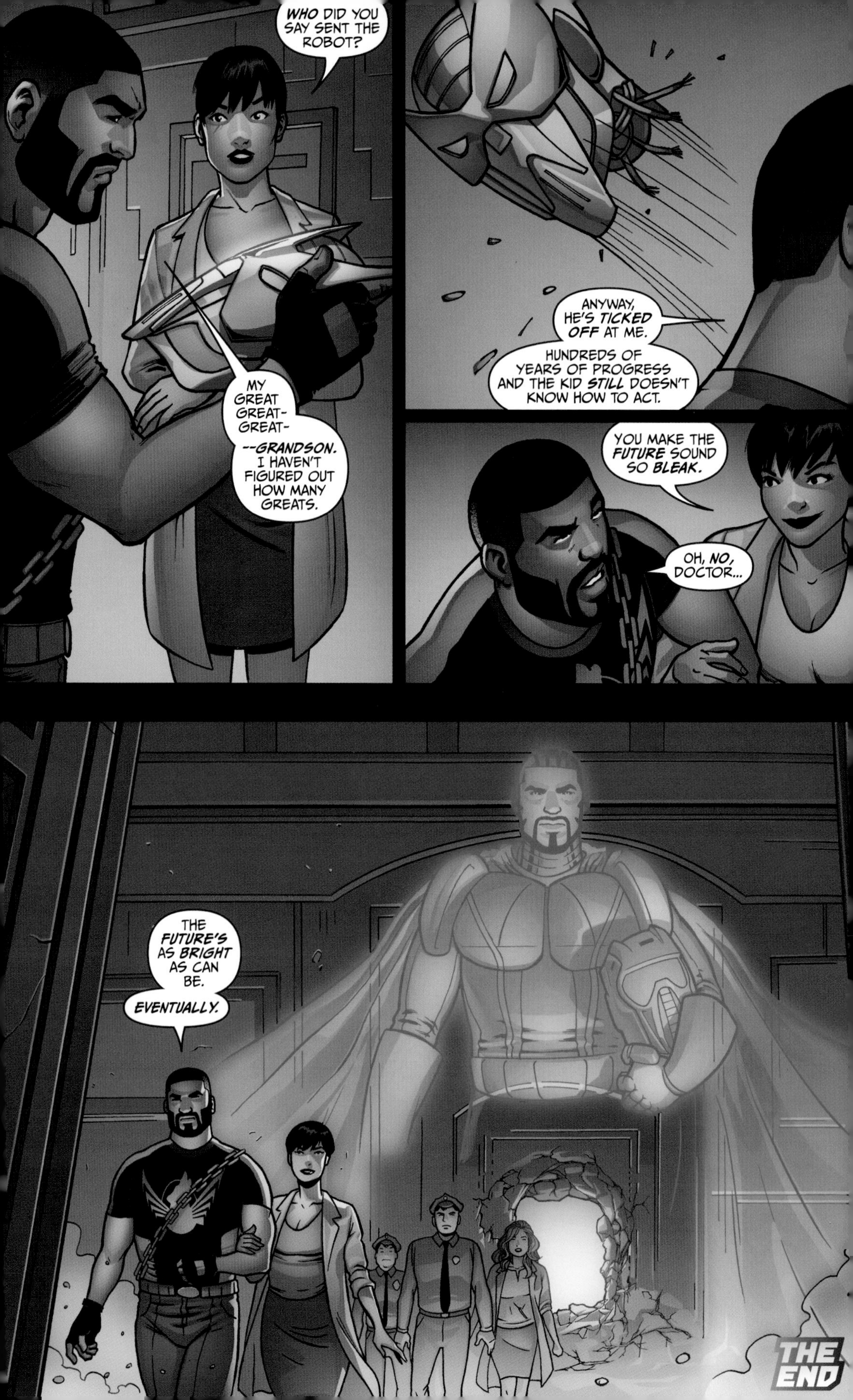
WHO DID YOU SAY SENT THE ROBOT?
MY GREAT GREAT-GREAT-
--GRANDSON. I HAVEN'T FIGURED OUT HOW MANY GREATS.
ANYWAY, HE'S TICKED OFF AT ME.
HUNDREDS OF YEARS OF PROGRESS AND THE KID STILL DOESN'T KNOW HOW TO ACT.
YOU MAKE THE FUTURE SOUND SO BLEAK.
OH, NO, DOCTOR...
THE FUTURE'S AS BRIGHT AS CAN BE.
EVENTUALLY.
THE END

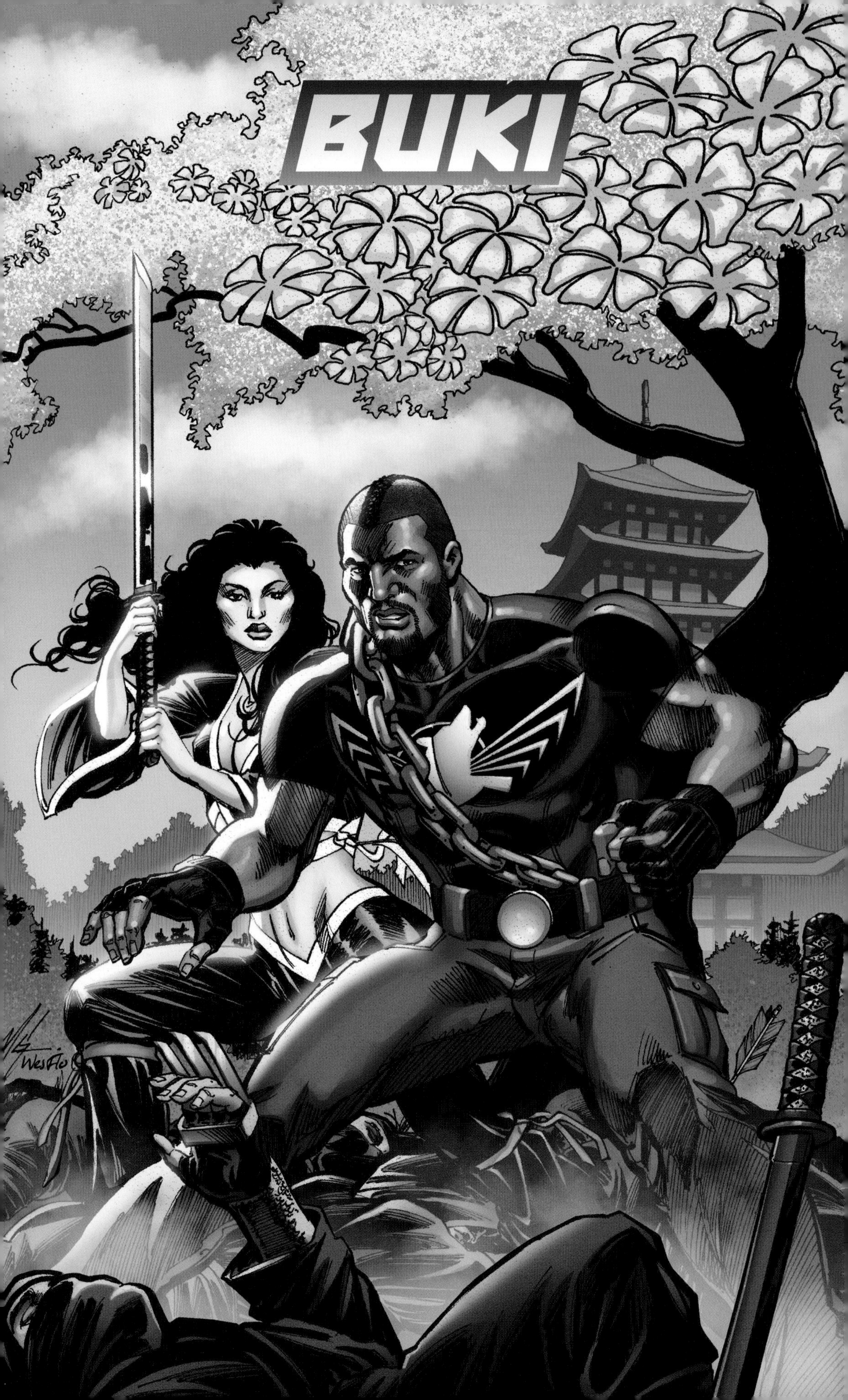
BUKI
WesFlo

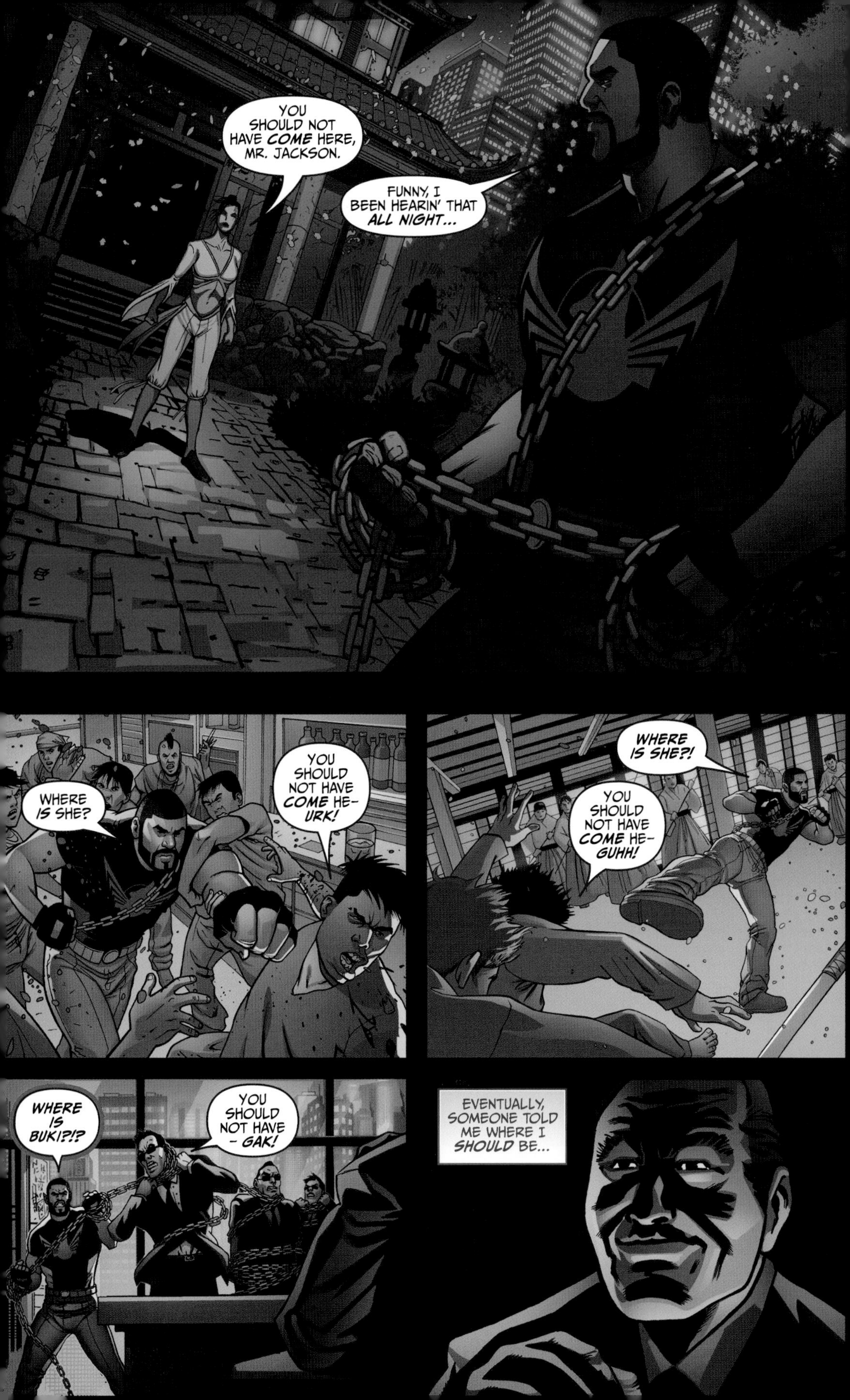
YOU SHOULD NOT HAVE COME HERE, MR. JACKSON.
FUNNY, I BEEN HEARIN' THAT ALL NIGHT...
WHERE IS SHE?
YOU SHOULD NOT HAVE COME HE-URK!
WHERE IS SHE?!
YOU SHOULD NOT HAVE COME HE-GUHH!
WHERE IS BUKI?!?
YOU SHOULD NOT HAVE - GAK!
EVENTUALLY, SOMEONE TOLD ME WHERE I SHOULD BE...

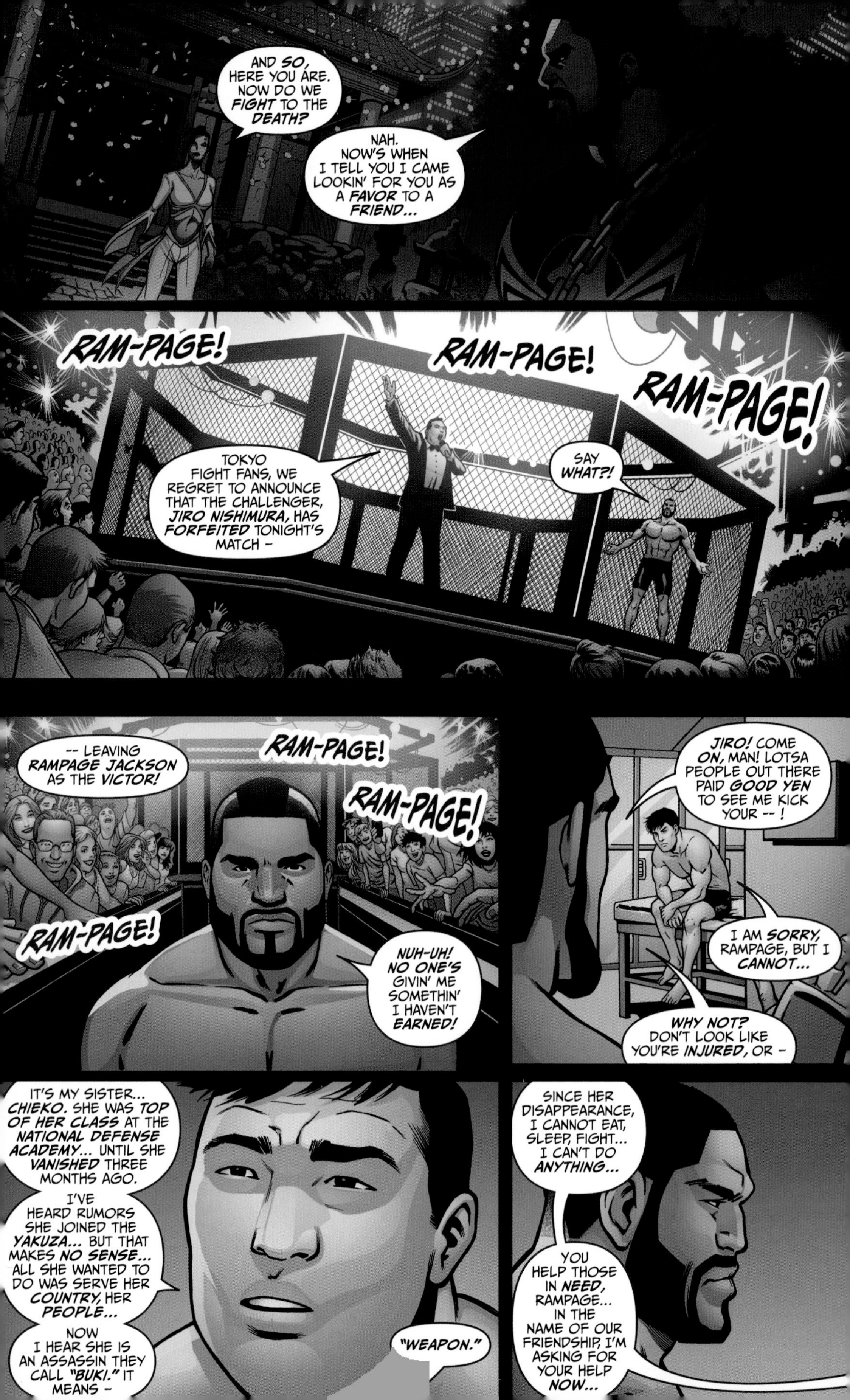
AND SO, HERE YOU ARE. NOW DO WE FIGHT TO THE DEATH?
NAH. NOW'S WHEN I TELL YOU I CAME LOOKIN' FOR YOU AS A FAVOR TO A FRIEND...
RAM-PAGE!
RAM-PAGE!
RAM-PAGE!
TOKYO FIGHT FANS, WE REGRET TO ANNOUNCE THAT THE CHALLENGER, JIRO NISHIMURA, HAS FORFEITED TONIGHT'S MATCH –
SAY WHAT?!
-- LEAVING RAMPAGE JACKSON AS THE VICTOR!
RAM-PAGE!
RAM-PAGE!
RAM-PAGE!
NUH-UH! NO ONE'S GIVIN' ME SOMETHIN' I HAVEN'T EARNED!
JIRO! COME ON, MAN! LOTSA PEOPLE OUT THERE PAID GOOD YEN TO SEE ME KICK YOUR -- !
I AM SORRY, RAMPAGE, BUT I CANNOT...
WHY NOT? DON'T LOOK LIKE YOU'RE INJURED, OR –
IT'S MY SISTER... CHIEKO. SHE WAS TOP OF HER CLASS AT THE NATIONAL DEFENSE ACADEMY... UNTIL SHE VANISHED THREE MONTHS AGO.
I'VE HEARD RUMORS SHE JOINED THE YAKUZA... BUT THAT MAKES NO SENSE... ALL SHE WANTED TO DO WAS SERVE HER COUNTRY, HER PEOPLE...
NOW I HEAR SHE IS AN ASSASSIN THEY CALL "BUKI." IT MEANS –
"WEAPON."
SINCE HER DISAPPEARANCE, I CANNOT EAT, SLEEP, FIGHT... I CAN'T DO ANYTHING...
YOU HELP THOSE IN NEED, RAMPAGE... IN THE NAME OF OUR FRIENDSHIP, I'M ASKING FOR YOUR HELP NOW...

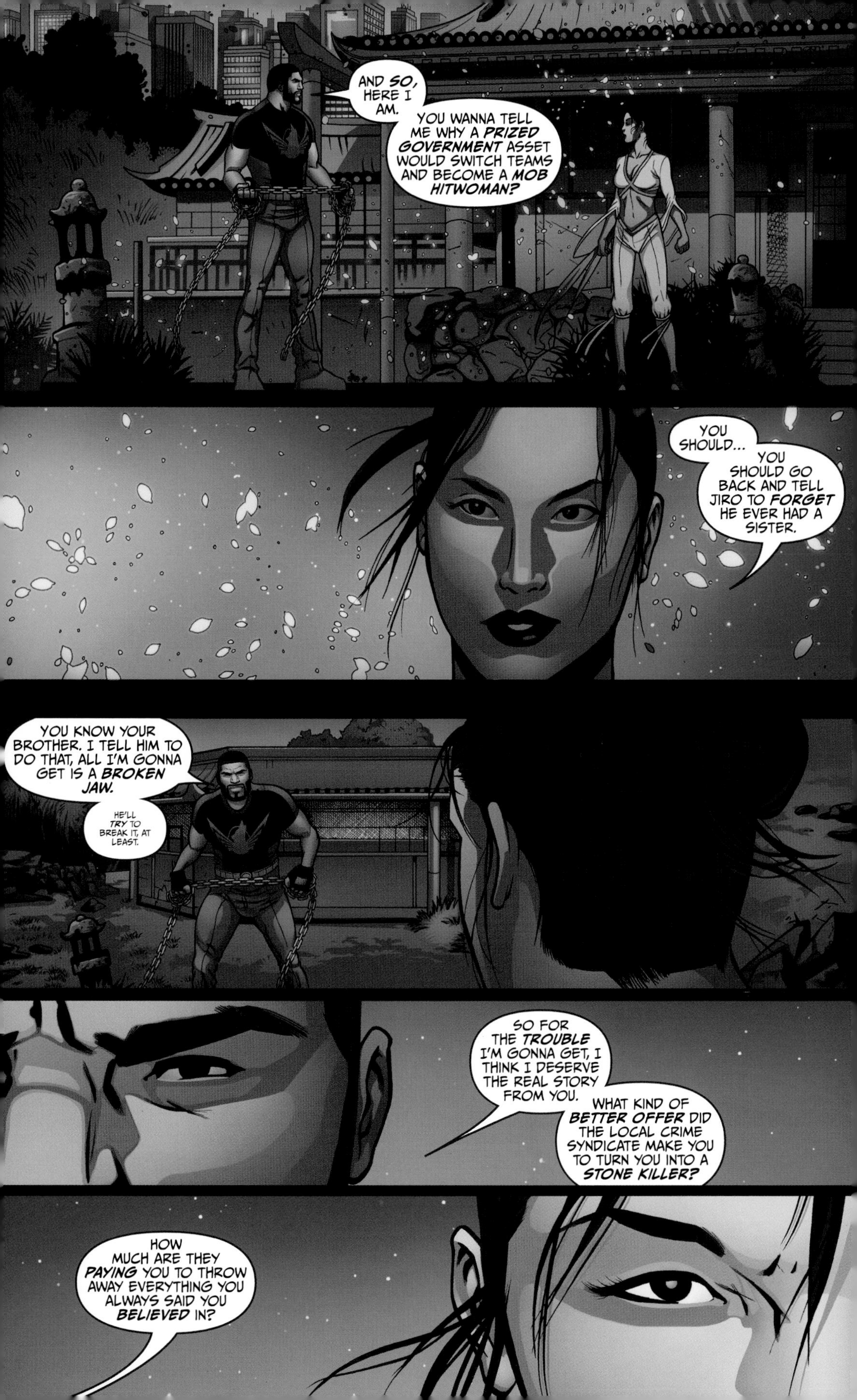
AND SO, HERE I AM.
YOU WANNA TELL ME WHY A PRIZED GOVERNMENT ASSET WOULD SWITCH TEAMS AND BECOME A MOB HITWOMAN?
YOU SHOULD...
YOU SHOULD GO BACK AND TELL JIRO TO FORGET HE EVER HAD A SISTER.
YOU KNOW YOUR BROTHER. I TELL HIM TO DO THAT, ALL I'M GONNA GET IS A BROKEN JAW.
HE'LL TRY TO BREAK IT, AT LEAST.
SO FOR THE TROUBLE I'M GONNA GET, I THINK I DESERVE THE REAL STORY FROM YOU.
WHAT KIND OF BETTER OFFER DID THE LOCAL CRIME SYNDICATE MAKE YOU TO TURN YOU INTO A STONE KILLER?
HOW MUCH ARE THEY PAYING YOU TO THROW AWAY EVERYTHING YOU ALWAYS SAID YOU BELIEVED IN?

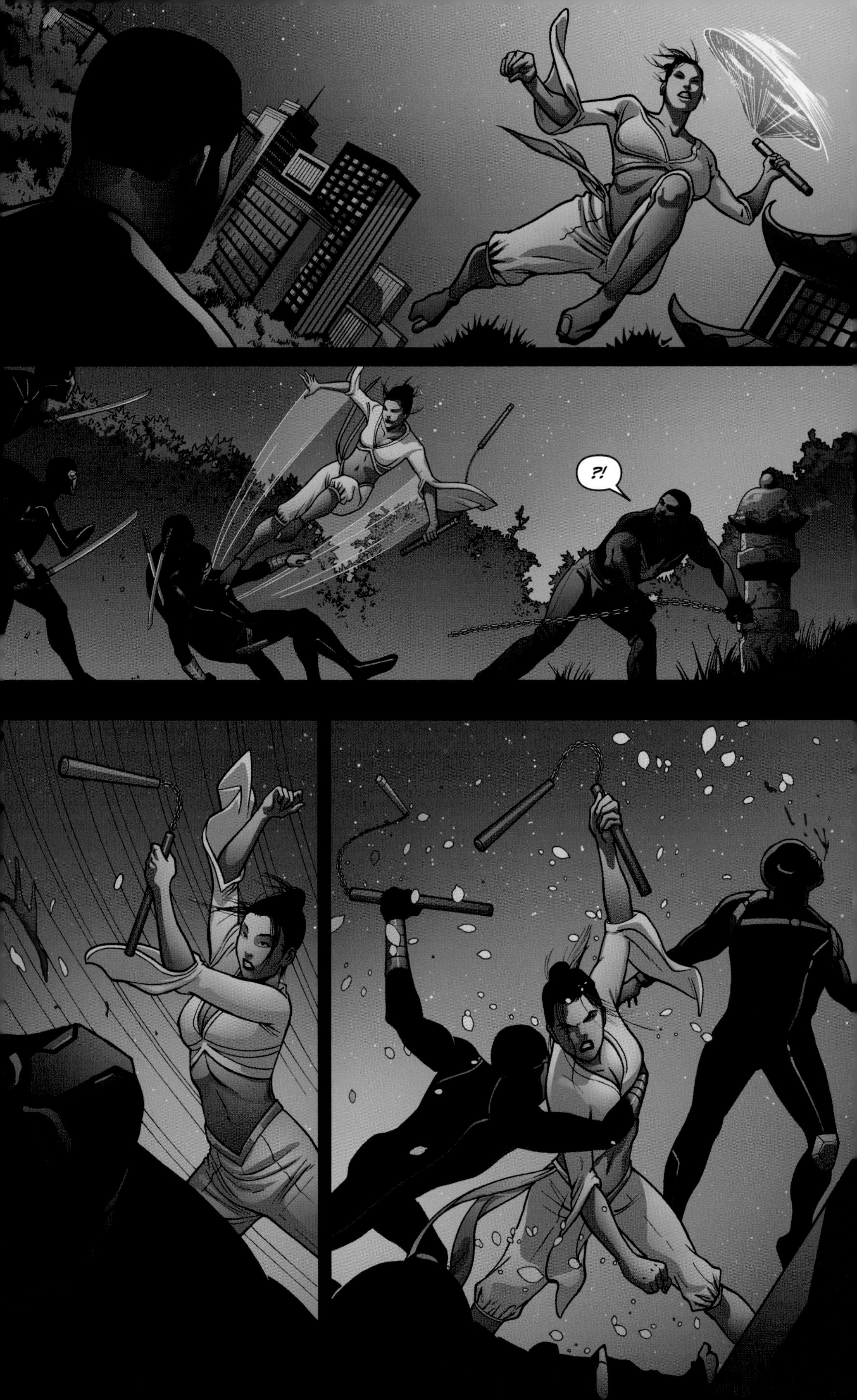
?!

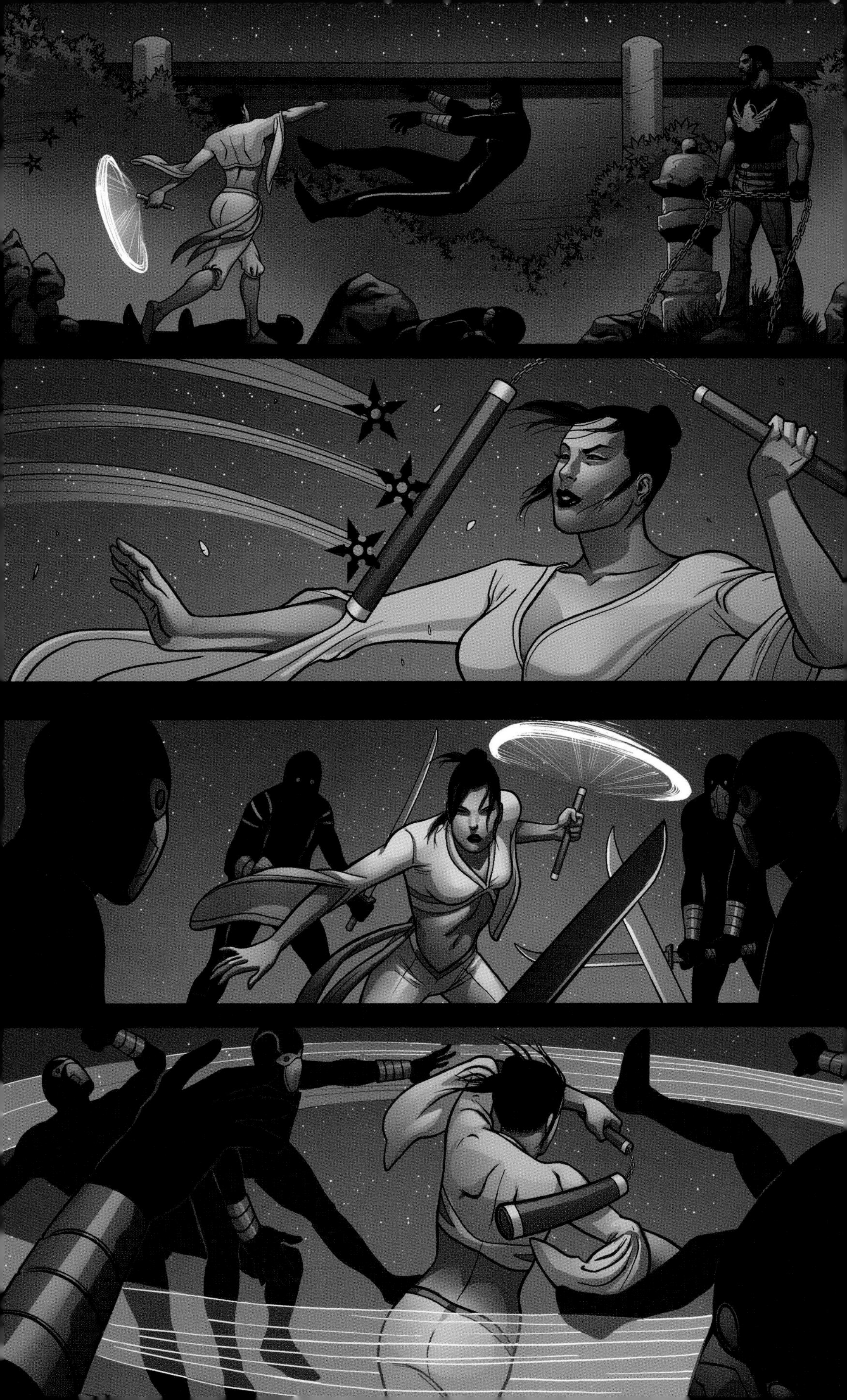

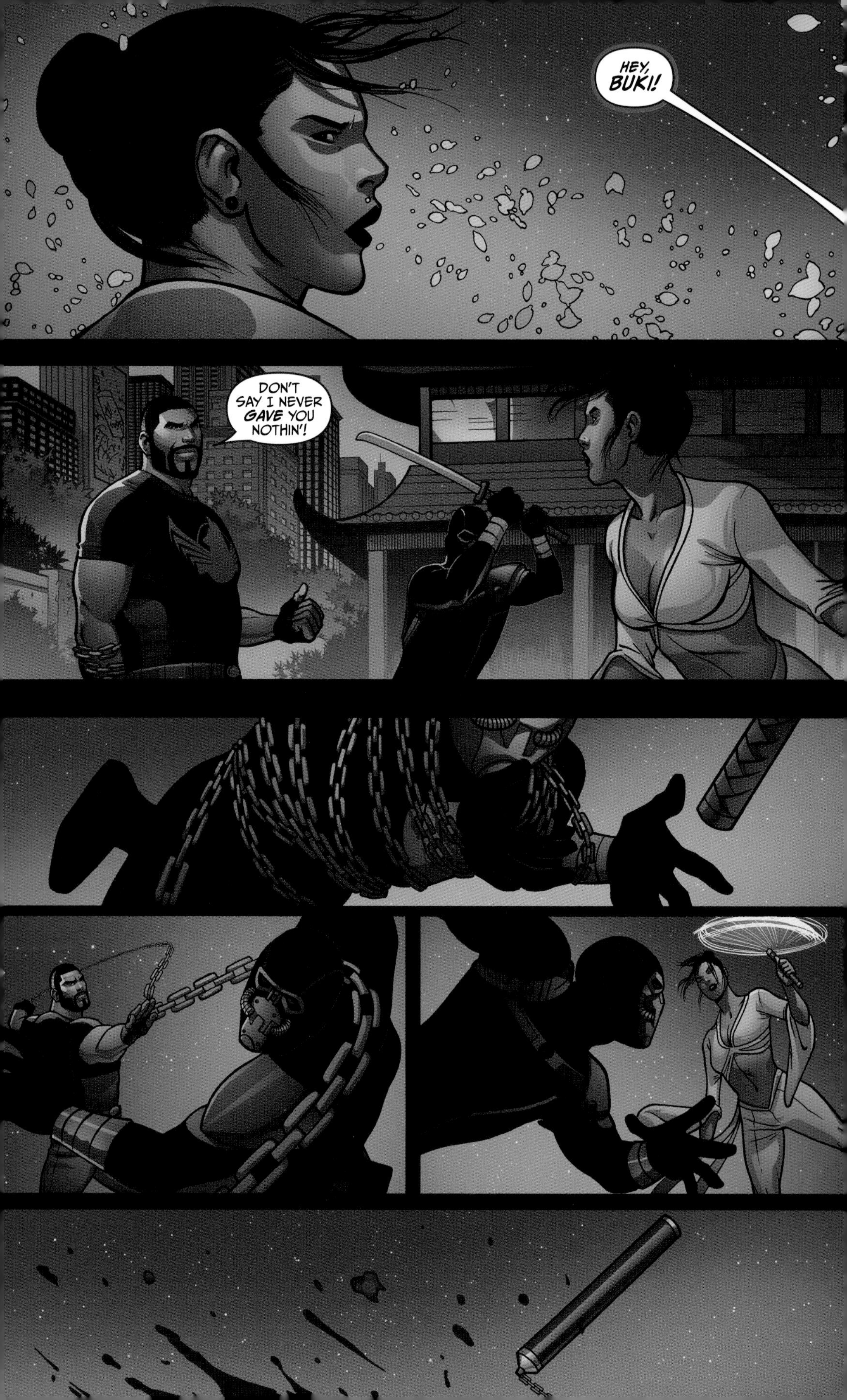
HEY, BUKI!
DON'T SAY I NEVER GAVE YOU NOTHIN'!

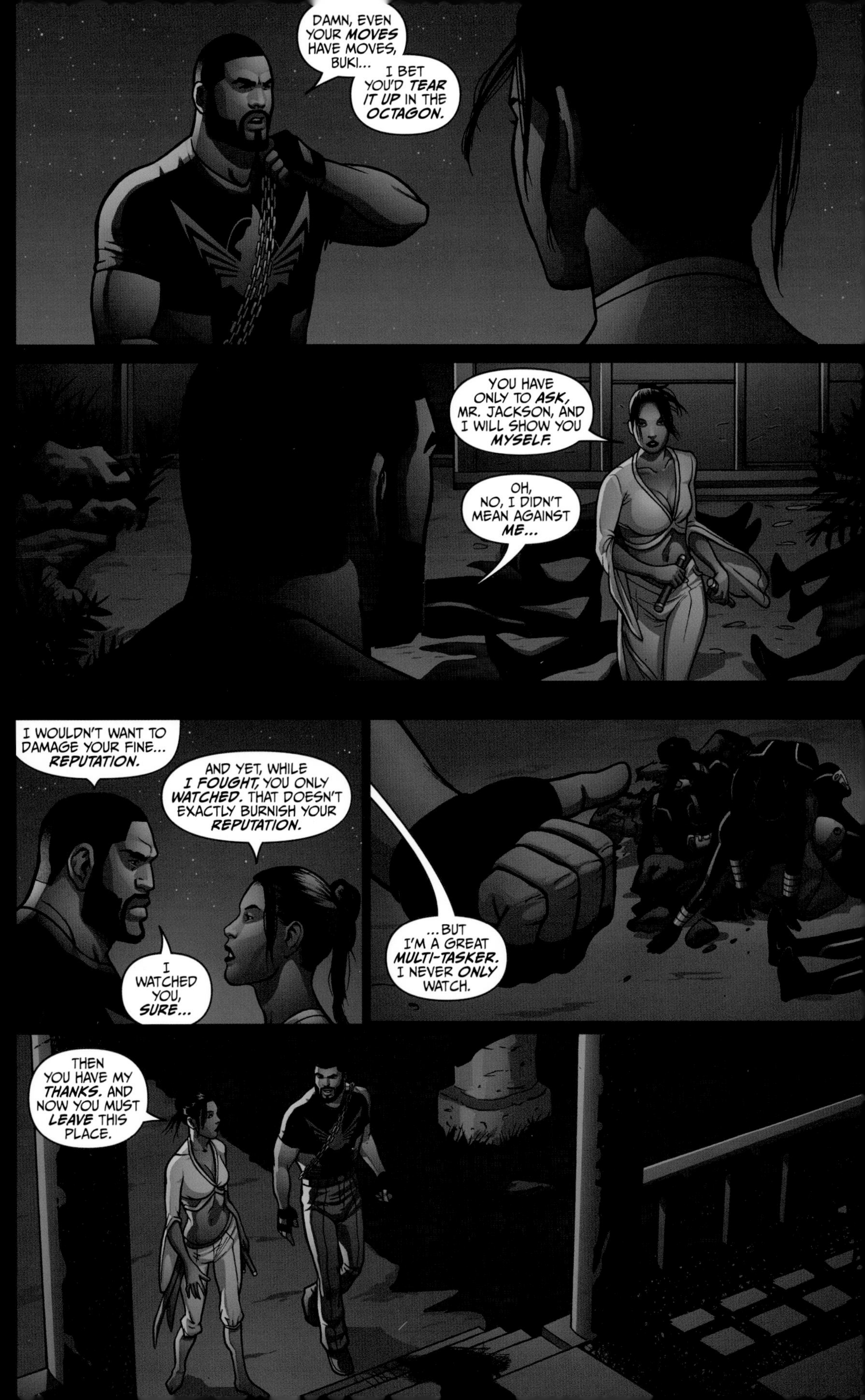

DAMN, EVEN YOUR MOVES HAVE MOVES, BUKI...
I BET YOU'D TEAR IT UP IN THE OCTAGON.
YOU HAVE ONLY TO ASK, MR. JACKSON, AND I WILL SHOW YOU MYSELF.
OH, NO, I DIDN'T MEAN AGAINST ME...
I WOULDN'T WANT TO DAMAGE YOUR FINE... REPUTATION.
AND YET, WHILE I FOUGHT, YOU ONLY WATCHED. THAT DOESN'T EXACTLY BURNISH YOUR REPUTATION.
I WATCHED YOU, SURE...
...BUT I'M A GREAT MULTI-TASKER. I NEVER ONLY WATCH.
THEN YOU HAVE MY THANKS. AND NOW YOU MUST LEAVE THIS PLACE.

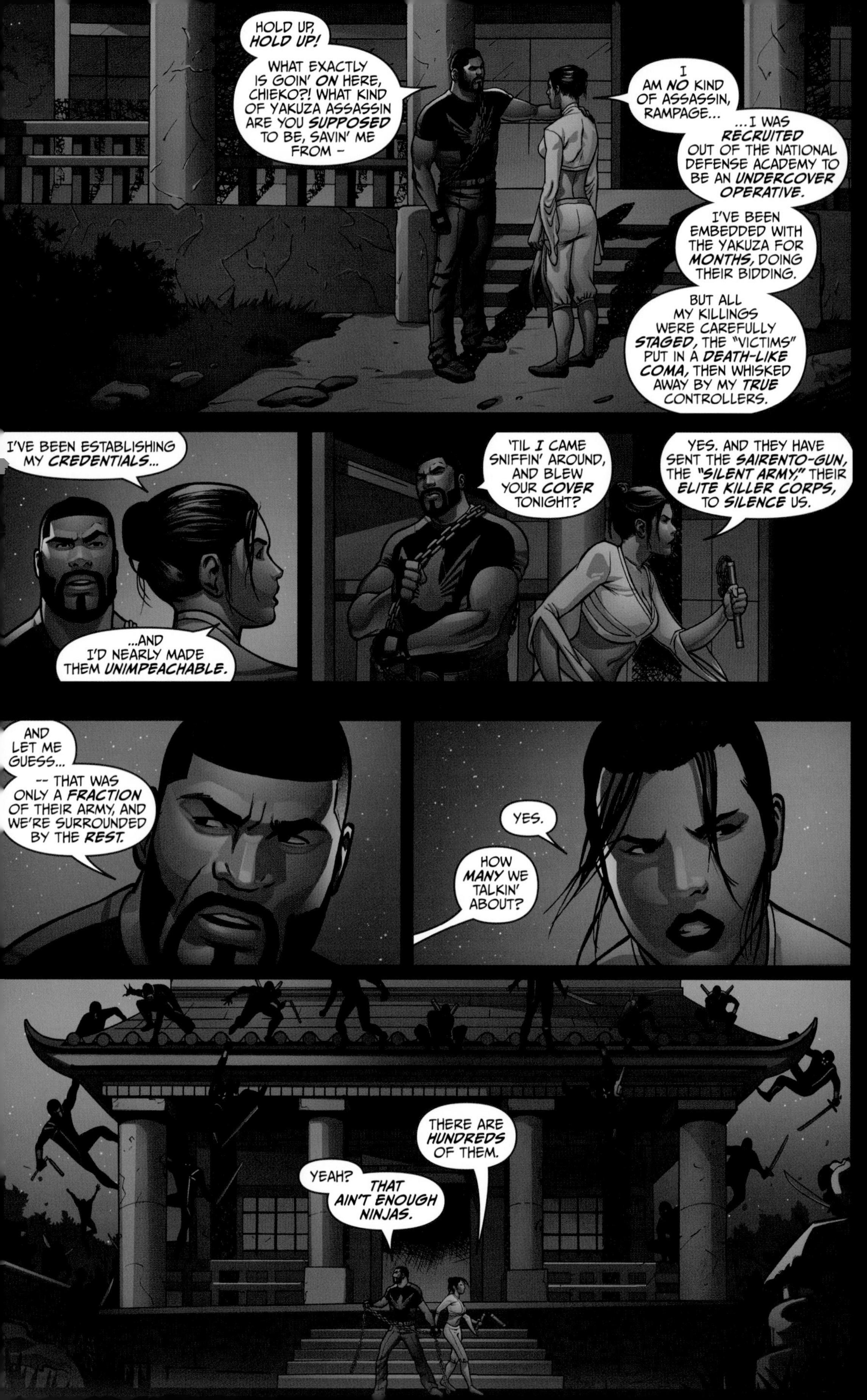

HOLD UP, HOLD UP!
WHAT EXACTLY IS GOIN' ON HERE, CHIEKO?! WHAT KIND OF YAKUZA ASSASSIN ARE YOU SUPPOSED TO BE, SAVIN' ME FROM –
I AM NO KIND OF ASSASSIN, RAMPAGE...
...I WAS RECRUITED OUT OF THE NATIONAL DEFENSE ACADEMY TO BE AN UNDERCOVER OPERATIVE.
I'VE BEEN EMBEDDED WITH THE YAKUZA FOR MONTHS, DOING THEIR BIDDING.
BUT ALL MY KILLINGS WERE CAREFULLY STAGED, THE "VICTIMS" PUT IN A DEATH-LIKE COMA, THEN WHISKED AWAY BY MY TRUE CONTROLLERS.
I'VE BEEN ESTABLISHING MY CREDENTIALS...
...AND I'D NEARLY MADE THEM UNIMPEACHABLE.
'TIL I CAME SNIFFIN' AROUND, AND BLEW YOUR COVER TONIGHT?
YES. AND THEY HAVE SENT THE SAIRENTO-GUN, THE "SILENT ARMY," THEIR ELITE KILLER CORPS, TO SILENCE US.
AND LET ME GUESS...
-- THAT WAS ONLY A FRACTION OF THEIR ARMY, AND WE'RE SURROUNDED BY THE REST.
YES.
HOW MANY WE TALKIN' ABOUT?
THERE ARE HUNDREDS OF THEM.
YEAH? THAT AIN'T ENOUGH NINJAS.

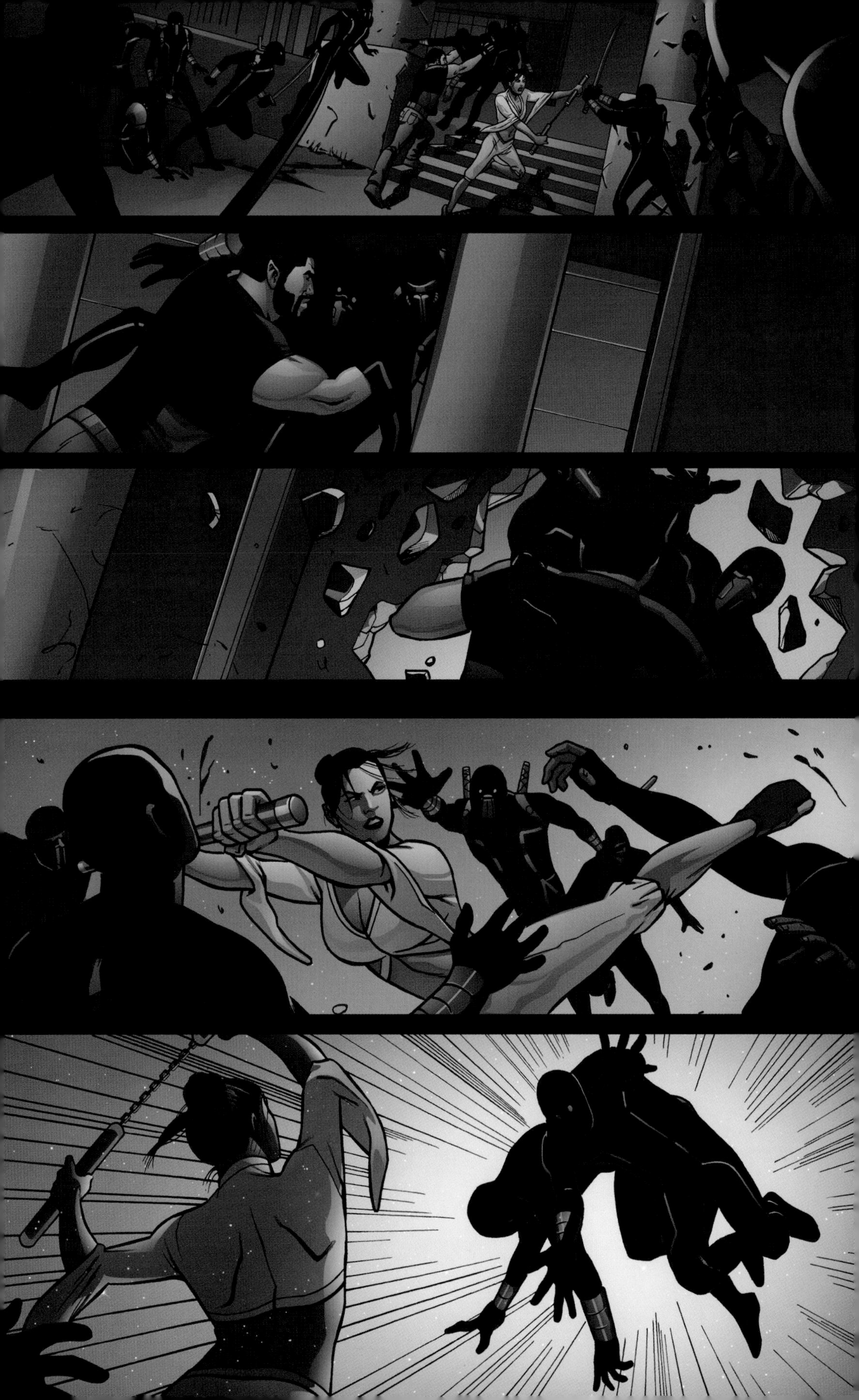

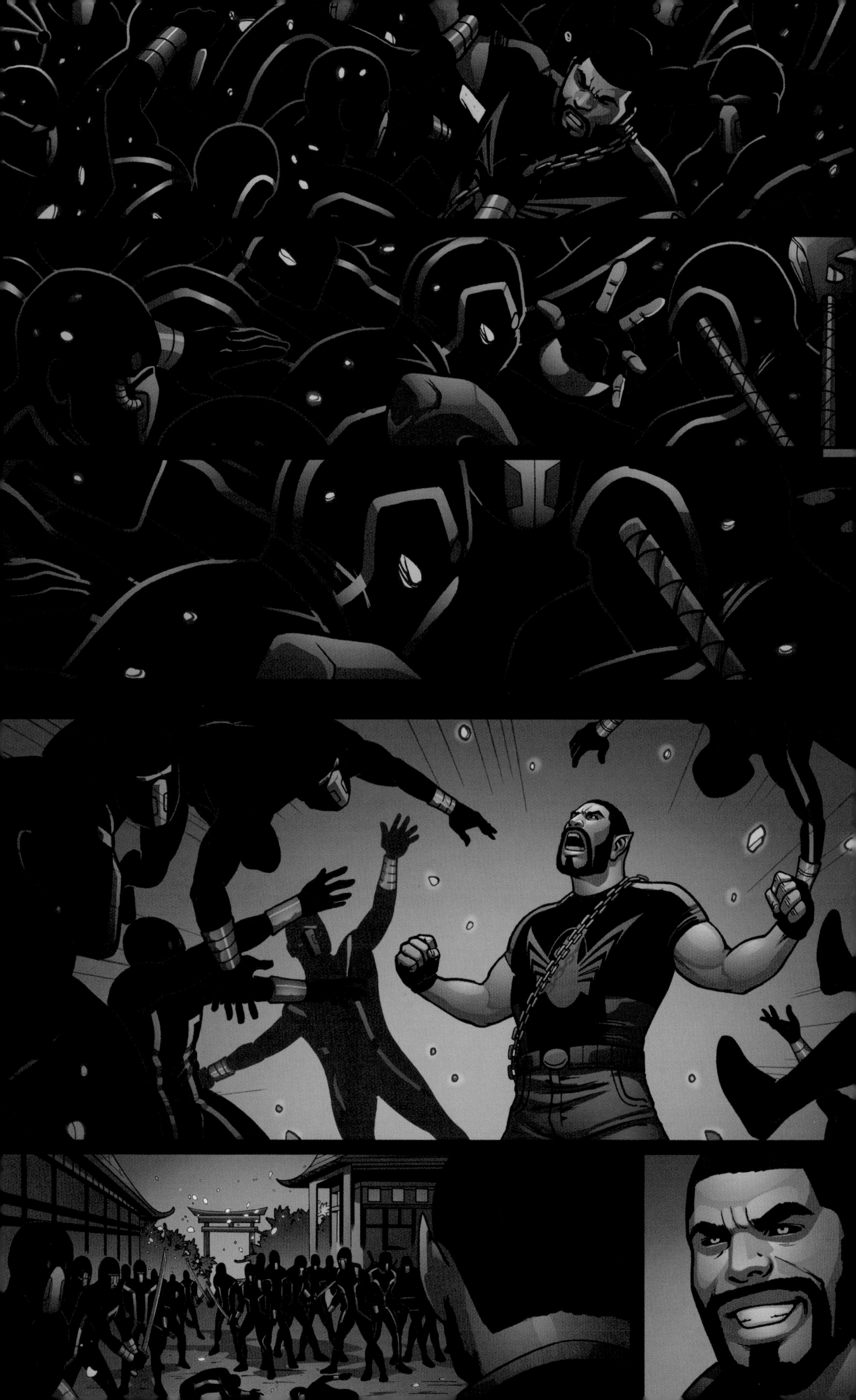

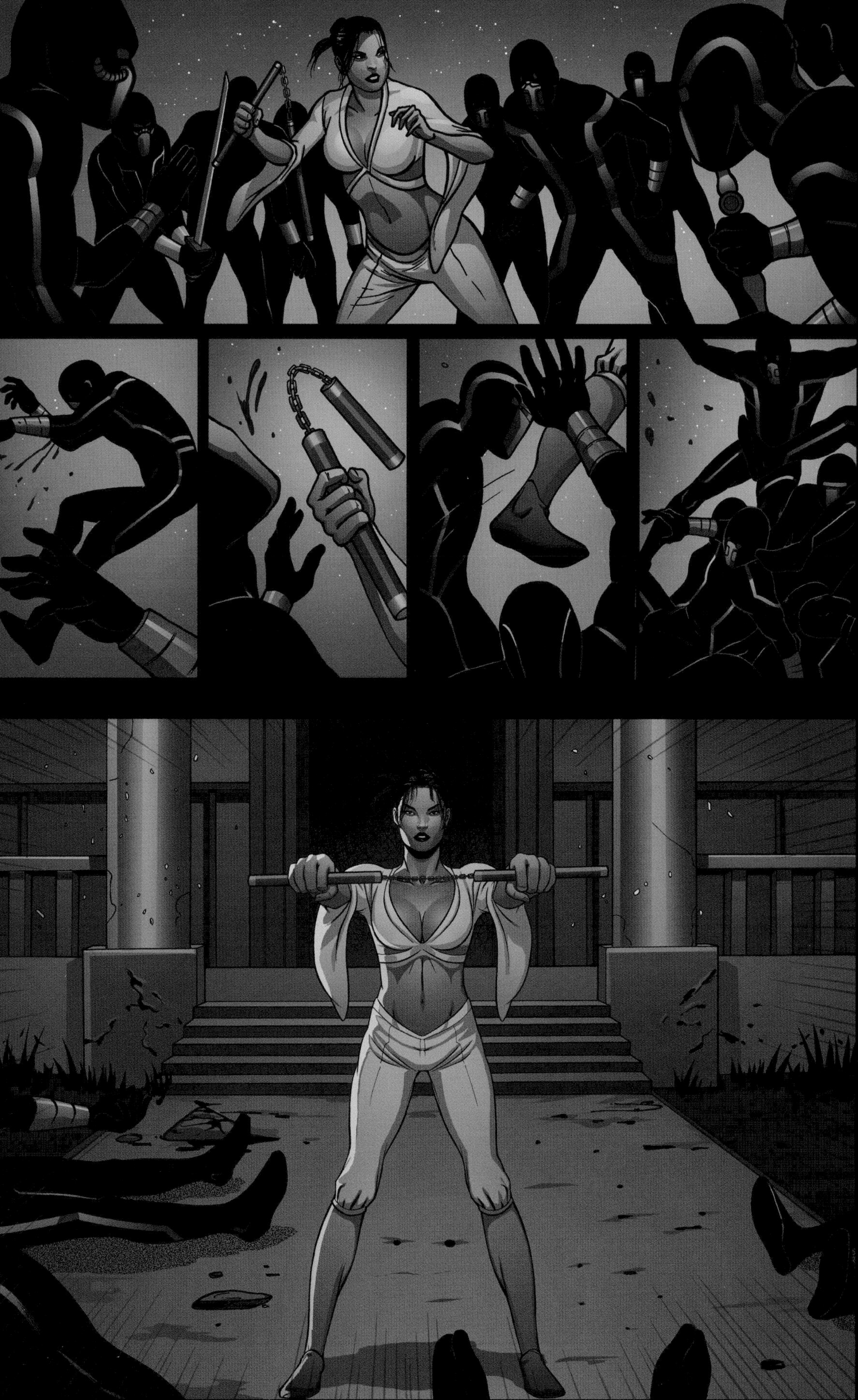

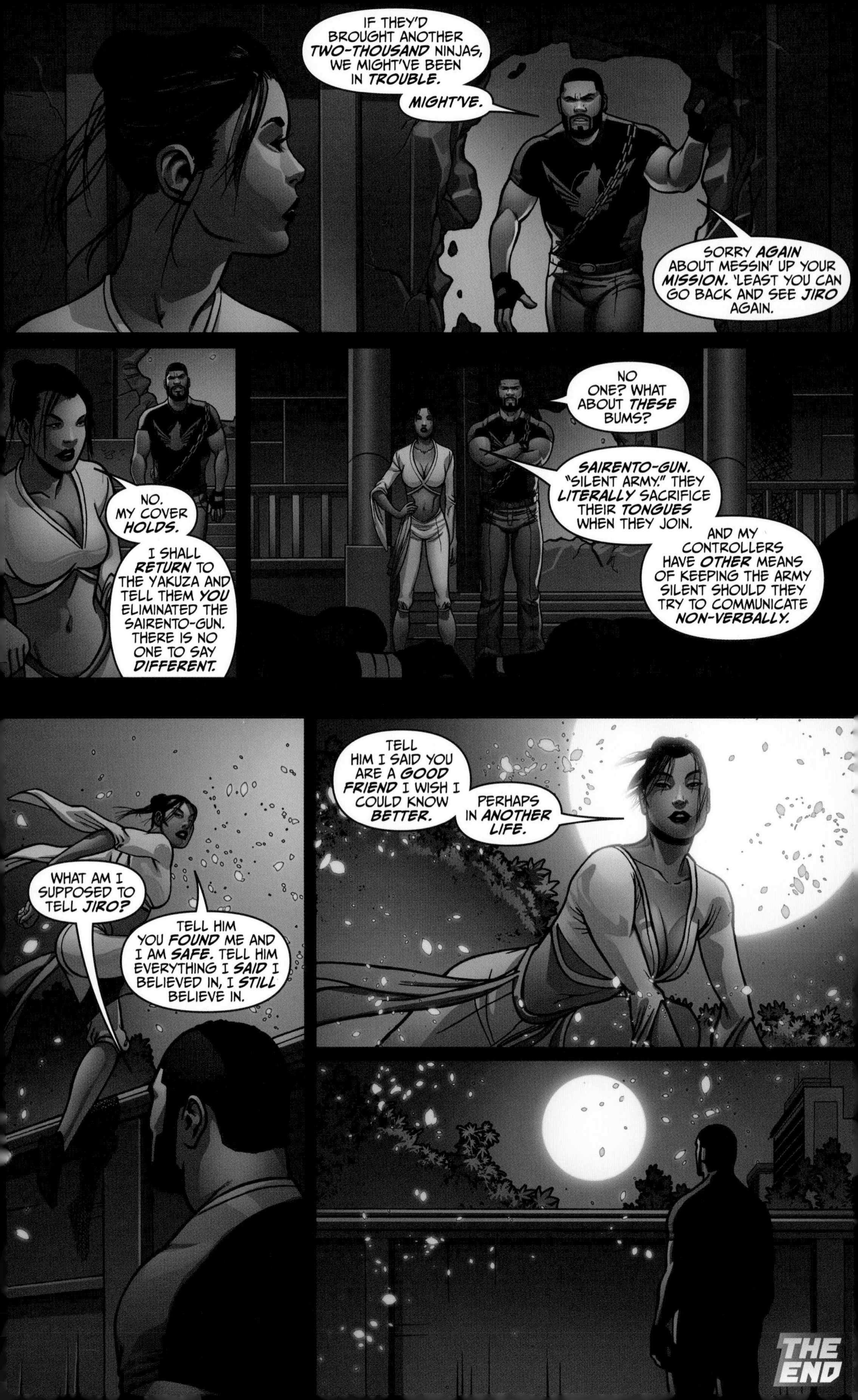

IF THEY'D BROUGHT ANOTHER TWO-THOUSAND NINJAS, WE MIGHT'VE BEEN IN TROUBLE.
MIGHT'VE.
SORRY AGAIN ABOUT MESSIN' UP YOUR MISSION. 'LEAST YOU CAN GO BACK AND SEE JIRO AGAIN.
NO. MY COVER HOLDS.
I SHALL RETURN TO THE YAKUZA AND TELL THEM YOU ELIMINATED THE SAIRENTO-GUN. THERE IS NO ONE TO SAY DIFFERENT.
NO ONE? WHAT ABOUT THESE BUMS?
SAIRENTO-GUN. "SILENT ARMY." THEY LITERALLY SACRIFICE THEIR TONGUES WHEN THEY JOIN.
AND MY CONTROLLERS HAVE OTHER MEANS OF KEEPING THE ARMY SILENT SHOULD THEY TRY TO COMMUNICATE NON-VERBALLY.
WHAT AM I SUPPOSED TO TELL JIRO?
TELL HIM YOU FOUND ME AND I AM SAFE. TELL HIM EVERYTHING I SAID I BELIEVED IN, I STILL BELIEVE IN.
TELL HIM I SAID YOU ARE A GOOD FRIEND I WISH I COULD KNOW BETTER.
PERHAPS IN ANOTHER LIFE.
THE END

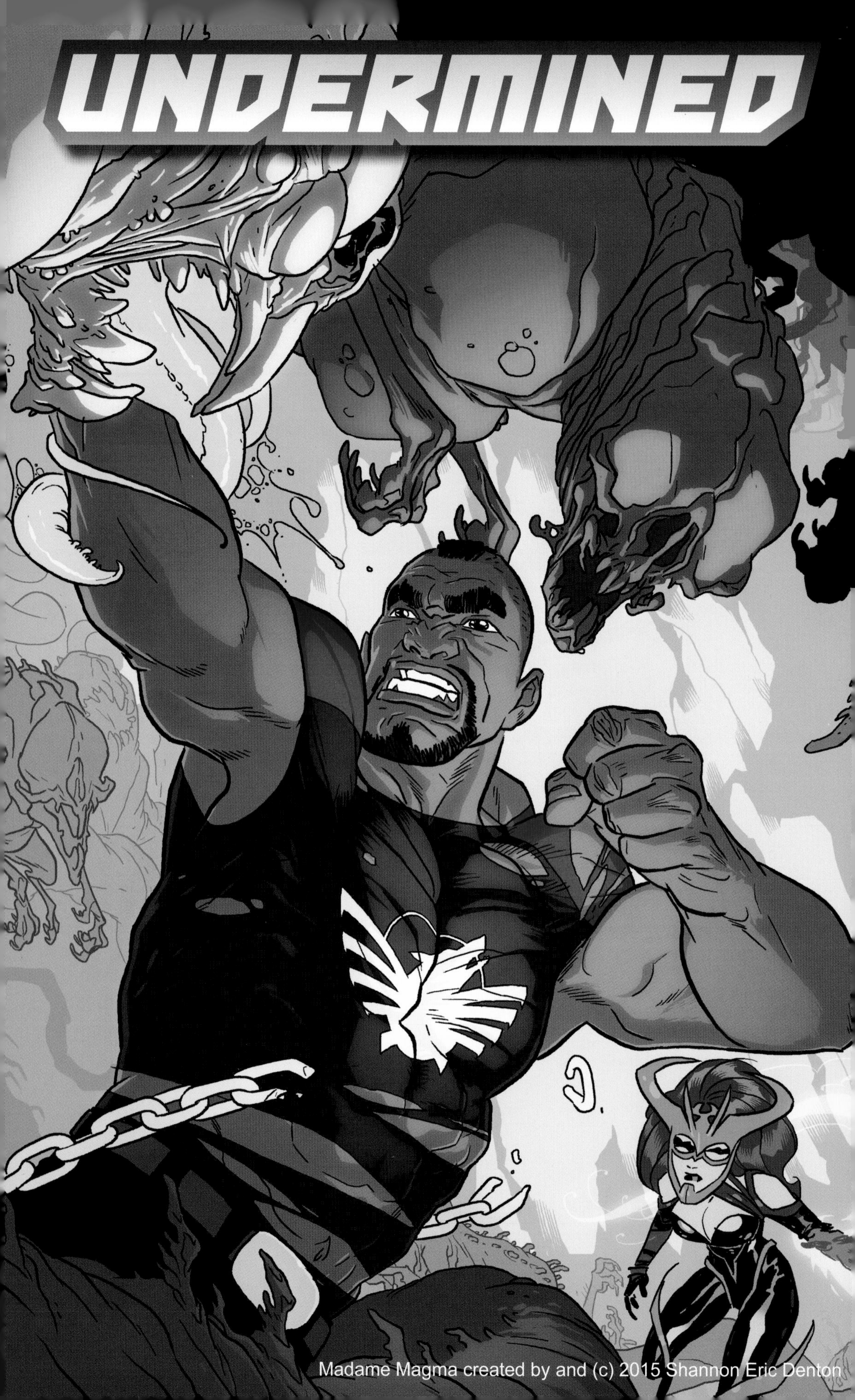
UNDERMINED

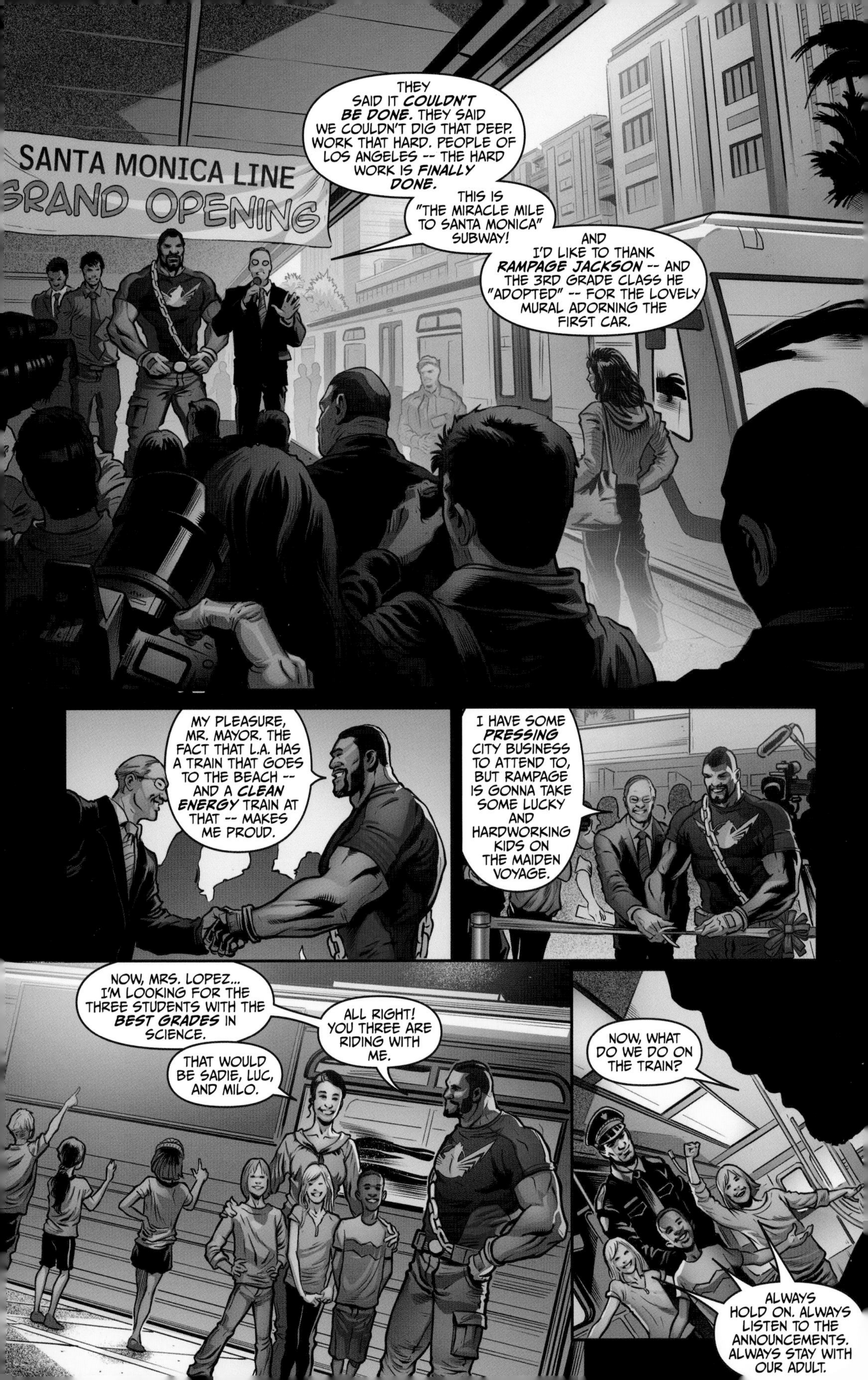
SANTA MONICA LINE
GRAND OPENING
THEY SAID IT COULDN'T BE DONE. THEY SAID WE COULDN'T DIG THAT DEEP. WORK THAT HARD. PEOPLE OF LOS ANGELES -- THE HARD WORK IS FINALLY DONE.
THIS IS "THE MIRACLE MILE TO SANTA MONICA" SUBWAY!
AND I'D LIKE TO THANK RAMPAGE JACKSON -- AND THE 3RD GRADE CLASS HE "ADOPTED" -- FOR THE LOVELY MURAL ADORNING THE FIRST CAR.
MY PLEASURE, MR. MAYOR. THE FACT THAT L.A. HAS A TRAIN THAT GOES TO THE BEACH -- AND A CLEAN ENERGY TRAIN AT THAT -- MAKES ME PROUD.
I HAVE SOME PRESSING CITY BUSINESS TO ATTEND TO, BUT RAMPAGE IS GONNA TAKE SOME LUCKY AND HARDWORKING KIDS ON THE MAIDEN VOYAGE.
NOW, MRS. LOPEZ... I'M LOOKING FOR THE THREE STUDENTS WITH THE BEST GRADES IN SCIENCE.
THAT WOULD BE SADIE, LUC, AND MILO.
ALL RIGHT! YOU THREE ARE RIDING WITH ME.
NOW, WHAT DO WE DO ON THE TRAIN?
ALWAYS HOLD ON. ALWAYS LISTEN TO THE ANNOUNCEMENTS. ALWAYS STAY WITH OUR ADULT.

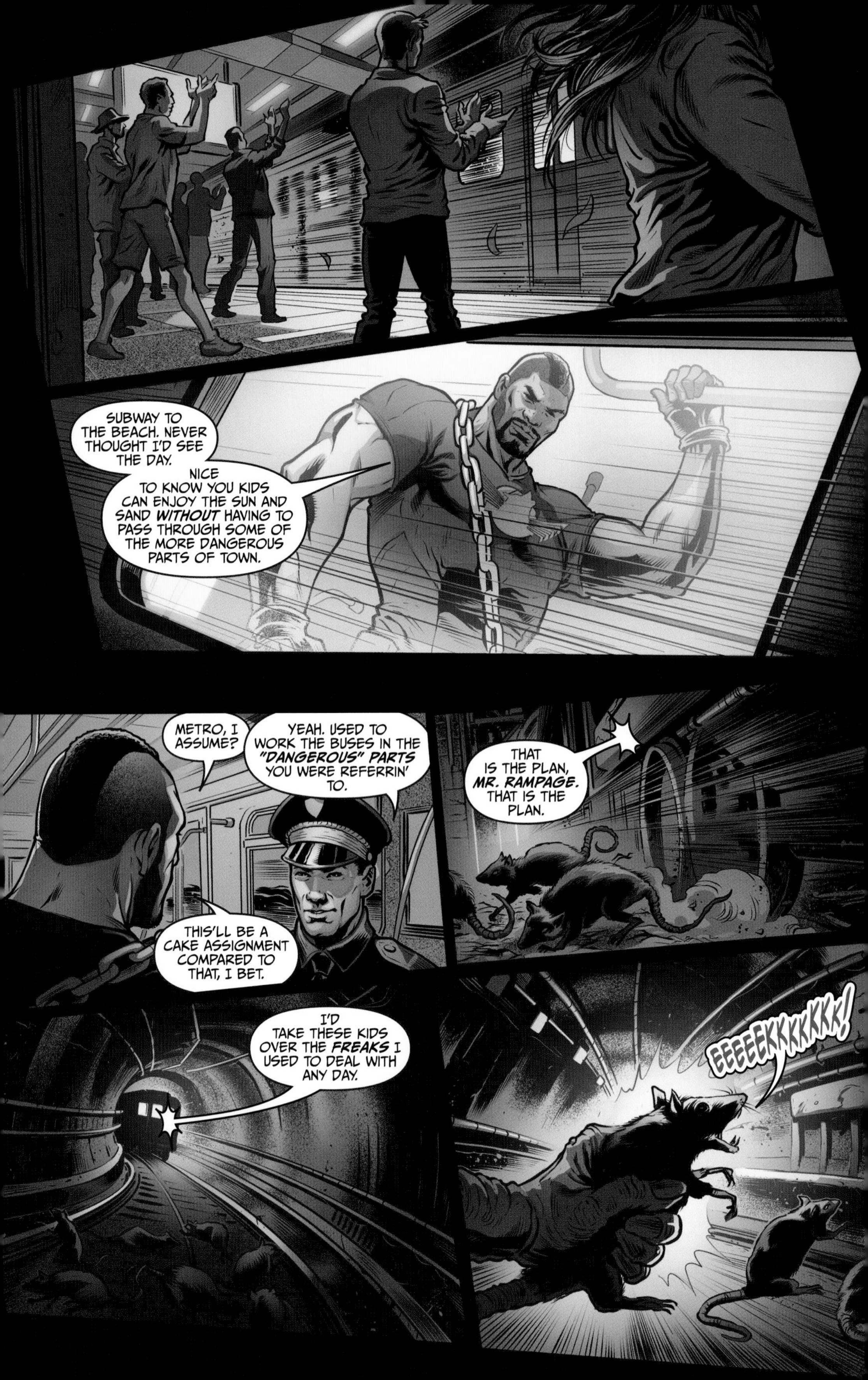
SUBWAY TO THE BEACH. NEVER THOUGHT I'D SEE THE DAY.
NICE TO KNOW YOU KIDS CAN ENJOY THE SUN AND SAND WITHOUT HAVING TO PASS THROUGH SOME OF THE MORE DANGEROUS PARTS OF TOWN.
METRO, I ASSUME?
YEAH. USED TO WORK THE BUSES IN THE "DANGEROUS" PARTS YOU WERE REFERRIN' TO.
THIS'LL BE A CAKE ASSIGNMENT COMPARED TO THAT, I BET.
THAT IS THE PLAN, MR. RAMPAGE. THAT IS THE PLAN.
I'D TAKE THESE KIDS OVER THE FREAKS I USED TO DEAL WITH ANY DAY.
EEEEEKKKKKKK!

CAN WE BODY SURF?
DUH. WE DIDN'T BRING BATHING SUITS, SADIE.
I DON'T LIKE THESE JEANS, ANYWAY.
NO BATHING SUITS, NO SWIMMING. TOES ONLY, KIDS.
GRRRRRRR...
RWRRRRR...

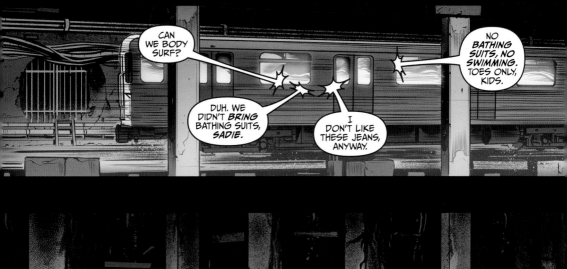

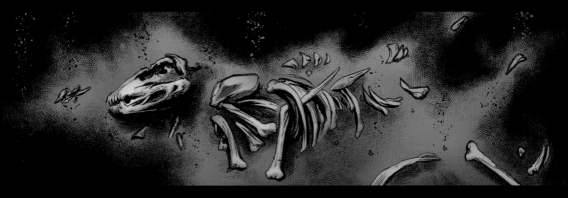

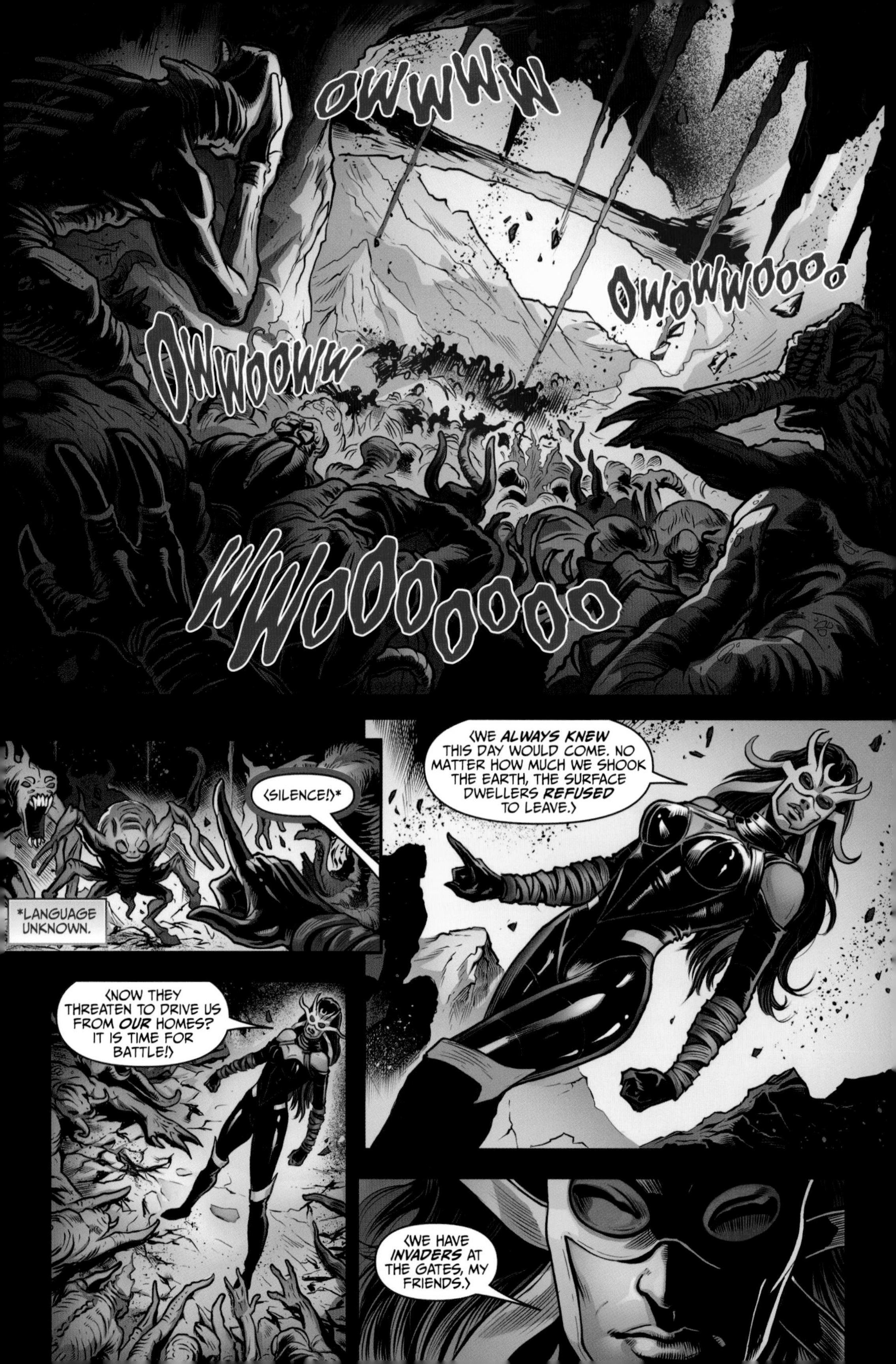
OWWWW
OWOWWOOOo
OWWOOWW
WWOOOOOOO
⟨SILENCE!⟩*
*LANGUAGE UNKNOWN.
⟨WE ALWAYS KNEW THIS DAY WOULD COME. NO MATTER HOW MUCH WE SHOOK THE EARTH, THE SURFACE DWELLERS REFUSED TO LEAVE.⟩
⟨NOW THEY THREATEN TO DRIVE US FROM OUR HOMES? IT IS TIME FOR BATTLE!⟩
⟨WE HAVE INVADERS AT THE GATES, MY FRIENDS.⟩

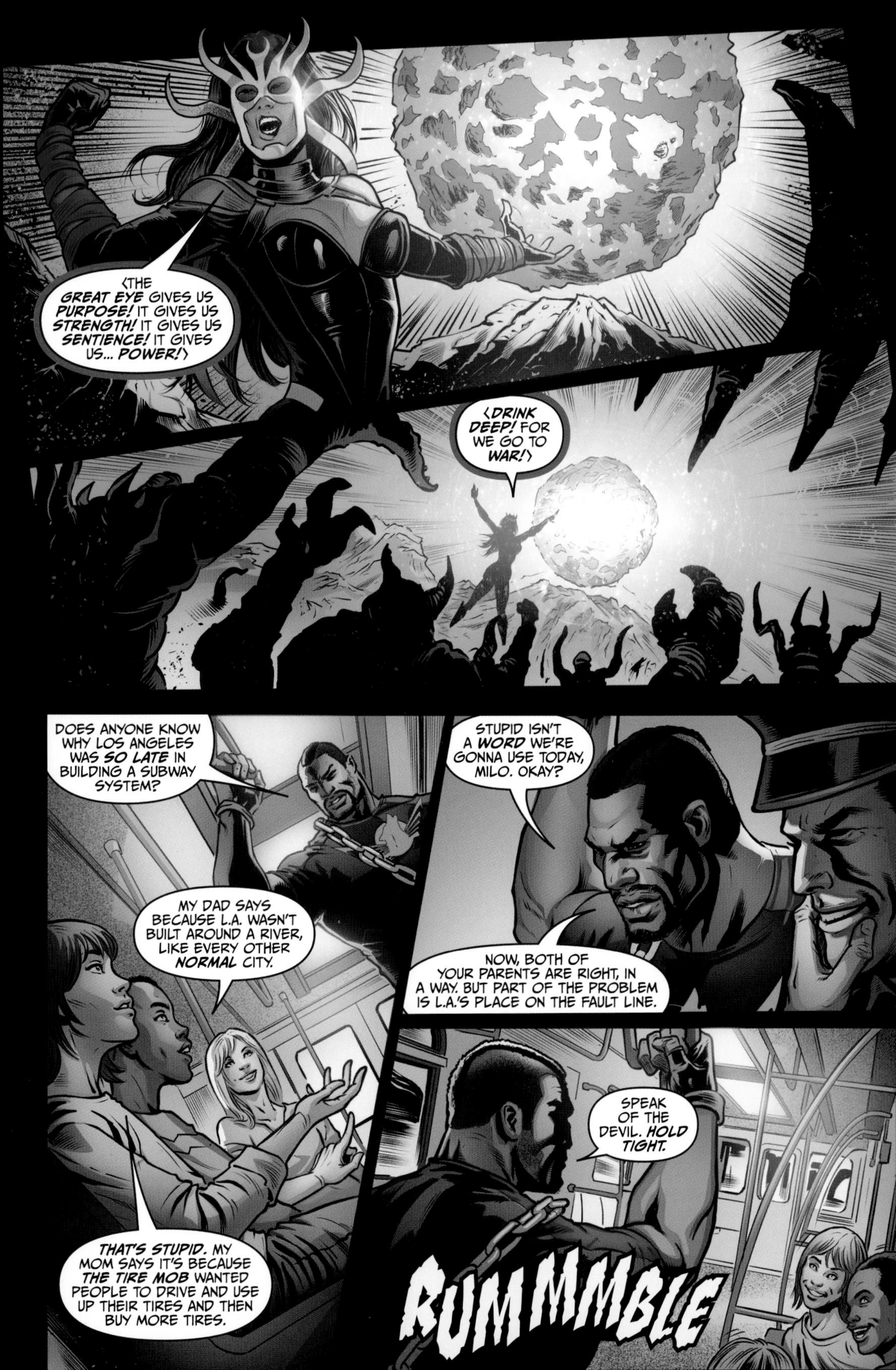

‹THE GREAT EYE GIVES US PURPOSE! IT GIVES US STRENGTH! IT GIVES US SENTIENCE! IT GIVES US... POWER!›
‹DRINK DEEP! FOR WE GO TO WAR!›
DOES ANYONE KNOW WHY LOS ANGELES WAS SO LATE IN BUILDING A SUBWAY SYSTEM?
MY DAD SAYS BECAUSE L.A. WASN'T BUILT AROUND A RIVER, LIKE EVERY OTHER NORMAL CITY.
THAT'S STUPID. MY MOM SAYS IT'S BECAUSE THE TIRE MOB WANTED PEOPLE TO DRIVE AND USE UP THEIR TIRES AND THEN BUY MORE TIRES.
STUPID ISN'T A WORD WE'RE GONNA USE TODAY, MILO. OKAY?
NOW, BOTH OF YOUR PARENTS ARE RIGHT, IN A WAY. BUT PART OF THE PROBLEM IS L.A.'S PLACE ON THE FAULT LINE.
SPEAK OF THE DEVIL. HOLD TIGHT.
RUMMMBLE

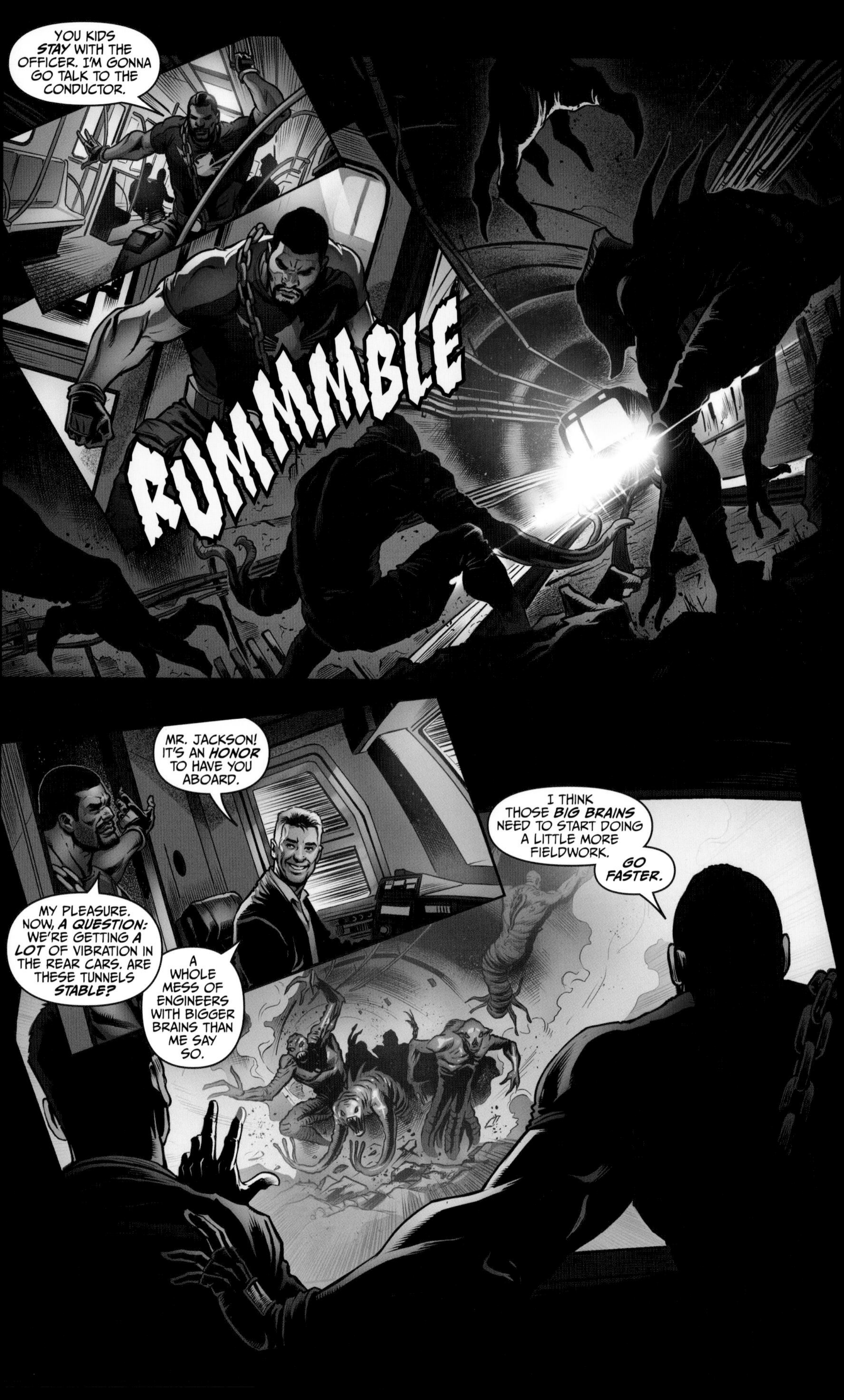
YOU KIDS *STAY* WITH THE OFFICER. I'M GONNA GO TALK TO THE CONDUCTOR.
RUMMMBLE
MR. JACKSON! IT'S AN *HONOR* TO HAVE YOU ABOARD.
MY PLEASURE. NOW, *A QUESTION:* WE'RE GETTING *A LOT* OF VIBRATION IN THE REAR CARS. ARE THESE TUNNELS *STABLE?*
A WHOLE MESS OF ENGINEERS WITH BIGGER BRAINS THAN ME SAY SO.
I THINK THOSE *BIG BRAINS* NEED TO START DOING A LITTLE MORE FIELDWORK.
GO FASTER.

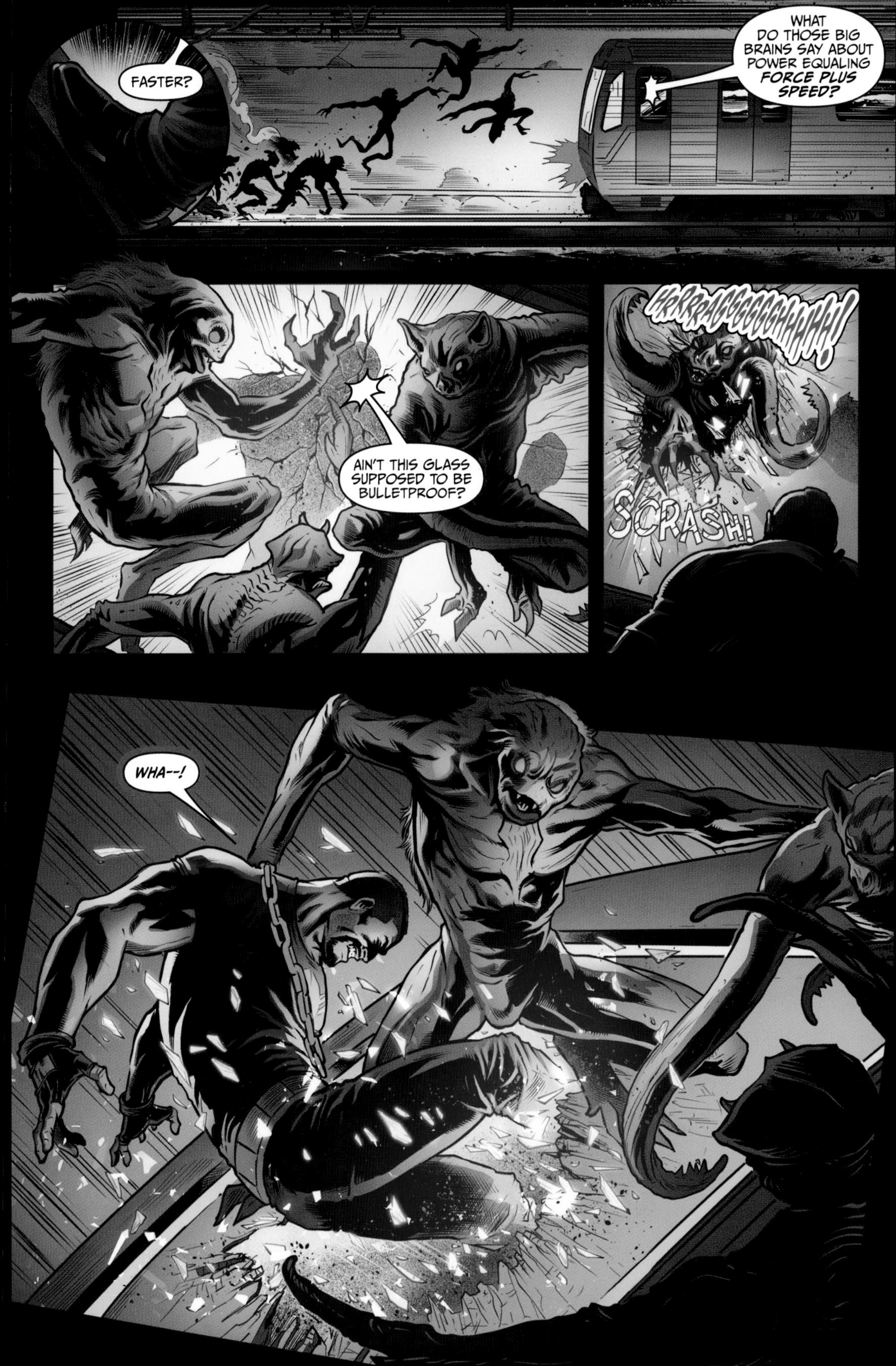
FASTER?
WHAT DO THOSE BIG BRAINS SAY ABOUT POWER EQUALING FORCE PLUS SPEED?
AIN'T THIS GLASS SUPPOSED TO BE BULLETPROOF?
HRKRRAGGGGGHHHH!
SCRASH!
WHA--!

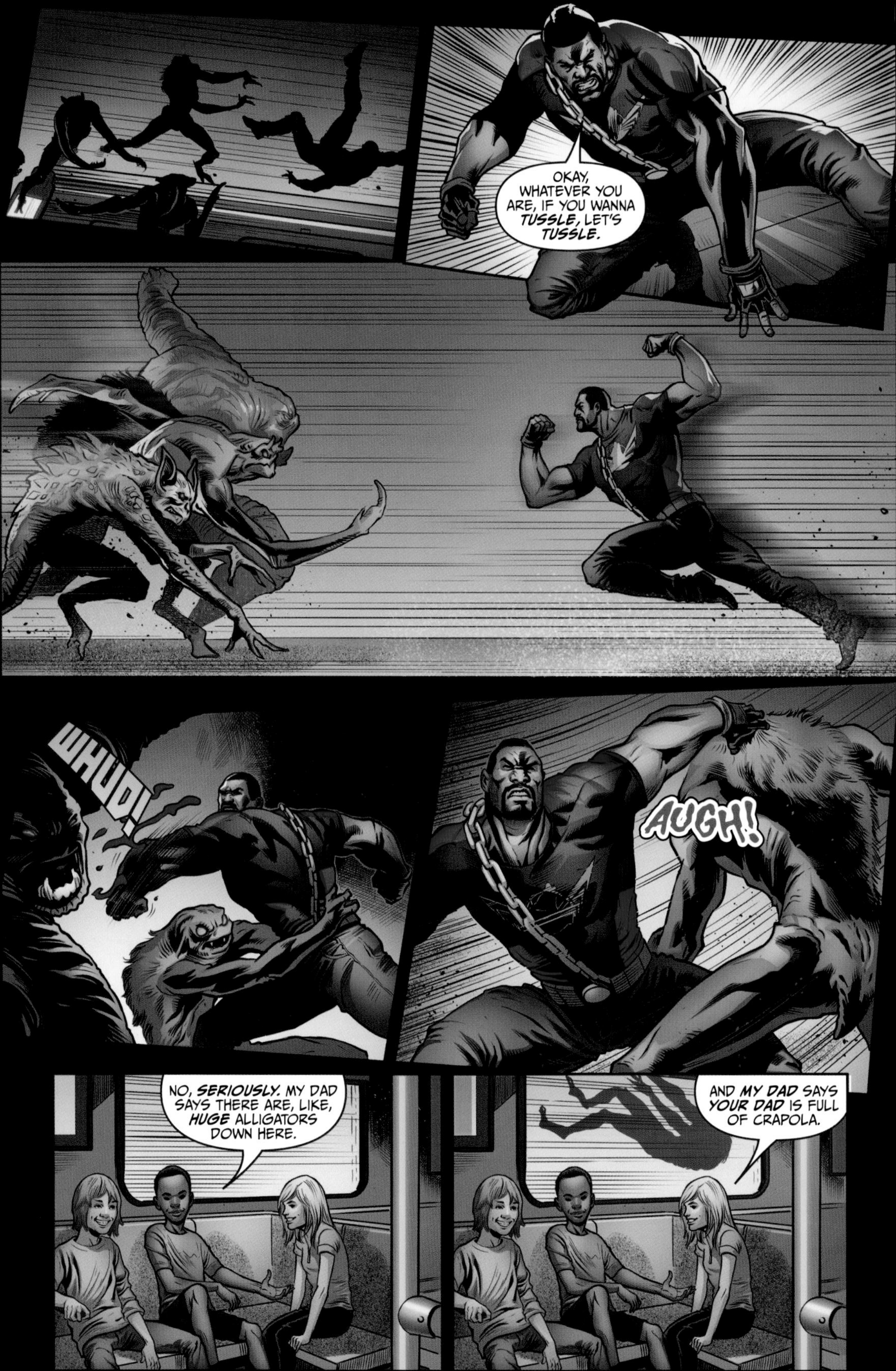
OKAY, WHATEVER YOU ARE, IF YOU WANNA TUSSLE, LET'S TUSSLE.
WHUD!
AUGH!
NO, SERIOUSLY. MY DAD SAYS THERE ARE, LIKE, HUGE ALLIGATORS DOWN HERE.
AND MY DAD SAYS YOUR DAD IS FULL OF CRAPOLA.

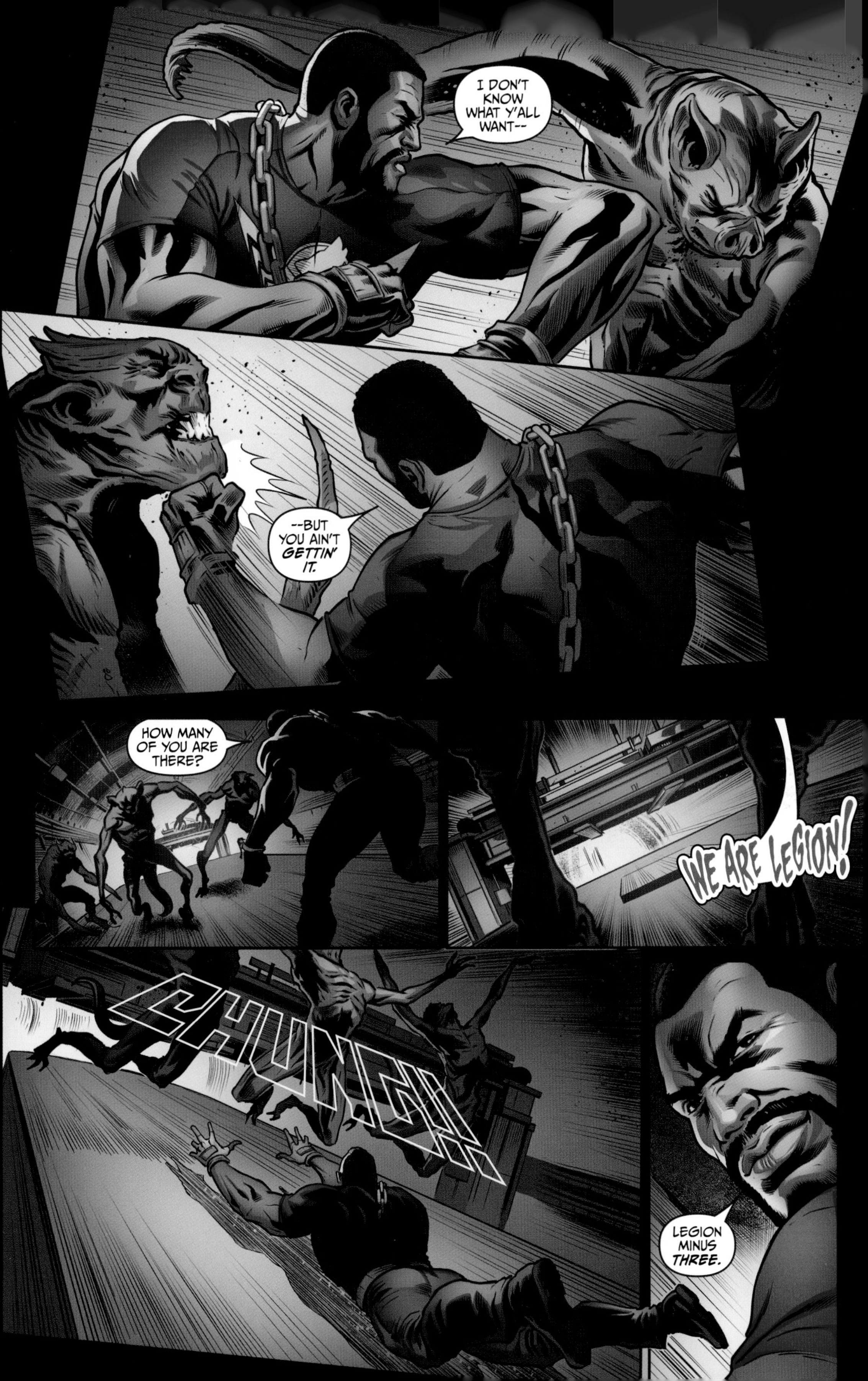
I DON'T KNOW WHAT Y'ALL WANT--
--BUT YOU AIN'T GETTIN' IT.
HOW MANY OF YOU ARE THERE?
WE ARE LEGION!
CHUNG!!
LEGION MINUS THREE.

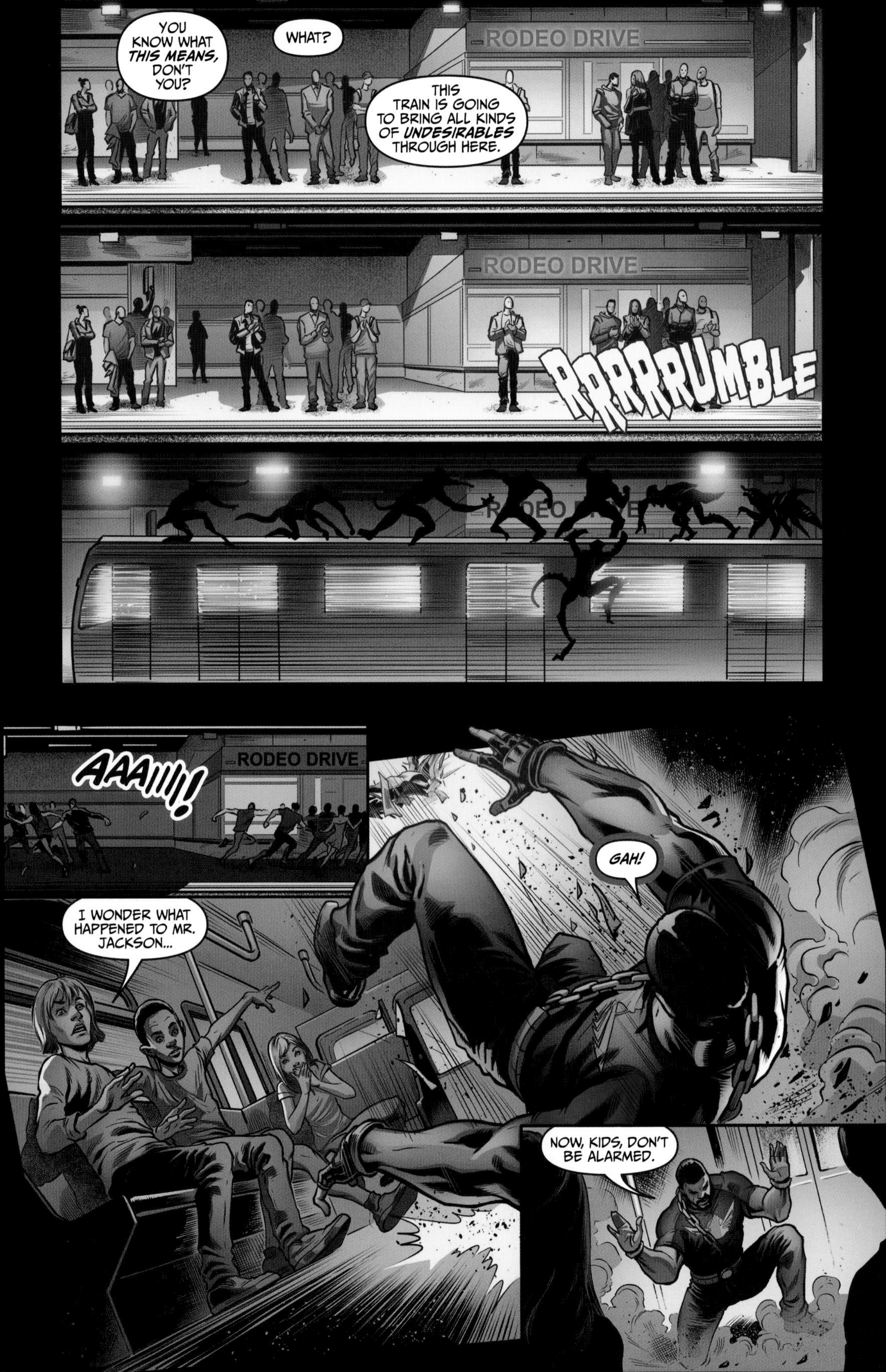
YOU KNOW WHAT *THIS MEANS,* DON'T YOU?
WHAT?
RODEO DRIVE
THIS TRAIN IS GOING TO BRING ALL KINDS OF *UNDESIRABLES* THROUGH HERE.
RODEO DRIVE
RRRRRUMBLE
RODEO DRIVE
AAAIIII!
GAH!
I WONDER WHAT HAPPENED TO MR. JACKSON...
NOW, KIDS, DON'T BE ALARMED.

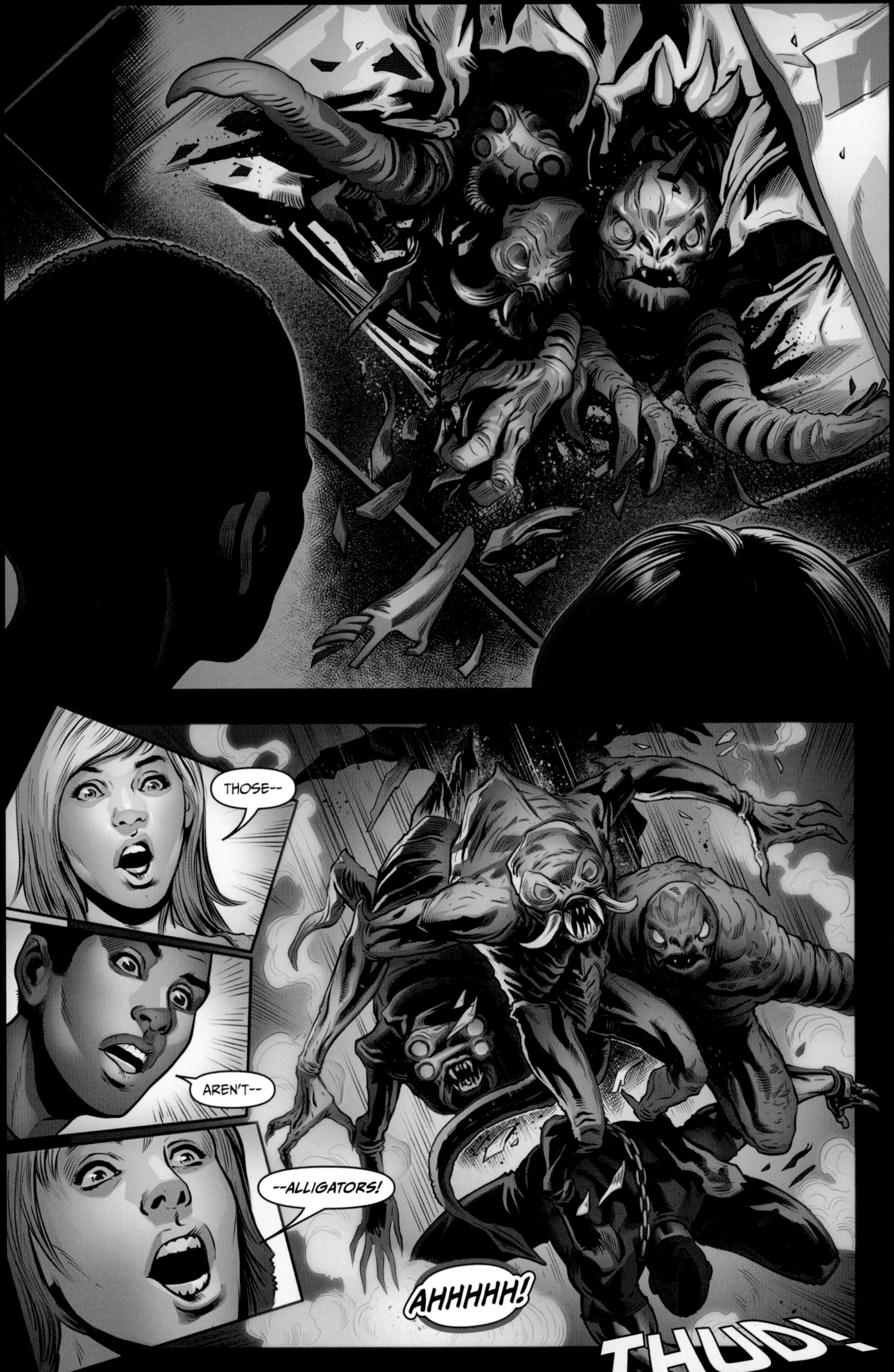
THOSE--
AREN'T--
--ALLIGATORS!
AHHHHH!
THUD!

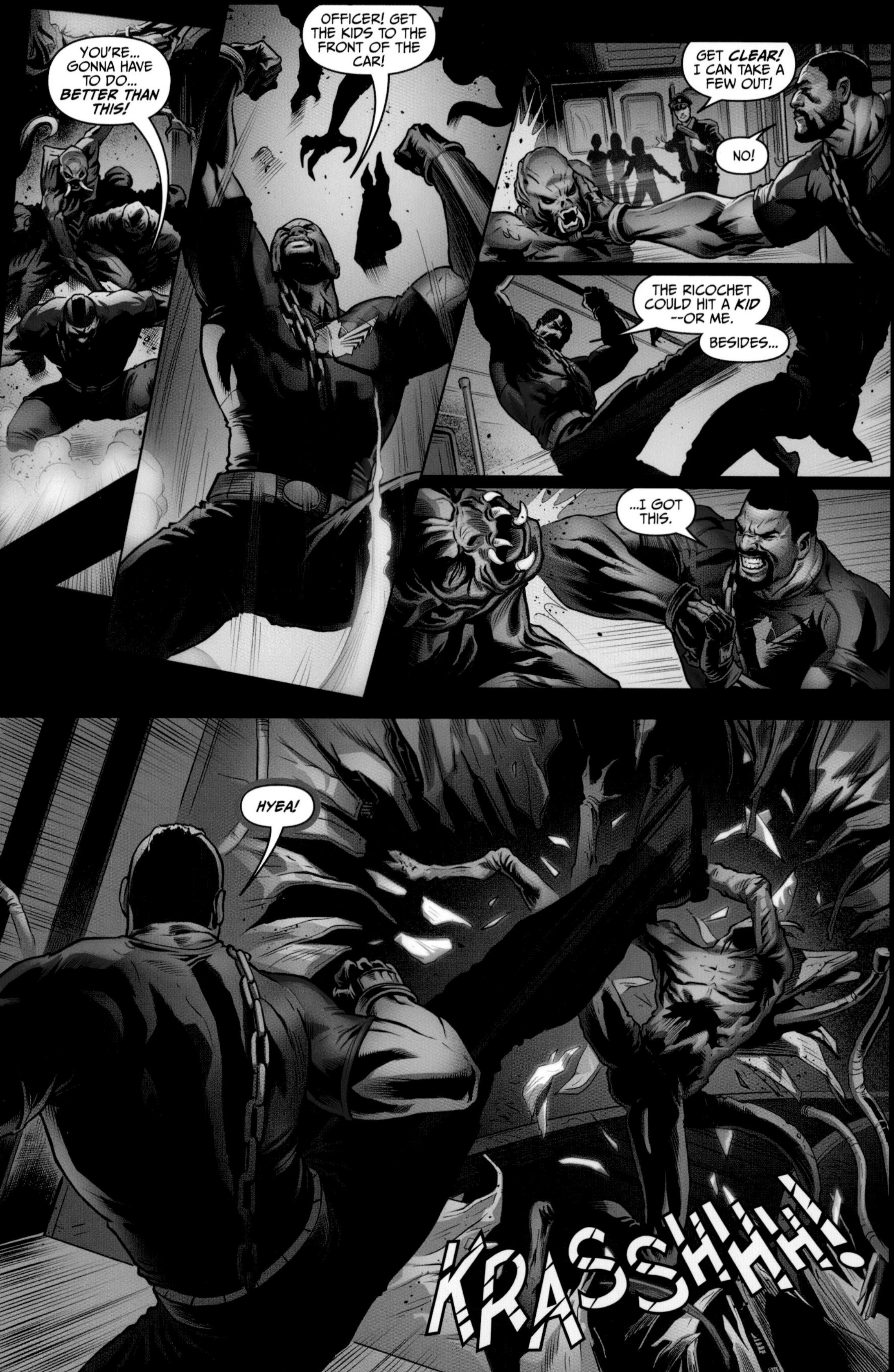
YOU'RE... GONNA HAVE TO DO... BETTER THAN THIS!
OFFICER! GET THE KIDS TO THE FRONT OF THE CAR!
GET CLEAR! I CAN TAKE A FEW OUT!
NO!
THE RICOCHET COULD HIT A KID --OR ME.
BESIDES...
...I GOT THIS.
HYEA!
KRASSHHH!

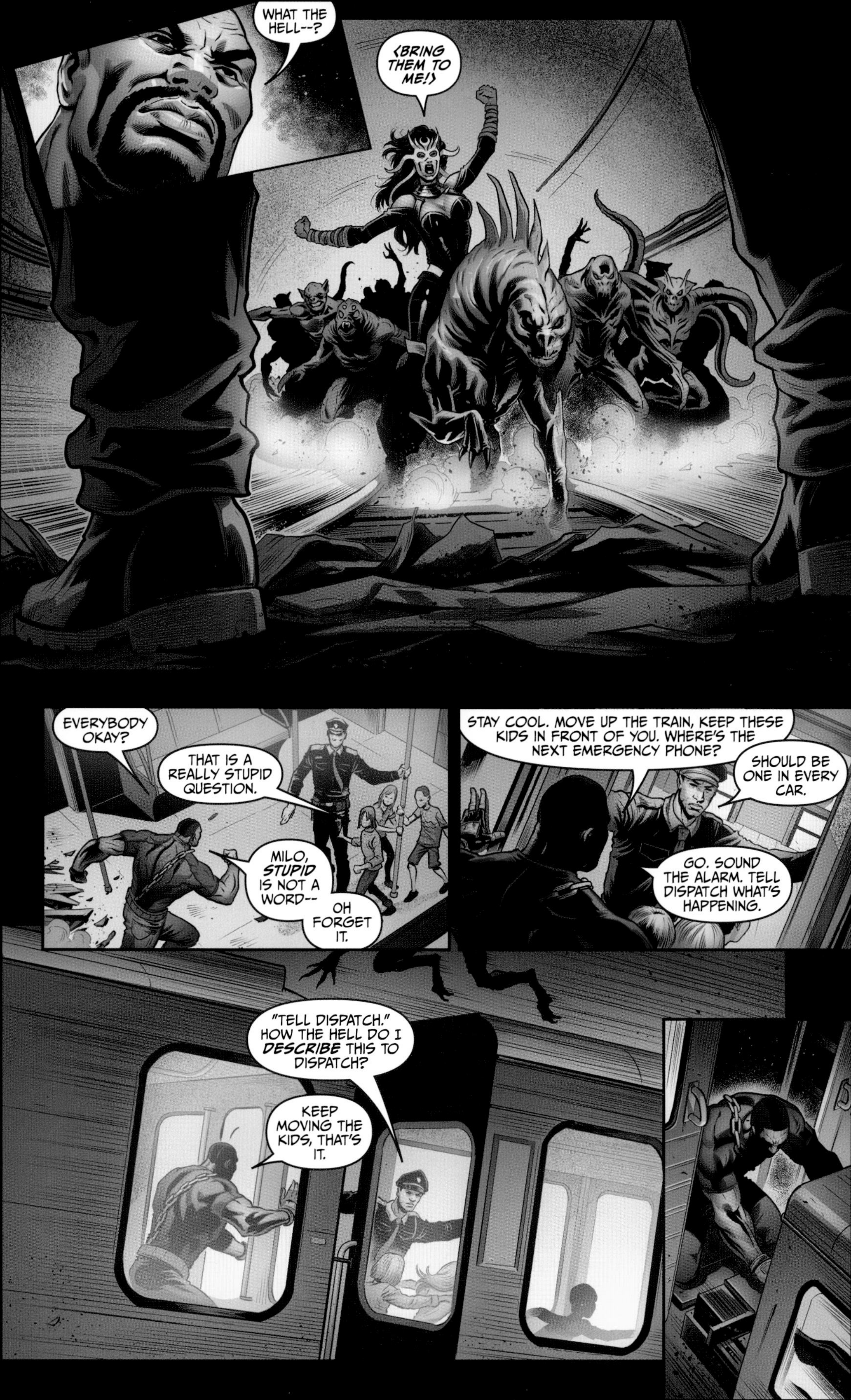
WHAT THE HELL--?
‹BRING THEM TO ME!›
EVERYBODY OKAY?
THAT IS A REALLY STUPID QUESTION.
MILO, *STUPID* IS NOT A WORD--
OH FORGET IT.
STAY COOL. MOVE UP THE TRAIN, KEEP THESE KIDS IN FRONT OF YOU. WHERE'S THE NEXT EMERGENCY PHONE?
SHOULD BE ONE IN EVERY CAR.
GO. SOUND THE ALARM. TELL DISPATCH WHAT'S HAPPENING.
"TELL DISPATCH." HOW THE HELL DO I *DESCRIBE* THIS TO DISPATCH?
KEEP MOVING THE KIDS, THAT'S IT.

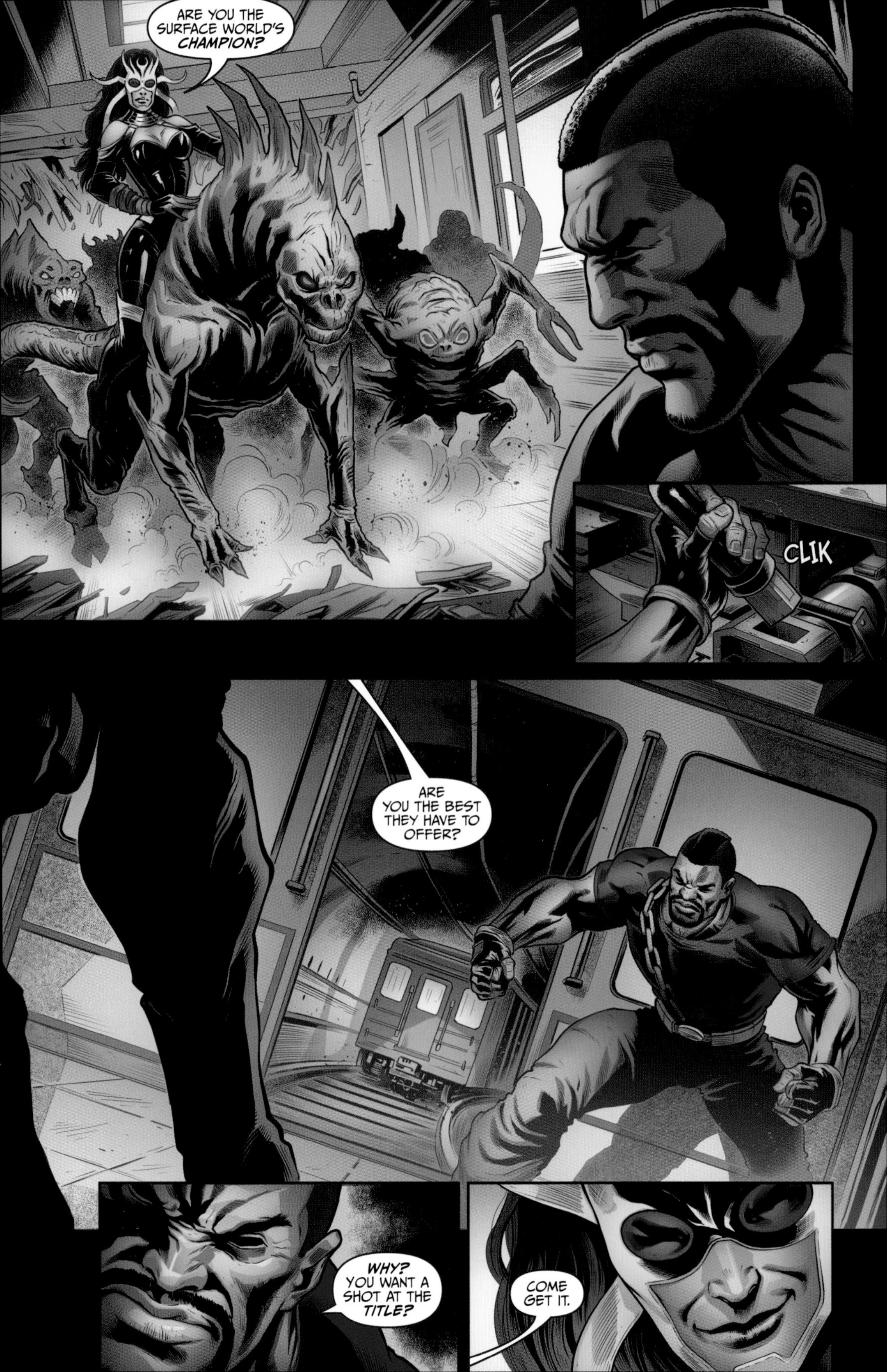
ARE YOU THE SURFACE WORLD'S *CHAMPION?*
CLIK
ARE YOU THE BEST THEY HAVE TO OFFER?
WHY? YOU WANT A SHOT AT THE *TITLE?*
COME GET IT.

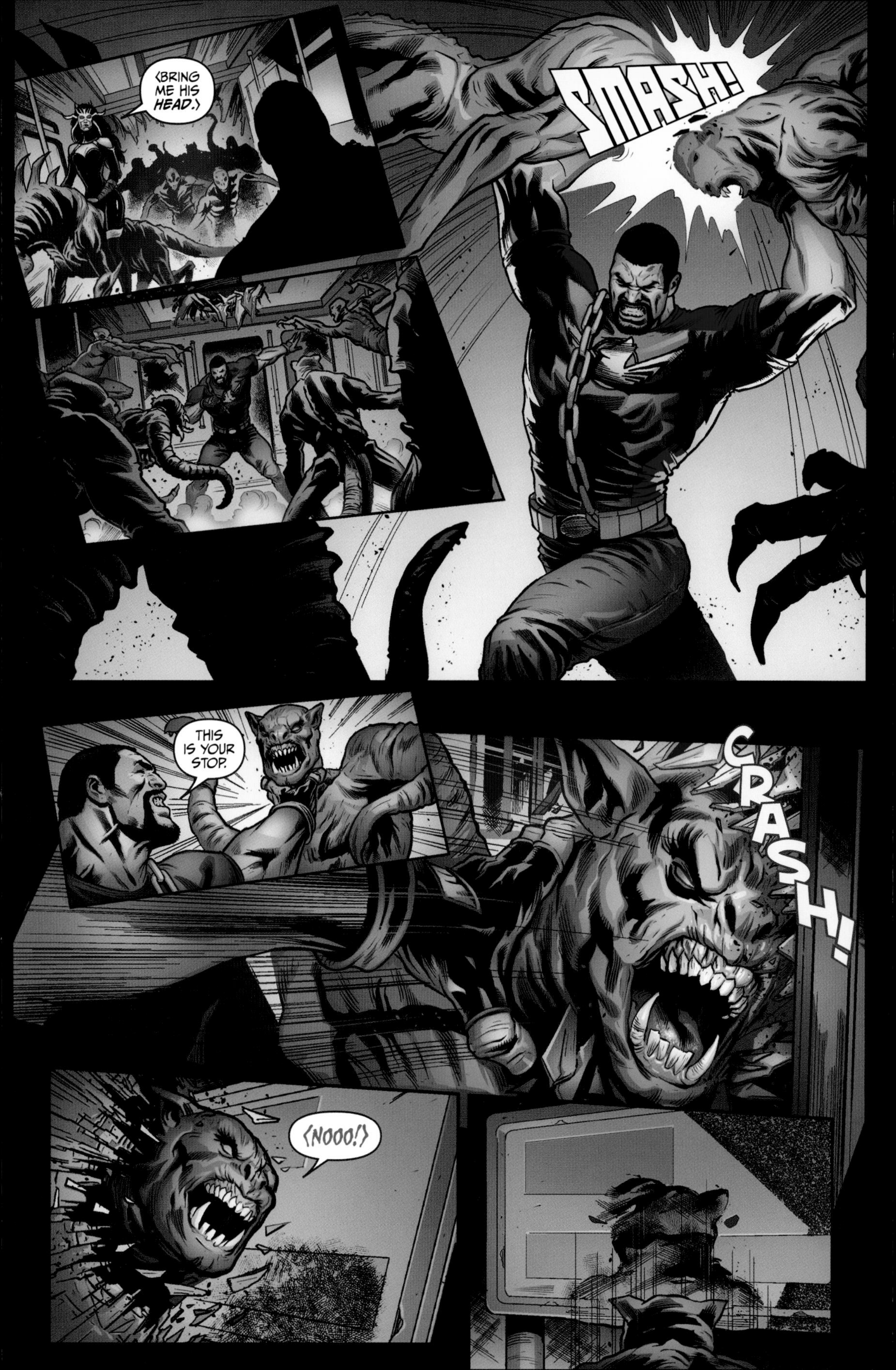
‹BRING ME HIS HEAD.›
SMASH!
THIS IS YOUR STOP.
CRASH!
‹NOOO!›

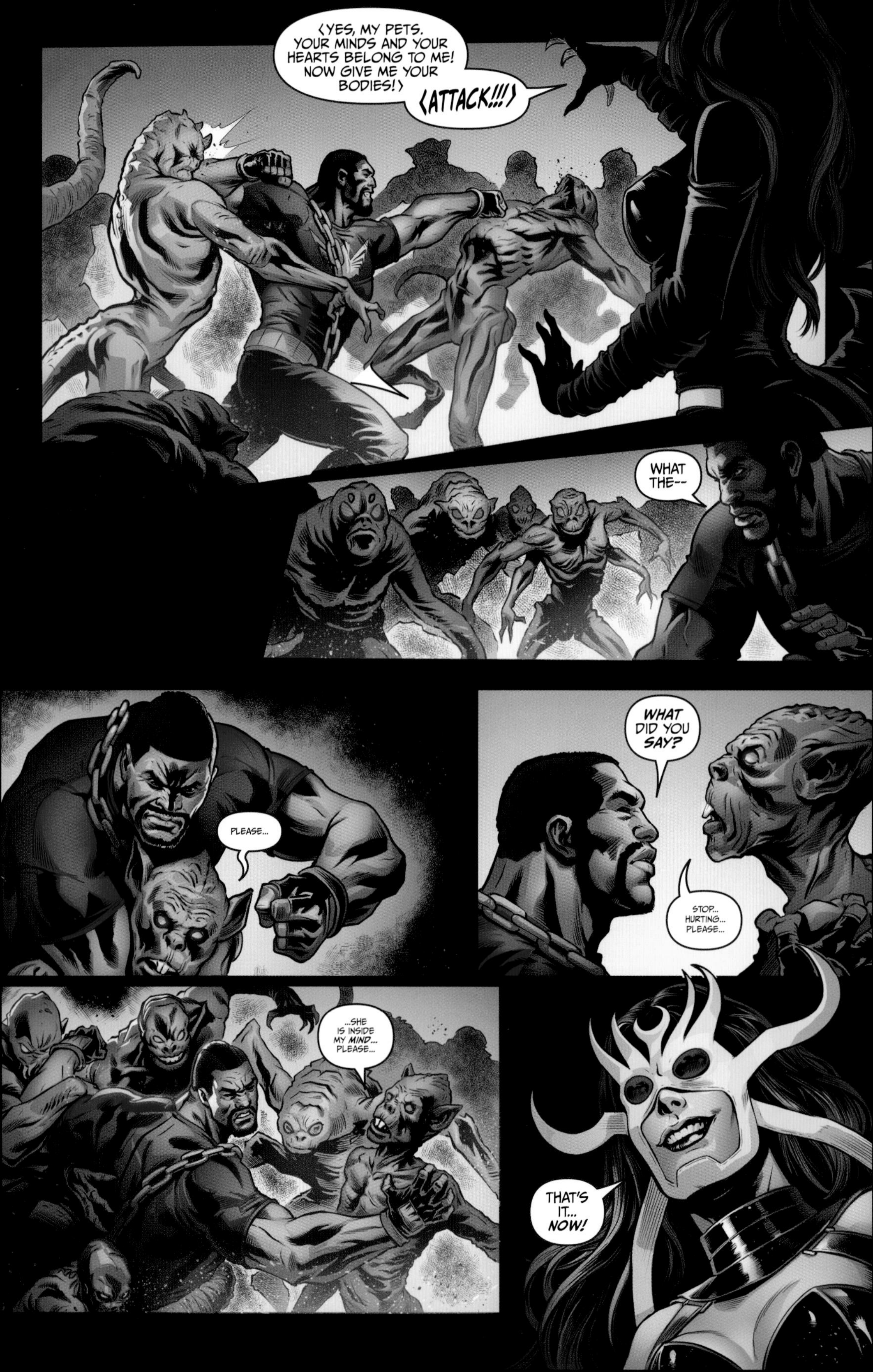
⟨YES, MY PETS. YOUR MINDS AND YOUR HEARTS BELONG TO ME! NOW GIVE ME YOUR BODIES!⟩
⟨ATTACK!!!⟩
WHAT THE--
PLEASE...
WHAT DID YOU SAY?
STOP... HURTING... PLEASE...
...SHE IS INSIDE MY MIND... PLEASE...
THAT'S IT... NOW!

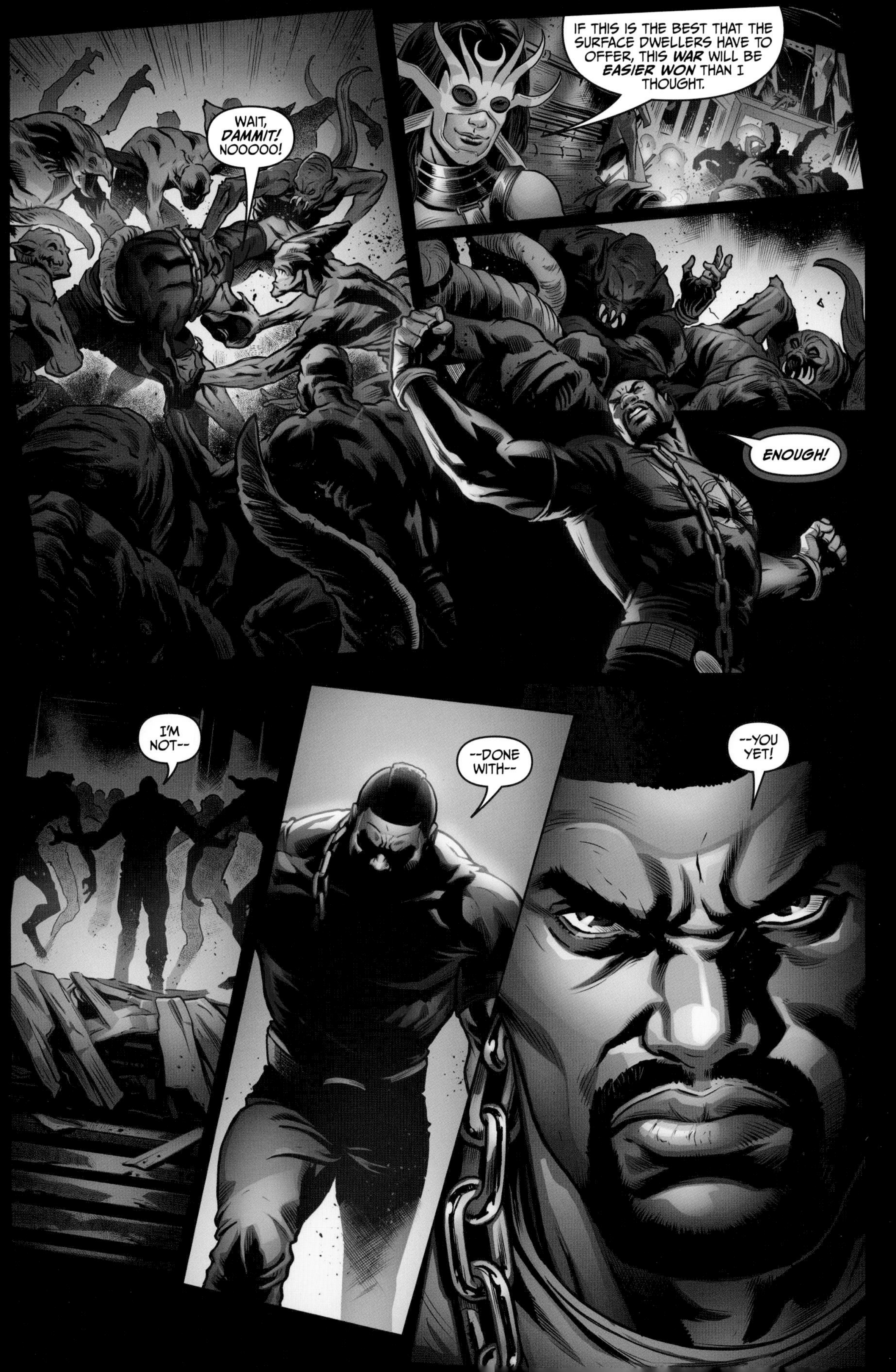
WAIT, DAMMIT! NOOOOO!
IF THIS IS THE BEST THAT THE SURFACE DWELLERS HAVE TO OFFER, THIS WAR WILL BE EASIER WON THAN I THOUGHT.
ENOUGH!
I'M NOT--
--DONE WITH--
--YOU YET!

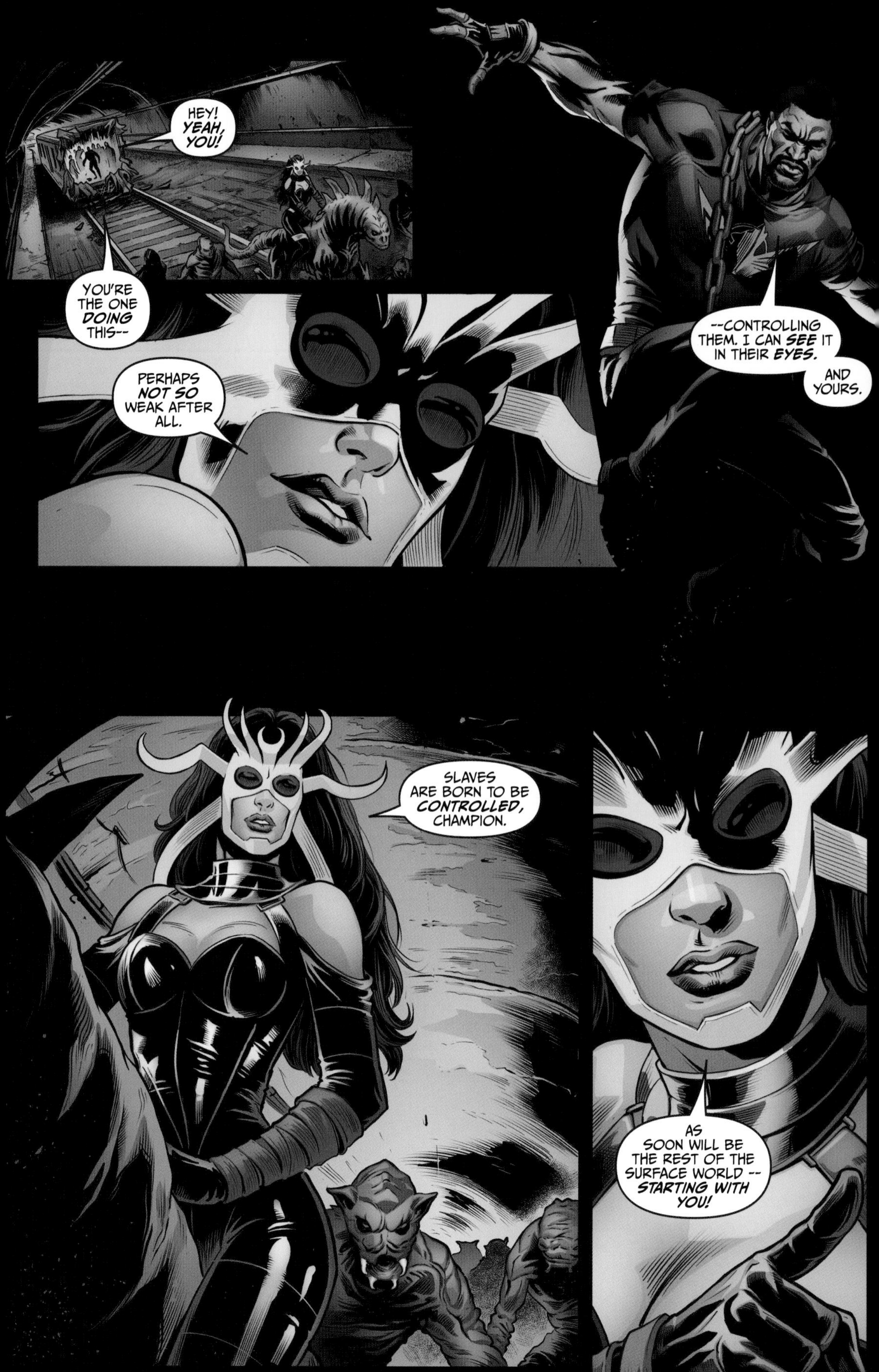
HEY! YEAH, YOU!
YOU'RE THE ONE DOING THIS--
--CONTROLLING THEM. I CAN SEE IT IN THEIR EYES.
AND YOURS.
PERHAPS NOT SO WEAK AFTER ALL.
SLAVES ARE BORN TO BE CONTROLLED, CHAMPION.
AS SOON WILL BE THE REST OF THE SURFACE WORLD -- STARTING WITH YOU!

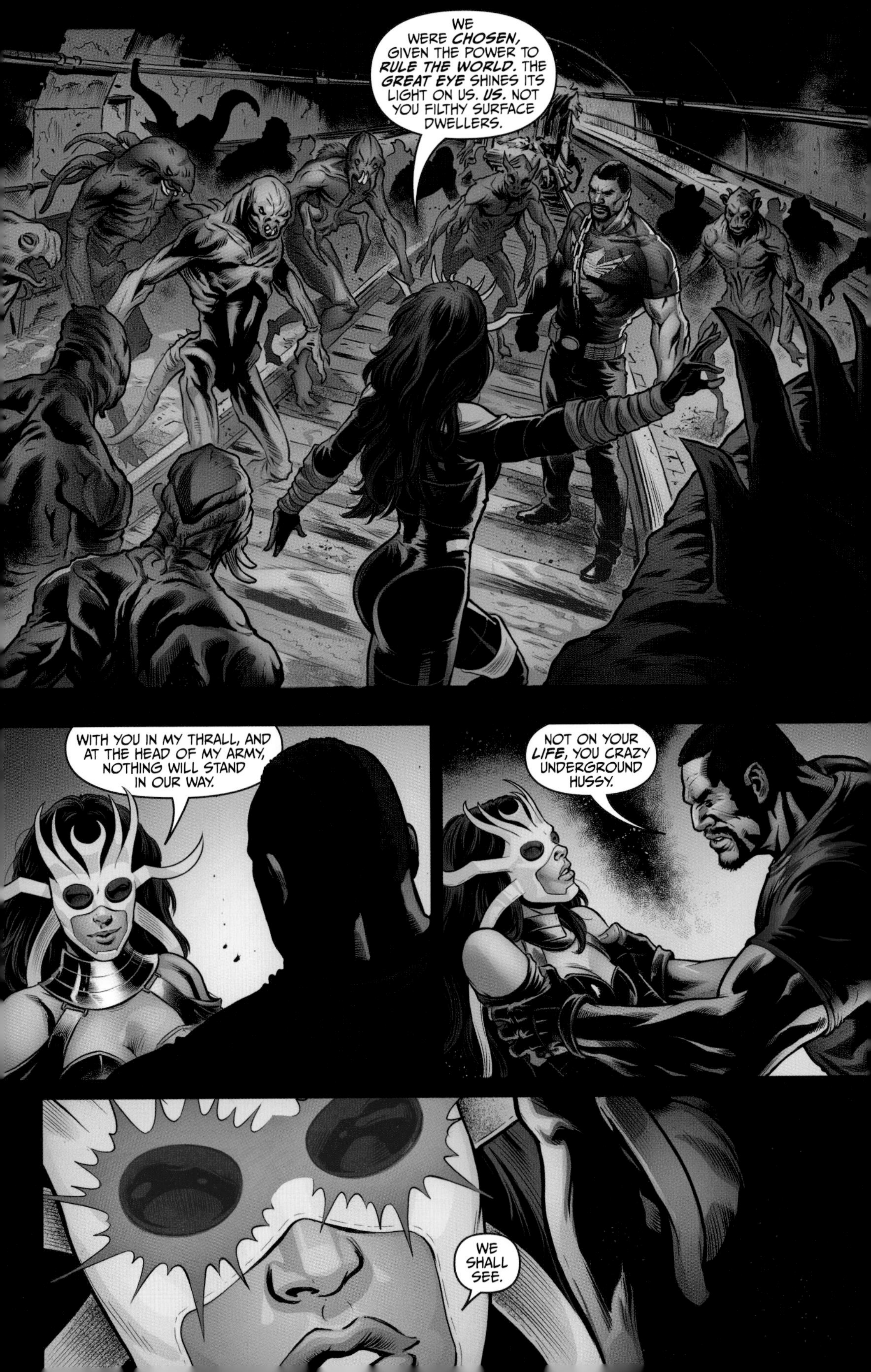
WE WERE *CHOSEN,* GIVEN THE POWER TO *RULE THE WORLD.* THE *GREAT EYE* SHINES ITS LIGHT ON US. *US.* NOT YOU FILTHY SURFACE DWELLERS.
WITH YOU IN MY THRALL, AND AT THE HEAD OF MY ARMY, NOTHING WILL STAND IN OUR WAY.
NOT ON YOUR *LIFE,* YOU CRAZY UNDERGROUND HUSSY.
WE SHALL SEE.

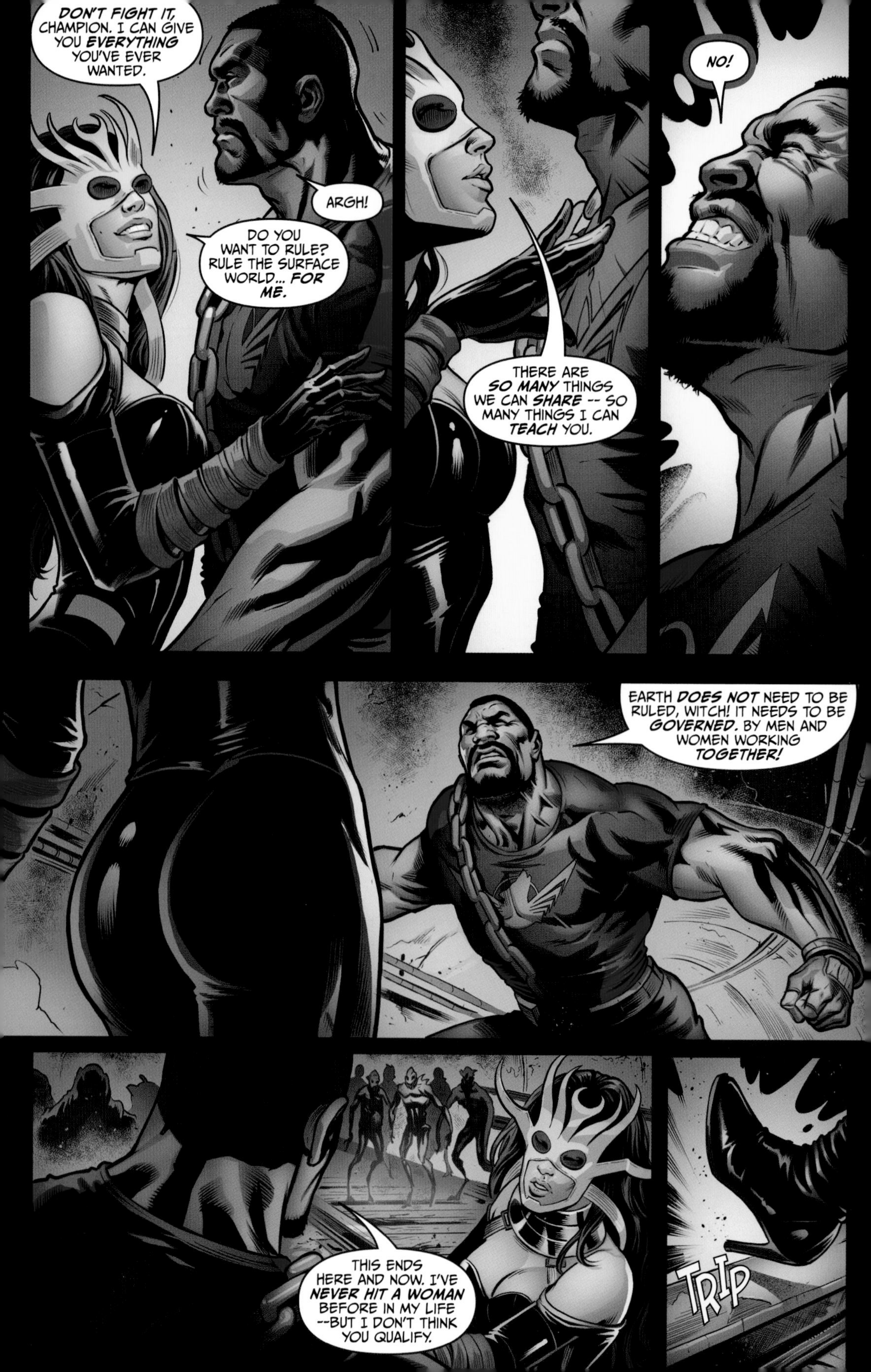

DON'T FIGHT IT, CHAMPION. I CAN GIVE YOU EVERYTHING YOU'VE EVER WANTED.
ARGH!
DO YOU WANT TO RULE? RULE THE SURFACE WORLD... FOR ME.
THERE ARE SO MANY THINGS WE CAN SHARE -- SO MANY THINGS I CAN TEACH YOU.
NO!
EARTH DOES NOT NEED TO BE RULED, WITCH! IT NEEDS TO BE GOVERNED. BY MEN AND WOMEN WORKING TOGETHER!
THIS ENDS HERE AND NOW. I'VE NEVER HIT A WOMAN BEFORE IN MY LIFE --BUT I DON'T THINK YOU QUALIFY.
TRIP

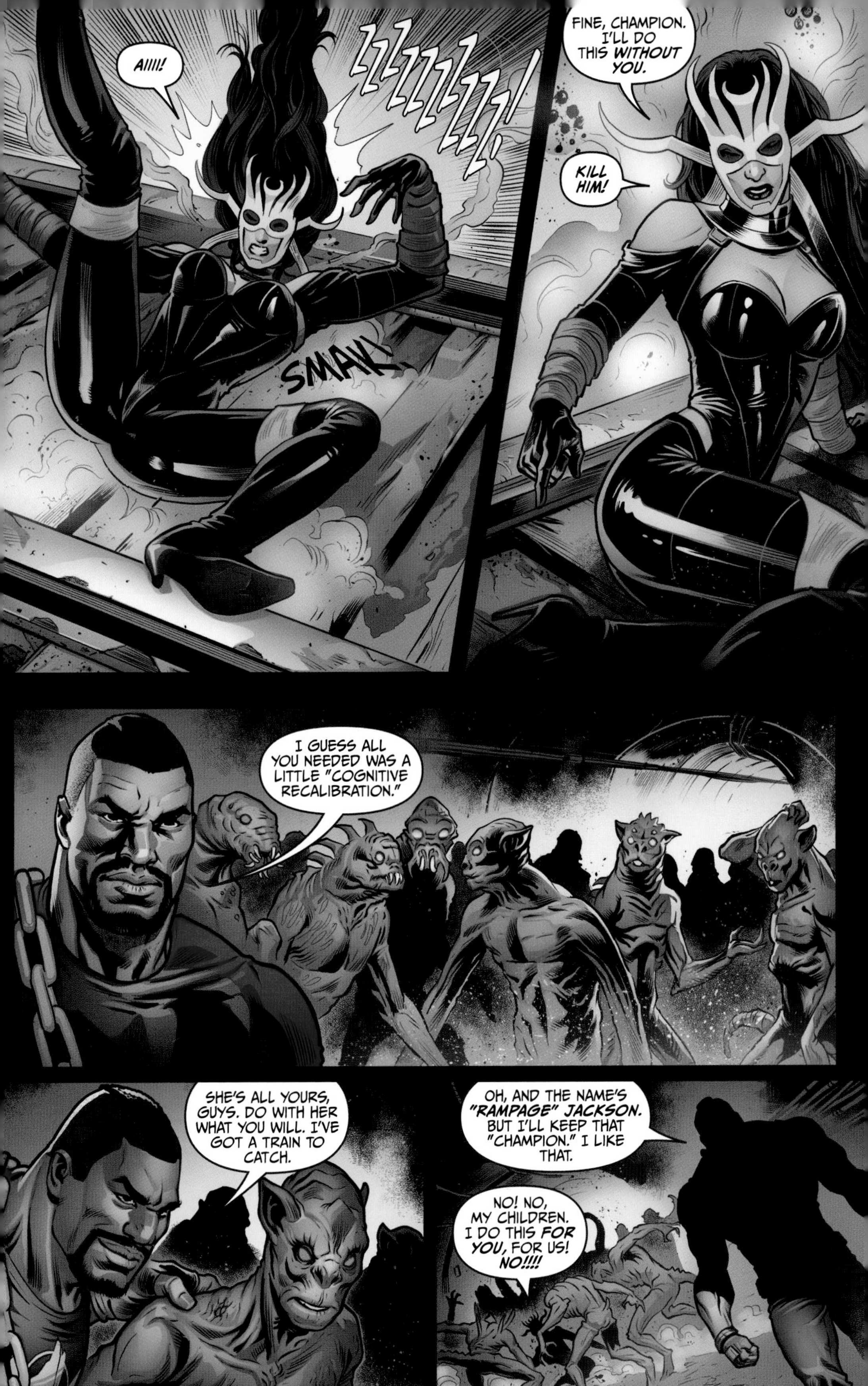
AIIII!
ZZZZZZZZZZZ!
SMAK
FINE, CHAMPION. I'LL DO THIS WITHOUT YOU.
KILL HIM!
I GUESS ALL YOU NEEDED WAS A LITTLE "COGNITIVE RECALIBRATION."
SHE'S ALL YOURS, GUYS. DO WITH HER WHAT YOU WILL. I'VE GOT A TRAIN TO CATCH.
OH, AND THE NAME'S "RAMPAGE" JACKSON. BUT I'LL KEEP THAT "CHAMPION." I LIKE THAT.
NO! NO, MY CHILDREN. I DO THIS FOR YOU, FOR US! NO!!!!

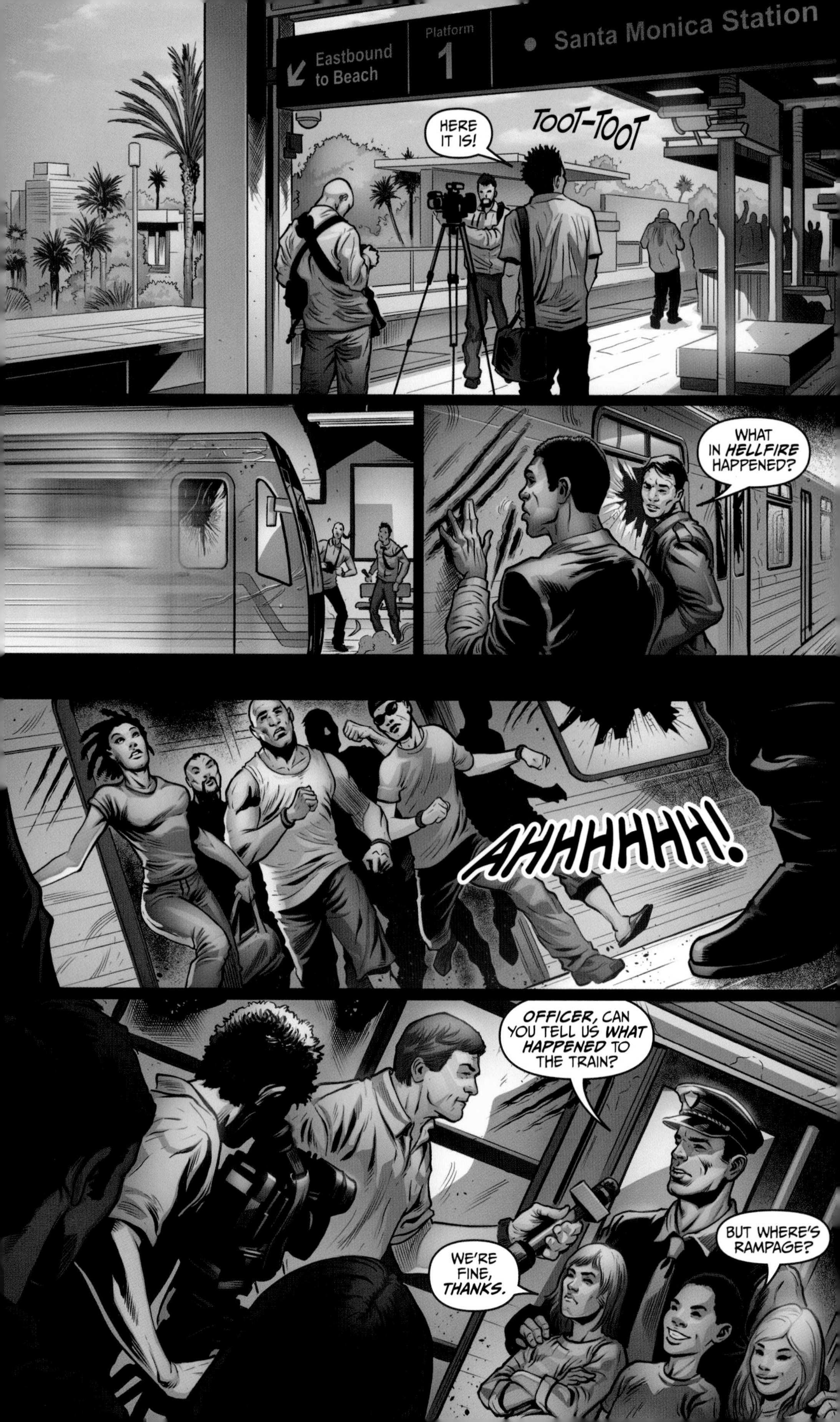
Eastbound to Beach
Platform 1
Santa Monica Station
HERE IT IS!
TOOT-TOOT
WHAT IN HELLFIRE HAPPENED?
AHHHHHH!
OFFICER, CAN YOU TELL US WHAT HAPPENED TO THE TRAIN?
WE'RE FINE, THANKS.
BUT WHERE'S RAMPAGE?

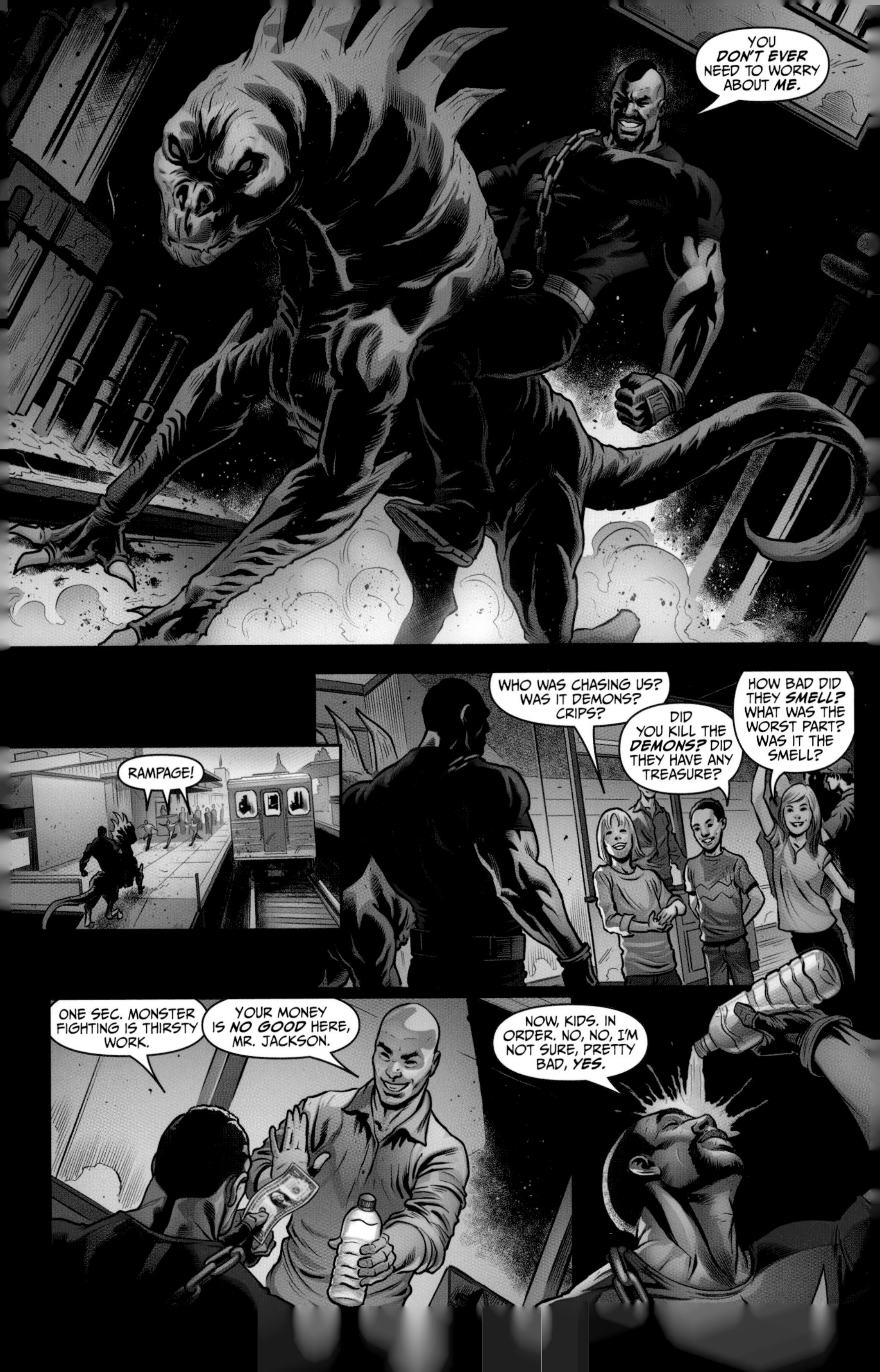

YOU DON'T EVER NEED TO WORRY ABOUT ME.
RAMPAGE!
WHO WAS CHASING US? WAS IT DEMONS? CRIPS?
DID YOU KILL THE DEMONS? DID THEY HAVE ANY TREASURE?
HOW BAD DID THEY SMELL? WHAT WAS THE WORST PART? WAS IT THE SMELL?
ONE SEC. MONSTER FIGHTING IS THIRSTY WORK.
YOUR MONEY IS NO GOOD HERE, MR. JACKSON.
NOW, KIDS. IN ORDER. NO, NO, I'M NOT SURE, PRETTY BAD, YES.

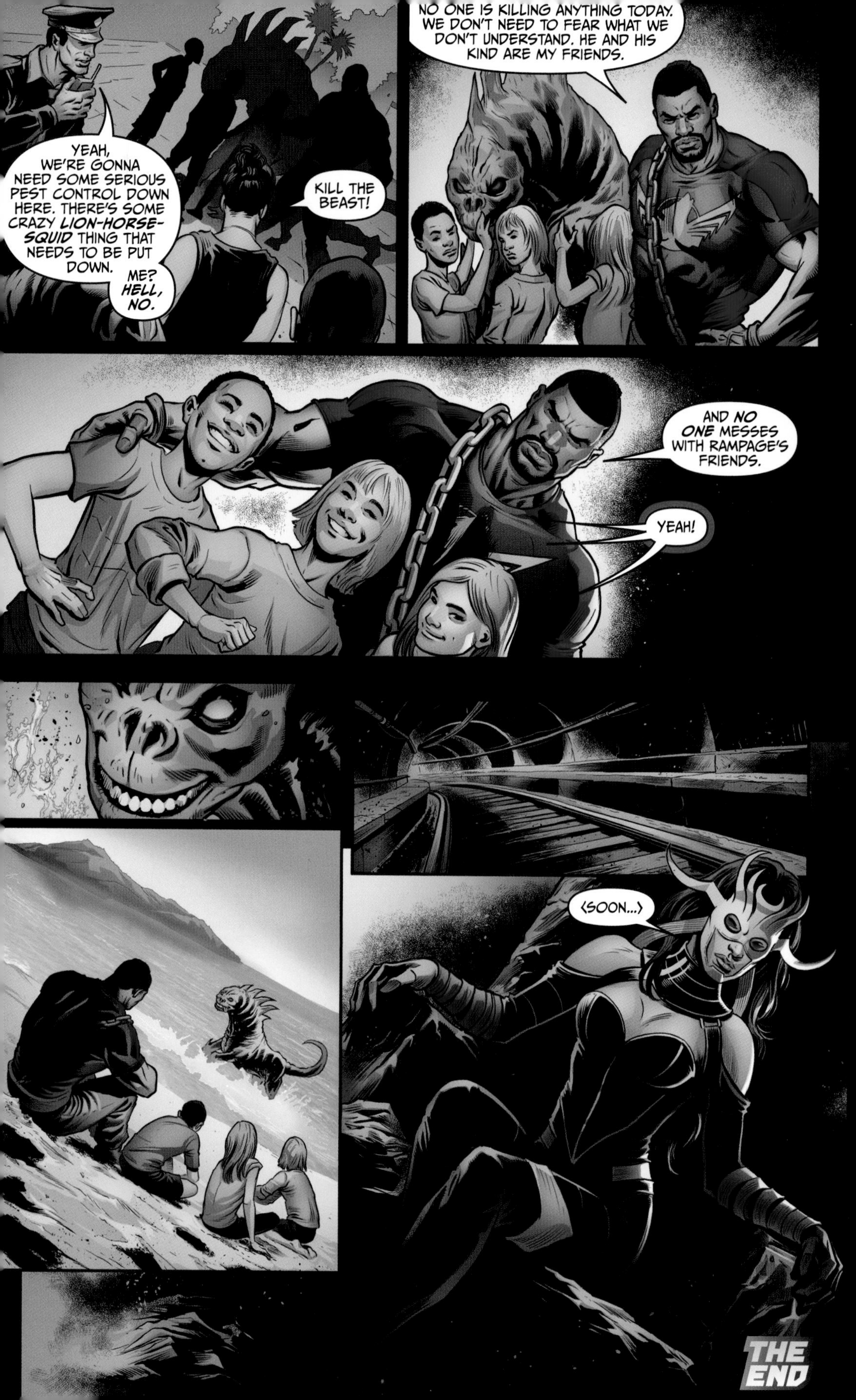
YEAH, WE'RE GONNA NEED SOME SERIOUS PEST CONTROL DOWN HERE. THERE'S SOME CRAZY ***LION-HORSE-SQUID*** THING THAT NEEDS TO BE PUT DOWN.
ME? ***HELL, NO.***
KILL THE BEAST!
NO ONE IS KILLING ANYTHING TODAY. WE DON'T NEED TO FEAR WHAT WE DON'T UNDERSTAND. HE AND HIS KIND ARE MY FRIENDS.
AND ***NO ONE*** MESSES WITH RAMPAGE'S FRIENDS.
YEAH!
<SOON...>
THE END

COVERS

DAN PANOSIAN

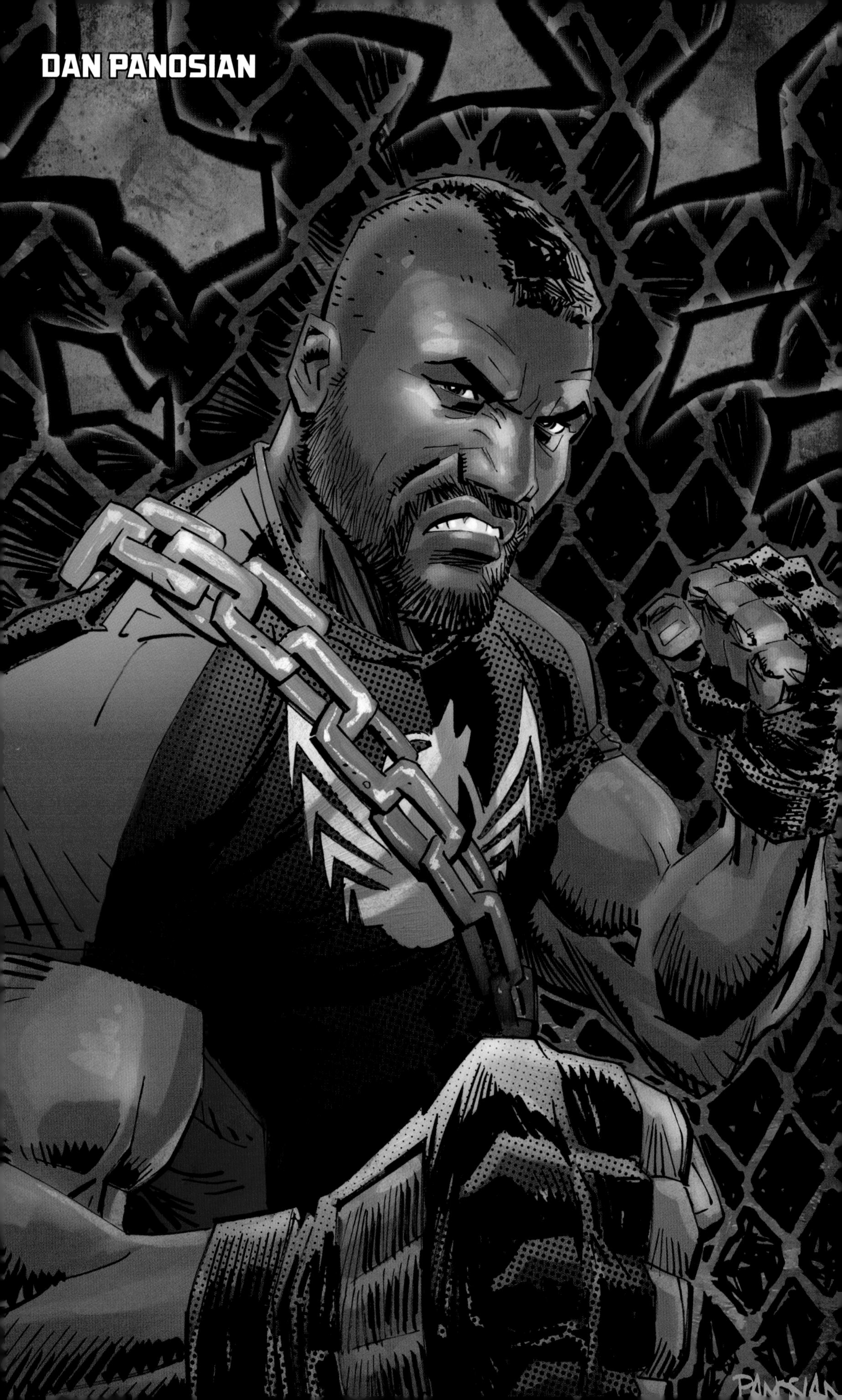

MIKE NORTON

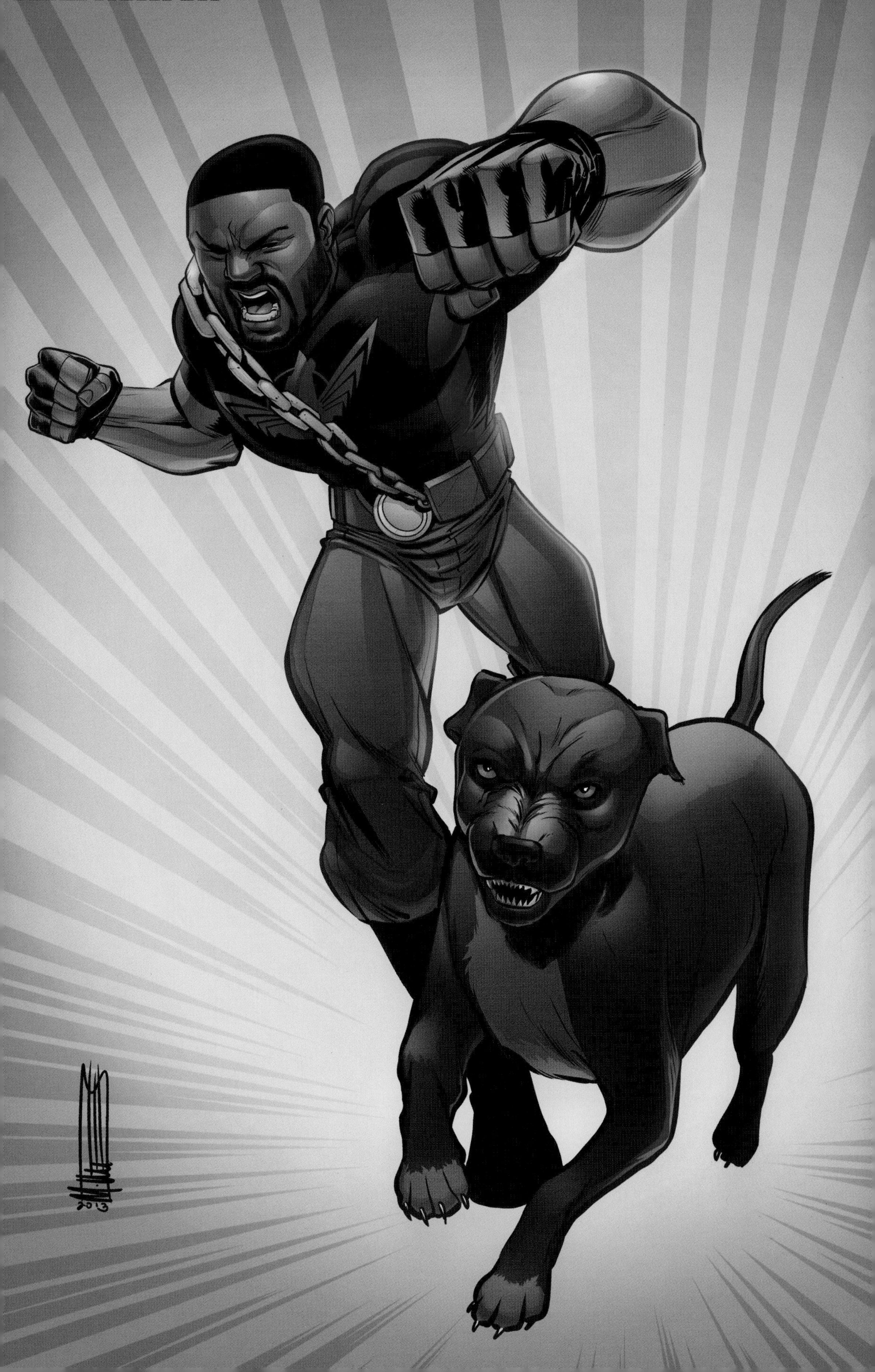

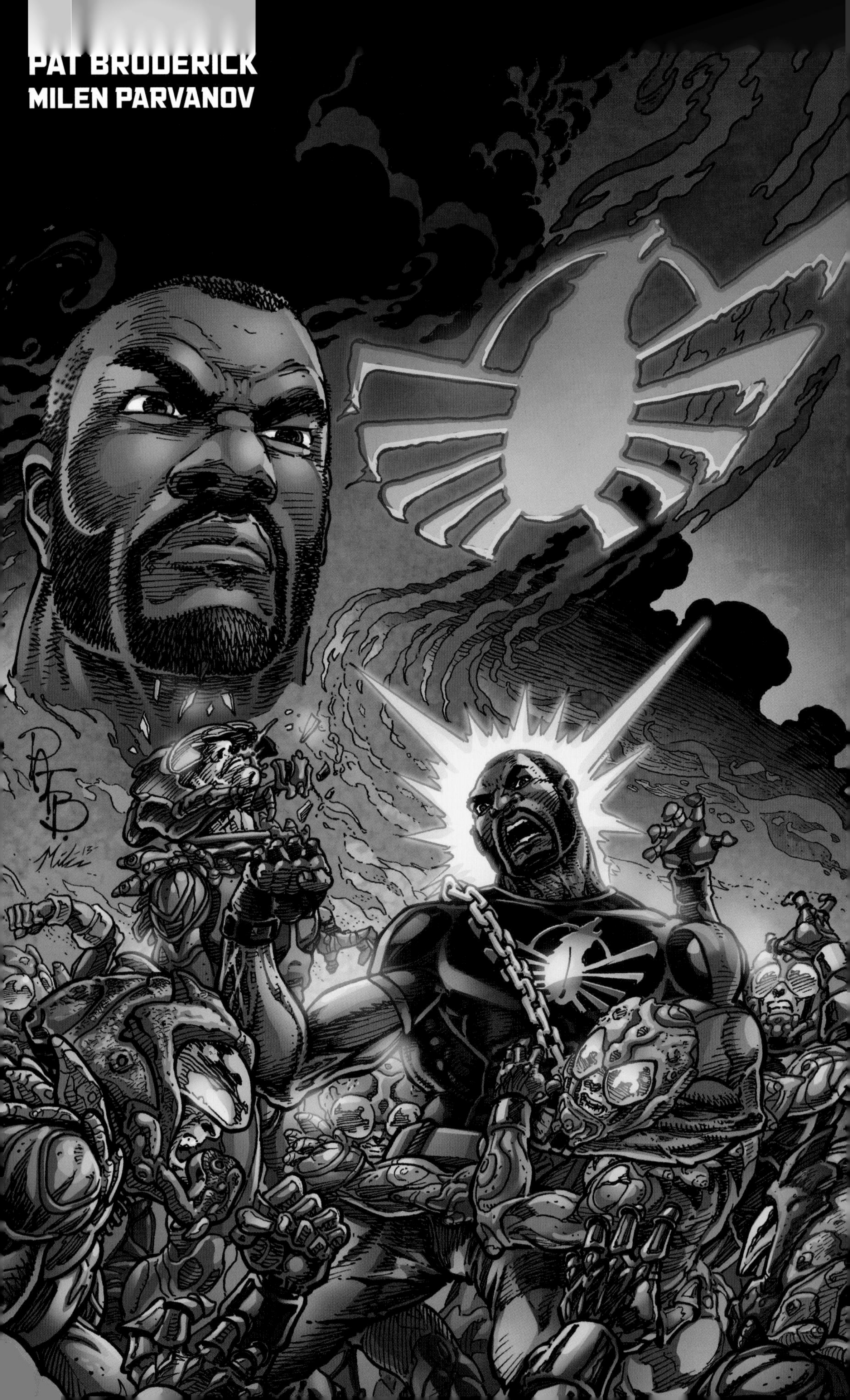
PAT BRODERICK
MILEN PARVANOV

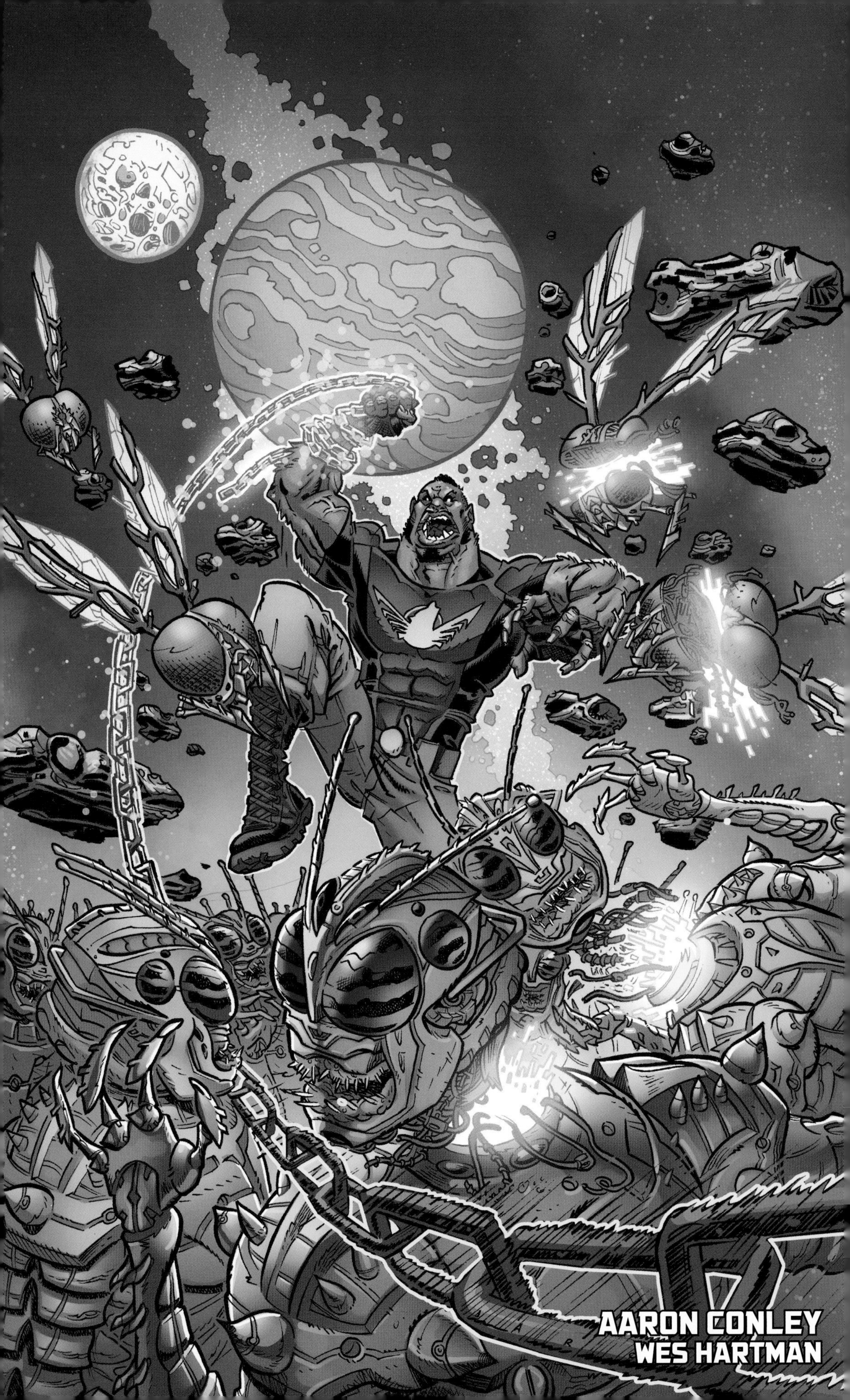
AARON CONLEY
WES HARTMAN

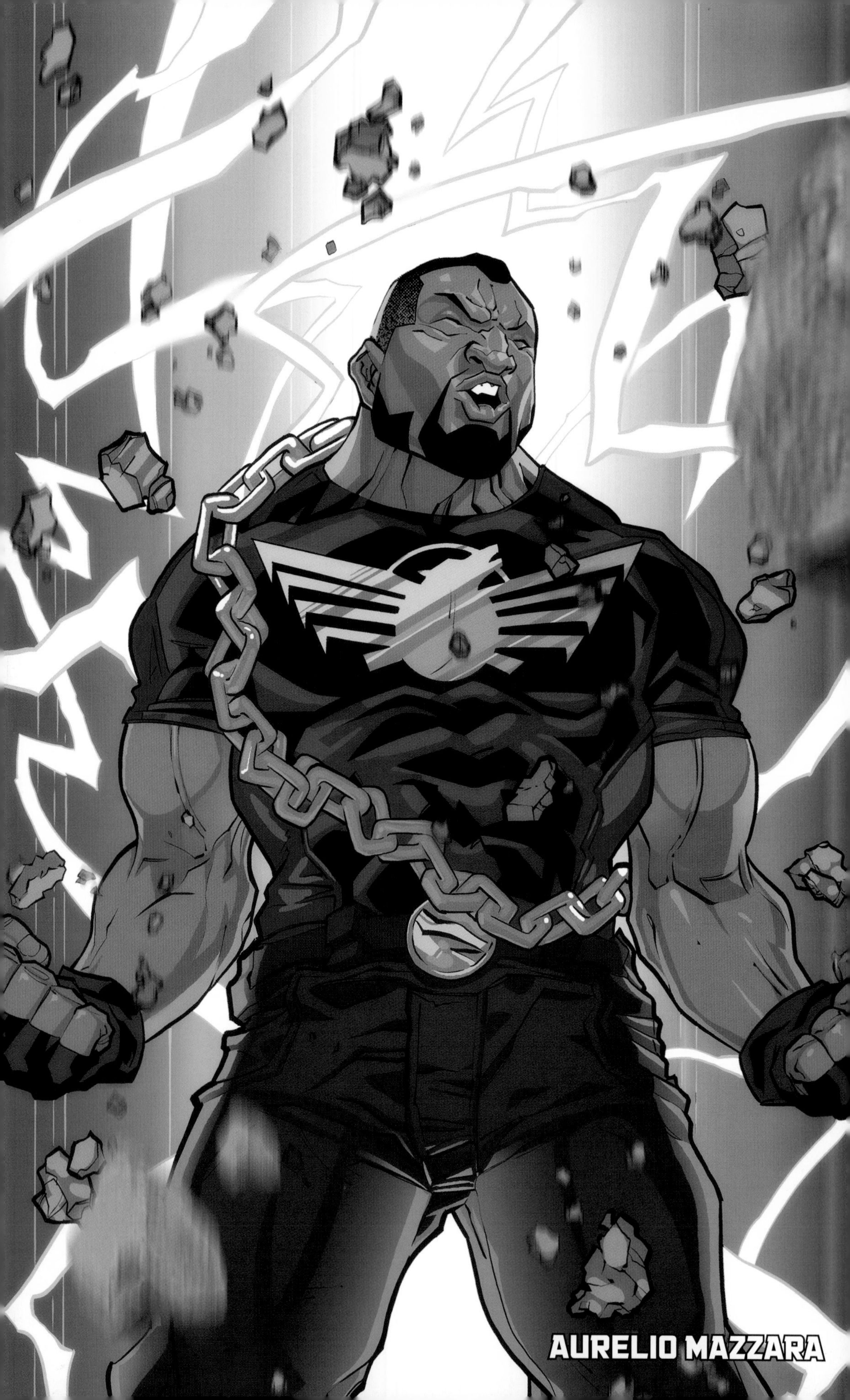
AURELIO MAZZARA

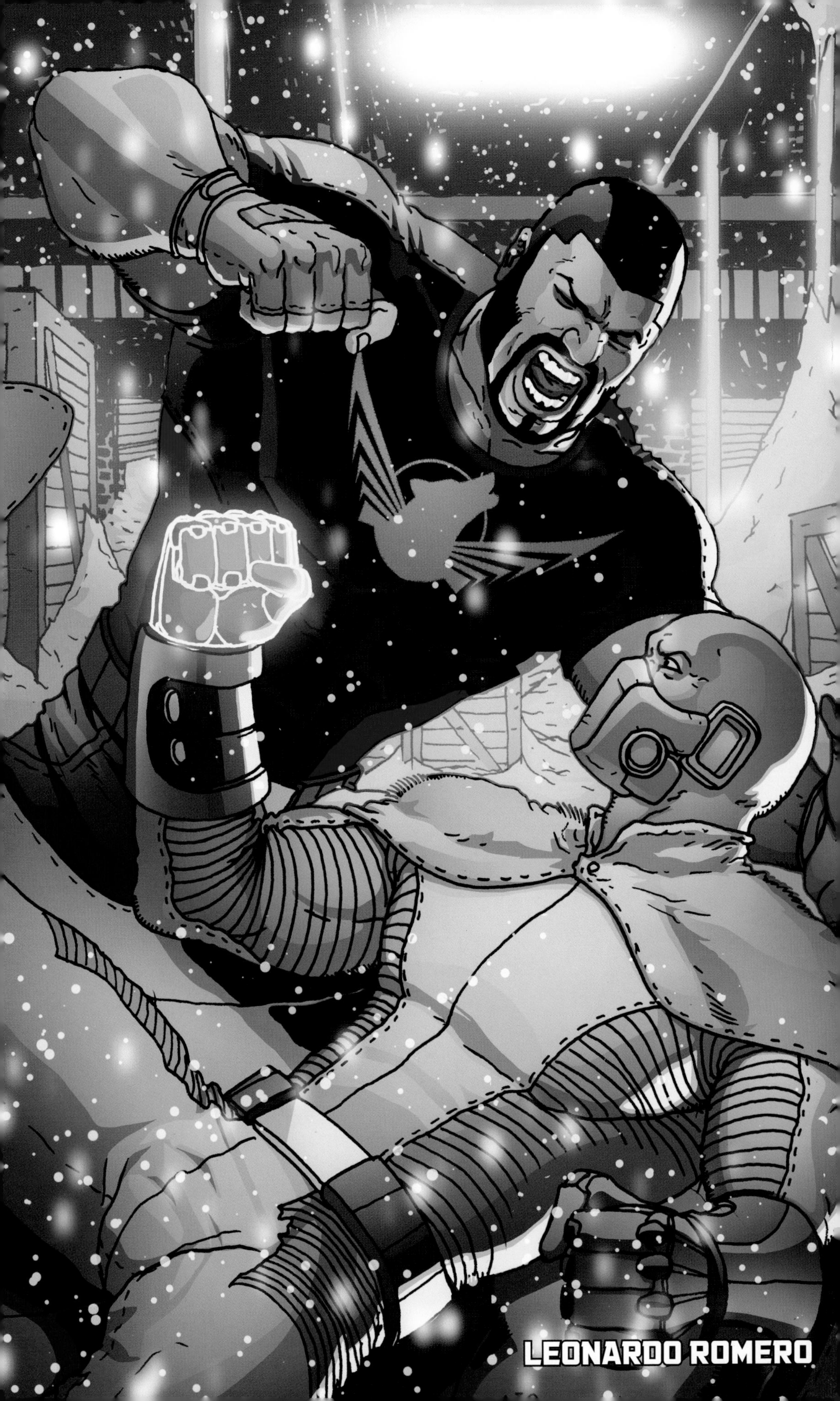

LEONARDO ROMERO

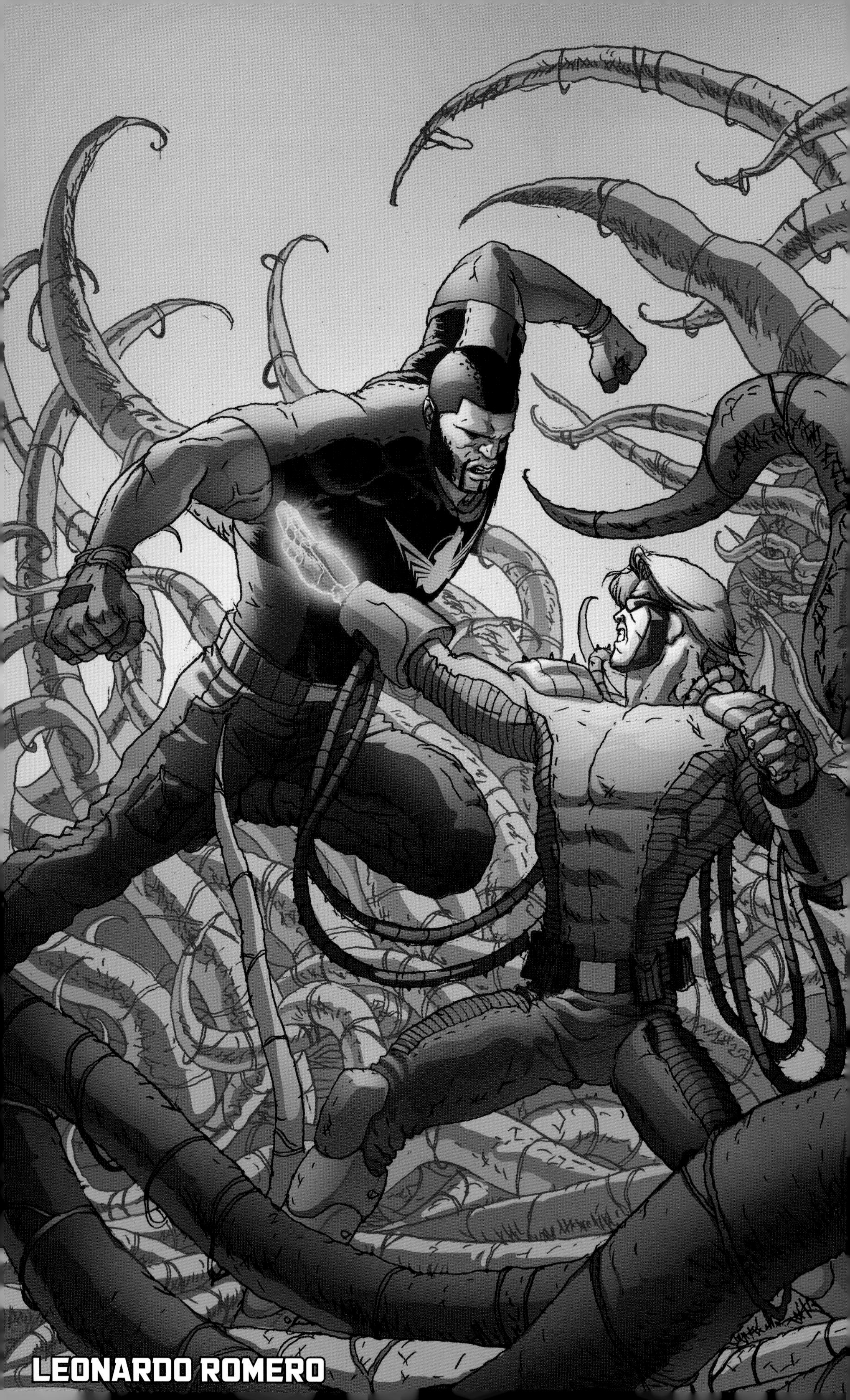
LEONARDO ROMERO

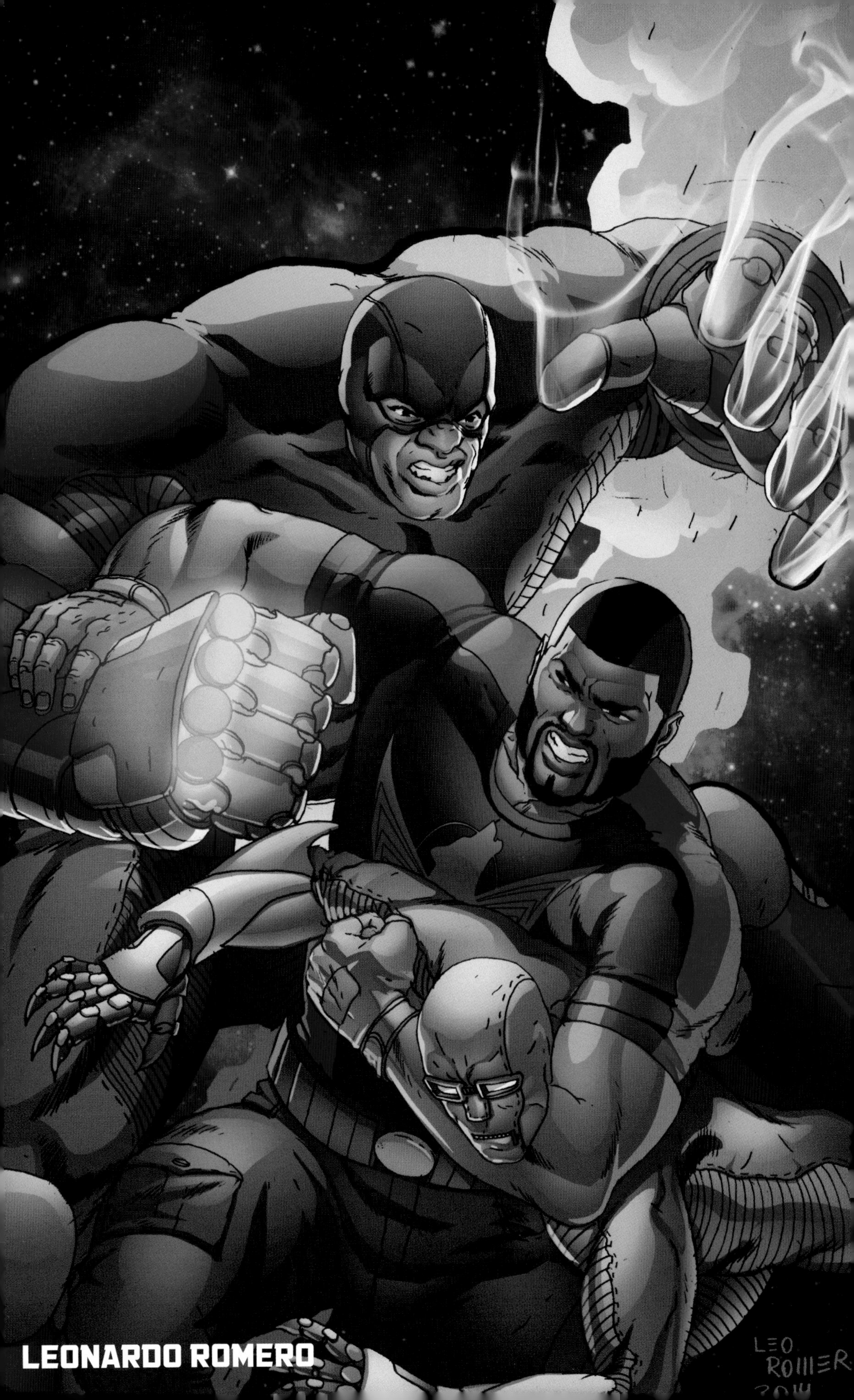

LEONARDO ROMERO

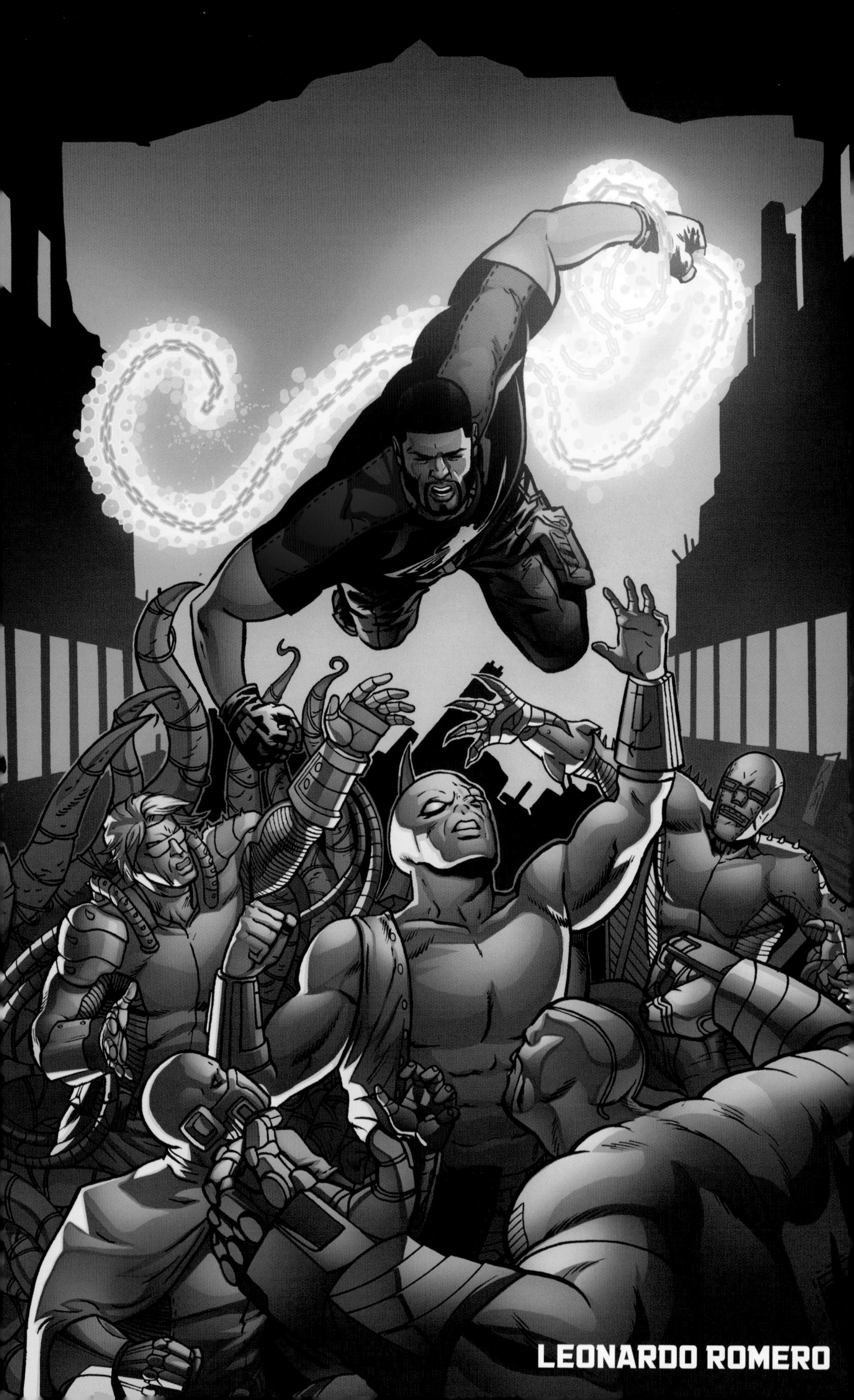

LEONARDO ROMERO

LEONARDO ROMERO

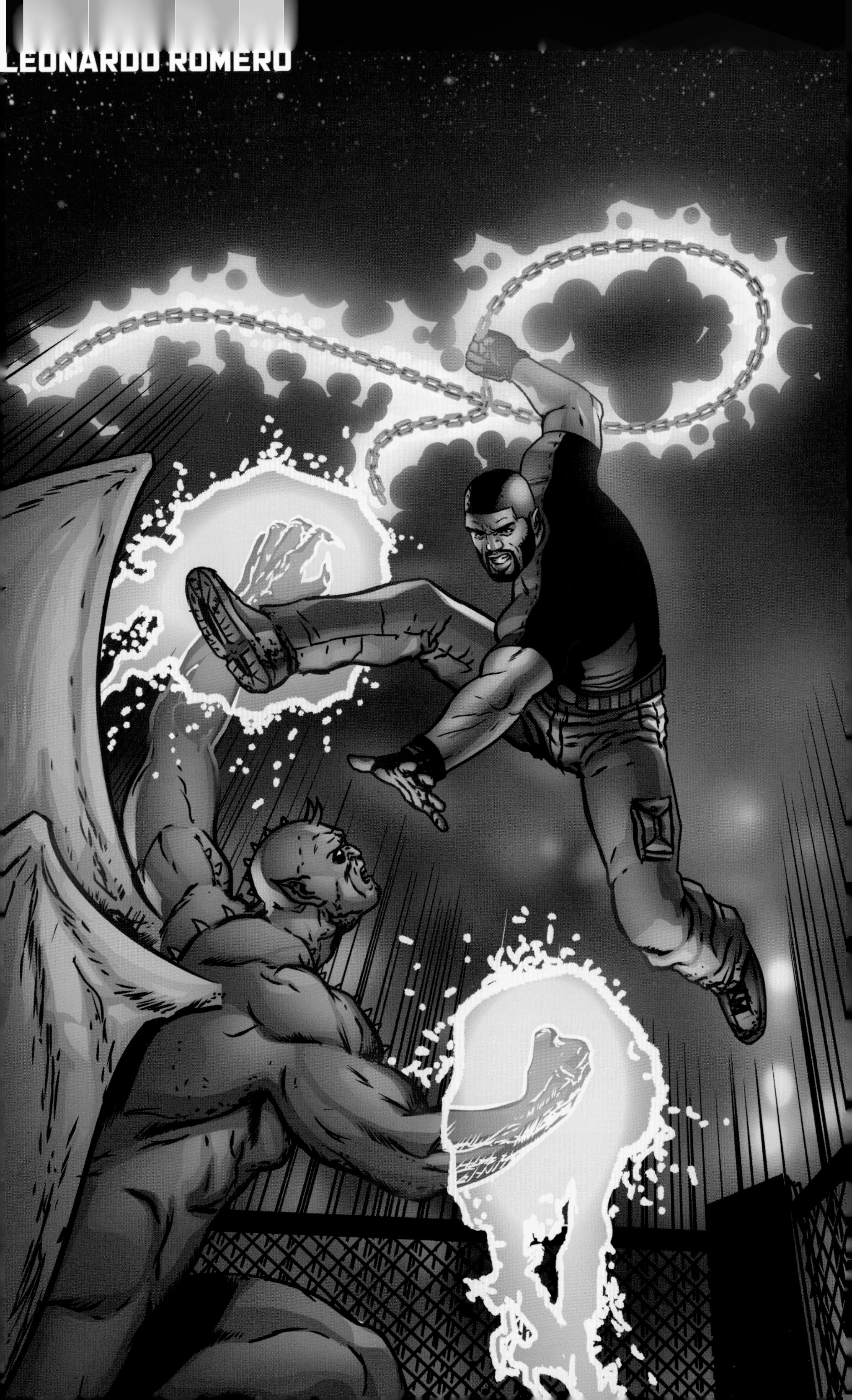

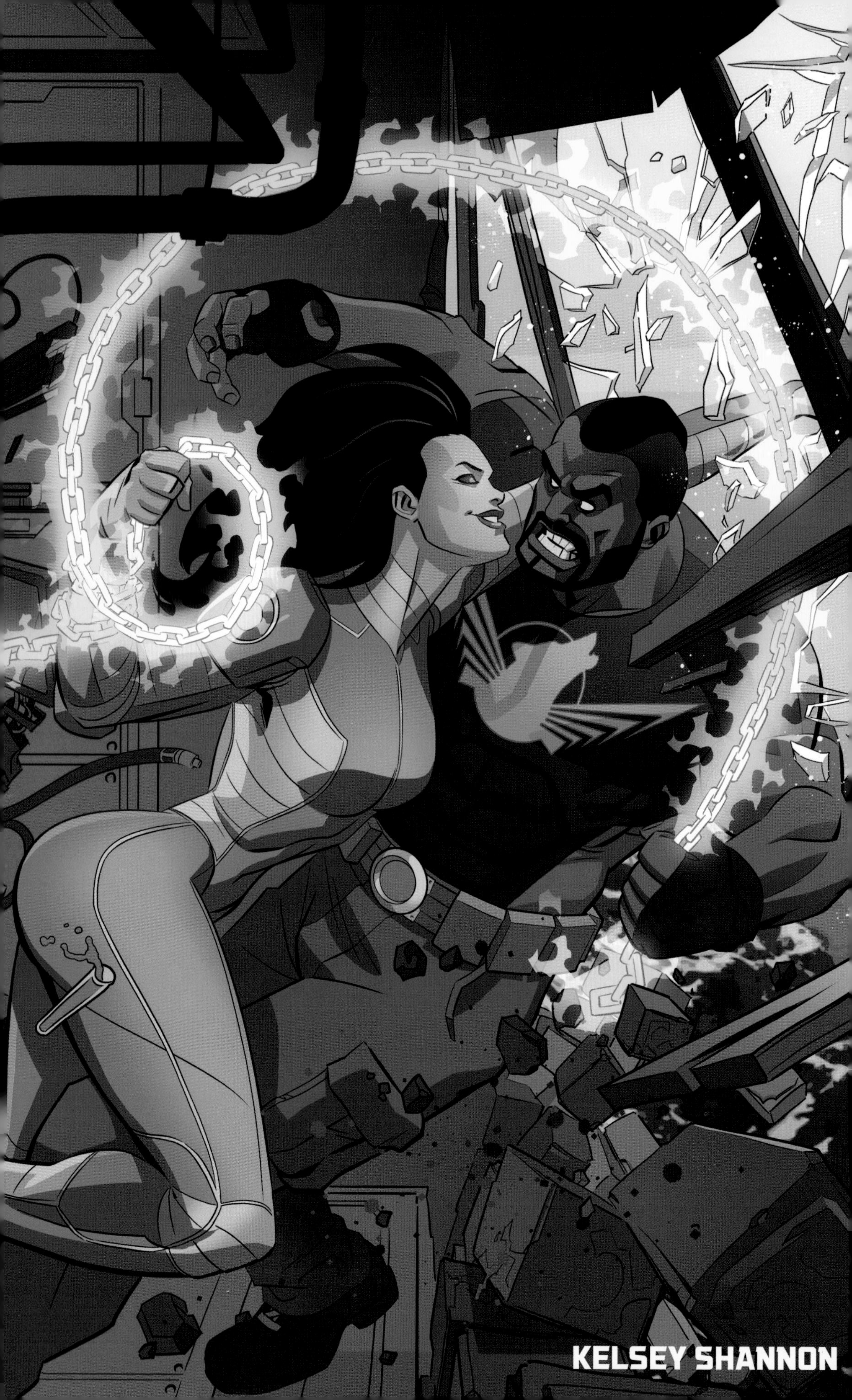

KELSEY SHANNON

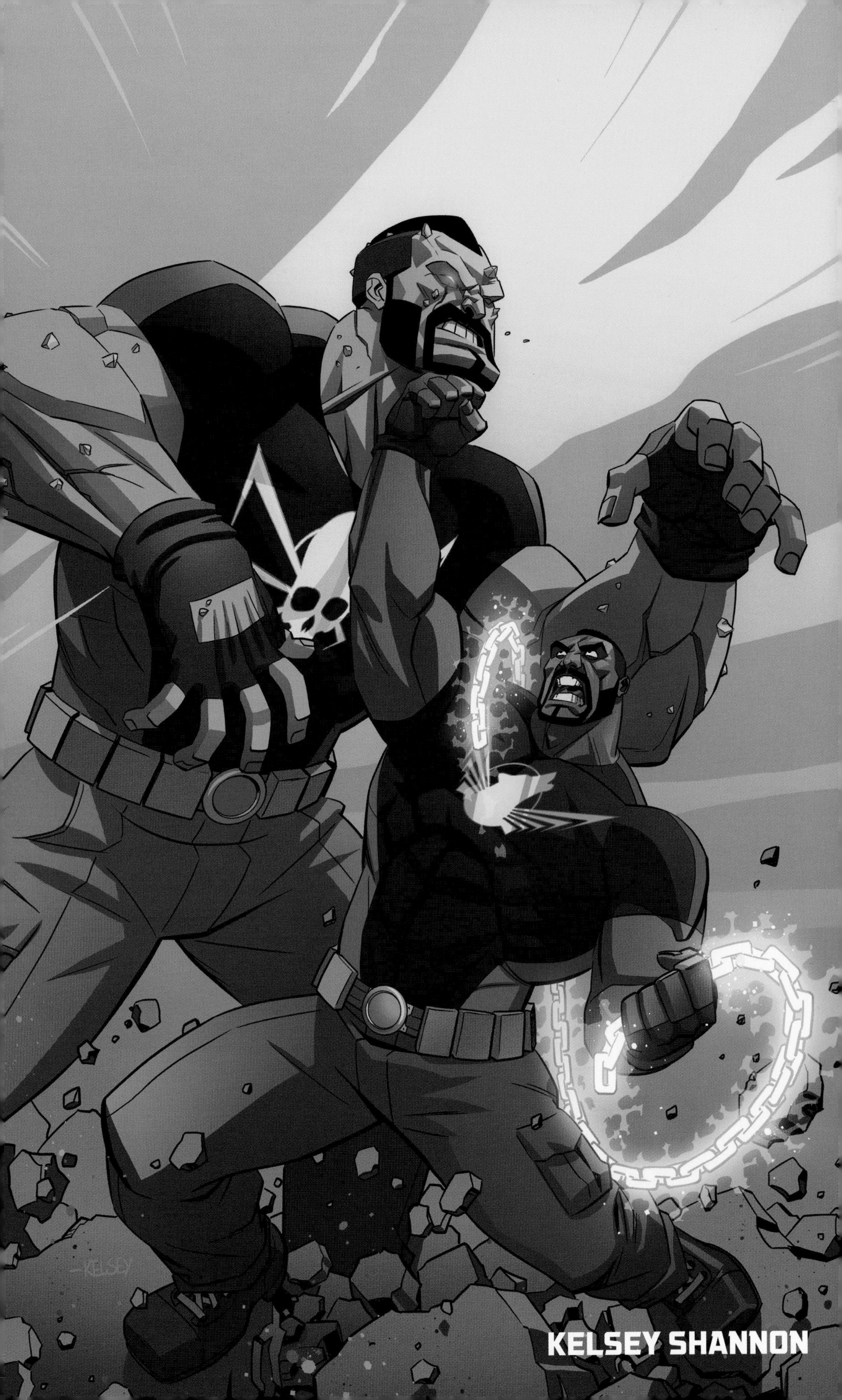
KELSEY
KELSEY SHANNON

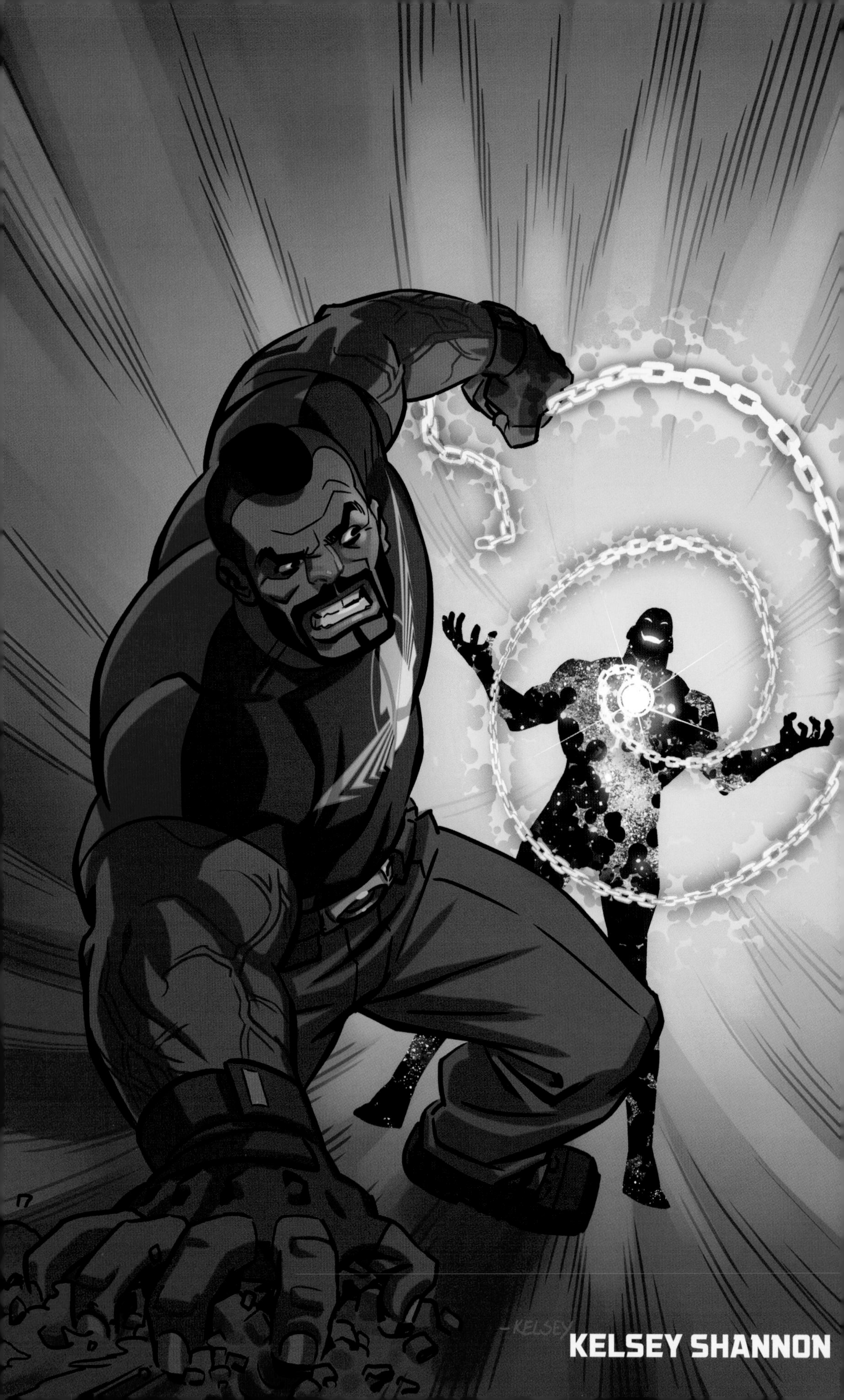
– KELSEY

KELSEY SHANNON

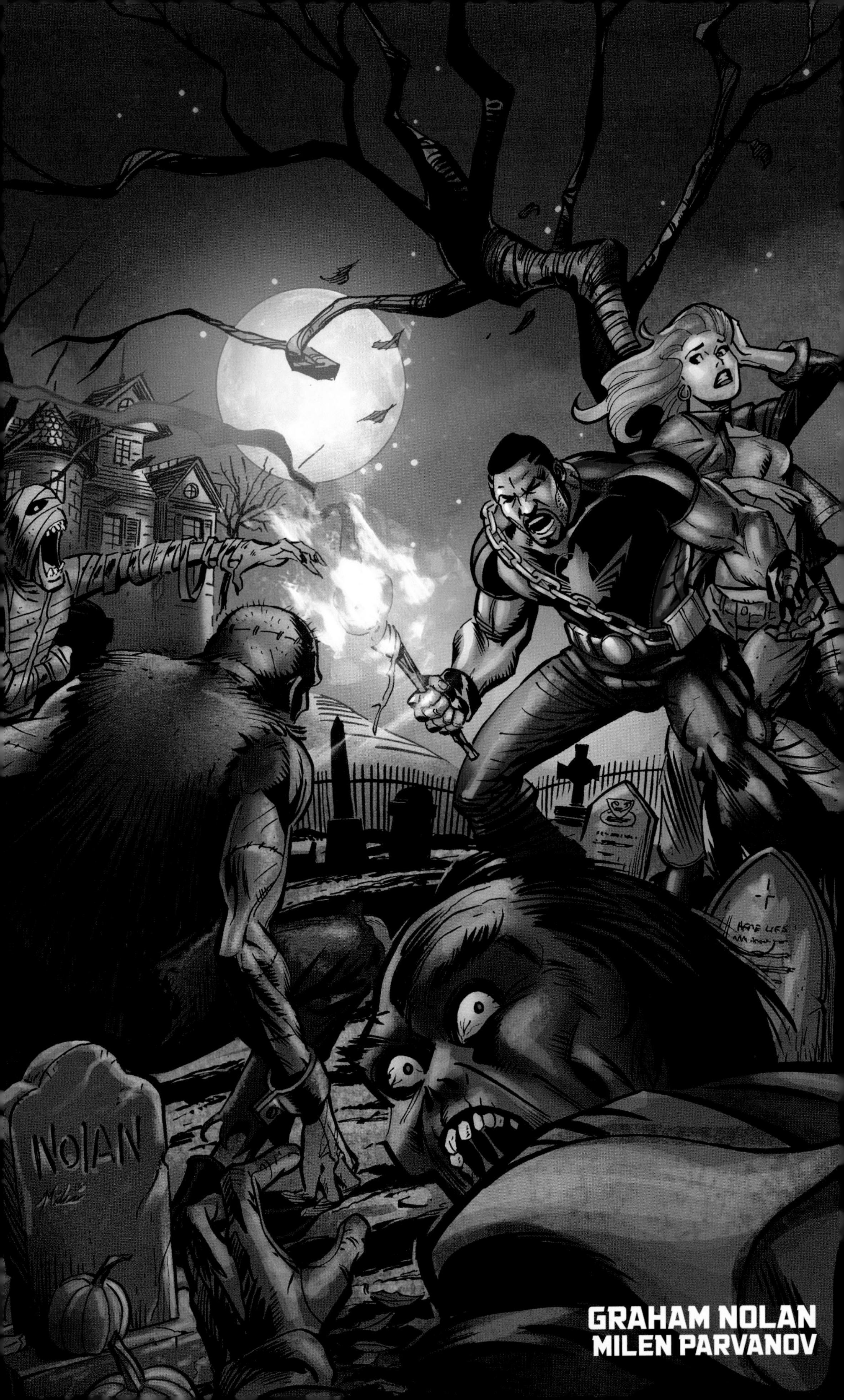
NOLAN
GRAHAM NOLAN
MILEN PARVANOV

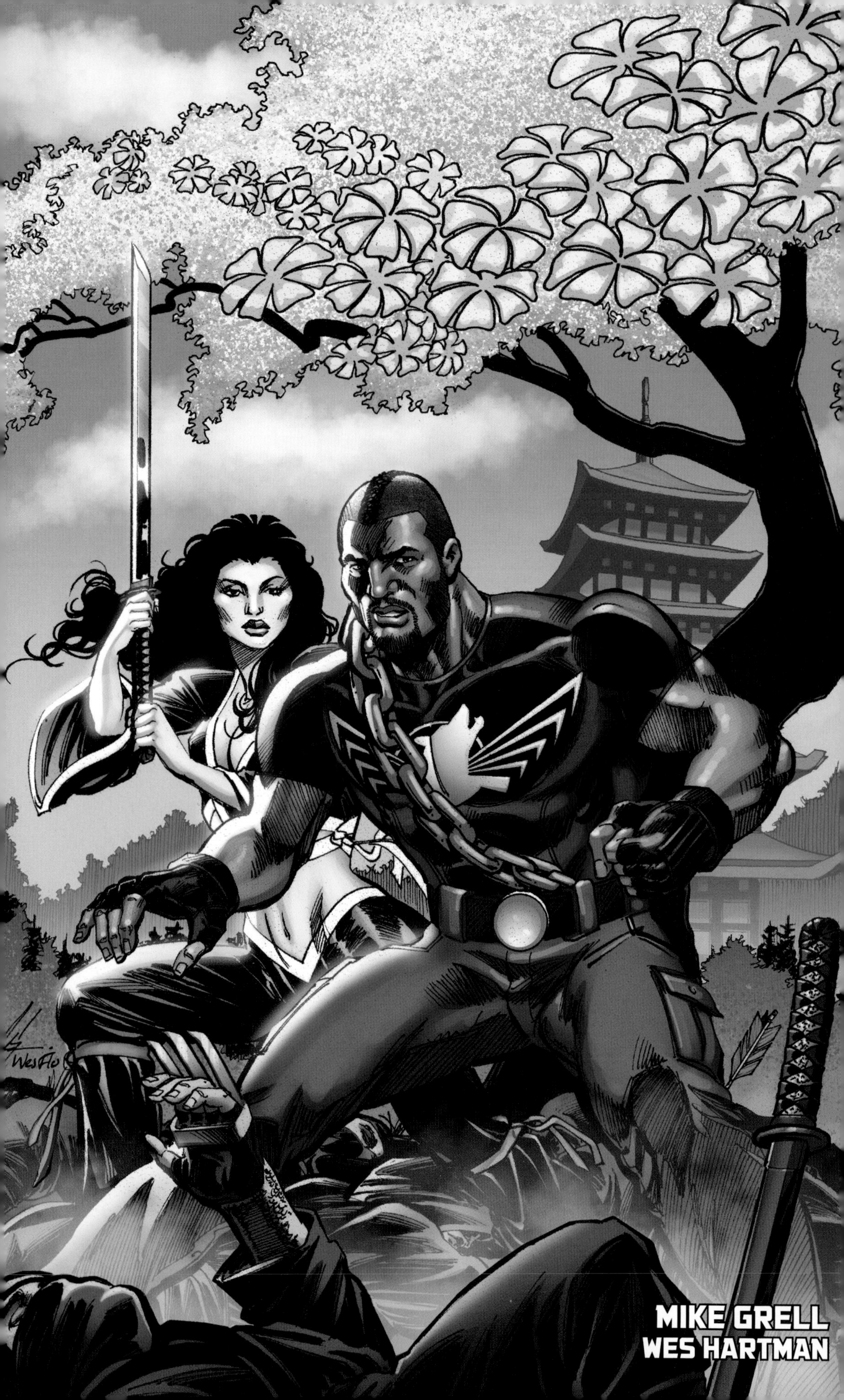
MIKE GRELL
WES HARTMAN

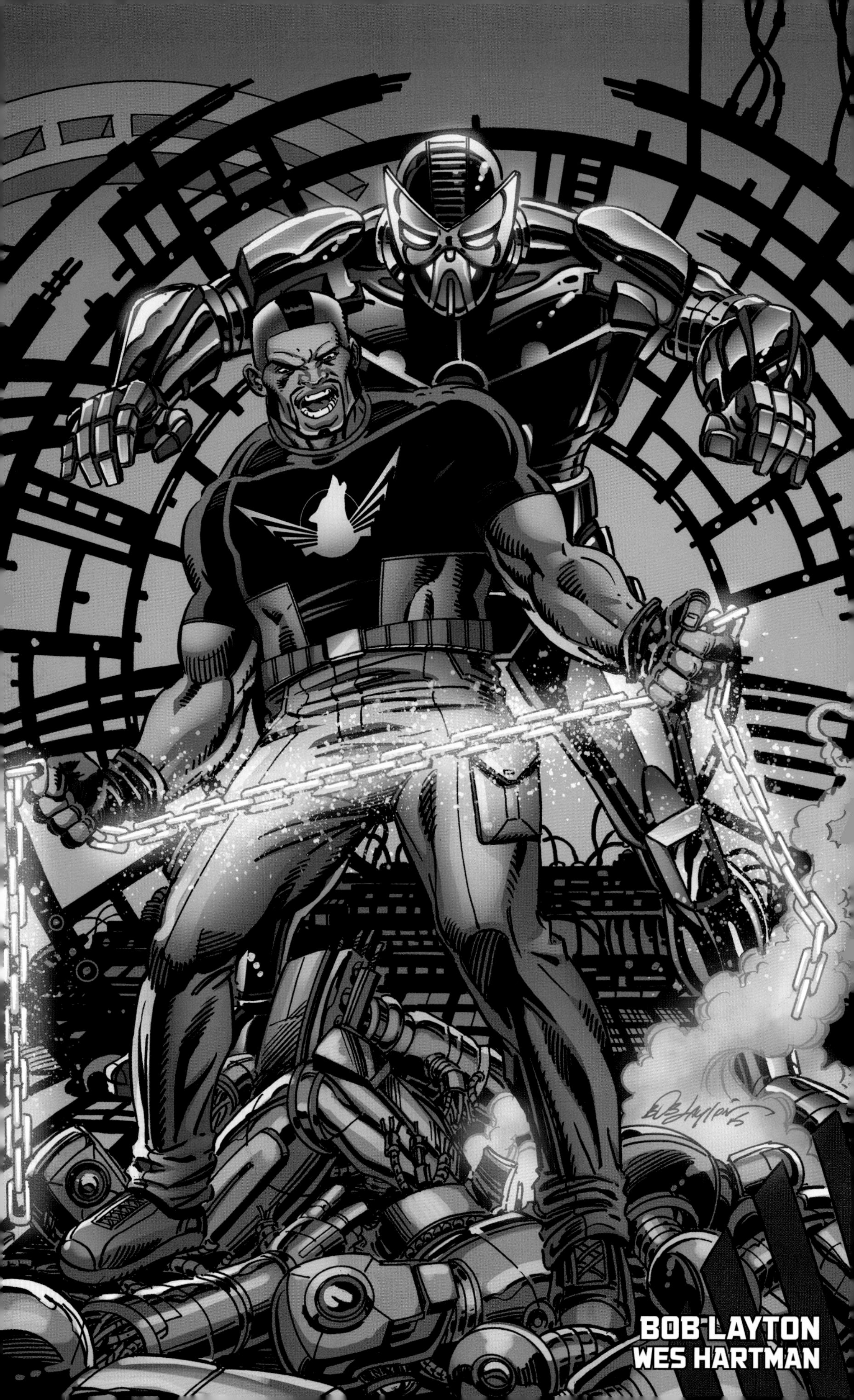
BOB LAYTON
WES HARTMAN

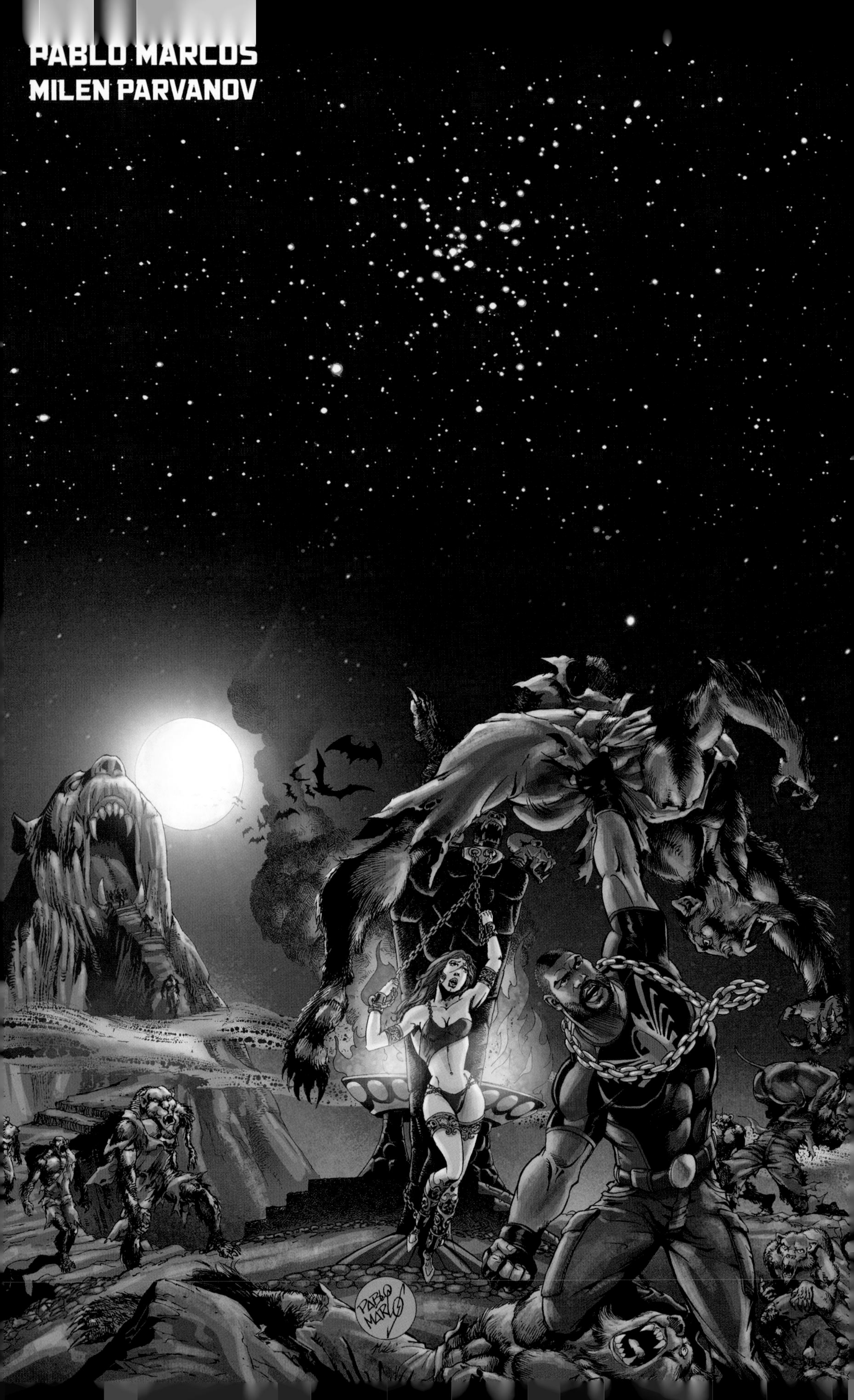
PABLO MARCOS
MILEN PARVANOV

PHIL HESTER
MILEN PARVANOV

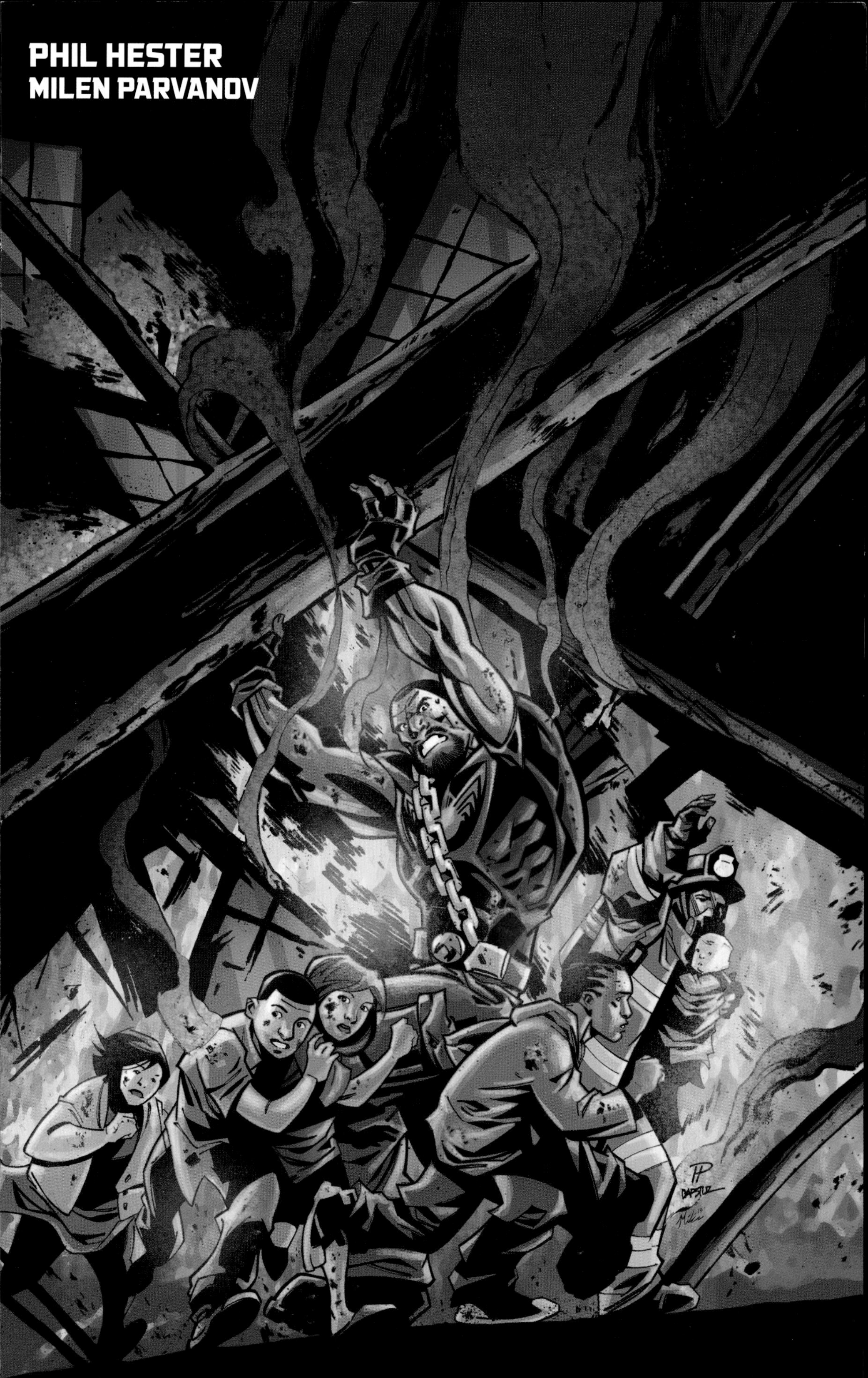

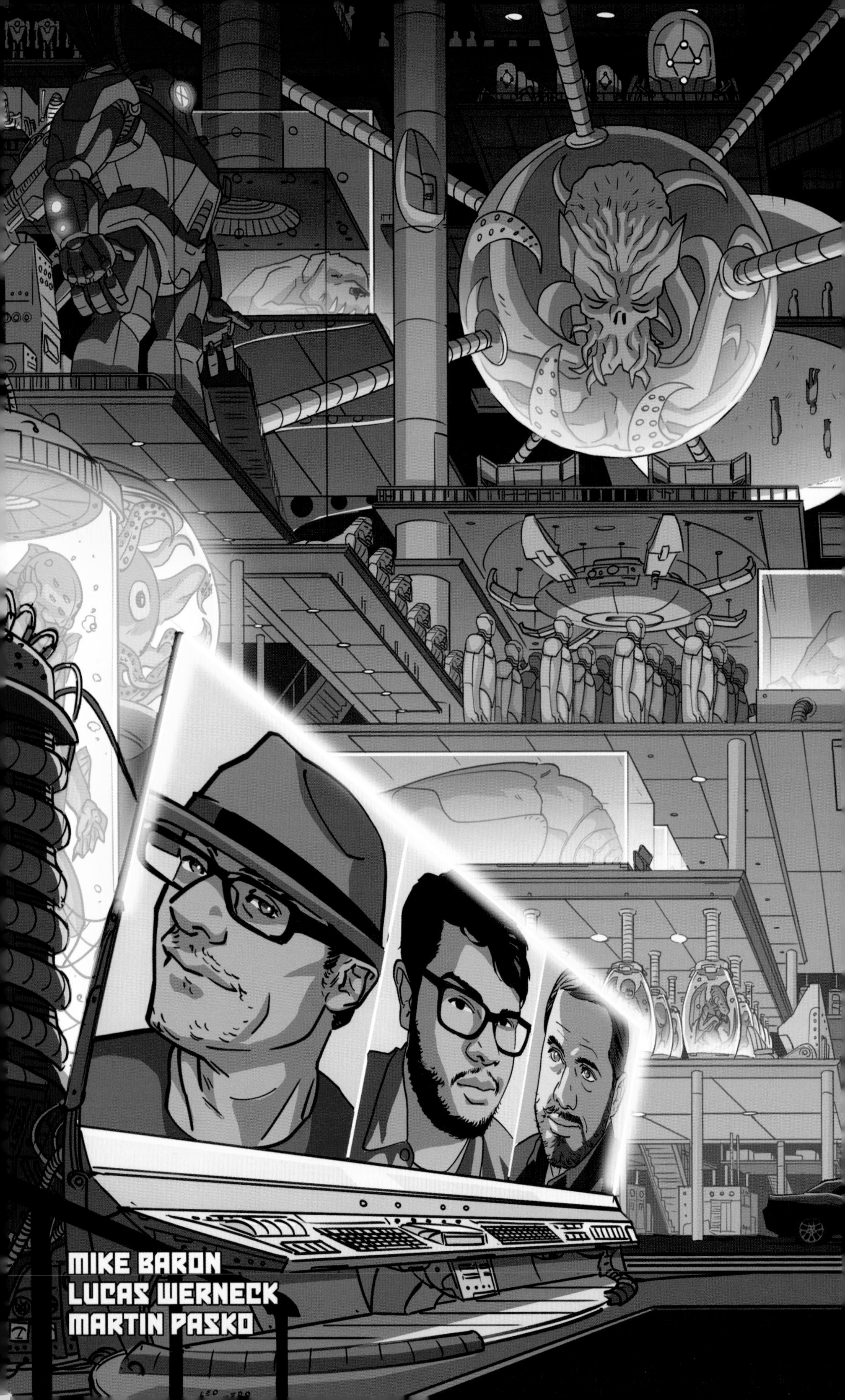
MIKE BARON
LUCAS WERNECK
MARTIN PASKO

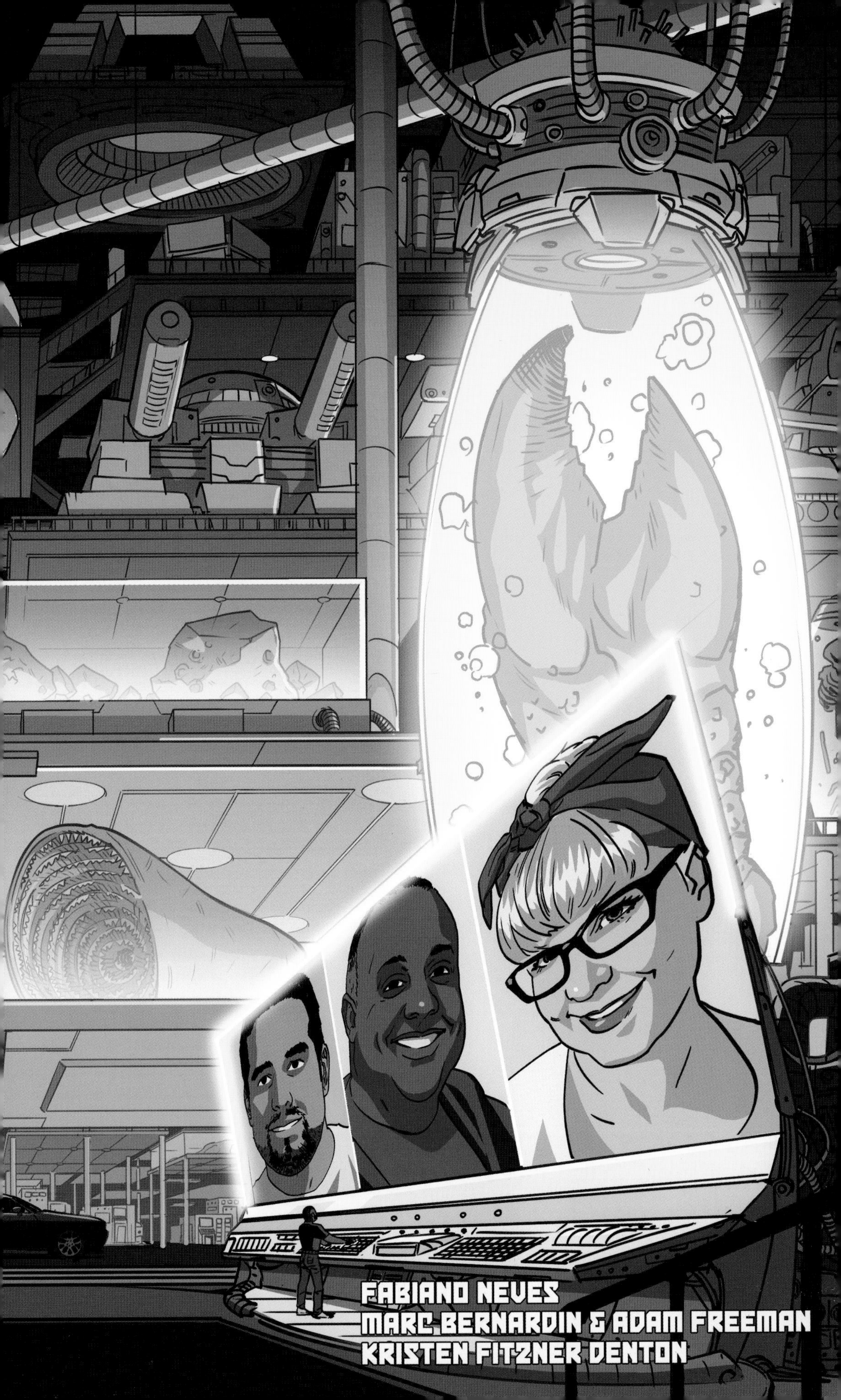
FABIANO NEVES
MARC BERNARDIN & ADAM FREEMAN
KRISTEN FITZNER DENTON

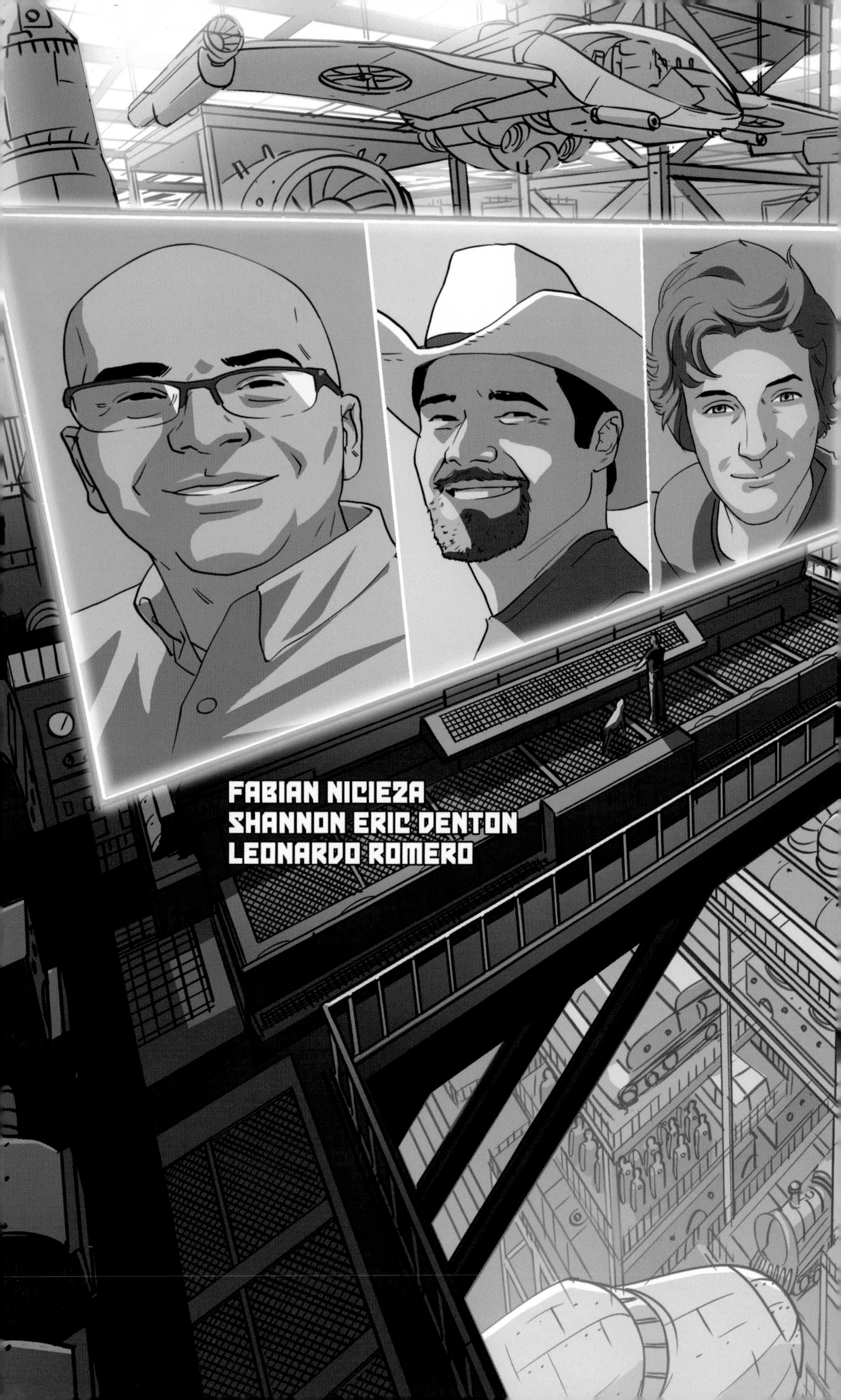
FABIAN NICIEZA
SHANNON ERIC DENTON
LEONARDO ROMERO

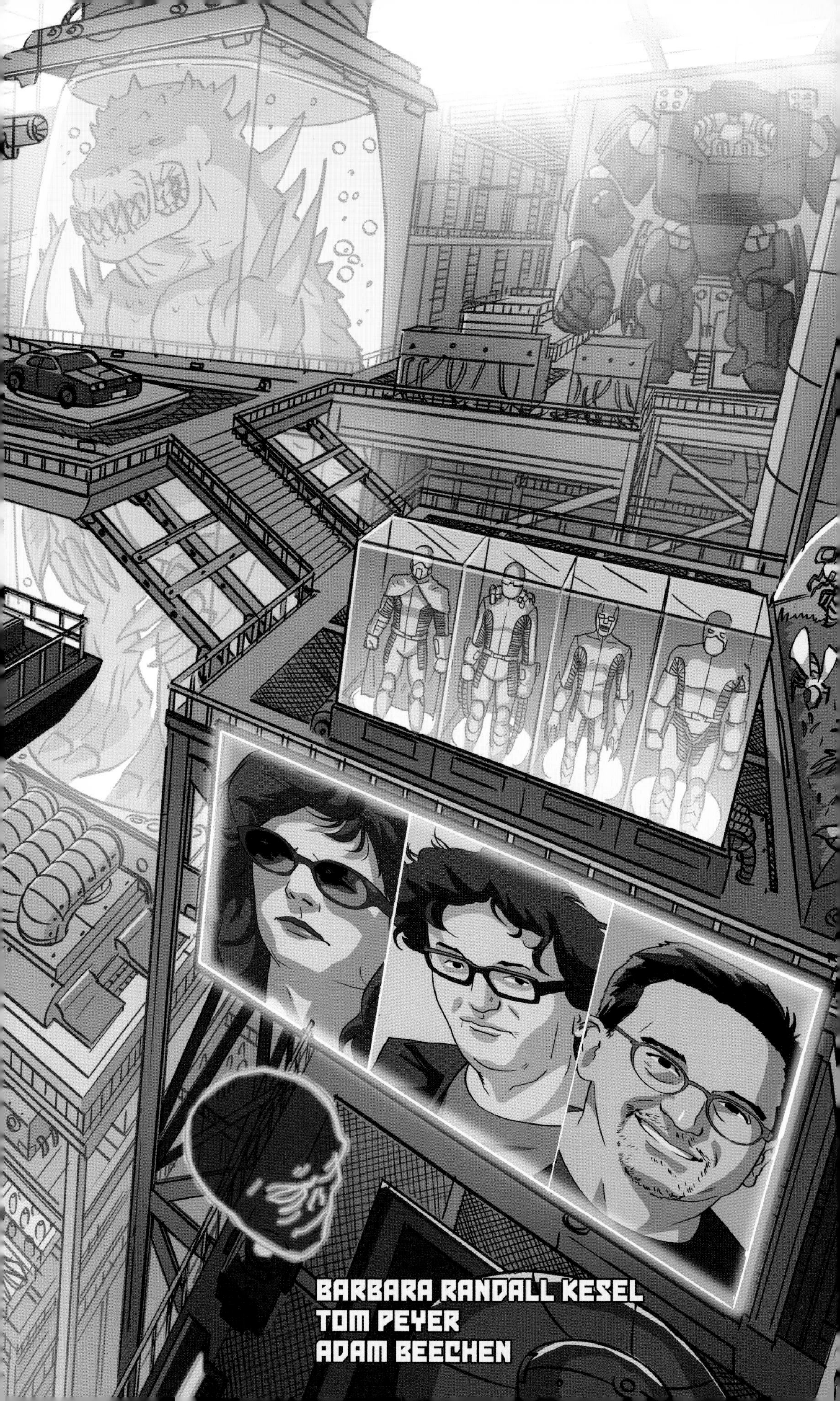
BARBARA RANDALL KESEL
TOM PEYER
ADAM BEECHEN

RAMPAGE JACKSON
STREET SOLDIER

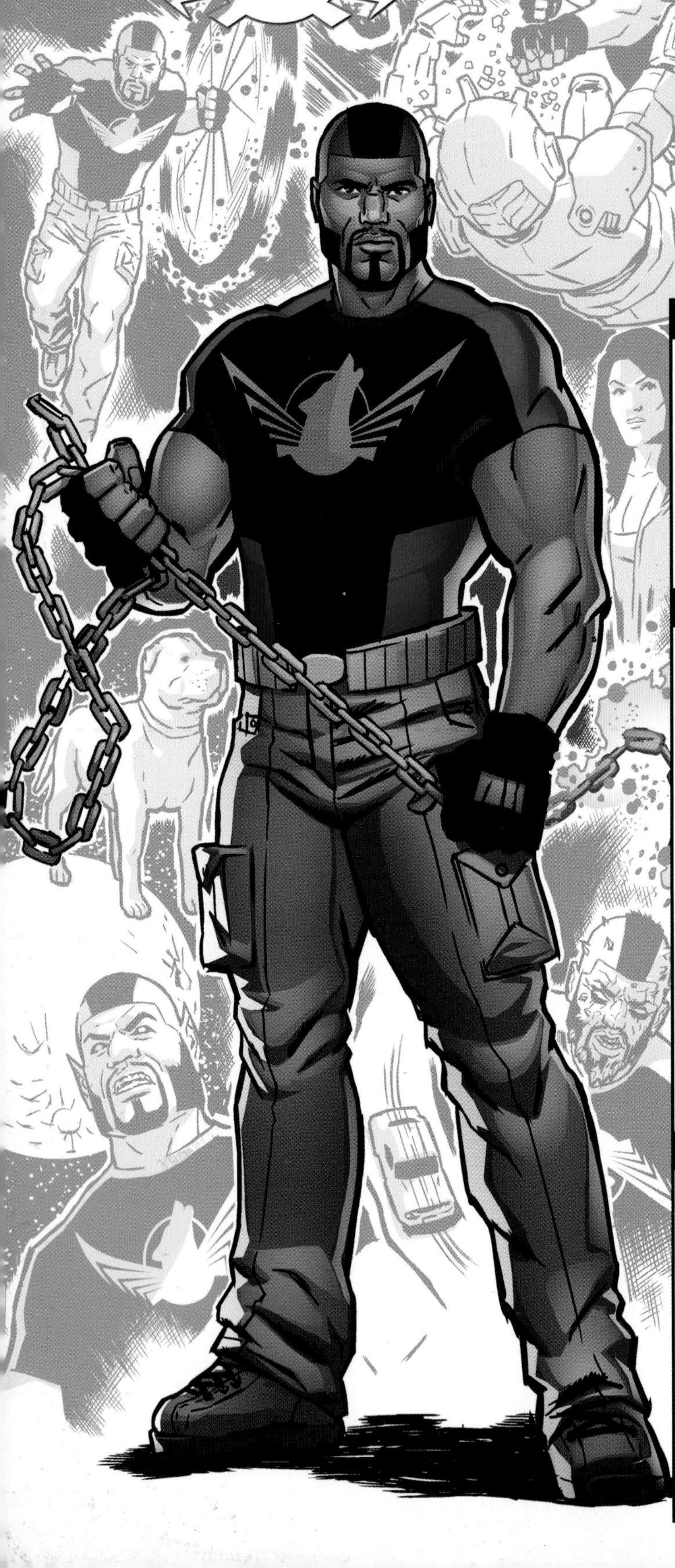

PERSONAL DATA

Real Name: Quinton "Rampage" Jackson
Occupation: Professional MMA fighter, wrestler, actor, adventurer
Marital Status: Single
Known Relatives: Numerous
Group Affiliation: None
First Appearance: Rampage Jackson: Street Soldier One Shot
Height: 6'4" Weight: 230 Lbs.
Eyes: Brown Hair: Black

HISTORY

Quinton "Rampage" Jackson is a world class fighter and wrestler who has toured all over the world showing off his incredible skill in the ring. He has racked up several wins with his superior hand to hand combat skills. He's also starred in motion pictures and is adored by his fans all over the world.

One night he was running late for a tour date and had to charter a private plane to get him there on time. While driving to the airport his van swerved to miss hitting a deer in the road and slid off the icy road and into a ravine. The accident threw Rampage and his faithful dog Andronicus out of the back of the van as the engine burst into flame. Before Rampage could help his friends he fell into a fissure in the ground that contained a fallen meteorite that mutated his DNA. Rampage emerged from the fissure and quickly saved his friends. He then decided to use his extraordinary powers to protect the innocent in this new world of super powered individuals.

POWERS

Rampage has the ability to transform his shape at will into any living form he chooses. People tend to think he is a werewolf because he is always choosing wolf like forms but in reality this is only because Rampage is really a fan of wolves and consciously chooses these differing wolf forms as he most widely identifies with them. Rampage also has the ability to channel energy through his chain and can use it as a powerful offensive and defensive weapon. Rampage's dog Andronicus was also empowered by the meteorite and has the ability to change size and form at will and shares a slight psychic link with Rampage allowing the two to communicate on a subconscious level.